第十八届
国际粤方言研讨会论文集

DISHIBAJIE GUOJI YUEFANGYAN YANTAOHUI LUNWENJI

孙景涛　姚玉敏 

暨南大學出版社
JINAN UNIVERSITY PRESS

中国·广州

图书在版编目（CIP）数据

第十八届国际粤方言研讨会论文集/孙景涛，姚玉敏主编．—广州：暨南大学出版社，2015.9

ISBN 978－7－5668－1494－4

Ⅰ．①第…　Ⅱ．①孙…②姚…　Ⅲ．①粤语—国际学术会议—文集　Ⅳ．①H178－53

中国版本图书馆 CIP 数据核字（2015）第 142293 号

出版发行：暨南大学出版社

地　址：中国广州暨南大学
电　话：总编室（8620）85221601
　　　　营销部（8620）85225284　85228291　85228292（邮购）
传　真：（8620）85221583（办公室）　85223774（营销部）
邮　编：510630
网　址：http：//www.jnupress.com　http：//press.jnu.edu.cn

排　版：广州市天河星辰文化发展部照排中心
印　刷：佛山市浩文彩色印刷有限公司

开　本：787mm×1092mm　1/16
印　张：19
字　数：448 千
版　次：2015 年 9 月第 1 版
印　次：2015 年 9 月第 1 次

定　价：60.00 元

目　录

继往开来，不断开拓，不断前进！

——第十八届国际粤方言研讨会开幕词

詹伯慧

（暨南大学汉语方言研究中心）

各位同道朋友：

南国冬暖，花红草绿，我们一众粤语学人以文会友，又聚集到香港科技大学来，共庆粤语研究取得的新成就，共享丰盛的学术大餐。大会召集人孙景涛教授要我来致开幕词，大概是因为我是这次盛会中年事较高的一位吧！我不敢倚老卖老，但我倒真是咱们这个会缺席次数最少的一个。打从1987年首届国际粤方言研讨会在香港中文大学祖尧堂拉开帷幕以来，除了前年在红磡理工举行的第十六届外，我是每会必到的。第十六届那次由于会期和另一个重要会议完全重叠，我无法分身，不得已才写了一个书面发言稿请张群显博士替我在会上宣读。

我们的粤语研讨会已经开到第十八届了，真可以用“不简单”来形容！在所有汉语方言学科的学术会议中，还没有哪一种方言能够连续不断地在二十多年中举行十八次规模盛大的学术研讨会。这说明我们的粤语研究是多么的充满活力！多么的经久不衰！当年举行第一届研讨会时，大家都说万事起头难，期望着有了第一次，从此可以持续不断地把这一国际性的粤方言研讨会开下去，以达到定期检阅研究成果、及时交流心得体会的目的。果然不负众望，在粤语研究这块肥沃的园地上，我们大家齐心协力，精耕细作，年复一年地开花结果，如今终于迎来了济济一堂，喜迎第十八届盛会开幕的欢乐时刻。现在，请允许我作为粤语园地上的一名“老园丁”，简略回顾一下我们的粤方言研讨会近三十年来走过的历程，并就今后前进的路向略抒管见：

第一，这次盛会是第十八届，离首届研讨会的时间是26年。没有记错的话，在我的记忆中，这十八届会议在香港举行过第一、四、七、十、十三、十六届和这次的十八届等7届，在广东举行过第二、五、八、十二、十七届等5届，在澳门举行过第三、六、九、十五等4届，在广西举行过第十一、十四届等2届。这十八届按照原先两年一届计算，开到第十八届应该用上36年，之所以能够在26年间就开到第十八届，关键在于第十届回到香港中文大学举行时，广西的粤语同道来到会上，强烈要求第十一届会议移师广西首府南宁举行，而在南宁举行第十一届会议期间，香港的同道又提出香港此前举行过的5届会议，是由香港中文大学、香港大学和城市大学主办的，现在香港光是政府注资的大学就有八所，这些大学越来越重视科研活动的开展和学术交流，大家都希望能有机会主办粤方言的研讨会。为适应形势的发展，满足香港同道的愿望，经协商我们又对粤语研讨会举行的周期和轮值次序进行了调整，从第十一届以后，改为每年一届，轮流在港、粤、澳、桂举行，并且明确每隔一年由香港方面主办一次，轮值的次序调整为“港—粤—港—澳—港—桂”的格局。会议周期的加密和轮值次序的调整反映出粤语研究的持续发展和不断深化，是近三十年来粤语研究突飞猛进的显著标志。想当初首轮“港—粤—澳”轮值过后，再轮回香港时，到底有没有大学愿意接会就颇费脑筋，没料到现在竟发展到香港各大学都乐于承办粤语盛会，还担心按照原先两年一届由“港—粤—澳”三地轮流主办的程序，香港八所大学，真不知何年何月才有机会接过主办盛会的接力棒呢！经过调整以后，原先争取不到“接棒”机会的大学，如今很快就会有办会的机会了。从担心没人接会到纷纷争取“接棒”，不正是粤语事业飞跃发展的生动写照吗？事实上，我们在这方面一直是走在全国各大方言的前列，并对其他方言的研究有影响的。打从1987年粤语首开“以一个大方言”为主题举办研讨会的先例以后，汉语其他大方言就闻风而动，陆续跟上，终于形成了今天各大方言都有定期举行研讨会的格局，这无疑大大加快了全国汉语方言研究的步伐。近三十年间粤语研究队伍不断壮大，研究领域不断扩展，研究水准不断提升，研究成果不断增加的历程，确实称得上是硕果累累、成绩斐然。这跟我们长期坚持定期不间断地举行粤方言研讨会，是不无关系的。在这里，我还想特别一提的，就是如今我们不但能够连续不断地定期举行研讨会，其间，我们还在香港大学建立起粤方言研究的网站，又在以粤语为社会通用语的澳门建立起粤方言研究的学会，并由这个学会主办定期出版的专业刊物《粤语研究》。从今年起，澳门粤方言学会还组织起主题较集中、规模较小的“粤语论坛”，计划每年一次，作为我们这个大型研讨会的补充。这样一来，我们每年就有一大一小两个粤语研讨会，真可谓锦上添花！每年两期的《粤语研究》迄今已经出刊到十四期，深受学术界的瞩目。不言而喻，一个学会，一份期刊，为学术研究和学术交流提供了重要的平台，在粤语研究的蓬勃发展中，该发挥着多么重要的作用啊！面对粤语研究如此繁荣发达的大好形势，像我这样有幸亲历其境的老头儿，宁不欣喜万分！当年参与首届粤语盛会的张洪年教授、余霭芹教授、张日升教授、邹嘉彦教授、单周尧教授、徐云扬教授等一大批同道，想必也同样会欣喜万分。可惜有几位活跃在首届研讨会上的前辈学者，像高华年教授、黄家教教授、黄伯荣教授、李新魁教授，还有演艺界的黄霑先生等，都已不幸先后作古，无缘和我们一起检阅新成果，欢庆新丰收了！我们深深怀念他们，他们的业绩将永远载入粤语研究的史册！长江后浪推前浪，幸喜我们的队伍新秀辈出，后继有人。此刻看到会上许多朝气蓬勃的新鲜面孔，我们完全有信心持续保持粤语研究兴旺发达的局面。我们的事业一定会在继往开来中不断获得新的进展，不断登上新的台阶。

第二，回顾过去，为的是展望未来。以往的辉煌不是事业的终结，只是继续发展的良好基础。在这个基础上，我们更要加倍努力，以更上一层楼的姿态来创造新的辉煌。在此请允许我提几点粗浅的看法：

首先，面对粤语研究繁花似锦、不断开拓、不断升温的大好形势，我们对粤语的认识也应该有所发展，有所提高。要从语言资源的高度来认识粤语在汉语诸方言中的重要性和突出地位。把语言看作珍贵资源，而不仅仅看作是一种交际工具，这一观念日益深入人心。就我国丰富的语言资源来说，不仅全社会通用的民族共同语是资源，遍布全国各地的地方方言同样也是资源。特别是像粤语这样在海内外广为使用、社会影响很大的强势方言，更应该被视为重要的语言资源。既然是资源，就要在调查资源、开发资源、保护资源、使用资源等方面都有所策划，有所研究，有所实践。在这一新的理念下，粤语研究的思路自然会更加开阔，研究的内容也必然会更加丰富。

其次，语言研究的主要任务是为语言的应用服务。支撑语言研究的主要动力也是语言的应用，缺乏应用价值的语言，很难激发人们的研究热情。古往今来，研究语言的学者总是格外关注所研究语言的应用情况，古代编修韵书以“正音”为宗旨，20世纪50年代以来，中国大力开展语言规范化工作，汉语方言的调查也常常是围绕着“推普”和汉语规范化的需要来开展的。粤语既是粤语地区的交际工具，又是岭南地域文化的重要载体，粤语的社会应用范围十分广泛，粤语的研究更应该在服务于应用方面多下功夫。此刻回顾几十年来粤语研究走过的历程，盘点我们的研究成果时，我们会发现，在粤语本体的研究方面，例如深入调查粤语语音、词汇、语法现象，揭示粤语各式各样的语言特点，对粤语的发展作共时和历时的探讨等等，已经发表的著述很多，堪称硕果累累；可是，深入讨论粤语在各个方面应用情况的著述，相对就比较少了。我们认为，今后的粤语研究有必要多多面对粤语应用中出现的问题，特别是粤语在社会应用中常见的问题。我们粤语专业人士更要多加关注，多加研究，着力解决。

再次，当前在粤语的应用中，有哪些问题值得我们认真研究、认真解决呢？

（1）记录地域文化、承载地域文化、弘扬地域文化是发挥地方方言作用的重要一环。粤语地区积淀着的丰富的广府文化，都离不开粤语这一载体。粤语在记录、承载、反映广府文化中如何发挥作用？各种不同内容的广府文化跟它的载体之间关系如何？彼此间如何密切配合，相得益彰？这里面是大有文章可做的。拿粤曲粤剧来说，其载体无疑是粤语，粤语音韵和粤曲的关系如何？粤语音韵的研究如何为粤曲的创作服务，使之达至最佳的艺术效果？这方面的课题，据我所知，我们的同道是有人“染指”过的。类似粤语与粤曲粤剧挂钩这样的研究课题不少，研究的天地相当广阔，是值得我们多多关注的。

（2）在“两文三语”的框架下，香港的粤语研究如何面对这一社会语言生活的重大变化？这就要研究在贯彻这一政策中可能出现的问题，“三语”中有普通话，普通话在社会语言生活中跟粤语的关系如何？可以肯定的是：在“两文三语”中，粤语依然会是香港社会最通用的交际工具，而随着学习普通话的人越来越多，普通话日渐普及也是大势所趋。一方面，粤语的研究必须着力于帮助说惯粤语的人学好普通话；另一方面，进入香港还不会说粤语的人，也需要粤语的研究来提供学习粤语的帮助。粤语的研究应该在两语的相互学习中发挥积极的作用。近期有教师提倡用普通话上中小学的语文课，理由是选进中小学语文课本中的课文大都是以普通话为基础的现代典范白话文，用粤语教学不如用普通话教学效果好。但也有人持反对意见，提出种种理由，论证母语（粤语）教学的优越性，用粤语教语文课仍是最佳选择。在这一争议中，作为粤语专业人士，就该本着粤语研究为粤语应用服务的精神来介入，通过调查研究、比较得失等来进行讨论，发表意见。还有，在“两文”的层面，“中文”指的是什么并无明确界定。是标准的白话文吗？所谓“港式中文”算不算？粤语口语入文的现象相当普遍，又应该如何看待？香港学生笔下往往因粤语口语的干扰而造成语文习作中出现形形色色的差错，该如何引导改正？这类语文教学中出现的问题，都有必要进行认真的剖析，以求合理的解决方法。

（3）粤语的正音和粤方言字的使用，有必要通过深入细致的研究，进行一定的规范。编写粤语正音字典，厘定通用粤方言字表等都是有助于粤语社会应用的事，值得大力提倡。拿粤语的正音来说，由于它直接影响到中小学语文课的教学，某些字的读音出现分歧，学生和老师无所适从，自然不能听之任之。不但老师、学生关注，社会各界、凡是跟粤语的应用有关系的人士，如为数众多的传媒、影视界人士，也都十分关切。这是一个专业性很强的粤语学术问题，也是一个突出的粤语应用问题，要解决好这一问题，有赖于我们粤语学者的切磋研究。早在20世纪90年代，我们粤、港、澳三地的粤语专业人士，就曾经组织起一个粤语的审音委员会，以“既要考虑粤音与古代音韵（主要是《广韵》系统）之间的继承关系，更要考虑当今广大人民群众的实际读音”的原则，从现实的读音出发，在强调“从今从众”的理念下，经过多年的切磋讨论，为每一个读音有分歧的字拟定了正音，并在此基础上编撰了《广州话正音字典》，在2002年正式出版。这项前后历时十载的正音工程，在香港似乎并未引起足够的重视，而与此同时，本地另一些由标明“从切”的学者编写的粤语“正读”字典，却在全港大为畅销，对香港粤语的教学和社会应用影响很大。一个时期以来，社会上对粤语的正音问题议论纷纷，沸沸扬扬，俨然成为社会关注的热点。这就说明在正音问题上，还有许多值得深入探讨的空间。期待我们粤语学界能本着粤语研究为粤语应用服务的精神，多加关注，多加研究。粤语的方言用字问题，也是粤语应用中一个引人注目的问题。众所周知，粤语中有许多独特的方言词，体现出鲜明的地域文化色彩。粤语区用来记录这些方言词的方言字，据统计常见的少说也有两三百个。这些方言字形形色色，有的同一个方言词用了几种不同的表达方式，例如表示“现在”的粤语词就有几种不同的写法，到底应该写作“而家”，还是“依家”、“宜家”、“伊家”呢？一个读成ham，表示“盖得严密、不透风”的粤方言词，和另一个读成kam，作动词“盖”用的粤方言词，同样写成方言字“冚”。这类方言用字的混乱现象，要不要有所规范？如何进行规范？这类方言用字问题，我们希望也能引起大家的关注。

（4）粤语教材的编写，也是粤语应用中的一个重要问题。随着粤语的学习在海内外越来越受到重视，为各种不同需要的对象编写出能够突出粤语特点，反映粤语实际情况，体现粤语研究成果，并能够与时俱进的优质教材，为粤语的教学工作提供服务，无疑应是粤语学者责无旁贷的任务。说实在的，时下坊间虽然充斥着各种粤语课本教材，但其中不少是粗制滥造之作，质量大成问题。要改变这种局面，有赖于各位粤语研究有成的专业人士。我们在此呼吁：大家都来关心粤语教学工作，都来着力编写学术性与应用性俱佳的粤语教材。

以上拉拉杂杂，略抒管见，请各位多多指教。

2013年12月7日于香港科技大学

"至/正"与"莫个"：早期粤语语料中残留的语法现象

张洪年

（加州大学柏克莱　香港中文大学）

提　要：研究语言的历时发展，一般多致力于语言中的新现象，分析新旧交替之间变化的年代和轨迹。至于旧有的用法本身有什么特质，来源究竟本自什么，一般不太深究。殊不知，语言演变本来就是一个渐变的过程，老旧用语，很可能就是变化过程中某一个阶段的如实写照。等到新旧替换以后，我们只听新语，不闻旧说。旧日变化，也就湮没无闻了。对一个研究历史的人来说，任何材料的消失都是最可惜的事。对一个研究语言发展演变的学者来说，淘沙觅金，能找到任何一点旧材料，从中发现些许变化的蛛丝马迹，最是兴奋不过的事。我从 19 世纪以来的粤语语料中一共选用 27 种，挖取一些例句，排列梳理，试着说明早期粤语语法变化的一些现象。第一个现象是"至/正"的用法，用以表示条件；第二个现象是"莫个"的组合，用以表示否定命令句。这两种用法上下两百年，变化甚为繁复。

关键词：早期粤语　至　正　莫个　条件句　否定命令句

1　引　言

地有南北，时有古今，任何一种语言都会因时随地而逐渐嬗变。同一时同一地的人也许并不感觉到周遭语言有什么不同，但只要把异时异地的话语拿来对比，变化痕迹，了然可见。我们研究粤语，可以从共时的角度来比较各处语言的异同，也可以从历时的层面来研究语言长时期以来所经历的变化。上一个世纪的学者，许多是专力描述、分析共时语言中的特点，界定大小方言之间的分别的，成绩斐然。从 20 世纪 90 年代开始，学者的着眼点开始转向历时的探讨，发现许多由早年传教士编写的口语教材，于是努力汇集语料，进行分析，成果也有目共睹。近年有心之士更编写程序，建立语料库，以便网上搜索。①综观前人在这一方面的研究成果，从语音到语法到词汇，都多有发现。尤其是语法方面的讨论，包括对动词时态、趋向补语、给字句、指示词、语气助词等的研究，更让我们对早期粤语的面貌有了一种新的认识。我自己在这一方面，也曾写过一些文章，参与探溯重构的工作。

① 重要的粤语语料库有：《早期粤语口语文献资料库》，http：//pvs0001. ust. hk/Candbase/；《早期粤语标注语料库》，http：//pvs0001. ust. hk/WTagging；《香港二十世纪中期粤语语料库》，http：//corpus. ied. edu. hk/hkcc/。

粤语涵盖的范围很大，包括大小许多方言。一般所谓的广东话，专指广州、香港、澳门一带的语言。就珠三角这一小地域而言，广州和香港的粤语，已经渐渐分家。从时间上来看，今天年轻人的话语和我们父母、祖父母一代说的粤语，也有所差异。假如我们把时间线拉长，往上推移，因为材料有限，也只能推到19世纪早期而已。从语言发展的过程来说，两百年是一个相当短的时段。不过短并不代表少，就这一个两百年的发展来说，还是蕴藏着许多有趣的语言现象。我们当然得感谢19世纪以来中外学者为编写语料所做出的努力，在书籍文字上保留了当日语言的原貌。本文的研究主要集中在19世纪和20世纪30年代以前的材料，前后参看的语料一共有26种（书目见附录）。①本文试从这些早期粤语语料中发掘旧日语言残留的语法现象。

2　早期粤语语法变化的两个现象："至"与"莫"

一般历时语法研究的重点往往是希望能从语言中找到非同寻常的新语法现象，分析新旧交替之间语法变化的年代和轨迹。至于旧有的用法本身有什么特质，来源究竟本自什么，一般不太深究。还有一些老旧的用语说法，今日虽然不复流行，因为自己不说，别人也不这样说，于是等闲抛开，就算是见诸文字记载，也往往轻易掀过，不明白就不加注意。殊不知，淘沙觅金，一些看来陌生的用字，正因为它有异寻常，细究起来，可能正是躲藏在"今日寻常"背后的旧时面貌。语言演变本来是一个渐变的过程，需时费日，不可能一蹴而就。每一个年代的用语，都代表着那一个年代的语言特征。今日看来是老旧的用语，很可能是变化过程中某一个阶段的如实写照。等到有一天新旧替换以后，我们只听新语，不闻旧说。旧日变化，也就湮没无闻了。对一个研究历史的人来说，任何材料的消失都最是可惜的事。对一个研究语言发展演变的学者来说，能找到任何一点旧材料，从中发现些许蛛丝马迹，是最兴奋不过的事。本文从19世纪的语料中挖取一些例句，排列梳理，试着说明早期粤语语法变化的一些现象。第一个现象是"至"字和"正"字的用法，第二个现象是"莫"字的用法。这两种用法，乍看之下，并没有什么特别之处。但是翻检两百年的材料之后，我们这才发现个中变化至为繁复，紧扣粤语发展的总体趋势，实在莫能等闲视之。

2.1　表条件句式的标志："至"

2.1.1　"至"的三种用法

"至"字的本义是"到达"的意思。例如，《左传》文公二年："秦师又至。"这种用法至今还保留在某些汉语用语中。例如，"从古至今"、"福至心灵"等等，口语比较少用。粤语亦然，"至"只出现在某些现成的句构或一定用语中。例如（1）中的"由……至"句子，换成别的场合，一定要改用别的字眼，如（2）中的"到"。

---

① 承蒙姚玉敏和片冈新二位先生提供许多资料，谨此表示谢忱。

(1) 由香港至广州嘅火车，几点钟开出？(由香港到广州的火车，几点开出？)
(2) 到咗广州之后，记得打电话俾我。(到了广州以后，记得给我打电话。)

在古代汉语里，"至"还有一个用法，表示"最"。《荀子正论》："罪至重而刑至轻。"这种用法，还见于今日汉语某些用语中，例如，"至亲"、"感情至深"、"至高无上"等等。口语一般不用。但是粤语口语用"至"却相当普遍。例如：

(3) 你至肥吓阵时有几肥？(你最胖的时候有多胖？)
(4) 至叻系你喇。(最能干的就是你。)

"至"这两种用法之间的关系，当然是由"到达"引申到"最"。其间的语义变化也不难理解。以"至高无上"为例，假如"高"处只有一点，到达这个"高"点，也就是达到"最高"的一点，所以不可能再有更"上"之处。换言之，"至"后面加上一个表状态的词——一般是形容词，就可以从"达到这个状态"的过程引申为"最＋形容词"的描述。所以《庄子》的"水至清则无鱼"一句，可以有两种解释：①"水到了清澈的阶段就没有鱼"；②"水最清澈的时候就没有鱼"。在前一个解释中，"至"是动词；在后一个解释里，"至"转为"副词"，表示"最"。

(5) 至 + Adj → 至 + Adj
[+V]　　　　[+Adv]

这种表副词的用法，在19世纪的粤语语料中很常见。

(6) a. 至可恶系佢。(Bridgman，1841：Ⅷ)[①]
Most worthy of hatred is he.
b. 吩咐一个奴仆话，去归抬件至好嘅衫来俾佢着。(浪子悔改，1840：2)
c. 至多不过五十。(Bonney，1853：54)
At the most，there are no more than 50.
d. 个一本至大。(*EPCD*，1877：L. 8)
That one is the largest of all.
e. 至紧依期煮饭食。(Stedman/Lee，1888：27)
You must be very punctual in having meals on time.
d. 至凄凉系无辜刑狱。(Kerr，1889：32)
It is very miserable to be punished without cause.

① 例句后附原书年份并页数。如材料不列页码，则列明出自书中第几部分或第几课，供参考。

如上所述，今日粤语中依然保留着“至”表副词的用法。[1]现请看以下所举二例：

（7）病人食牛奶至有益嘅。（Kerr，1889：45）
Milk is the best food for invalids.

（8）要食好耐药至得好呀。（Kerr，1889：45）
You must take physics for a long time before you expect complete recovery.

从英文翻译来看，句（7）的“至”正是表示程度，但是句（8）却用“before”来翻译“至”的用法。换言之，“至”表示时间先后的次序，用法相当于现代汉语的“才”。

（8）a. 要吃很久的药，病才会好。

这种用法，在早期粤语语料中颇为常见。下面再举数例说明。

（9）a. 你络住下耙至好讲啊。（Bridgman，1841：Ⅷ）
Tie up your jaws and then speak freely.（For there is danger of their falling from your face as a judgment for the lies you tell.）

b. 忽然间有个跌落山庶死哓个阵时，你然后至叫佢咪行咁开咩？（亲就耶稣，1865：36）

c. 要照直讲，亲眼见，亲耳听，至好讲出嚟。（*CME*，1883：30）
You must tell the truth，and only say what you have seen and heard.

d. 唔好前时好，后来又唔好，噉致系真真嘅孝子，真真嘅好兄弟。[2]（*RCC*，1894：160）
Preserve in goodness. He who does so is truly a good brother，truly a dutiful son.

e. 佢等齐人客，等到够客至开身咩？（*HSC*，1912：50）
They wait till there are sufficient passengers before they start.

这种用法，仍然保留在今日粤语中。例如：

（10）你揾到工至好揾老婆。（你先找到工作，然后再找老婆。）

这些例子每句都可以分为两小段，后一部分以“至”为标志。前后两段有时序先后相承的关系。以句（8）为例，要先吃药，然后病才会好转。吃药和病愈，先后发生。但正因为这先后的陈述，所以“病愈”是果，“吃药”是因。若要病好，先得吃药。这也就是说，“吃药”可以是“病愈”的先决条件。时序前后的排列，成了表达条件的句式，陈述

① 今日粤语中表示最高级的程度副词是“最”。早期粤语中亦有用“最”的例句，但并不常见，而且常用于书面语。例如：“为人须要令人见重，最怕俾人体轻。”（He who is a man must desire to cause others to view him with respect；the worst thing to be feared is to cause others to look at him lightly.）（Morrison，1828：I）

② 请注意（9）d 句的“至”作“致”。语料中也还有一些例子作“致”，但不常见。

句因而转化为条件句，而"至"正是这个条件句式的标志。上述各例，有的似乎是表示时序，有的是说明条件，有的两者皆可，其实都可以从这个语用转化的模式来理解。

2.1.2 "至"用法的演变

如上所说，"至"的一般用法是表"移动"的动词，或是表"最"的副词。这两种用法由来已久。但是用来标志"时序"、"条件"的句子，却似乎是粤语的特有用法，不见于古书或其他方言。假如说这是语义或语用的延伸，我们应该怎么去理解？下面，我们试从另一个角度来解释"至"这种新的延伸用法。

我们试比较下列两句粤语：

（11）a. 噉最靓。
　　　b. 噉至靓。

表面看来，"最"和"至"都是表示形容词最高级的标志，意思完全一样："这样再漂亮不过。"不过，仔细想一下，（11）b 还可以另有一种解释。假如在我们面前有各种选择，可是都不太理想，但相比之下，只有"噉样"还可以考虑；又或者是"噉样"本来不怎么漂亮，但做了某些调整以后，还可以比较中选。比如：

　　　c. 本来一啲都唔靓，要搽多啲粉，噉至靓。（本来一点儿都不漂亮，要多搽点儿粉，这才漂亮。）

所以这里使用"至靓"是强调在某种条件之下的"至靓"，而并非指绝对性的"至靓"。换言之，（11）b 有两种解释，可以是"绝对性"的"至靓"，也可以是"相对性"的"至靓"。而（11）a 的"最靓"只有"绝对性"的一种解释。绝对性的"至靓"可以和"最靓"对换，但是相对性的"至靓"却不可以。

这种相对性的用法，还可以从下面的对比中看出来。

（12）a. *噉最靓啲。
　　　b. 噉至靓啲。（这样才比较漂亮。）

"最"是强调绝对的顶点，不可能再有等级的差异，所以不能在句子后面再添加表示程度性的词尾"啲"（"一点儿"）。但是"相对性"的"至"，既然是相对而言，当然可以说"漂亮一点"。

"至靓"从"绝对性的最美"转换到"相对性的美"，是从"肯定式"转换到"条件式"。如上所述，这种条件可以是时间上的先后，只有到了某一个时间才会有这种情形，如（13）a，或者是在某种环境或条件之下，才能作如是观，如（13）b：

（13）a. 呢处嘅风景，而家麻麻，夏天至靓。（这里的风景，现在一般般，夏天才漂亮。）
　　　b. 幅画要加多啲红叶，噉嘅风景至靓。（这幅画，要多添点红叶，风景才会漂亮。）

这也就是说，“至”已经从表“绝对最高级”的副词，慢慢转变成表“条件”的副词。这一转化，也让“至”的用法从修饰“形容词”表“最”，扩大到修饰任何动词，表“才”。例如：

（14）a. 而家太夜，听朝至打电话。（现在太晚，明天早上再打电话。）
b. 几时得闲，至去揾佢。（什么时候有空，再去找他。）

这种扩大的用法，在早期粤语材料中，遍拾皆是。

（15）a. 带笑面至见得人。（Morrison，1828：I）
Put on a mask to see people.
b. 个裁缝拧番张被面嚟未呀？唔曾。佢话挨晚至拧嚟和。（Bridgman，1841：158）
Has the tailor brought back the coverlet? No，not yet，but he promised to bring it this evening.
c. 剩返呢地，听日至使。（Devan，1847：91）
Save this for tomorrow.
d. 我哋唔使等到改晓的恶事至去耶稣庶。（亲就耶稣，1865：30）（我们不必等到把坏事全改了以后才去耶稣那里。）
e. 等人客饮到将醉，然后至出淡酒吖。（述史浅释，1888：35）（等客人喝得快醉的时候，这才拿出淡酒。）
f. 亦不必定要噉样做致叫做孝。（*RCC*，1894：142）
Nor is it necessary thus to act in order that it may be denominated filial piety.

换言之，我们可以把这种用法写成这样的句式，P1 和 P2 代表前后两个小句：P1，至 P2。

这种条件式的用法，最常出现在表示“可以”的“得”字句子中，表示只有在某种条件之下，才会有这样的结果。例如：

（16）a. 脚大至跂得稳。（Morrison，1828：XII）
A larger foot will stand the firmer.
b. 我唔俾得咁高。至高俾你七个二毫半。你要添起的至做得。（Bridgman，1841：239）
I cannot give you so high a price. The very utmost I can give you is seven dollars and twenty-five cents. You ought to add a little to your price. Then it will do very well.
c. 你去几耐至得呢？（*EPCD*，1877：30）①

① 1877 年出版的 *Easy Phrases in the Canton Dialect of the Chinese Language*（*EPCD*），没有编写页数，只列第几课。又引句中的“几耐”，原文作“己耐”，按翻译，当是“几耐”笔误。

(你要去多长时间才行?)

d. 先使把荷包锁，锁紧个度门至得。(*CME*，1888：28)

First take a padlock and lock the door first (before it will do).

e. 水紧至少要两日至开得身。(Fulton，1888：28)

The water is swift，must wait at least two days before we can go.

(16)e 句中，有两个"至"，第一个是"至少"，表示程度，第二个是"至V得"，表示条件。同样，(16)b 句中，也有两个"至"，第一个是"至高"，表示"最高"，第二个是"至做得"，表示"才"。绝对性的"至"和条件式的"至"，前后两例，都是一句并存。又如下列两句，"至安乐"和"至安心"，意思看来极相似，但是用法有别：

(17) a. 我而家至安乐啫。(Morrison，1824：Ⅷ)

I am now quite at ease and happy being delivered from some dreaded evil.

b. 等到你身子好哓，嗷至安心。(*RCC*，1894：140)

They waited (with anxiety) till you recovered，then their minds were composed.

(17)a 句没有上文交代，所以句子可以有程度和条件两种解释，但是(17)b 只有一种意思，条件分明。

2.1.3 表条件句的"正"

上文说明"至"在粤语中表条件式的用法，并尝试解释这种条件式用法，认为是从表示绝对性最高级的"至"，引申为表示相对性的"至"，由程度修饰转化为条件标志，涵盖范畴从形容词扩大到整个分句。

至 + Adj	(绝对性)	(描述性)
至 + Adj	(相对性)	(条件式)
至 + V		
	P1，至 + P2 (条件句)	↓

从语义和语用的演化过程来看，这种解释可以备为一说。但是根据历史语料，我们并不能看出在时代上其前后演化的轨迹。原因很可能是我们的历时材料只能上溯两百年，窗口窄，视深浅，无法重塑整个变化的过程和进度。不过，我们从现存语料中找到了另外一条线索，也许可以作为我们这种拟测的一个佐证。

在讨论"至"的演化过程中，我们可以从另一个角度来理解。"至"原来的意思是"到达"，而表示"条件"的用法也许是从"到达"的用法延伸而成的。以(13)b 为例，我们可以说在画中添上红叶，这才会"达到"所谓"漂亮"的标准。

(13) b. 幅画要加多啲红叶，嗷嘅风景至靓。

这个说法，看起来似乎更合理。但是我们参考语料，发现早期粤语中表示条件句的还有另一种句式。相比而言，这一种句式似乎更能说明从“相对”过渡到“条件”的演变过程。这一种句式，用“正”作为标志。我们先看下面几句：

(18) a. 佢哋几时正饮茶呢？(Bridgman，1841：182)
When do they drink tea?
b. 红萝卜要焓得一点钟正食得。(Bridgman，1841：151)
Carrots require boiling a full hour before they become fit to be eaten.
c. 点样至晓得呢？(Bridgman，1841：4)
How can knowledge of these be acquired?

(18)a 句中的“几时正”可以理解为“几点整”的意思；但是在（18)b 中，“一点钟正……”只有一个意思，就是“要一个小时才……”。换言之，“正”的用法和上文说的“至”一样。（18)c 和（18)b 都是“得”字句，同样的句型，利用“正/至”表示条件。

我们从早期语料中可以找到不少这样的“正”字用法：

(19) a. 一年要十万银正得够用。(Bonney，1853：92)
One hundred thousand dollars are yearly needed for use.
b. 我喺唐山学过，正嚟咯。(Stedman/Lee，1888：34)
I learnt it in China before I came here.
c. 大人，因顾命我正打佢啫。(Stedman/Lee，1888：34)
May it please Your Honor，I struck him in self-defence.
d. 但系佢唔知揾乜嘢法子正做得。(*RCC*，1894：37)
But they did not know how to get him into disgrace. —（but they did not to-find what means to do to-be-able）
e. 我两个痴梦痴得咁交关，未知何日正醒？（正粤讴，1900：10）
f. 总要长命又要长情，正可以渡得鹊桥。（正粤讴，1900：41）

从上下文意来看，这些“正”字句的用法正相当于“至”。同是 Stedman and Lee《英语不求人》（1888）的（19)b 和（19)c 两句，第一句表示时序前后，第二句表示在什么情形之下才出手打人。同样，(19)e 和（19)f 两句，都出自《正粤讴》（1900)，第一句表示时序，第二句表示条件。“正”字句和“至”字句的表现基本相同。

这种“正”字的用法已经不见于现代粤语，遍查坊间各种粤语字典，都没有开列这种例句。换言之，条件句的“正”已经从现代粤语中消失，但是语料中却给我们保存了使用实例，自是珍贵。不过更有意思的问题是，这个“正”的用法从何而来？

“正”原来的意思是“平正”、“不倾斜”、“正确”，引申为“的确”、“确实”的意思，是副词的用法。例如“正好”，就是“确实好”、“真正好”的意思。《现代汉语八百词》说这是"加强肯定的语气"的用法。[①] 早期粤语材料中颇有一些这种用法。例如1856年Williams的词典中，在词条"正"底下注明"correct"、"right"等意思；[②] 1924年*Cantonese Made Easy*也收有"正"的词条，批注是"正：right"（LXXXVII），同书第96页有这样的句子：

（20）真正好喇。（*CME*，1924：96）
It is really good.

这正是"加强语气"的用法。以"啱"为例，下面的句子是一个描述句，肯定事情的"正确"性。

（21）a. 噉正啱。
（这样十分正确。）

假如这个正确性要在某种特殊的情形之下才存在，那就是一个"条件句"。

b. 要噉正啱。
（要这样才十分正确。）

换言之，这种说法沿用既久，"正"就会从描述性的"非常"，慢慢延伸到表示条件，成为"条件句"的标志。下面一句是从1888年《英语不求人》中节录出来的：

（22）a. ……揽条白围裙正好。

从字面上看，意思是"系上白色围裙最好"。可是从全句上下文来看，意思很不一样。

b. 大凡企枱，要揽条白围裙，正好。（Stedman/Lee，1888：28）
When you wait on the table，Charley，you must wear a white apron.

显然，这个句子中的"正"并不是表示"非常"，而是说明"条件"：非要系上白围裙才合格。下例是同书"正好"类似的用法。

（23）好咧，记得带批来正好呀。（Stedman/Lee，1888：18）
Don't forget to bring your lease with you.

用"正"表示"条件"句的用法，19世纪以后已经不太普遍。说话人也许不知道"正"的来源，于是在书写上往往会用发音相近的假借字代替。例如：

---

① 吕叔湘：《现代汉语八百词》，北京：商务印书馆1981年版，第598页。

② S. W. Williams，*A Tonic Dictionary of the Chinese Language in the Canton Dialect*，Canton：The Office of the Chinese Repository，1856，p. 19。

（24）我哋惯多十二点钟净瞓。（*Lexilogus*，1841：103）
（我们常到晚上十二点钟方睡。）[①]

括号中的翻译见于原书，以“方”对“净”，正说明这种条件句的用法。[②]

早期粤语中表示“条件”的有“至”和“正”两种标志。“至”和“正”本来都没有“才”或“方”的意思，表条件应该是一种后起的用法。我们的设想是“至”和“正”原先是表程度的副词，是“最”或“非常”的意思，描述或加强形容后面形容词表示的情状。这样的描述句，要是放在一定的情境之下，或是时间前后的限制，或是有某种特殊的条件，描述于是就成了条件底下的结果，而“至”和“正”也就渐渐转化为“条件”的标志，原来在语义语用上的关联后来也鲜为人知，慢慢地也就被人们忘却。

这两个标志，在早期语料中并存，但是今日只留有“至”。下面我们把19世纪到20世纪初语料中表条件的“至”和“正”的出现情形，列表说明：

表1　19世纪到20世纪初语料中“至”和“正”出现的情形

年份	作者	书名（简称）	正	至
1828	Morrison	*Vocabulary*		×
1841	Bridgman	*Chrestomathy*	×	×
1841		*Lexilogus*	×	
1847	Devan	*Beginner's 1st Book*		×
1853	Bonney	*Colloquial Phrases*	×	
1865		亲就耶稣		×
1877		*Easy Phrases*		×
1883—1907	Ball	*Cantonese Made Easy*（*CME*）		×
1888		述史浅释		×
1888	Fulton	*Progressive Idiomatic*		×
1888	Stedman and Lee	*Phrase Book*	×	×
1894	Ball	*Readings in Cantonese Colloquial*（*RCC*）		×
1900		正粤讴	×	×
1903		粤音指南		×
1912	Ball	*How to Speak Cantonese*（*HSC*）		×
1926	Caysac	*Cantonaise*	×	

① *Lexilogus* 全书例句并列官话、粤语、闽语和马来语的说法。
② 粤语中“净”和“正”声母韵母俱同，但“净”属阳去，“正”属阴去，声调有异。

第一，根据材料来看，使用“正”的文本远比“至”少，而且“正”主要出现在19世纪中期左右的材料中，其后只偶尔出现而已。以1841年Bridgman的*Chrestomathy*为例，“正”、“至”两见，但用“正”的只有2例，用“至”的有14例。

（25）a. 佢哋几时正饮茶呢？（Bridgman，1841：182）
When do they drink tea?
b. 点样至晓得呢？（Bridgman，1841：4）
How can knowledge of these be acquired?

但在更早期的1828年Morrison的*Vocabulary*中，用“至”的共有13例，用“正”的则全然不见。

（26）做乜你咁耐至黎？（Morrison，1828：Ⅷ）
Why are you so long in coming?

第二，19世纪中叶以后，“正”、“至”两用的情形只见于1894年Ball编写的*Readings in Cantonese Colloquial*。但“正”只有一例，其他句子都用“至”。

（27）a. 但系佢唔知揾乜嘢法子<u>正</u>做得？（*RCC*，1894：37）
But they did not know how to get him into disgrace.
b. 点样亲爱<u>至</u>做得？（*RCC*，1894：150）
But in what manner is this love and kindness to be manifested to them?

Ball除了编写*Readings in Cantonese Colloquial*以外，还撰有其他一系列的粤语教科书，但是遍查各书，都没有“正”字的用例。①

（28）a. 要照直讲，亲眼见，亲耳听，<u>至</u>好讲出嚟。（*CME*，1888：30）
You must tell the truth, and only say what you have seen and heard yourself.
b. 打咀至好放佢出去咯。（*CME*，1907：12）
Only let him go when he has been beaten.

在各种材料中只有《正粤讴》一书中有一例用“致”［例（29）d］，其他全部用“正”。②

（29）a. 风流到底正算得老来娇。（正粤讴，1900：41）
b. 只望捱通世界正有的心机。（正粤讴，1900：35）

① Ball编写的书包括：*Cantonese Made Easy*（1883，1888，1907，1924），*Readings in Cantonese Colloquial*（1894），*How to Write Chinese*（1905），*Cantonese Made Easy Vocabulary*（1908），*How to Speak Cantonese*（1912）。Ball也曾撰写专文论述新会、东莞、香山、顺德等地的粤语。

② 例（29）c句中“方正”连用。

c. 悟破色空方正是乐景。（正粤讴，1900：1）

d. 凭柳丝你代诉，故此咁远致到得呢处离亭，我亦不惮劳。（正粤讴，1900：39）

《正粤讴》由广州五桂堂出版，确切年代不详，大概是19世纪末、20世纪初的刊物。全书收录粤讴，大都是有关妓院生涯、男欢女爱的故事。这些歌曲，相信在行中流传已久，19世纪末才搜集成书。这样看来，粤讴的唱词，可能是19世纪早期的语言。

究竟“正”、“至”的用法是什么时候在语言中最早出现？根据现有的材料，无从考证。但很明显的是，虽然在19世纪的材料中两者俱存，但是“至”已渐渐取代“正”。上文所引例句（24），见于1841年的词典，“正”写作“净”，正表示这种“条件”句的用法，在19世纪中期以后，已经不太普遍。说话人也许不知道“正”的来源，于是在书写上，转用音近的假借字代替。

（24）我哋惯多十二点钟净瞓。（*Lexilogus*，1841：103）

（我们常到晚上十二点钟方睡。）

20世纪以后，“正”的用法荡然无存。但一直到今天，语言中还保留着“至”这个特有标志。

2.1.4 “至”与“先”

其实，在今日粤语中，“至”的用法也略有改变。比如上文所举的例（10），口语中更自然的说法是：

（10）a. 你揾到工至好揾老婆。

b. 你揾到工<u>先</u>至好揾老婆。

语料中列举的19世纪以来的例子，用今天的粤语来说，都可以前加“先”，“先”和“至”前后相承，于是形成“先至”连用的表达方式。例如：

（9）a. 你络住下耙<u>至</u>好讲啊。（Bridgman，1841：Ⅷ）

Tie up your jaws and then speak freely.

a'. 你络住下耙先<u>至</u>好讲啊。

Tie up your jaws and then speak freely.

翻查语料，1841年的 *Chrestomathy* 和19世纪末的 Fulton 教科书，各有一例“先至”连用：

（30）若有小子相随，则小子<u>先至</u>叩门……（Bridgman，1841：183）

If he had a servant in attendance, the servant precedes him, and knocking at the gate …

（31）呢个字就<u>先至</u>读紧嚟，你就忘记咯。（Fulton，1888：50）

This character which you just read, you have forgotten.

细看上下文，(30) 句的"先至"是"先到达"的意思，虽然是连用，但各自独立。(31) 句的"先至"，"至"确实是表示"才"的意思，但"先"却是和前面的"就"连用，自成一词，"就先"就是"刚才"的意思。这也就是说，表示"条件"的"先至"连用到20世纪以后才慢慢流行。

我们知道在条件句的句式"P1，至P2"中，"至"是标志时序前后，说明非要到达某个时间或事件P1以后，才会有P2的结果。所以用"先"也可以理解。但是这样的理解，"先"应该属于P1，所以不会进入P2的范畴，"先至"不可能独立成词。这样一来，今日"先至"连用，又当如何解释？

我们知道在现代粤语中，副词"先"常常出现在动词之后："V + 先"，和现代汉语的词序"先 + V"正好相反。例如：

(32) a. 你先吃。(现汉)
b. 你食先。(粤语)

"先"字后置的用例，粤语早期语料中并不多见。19世纪的文本中，仅数见而已。

(33) a. 唔知写边的先呢？(Bridgman，1841：22)
Yet I do not know which part of the character should be written first?
b. 我想喺世界上快活一排先，等到老大时容乜易信呢？(亲就耶稣，1865：32)
c. 神至羔，未创世个时，就割定先嘅咯。(述史浅释，1888：24)

一般词序是"先"字先行，如：

(34) a. 向尾先入。(Morrison，1828：102)
(The tiger) enters (a den) tail foremost.
b. 阿哥先行。(Bridgman，1841：98)
The eldest brother walks foremost.
c. 你先打地。(Lobscheid，1871：77)
d. 唐人细仗仔先读个部嘅咯。(*CME*，1888：32)
That is …the book that a Chinese boy first reads.

我们试设想表示条件的"至"字句，前后两部分，前一部分先发生，可以加"先"，后一部分表示结果，带"至"。这样的句构应该是：

先P1，至P2。

假如"先"字移后，句构就成为：

P1先，至P2。

这样一来，“先”和“至”就会前后相靠紧，词序重新分析，“先至”连成一个双音节的词语，渐渐成为“条件”句的正式标志。

先 P1，至 P2 ↓
→ P1 先，至 P2 ↓
→ P1，先至 P2

我们试用下面的语料句子为例：

（35）a. 一个人欠人，应该先还番，后来至顾自己。（述史浅释，1888：71）
先 V1，至 V2

要是“先”字移后，时间词“后来”省略，句子会是这样：

b. 一个人欠人，应该还番先，至顾自己。
V1 先，至 V2

然后，词序经过重新调整，“先至”连用，就成了现代的新句式：

c. 一个人欠人，应该还番，先至顾自己。
V1，先至 V2

但是这样的句构，在语料中我们却找不到实例。“先”、“至”前后两句连用，整个语料中除（35）a 外，还有另一例句：

（36）先使把荷包锁，锁紧个度门至得。（*CME*，1888：28）
First take a padlock，and lock the door securely.

我们也可以按上述的步骤，移位重整，得出下面这样的句子：

a. 先 ……锁紧个度门，至得。
b. ……锁紧个度门先，至得。
c. ……锁紧个度门，先至得。

当然，这样的移位重整，只是推想而已，我们并没有实证支持这样的解释。不过，正如上文所说，现有的材料无论从年代上还是从概括范畴来说，都极为有限。将来随着发现的材料越多，一定能更进一步了解其整个发展的过程和时间进度。

2.2 表否定命令句式的标志："莫个"

现在讨论早期粤语中另一个语法现象。现代粤语表示否定式的命令句是在动词之前加"咪"或"唔好"，如：

（37）咪嘈。
（别吵！）

（38）唔好嘈。

"唔好"［m + hou］或可连读成［mou］，写成"冇"，不过这是近日的新变化。[①]古代汉语则一般用"勿"或"莫"，放在动词之前。如《孙子兵法》中的"穷寇勿追"、《满江红》中的"莫等闲"等等。这四个标志，在早期粤语中一并俱存。而四者之中，又以"咪"和"莫"最为常见。例如：

（39）a. 你咪嚟混我啰。（Bridgman，1841：251）
Don't you try to make game of me.
b. 请大人咪见怪。（粤音指南，1903：4.1）

（40）唔好撩佢啊。（Morrison，1828：I）
Don't annoy him.

（41）而家勿混我。（*EPCD*，1877：L.29）
Don't bother me now.

（42）a. 牛肉刀，莫磨薄。（Bridgman，1841：139）
Do not scour the case knives so thin.
b. 普劝世间人仔，莫误结个段水上丝箩。（正粤讴，1900：38）

但是，早期粤语语料中还有一个表否定的命令词"莫个"，今日不用。例如：

（43）a. 你莫个催我。（Morrison，1828：47）
Don't hurry me.
b. 你莫个开咁大价呀。（Bridgman，1841：247）
You do not charge an exorbitant price.
c. 莫个讲。（Lobscheid，1871：417）
Do not speak.
d. 莫个逢人就热，热到咁痴缠。（正粤讴，1900：37）

① "冇"的发音是阳上调，而在"唔好"这样压缩而成的新结合中，则读成阴上调，有的时候会写成"帽"。"帽"本是阳去，但在口语中转读阴上变调。

下面我们把语料中“莫”、“莫个”和“咪”出现的情形合成一表，以示比较。

表2　19世纪到20世纪初语料中“莫”、“莫个”和“咪”出现的情形

年份	作者	书名（简称）	莫	莫个	咪
1828	Morrison	*Vocabulary*	×	×	×
1841	Bridgman	*Chrestomathy*	×	×	×
1841		*Lexilogus*	×		
1847	Devan	*Beginner's 1st Book*	×		
1859	Chalmers	*Pocket Dictionary*			×
1865		亲就耶稣			×
1871	Lobscheid	*A Chinese and English Dictionary*	×	×	
1877		*Easy Phrases*			×
1888—1907	Ball	*Cantonese Made Easy*	×		
1888	Fulton	*Progressive and Idiomatic*			×
1889	Kerr	*Selected Phrases*			×
1894	Ball	*Readings in Cantonese Colloquial*			×
1900		正粤讴	×	×	
1903		粤音指南			×
1912	Ball	*How to Speak Cantonese*			×
1931	Wells	*English Cantonese Dictionary*			×
1936	Hoh/Belt	*Pocket Guide*			×

从表中分布来看，从19世纪以来，否定式的命令句当以“咪”为最常见的标志。20世纪以前，使用“莫”的材料也颇常见，但“莫个”仅见于四种语料，其中1871年Lobscheid书中只偶然出现，还是以“莫”为常。而在最早的Morrison的词典中（1828），虽然“莫”和“莫个”并见，但是用“莫个”的例子很多。全书共有14句用“莫个”，25句用“莫”，看起来，似乎以用“莫”为常，但仔细查看，用“莫”的句子多是熟语或文言句，如（44）a～c，口语句子只有个别几例而已，如（44）d。

（44）a. 命里有来终须有，命里无来莫强求。（Morrison，1828：I）
If it be your destiny to possess，you must at last possess，
if it be your destiny not to possess，don't seek it violently.
b. 非酒莫饮，非肉莫食。（Morrison，1828：Ⅶ）
Ill gotten wine don't drink it，ill gotten flesh don't eat it.
c. 英雄莫问出处。（Morrison，1828：XV）
An heroic man，ask not whence he came.
d. 你莫率佢阿。（Morrison，1828：I）
Don't meddle with him.

较晚的 Bridgman 的 *Chrestomathy*（1841），也是"莫"、"莫个"两见，但是全书只有两个例子用"莫个"，如（45）c，其他例句，不分文白，一律用"莫"，如（45）a～b。

（45）a. 莫欺白发人。（Bridgman，1841：72）
Do not insult a gray-headed man.
b. 黄姜汤，莫整咁辣嚡。（Bridgman，1841：164）
Do not make the mulligatawny so hot.
c. 莫个失手势。（Bridgman，1841：68）
Do not refuse to me what I desire.

这也就是说，在短短的十多年间，"莫个"已经被"莫"取代。1871 年 Lobscheid 的词典、19 世纪末的《正粤讴》，虽然也都是"莫"、"莫个"两见，但"莫个"都只有一例，而同时代或前后的语料中都没有"莫个"的用例。显然"莫个"已经在语言中消失殆尽。

翻检材料，20 世纪以后，"莫"的用法也不复多见。表示否定式的命令句就主要用"咪"为标志。其实，如上所述，"咪"字句早就见于 19 世纪的材料。一直到今天，历久弥新。不过，有一点应当注意的是，在个别文本中，也有"咪个"的组合。如：

（46）a. 我劝你各人，咪个遮瞒自己，咪个俾人遮瞒。（亲就耶稣，1865：20）
b. 求老爷千万赏面，咪个推辞。（粤音指南，1903：22）

"咪个"用例极少，但可见原先不管是"咪"或"莫"，都可以有"否定词＋个"的结合。

2.2.1 "莫个"的来源

"莫个"是一个很奇特的组合。"莫"是否定词，"个"是量词，应该是不可能前后相承组合成词的，古代文献中并没有这样的词语。①显然这是早期粤语的一个特有用法。但是究竟来自何处？此问题一直缠绕在心。近年我在整理早期粤语语料的时候，本来是研究另一个课题，突然有一种联想，也许可以解释"莫"怎么和"个"连接起来发生关系。现在就想借用一些篇幅，说明我的看法。

"个"本是汉语中一个很常用的量词，由来已久。但是在粤语中，"个"却经历过一连串的语法转型，获得了一些新的语法功能，并以新的语音形式出现。我最近写了两篇文章，讨论早期粤语中的"个"。简单而言，我以为"个"在近代粤语中，先从量词转化为指示词，表远指，书写形式从"个"改成"吓"，声调从原来的阴去调（调 3）转为阴上调（调 2），而声调转型当在 20 世纪早年完成。②下列两例，正表示这两个阶段的"个"［$kɔ^3$］和"吓"［$kɔ^2$］。

① 我曾经就"莫个"的出处，向蒋绍愚和曹广顺二位先生请教，承蒙他们检阅有关的语料库，都没有收获。

② 请参看张洪年：《早期粤语"个"的研究》，载于何大安、张洪年、潘悟云、吴福祥编《山高水长：丁邦新先生七秩寿庆论文集》，台北："中央研究院"语言学研究所 2006 年版，第 813～835 页。

（47） a. 挤好个的酒樽。（［kɔ^{3}］）（Bridgman，1841：136）

Arrange those wine bottles in good order.

b. 叫木工嚟，整翻好吤度们。（［kɔ^{2}］）（*CME*，1907：28）

Call the carpenter，to mend that door.

有关汉语中量词和指示词之间的关系，已有前人撰写文章，讨论汉语方言中指示词来自量词的变化。①但是像粤语这样有明文记录，甚至连转化过程和时代前后在语料中都有迹可寻，而别的方言到现在还没有这样的发现。所以，粤语中"个"和"吤"的传承，我们相当肯定。

与此同时，表指示远指的"个"又从简单的指代延伸到表"状态"和"程度"的用法，变化颇有类于现代汉语的"这/那"转成"这样/那样"和"这么/那么"的用法。不过这个变化在粤语中比较复杂。首先，粤语中表"这样/那样"和"这么/那么"的是"噉"［kɐm^{2}］和"咁"［kɐm^{3}］。从表面上来看，他们的语音形式和语法功能都与量词或指示词的"个"［kɔ］没有必然的关系。我在最近的一篇文章中指出"咁/噉"的发音，根据19世纪的语料，当时应该是［kɔm^{3}］，元音从［ɔ］转为［ɐ］，声调从原来的阴去（调3）分化为阴上（调2）和阴去（调3），都是后起的现象。而［kɔm^{3}］的双唇韵尾［-m］，原是来自双唇声母的"物"［mɐt］，② 这也就是说原来表"状态"和"程度"的应该是"个+物"［kɔ + mɐt］的合成词，后来经过语音连读的变化，产生了新的音节：③

个物	←	咁
［kɔ + mɐt］		［kɔm］→［kɐm］

其间的变化，可以列表图解如下：

kɔ^{3}（量） →	kɔ^{3}（远指） →	kɔ + m	
│	│	│	
│	│	kɔm^{3}	
│	│	│	╲
│	│	kɔm^{3}（程度）	kɔm^{3}（情态）
│	│	│	│
│	kɔ^{2}（指）	kɔm^{3}（程度）	kɔm^{2}（情态）
│	│	│	│
kɔ^{3}（量）	kɔ^{2}（指）	kɐm^{3}（程度）	kɐm^{2}（情态）
个	吤	咁	噉

① 张惠英（2001）对汉语方言中指示词和量词的关系，有详细的论述。

② 有关 -m 来自"物"的说法，请参看郭必之：《香港粤语疑问代词"点［tim^{35}］"的来源》，《语言学论丛》2003年第27辑。

③ 张洪年：《"咁"又如何？——再探早期粤语中的指示代词》，*Bulletin of Chinese Linguistics*，2013，7.2，Special Issue Celebrating the 10th Anniversary of the Li Fang-Kuei Society for Chinese Linguistics，pp. 165－201.

我现在的设想是，在更早期的粤语中，表示"状态"、"程度"的指代就是一个"个"［kɔ³］。所以"莫+个"并非"否定+量词"，而是"否定 +指代"，就是"别这样……"的意思，相当于后来的"莫 + 咁"。上文所举（43）a 例子，意思就是"你莫咁催我。"

（43）a. 你莫个催我。（Morrison，1828：47）

Don't hurry me.

按这样的分析，"个"是表状态的指代，修饰后面的动词"催"，而否定的"莫"是否定后面整个"个催"。所以句子的组合成分是：

莫+［个 + V］

用之已久，两个单音节的"莫"和"个"，合成一个双音节的"莫个"，这个表指代的"个"后来经过种种变化，语音形式转为［kɔm］，"莫个"就再一次经过语法重新分析，独立成词。

莫+［个 + V］ →
［莫+个］+ V →
［莫个+ V］ →
［莫个-m + V］ →
［莫噉 + V］

"莫个"这个新组合的产生，一方面是因为双音节化的趋势，但更重要的原因恐怕是表"状态"、"程度"的指代在语言中有进一步的变化，产生新的［kɔm］的语音组合，写成"咁"、"噉"，和原来的"个"关系渐远，这样一来，在"莫……个"的句构中，"个"的语法身份游离不明，于是更容易和前面的"莫"黏着成词，粤语中便多了一个表命令的否定词，和原来的"莫"平起平坐。我们推想这个"莫个"新组合，在早期粤语中一定颇为流行，所以 1828 年的词典，"莫个"的例子占尽优势。我们再翻查语料，发现下面这样的例子：例（48）中"莫个"和"咁"一起出现；例（49）中则"莫个"后加"如此"，而"如此"本就是"个"的意思。

（48）莫个咁生疏阿。（Morrison，1828：I）

Don't let your visits be so infrequent.

（49）自后莫个如此。（Morrison，1828：76）

Henceforth，or hereafter，not as thus.

从这些用例中可以看出在"莫个"这个新组合中，"个"的原意已经完全隐没。

我们的语料最早上溯到 19 世纪早期，但仔细翻阅整理，都没有发现"个"可以单独使用，标志"状态"、"程度"的用例。这也就是说，假如我们的说法成立，以为"莫个 + V"是来自"否定 + 指代 + V"，那么这一定是 19 世纪以前的情形。但是由于材料有限，我们无法肯定或否定这种可能。

不过，“个”作为表远指或表“状态”、“程度”的指代，在近代汉语中早有先例可援。

2.2.2 历史文献中“个”表指代的用法

1945年张相编成《诗词曲语辞汇释》，汇集唐宋以来诗词戏曲中的特殊语词，“详引例证，解释辞义与用法，兼谈其流变与演化”①。其中有词条“个”（第372～373页），说明如下：

个，指点辞，犹这也，那也。

他列举隋唐以来诗词例句为证，例如：

周邦彦《瑞龙吟》词：“暗凝伫，因记个人痴小，乍窥门户。”个人，那人也。
贺铸《鹤冲天》词：“个处频回首。”个处犹云此处。
朱敦儒《朝中措》词：“个是一场春梦，长江不住东流。”个是犹云此是。

这也就是说，隋唐以来，“个”是一个指代词，可以远指，也可以近指。

同书又指出“个”的另一个用法，并广征诗词曲语为证（第364～372页）。张相以为“个”是“估量某种光景之辞”，用法等于“价”或“家”。而他给“价”和“家”下的解释是：

估量某种光景之辞，犹云这般或那般，这个样儿或那个样儿。（第364页）

诗词举例如：

凡少则曰些儿个。李后主《一斛珠》词云：“晓妆初过，沉檀轻注些儿个。”
朱敦儒《鹊桥仙》词：“轻风冷露夜深时，独自个凌波直上。”独自则曰独自个。

这一种用法就相当于表“状态”的指代词，和粤语中的“噉”相同。虽然诗词举例中，“个”都是放在动词之后，整个短语修饰后面的字句，例如“独自个”修饰“凌波直上”，没有“个”直接放在动词之前，表示“这样做”或“这样的程度”，但是不容置疑的是：从唐宋以来，“个”的用法确实多元，除了是量词之外，还可以是表“这/那”和“这样/那样”的指代词。这样看来，早期粤语中“个”的用法似乎特别，其实很可能是由来已久，上有所承，只是我们并未察觉而已。当然，量词“个”可以延伸为指代的用法是不争的事实，但为什么会有这样的演变，量转指代，背后的动力是什么？这是汉语特有的变化，还是可以在其他语言中找到类似的发展，这点还需要做更多、更深入的研究，才能找到端倪。

---

① 张相：《诗词曲语辞汇释》，北京：中华书局1977年版。引文见书前“重印说明”。

3 结 语

这篇文章，主要是就早期粤语语料中两个比较特殊的例子，进行整理分析以后，提出我对粤语发展的一些看法。我虽然用了二十多种不同的材料，但时间窗口主要还是局限在19世纪到20世纪之间。时限很短浅，但就这百年语料所呈现的种种现象，我们还是可以看出19世纪的语言和今日的语言有明显的不同。我们可以在排比梳理之后，归纳出一些变化的类别，但如何解释这些不同，如何利用这些不同，进一步说明语言变化的轨迹和规律，这是我们需要特别努力的地方。从我们的语料中，我找到一些有关"正"和"莫个"的例句，有异于后代粤语的说法。诚然，这只是一些零星的异同，并不会影响我们对当日文本的了解，也不会让我们对整个粤语的发展趋势有什么新的大发现。其实，翻阅的时候，只要稍不注意，就会很容易忽视，匆匆带过。我用了一些时间前后对读，渐渐发现这些异同之处，除了说明语言演变的路向以外，偶尔还能透露出演变背后的一些道理。一百多年的语料就保留了这一百多年语言的真实现象。从前的说法，现在不说，那就是旧日语言的特质，今日已经消失。语料帮我们把这些消失的说法保存下来，难能可贵，因为没有这些材料，我们根本想象不到语言变化是怎么一回事。要是没有"正"表条件的用例，我们无法联想到今日"至"的用法也许是循着同样语义引申的路子发展而来的；要是没有"莫个"的用例，我们也无法明白在"嘅"以前，还有"个"这个可能单独使用的指代词。当然我们的分析和推论，还有待进一步考证。不过，正是因为语料给我们留下了这些历史残余证据，才会让我们发想无端，希望能把语法发展的每一个阶段和细节逐步逐步地建构起来。历史的残余也是历史的馈赠，我们小心把握、仔细考虑，根据现有的各种历时语料重拾旧步，重新认识从前，同时也可以为当下的发展重新定位。

附　录

本文所用历时语料共 27 种。括号中为论文中征引例句时所用简称。

年份	作者	语料	引用简称
1828	Morrison, Robert	*A Vocabulary of the Canton Dialect*.《广东省土话字汇》. Macao, China: The Honorable East India Company's Press.	(Morrison)
1840		《浪子悔改》. Chinese Protestant Mission.	(浪子悔改)
1840		《落炉不烧》. Chinese Protestant Mission.	(落炉不烧)
1841	Bridgman, E. C.	*Chinese Chrestomathy in the Canton Dialect*. Macao: S. Wells Williams.	(Bridgman)
1841		*A Lexilogus of the English, Malay, and Chinese Languages: Compendium*. Malacca: The Anglo-Chinese College Press.	(*Lexilogus*)
1847	Devan, Thomas T.	*The Beginner's First Book in the Chinese Language (Canton Vernacular)*. Hong Kong: The China Mail Office.	(Devan)
1853	Bonney, Samuel. W.	*Phrases in the Canton Colloquial Dialect*. Canton.	(Bonney)
1856	Williams, S. Wells	A *Tonic Dictionary of the Chinese Language in the Canton Dialect*.《英华分韵撮要》. Canton: The Office of the Chinese Repository.	(Williams)
1859	Chalmers, John	An *English and Cantonese Pocket Dictionary*.《英粤字典》. London Missionary Society's Press.	(Chalmers)
1865		《亲就耶稣》	(亲就耶稣)
1871	Lobscheid, William	*A Chinese and English Dictionary*.《汉英字典》. Hong Kong: Noronha & Sons.	(Lobscheid)
1877	Bruce, E. Donald	*Easy Phrases in the Canton Dialect of the Chinese Language*.《英华常语合璧》. San Francisco: Bruce's Printing House.	(*EPCD*)
1883	Ball, J. Dyer	*Cantonese Made Easy*. Hong Kong: China Mail Office.	(*CME*)
1888	Ball, J. Dyer	*Cantonese Made Easy*, 2nd edition. Hong Kong: China Mail Office.	(*CME*)
1888	Stedman, Thomas L. & K. P. Lee	*A Chinese and English Phrase Book in the Canton Dialect*.《英语不求人》. New York: Williams R. Jenkins.	(Stedman/Lee)
1888	花波氏	《述史浅译》, 广东长老会藏版.	(述史浅译)
1888	Fulton, Albert A.	*Progressive and Idiomatic Sentences in Cantonese Colloquial*. Shanghai: Presbyterian Press.	(Fulton)

（续上表）

年份	作者	语料	引用简称
1889	Kerr, J. G.	*Selected Phrases in the Canton Dialect*. Hong Kong, Shanghai, Yokohama, Singapore: Kelly & Walsh, Ltd.	(Kerr)
1894	Ball, J. Dyer	*Readings in Cantonese Colloquial*. Hong Kong: Kelly & Walsh, Ltd.	(*RCC*)
1900		《正粤讴》，广州：五桂堂.	（正粤讴）
1903		《粤音指南》，香港：聚珍书楼.	（粤音指南）
1907	Ball, J. Dyer	*Cantonese Made Easy*. 3rd Edition. Singapore, Hong Kong, Shanghai, Yokohama: Kelly & Walsh, Ltd.	(*CME*)
1912	Ball, J. Dyer	*How to Speak Cantonese: 50 Conversations in Cantonese Colloquial*. Hong Kong, Shanghai, Singapore, Yokohama: Kelly & Walsh, Ltd.	(*HSC*)
1926	Caysac, Georges	*Introduction a l'Etude du Dialecte Cantonais*. Hong Kong: Imprimerie de Nazareth.	(Caysac)
1927	Wisner, O. F.	*Beginning Cantonese (Rewritten)*.《教话指南》. Canton: China Baptist Publication Society.	(Wisner)
1931	Wells, H. R.	*An English Cantonese Dictionary*. Hong Kong, Singapore, Shanghai: Kelly & Walsh, Ltd.	(Wells)
1936	Hoh, F. T, & Walter Belt	*A Pocket Guide to Cantonese: The Revised and Enlarged Edition*. Canton: Lingnan University.	(Hoh)

参考文献

郭必之 2003 《香港粤语疑问代词"点［tim^{35}］"的来源》，《语言学论丛》第27辑，第69~78页。

张洪年 2006 《早期粤语"个"的研究》，载于何大安、张洪年、潘悟云、吴福祥编 《山高水长：丁邦新先生七秩寿庆论文集》，台北："中央研究院"语言学研究所，第813~835页。

张洪年 2013 《"咁"又如何？——再探早期粤语中的指示代词》，*Bulletin of Chinese Linguistics*, 7.2, pp. 165-201.

张惠英 2001 《汉语方言代词研究》，北京：语文出版社。

张　相 1977 《诗词曲语辞汇释》，北京：中华书局。

Ripples Riding on Waves: Cantonese Tone-melody Match Mechanism Illustrated

Kwan Hin CHEUNG

(The Hong Kong Polytechnic University)

Abstract: For tone-preservation in Cantonese songs, it is the four tone categories 1 + 2, 3 + 5, 6, 4, or "m(elodic)-tones" that count. They form a series of pitch heights that bears some resemblance with a musical scale, hence the name "pseudo-scale" and the self-explanatory names "sharp", "high", "low" and "deep". The two fundamental attributes of lexical tones elasticity and transposability are the keys to the research question: "How the four m-tones in the pseudo-scale are matched to a much larger variety of notes in a song while maintaining the within-scale order of pitch heights?" With the help of expository designs and conventions, it is posited that: ①The lyrics of a song is separated into m-tone groups. ②Group boundaries are where transposing (and tone range widening or compression) occurs. ③Within a group, a default matching relation holds between an m-tone and a musical note, with principled variation permitted by virtue of tone elasticity. The Cantopop classic *The Bund* (《上海滩》) is used for illustration.

Key words: Cantonese　tone-melody match　pseudo-scale　transposing　elasticity

1　Tone and Note

"Tone" in one sense is synonymous with "note" or "musical note". "Tone" in the phonological sense, however, refers to what we more explicitly label as "lexical tone" and is thus clearly different from "musical note". Nevertheless, both senses of "tone" have to do with "pitch". Musical notes are specified with reference to pitch (or pitch height, which means the same); so are lexical tones. That both senses of "tone" have to do with "pitch" partly justifies the extension of the word "tone" in everyday use to its phonological use standing for "lexical tones". In this paper we shall use "tone" solely in the sense of "lexical tone" and use "note" for "musical note".

The relationship between the two senses of tone was well noticed in early descriptions of lexical tone. As a matter of fact description of lexical tone in musical terms predates the non-musical descriptions we are familiar with nowadays. This is especially the case when it came to the description of relatively complex Sinitic tone systems with syllable (as opposed to word) as domain. A classic example is the staff representation of the six lexical tones of Cantonese in Jones and Woo (1912) as reproduced in Figure 1.

> I cannot help feeling that the difficulty of the tones is generally much exaggerated. Anyone who has a musical ear can learn them in a very short time by practising the following tune, singing it on any vowel or on one of the consonants m, n or ŋ until it is firmly fixed in his mind:
>
> 
>
> For ladies' voices this tune might be transposed thus:
>
> 

Figure 1

Jones and Woo (1912) were addressing to English speakers. For them it would be easy to isolate any vowel or nasal for pitch manipulation. For monolingual native speakers of Cantonese, however, isolating an [n] would be difficult as [n] alone does not make a syllable in Cantonese. Having said that, Jones and Woo's suggestion does serve to enable one to examine Cantonese tone in syllables with the simplest structure possible, given that all the long vowels and the nasals [m] and [ŋ] are well-formed single-segment syllables in Cantonese.

Jones and Woo (1912) has another representation of the Cantonese tones somewhere else, with falling allotones given to Tones 1 and 4, as reproduced in Figure 2.

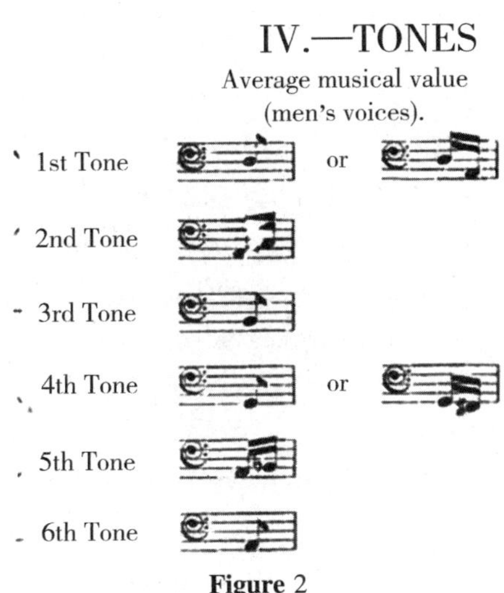

Figure 2

Figure 1 suggests that the level allotones are dominant. Let us initially look at the representation without the falling tones shown in Figure 1 and the left column of Figure 2. As the male voice and the female voice are just transposed counterparts of each other, we settle for looking at just the male voice for the sake of further examination. As Figure 3 shows, Tone 1 or T1 is a semitone higher than the offset of T2, and T3 is a semitone higher than the offset of T5. Note that in the case of the falling allotone of T1 as shown in Figure 2, it is its onset that is a semitone higher than the offset of T2.

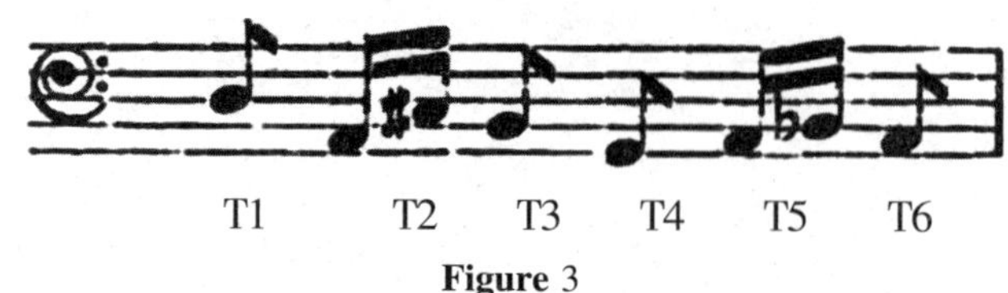

Figure 3

2 From Musical Notations to Chao Tone Letters

Chao (1930a) creates the Chao Tone Letters (CTL) in the course of and by way of notating Cantonese tones on the basis of their musical values as represented in musical notes, with Jones and Woo (1912) explicitly acknowledged. The representations of the six tones in Cantonese are shown in Table 1.

Table 1

Tone #	1	2	3	4	5	6
CTL	˥˧	˧˥	˧	˩	˩˧	˨
Tone name	53:	35:	33:	11:	13:	22:

In Chao's representation, T3 equals offset of T5 in pitch height, with the semitone difference dismissed. In a somewhat similar fashion the onset of T1 equals offset of T2 in pitch height. Here Chao has missed out the level allotone of T1, which should at least apply to the syllables with stops as coda, witness Chao (1930b) to be mentioned shortly. The level allotone of T1 is formally recognized in Chao (1947), where it is annotated as 55:. Thus, as far as the level allotone of T1 is concerned, T1 = offset of T2. The 1947 notation has later become the standard representation among workers on Cantonese tones.

3 Correspondence of Tones and Notes in Singsongs

It is no secret that Chao was a musician and composer. Chao (1930b:171 – 172), written in Chinese, provides an interesting description and demonstration of the somewhat mechanical melodization of speech in Pekinese and Cantonese as a function of the tonal identities of the morphosyllables uttered. He refers to this melodized style of speech as *jiaochangdiao* (叫唱调) or "singsong". In the case of Cantonese, he mentions "text recitation in private tutoring in Guangzhou" and "hawkers on the ferry shouting to sell Tiger Balm Ointment" as two common contexts for the use of such singsong. ① Thus, the six tones of Cantonese, with the two allotones of T1 differentiated, generate respective musical notes at a particular key, as shown in Table 2. ②

Table 2

		3(6)	3	13	1	5	61	6
Non-occluded	Jyutping	jam[1]		soeng[2]	heoi[3]	joeng[4]	joeng[5]	leoi[6]
	Character③	꜀阴		꜂赏	去꜄	꜁阳	꜃养	类꜅
Occluded	Character		北꜆ ↑④		百꜆			白꜇
	Jyutping		bak[1]		baak[3]			baak[6]

Chao's recognition of as many as nine categories (and hence his use of nine characters for demonstration) has somehow to do with the traditional philological preoccupation with maximally identifying the reflexes of the Middle Chinese four-*sheng* (声) (often loosely translated as "tone"), comprising *ping*, *shang*, *qu* and *ru*. Approaching Cantonese as a stand-alone synchronic system, Jones and Woo (1912) indicated over a century ago that the three *ru* categories (all with stop coda) are identifiable with three of the other six categories (all without stop coda). Thus, in Table 2 heoi[3] and baak[3] share the same column; so do leoi[6] and baak[6]. Unlike in Jones and Woo, Chao's (1930a, b) representation of *yin-ping* sheng (i. e. the non-occluded version of T1) as high-

---

① The original Chinese text reads, "广州私塾里读书跟渡船上卖药的讲万金油的万能也用一种简单化的语调"。

② The musical notes used in Chao (1930b) and in the rest of this paper are in numerical notation popular in East Asia, commonly referred to as *jianpu* (简谱) in Chinese. This numerical notation can be considered a numerical substitution (in writing but not in pronunciation) for the Tonic Sol-fa notation. The correspondence between the notes in the three systems is as follows:

Numerical	1	2	3	4	5	6	7
Tonic Sol-fa	d(o)	r(e)	m(i)	f(a)	s(o)	l(a)	t(i)
Western	C	D	E	F	G	A	B

In addition to the difference in representation of musical notes, the way rhythmic values are represented and scores written is also different between this East-Asian numerical notation and Western notations. Following conventions in the former, an underscored note has half the duration of a plain (i. e. non-underscored) note. Thus the "1" and "3", together in succession corresponding to T2, are each underscored, such that "13" form a rhythmic unit comparable to each of the singleton notes corresponding to level tones. The "6" and "1" together corresponding to T5 are underscored for the same reason.

③ Two conventions are adopted in this paper to convey (i) the four-*sheng* identity and (ii) level tone vs rising tone of a Chinese character. For (i), the traditional four-corner connotation (with *yin* vs *yang* subdivision) is used. For (ii) italics is used to specifically stand for a rising tone, namely either T2 or T5, which roughly correspond to *yin-shang* and *yang-shang* respectively but are less restrictive in that they can apply to items with a stop as coda.

④ There is no orthodox notation for the higher vs lower dichotomy of *yin-ru in* the traditional four-corner notation scheme, and the Unicode does not have separate characters for the higher vs lower *yin-ru shengs* either. An upward arrow is used here to signal that it is the higher of the two *yin-ru shengs*, which usually co-occurs with a short nucleus, as is the case for the morpho-syllables bak[1] in Table 2 here and ceot[1] in Table 4 below.

falling only would discourage one to equate the tone shape of the occluded and non-occluded version of T1. Nevertheless, for the other two occluded tones (e. g. 百꜆ and 白꜇) their conflating with the same-pitch non-occluded counterpart is uncontroversial. Adopting this seven-shape analysis, the same raw materials as given in Table 2 above can be rearranged in another way, with the musical notes arrayed from high to low and with lexical items fitted to them, as shown in Table 3.

Table 3

	36̣	3	13	1	5̣	6̣1	6̣
3		北꜆ ↑					
3↘	꜀阴						
↗3			꜂赏				
2							
1				去꜄/百꜆			
↗1						꜃养	
7̣							
6̣							类꜅/白꜇
5̣					꜁阳		
(Jyutping)	jam¹	bak¹	*soeng*²	heoi³/baak³	joeng⁴	*joeng*⁵	leoi⁶/baak⁶

Note that in Table 3 the characters only occupy seven of the rows from 3 to 5̣. The Cantonese singsong that Chao (1930b) demonstrated follows and is displayed in the frame of Table 3, as shown in Table 4.

Table 4

	6̣	3	5̣	5̣	6̣1	3(6̣)	6̣	6̣1	1	5̣	3(6̣)	13	6̣	3(6̣)
3		出꜆ ↑												
3↘						꜀心					꜀歌			꜀心
↗3												꜂解		
2														
1									唱꜄					
↗1					꜃我			꜃我						
7̣														
6̣	日꜇						乱꜅;						乱꜅	
5̣			꜁黄	꜁黄						꜁条				
	jat⁶	ceot¹	wong⁴	wong⁴	*ngo*⁵	sam¹	lyun⁶	*ngo*⁵	coeng³	tiu⁴	go¹	*gaai*²	lyun⁶	sam¹

With the noticeable monotony duly recognized, Chao makes a very interesting comment on the relative monotony between Cantonese singsong and Pekinese singsong, which I translate here: "There are more tones in Cantonese [than in Pekinese]; therefore, granted the simplistic correspondence [of tone and note] it is not as monotonous as that of Pekinese; also, the entire pitch range is no narrower than that used for actual intonation in authentic speech. As a result, it sounds better than that of Pekinese." ①

Singsong lies between speech and singing. Because Sinitic languages are tonal, Sinitic singsongs are somehow melodic, albeit somewhat monotonous. And because Cantonese has more tones than Pekinese, Cantonese singsong is less monotonous and closer to authentic singing. It is clear from the above exposition and demonstration that even Cantonese singsong as singsong par excellence has the following characteristics that contribute to monotony:

(1) The tone-note correspondence is too rigid to be pleasantly melodious.

(2) It does not manipulate rhythm (as an essential element of music) in a musical manner.

If singsong is not singing in the real sense, Cantonese *shuochang* (说唱) definitely is. Cantonese *shuochang* resembles Cantonese singsong in two respects:

(1) Words (lyrics) take precedence over melody, which has no independent, fixed tune.

(2) The melody is a function of (i. e. derived from) the tone of the respective morpho-syllables sung.

For *shuochang*, however, the tone-note correspondence in operation permits principled variation and musical rhythm applies, thus qualifying it to be singing in the real sense. As such its tone-note correspondence operates in such a way that one recognizes the existence of what we call today "tone-melody match mechanism". At the time when Chao (1930b) was published, the time-honoured song-type *shuochang* has been firmly assimilated into Cantonese operatic singing, with its tone-melody match mechanism transplanted to the "aria types(梆黄)" core of Cantonese operatic singing. See Cheung and Wong (2008) for details. Also by that time, Cantonese-toned② fixed-tune singing had emerged and was fast developing, chiefly in the context of Cantonese operatic singing. Chao (1930b) does not touch on either Cantonese *shuochang* or Cantonese-toned fixed-tune singing, where the tone-melody match mechanism operates in an intriguing manner. That said, it

---

① The original Chinese text reads, "广东音声调较多,所以虽简单化了,而比北平的不单调一点,并且全音域不比真语调缩小,所以比北平的好听"。

② I use the word "Cantonese-toned" to refer to the kind of singing with Chinese or Cantonese lyrics in Cantonese pronunciation both segmentally and tonally. This reference makes sense because there exists a way of singing where only the segments are pronounced as in Cantonese, without preserving the Cantonese tonal distinction.

would be fair to say that Chao (1930b) is an important initial step towards our understanding of "tone-melody match" for singing in Cantonese.

4 Before and During the 1980s

After this initial step, there has been no mention of Cantonese tone-melody match or its embryonic form "tone-note correspondence" in the literature, as far as I know, until the 1980s. The 1980s is preceded by certain important milestones in relation to Cantonese-toned singing. In the 1950s Cantonese Opera reached its peak of popularity and artistic achievement. The theme song 《香夭》hoeng^{1}jiu^1 of the opera *The Flower Princess*(《帝女花》dai^{3}neoi^{2}faa^1), launched in 1957, is probably the most sung Cantonese-toned song in history. 1974 is generally held to be the birth-year of modern Canto-pop, the popularity of which among Chinese (not just Cantonese) speakers worldwide continues till at least the turn of the century. The 1970s also saw the entrance of Cantonese opera studies into academia. ① The 1980s is the golden age of Canto-pop when it soared to great heights and gained large followings in Chinese communities worldwide. These milestones paved the way for the initial harvest in the quest for Cantonese tone-melody match in the 1980s.

Yung (1983) observes some correlation between certain *shengs* and certain musical notes. He, however, stopped short of relating the nine *shengs*(九声) to six tones and his interest does not extend from Cantonese opera to Cantonese-toned songs in general. These two characteristics have hindered him from going further in explicitly characterizing the tone-melody match mechanism of Cantonese-toned songs in general. Chi Wah Wong(黄志华), a writer and Canto-pop lyricist, wrote in 1984 of the folk understanding (witness certain tunes with such lyrics popular at the time) that the four Cantonese morpho-syllables saam^1, sei^4, ji^6, ling^4 (i. e. the numerals 3,4,2,0) suffice as the only items used in the lyrics to be set to any tune, literally. He believed he was the first to report on this folk understanding in writing but acknowledged that his set(3,4,2,0) is the result of conflating "1" and "3" in the set "0,1,2,3,4" earlier discovered by a columnist with the pen-name 秋子(cau^{1}zi^2). While the songs with 3-4-2-0 as lyrics enjoyed some popularity at the time, they have not been commercialized until the short tune extracted from the instrumental piece《昭君怨》(ciu^{1}gwan^{1}jyun^3) set to a permutation of the numerals 3,4,2 and 0 appeared in a 1988 movie *The Crazy Companies*(《最佳损友》zeoi^{3}gaai^{1}syun^{2}jau^5). A more successfully commercialized full-length song《数字人生》(sou^{3}zi^{6}jan^{4}sang^1), launched in 1986, has a long stretch of melody set to the numerals from 0 to 9. As "0 to 9" covers not just "3,4,2,0" or the six tones but also the nine *shengs*, it is difficult to say whether the workers behind this song were aware of the said folk under-

① In particular, ethnic musicologist Bell Yung (荣鸿曾) received his Ph. D. from Harvard University in 1976 and began to offer courses in Cantonese Opera in the Chinese University of Hong Kong and later the University of Hong Kong. Leung (梁沛锦, 1979) is probably the first academic book in Cantonese opera published in Chinese, followed by Leung (1982).

standing in terms of four items.

Folk understanding is one thing; explicit formulation of hypothesis is another. Note that the tones of the numerals "3,4,2 and 0" are T1,T3,T6 and T4 respectively. It takes a modern linguist (as opposed to traditional philologist) to observe that the four categories are the result of conflating T1 and T2, which have the same offset, and conflating T5 and T6, which also have the same offset, on the basis of a six-tone system with T1 as 55:. This is exactly what M. Chan (1987) does. She has not referred to the folk understanding mentioned above. Apparently she is not aware of such folk understanding. She actually develops her hypothesis on the basis of a modest corpus. What matters pitch-wise are the six tones, not the nine *shengs*. What matters in Cantonese tone-melody match are the four categories after the two offset-determined conflatings. The resultant categories are distinguished and defined by their offset. The folk understanding and her hypothesis corroborate each other.

5 Nine *shengs* vs Six Tones

Jones and Woo (1912) is little known or cited in writings in Chinese. It is interesting that Chao (1930a) speaks of six tones in Cantonese on the basis of Jones and Woo (1912) but Chao (1930b) still clings to the nine *shengs* of Cantonese. Judging from this difference I tend to believe that Chao (1930b) predates Chao (1930a). In Chao (1930a) he is so conscious of *yin-ping* being 53: as different from upper *yin-ru* being 55: that he only gives the shape 53: to T1, without any reference to the 55: shape, which he well recognizes in Chao (1930b) and later works. The nine-*sheng* preoccupation and the lack of reference to 55: for *yin-ping* have hindered him from conflating *yin-ping* and upper *yin-ru*. Chao finally admits a T1 (in a six-tone system) as 55: in Chao (1947). If Jones and Woo's six tones system and T1 as 55: had been accepted in Chao (1930b), then the top two rows pitched at the (musical) notes 3 and 3 ↘ respectively in Table 3 above could have been combined as a single row pitched solely at the note 3, as shown in Table 5 below, whereby reducing the number of occupied rows in Table 3, each representing a distinct tone shape, from seven to six.

Table 5

	3	13	1	5̣	61̣	6̣
3	꜀阴 jam^{1}/北꜄ ↑ bak^{1}					

In the same vein, the top two rows pitched at the notes 3 and 3 ↘ respectively in Table 4 above could also be combined as a single row pitched solely at the note 3, as shown in Table 6 below, whereby reducing the number of occupied rows or distinct tone shapes from seven to six.

Table 6

	6̣	3	5̣	5̣	61	3	6̣	61	1	5̣	3	13	6̣	3
3		出꜆ ↑ ceot1				꜀心 sam1					꜀歌 go1			꜀心 sam1

After the said conflating of two rows into one as shown in Tables 5 and 6, both of the tables that they belong, namely Tables 3 and 4, would then have six rows occupied (representing six distinct tone shapes) instead of seven. With the two versions of T1 now deemed to be equivalent, the six occupied rows or tone shapes would then be co-extensive with the six tones indicated in the Jyutping romanization, as shown in Table 7.

Table 7

	Table 3 After Revision	Table 4 After Revision	Tones 1 – 6
3	꜀阴/北꜆ ↑	出꜆ ↑, ꜀心, ꜀歌	T1
↗3	꜂赏	꜂解	T2(= ↗T1)
2			
1	去꜄/百꜆	唱꜄	T3
↗1	꜃养	꜃我	T5(= ↗T3)
7̣			
6̣	类꜅/白꜇	日꜇, 乱꜅	T6
5̣	꜁阳	꜁黄, ꜁条	T4

With data thus presented the observable would be much better placed to note the relationship between the notes "3" and "↗3" and that between the corresponding tones T1 and T2, and in parallel fashion the relationship between the notes "1" and "↗1" and that between the corresponding tones T3 and T5. Observation of such relationship is crucial for the far-reaching further conflating of T1 and T2 into one category and of T3 and T5 into another category for tone-melody match as mentioned above.

The nine *shengs* vs six tones positions does make a difference in phonology and in the quest for tone-melody match, as summarized in Table 8.

Table 8

Discipline	Nine *Shengs*(or More)	Six Tones
	Philology	Linguistics
Representation of aak2 (钜 bracelet)	No problem	Cannot cope
Sensitivity towards 55: vs 53:	Lower	Higher
Even-oblique(平仄) dichotomy	Less sensitive	More sensitive
Applicability in Cantonese-toned singing	All Cantonese-toned songs	Cantonese opera only
The four categories for matching with melody	Paving the way for their recognition	Masked

It has taken 57 years for the advancement of tone-melody match from Chao (1930b) to the recognition of the four tonal categories for matching with melody. Perhaps analysts' common preoccupation with nine *shengs* has been the chief hindrance.

Yet one more observation was made in the 1980s which has contributed to a deeper understanding of the mechanism of tone-melody match for Cantonese-toned songs. Thus, Sau Yan Chan (陈守仁) in 1987 observed and commented publicly in the First International Conference on Yue Dialects that an intended "T4" item is sometimes represented as if it was "T6" (in the sense of occupying a slot best suited to T6) and he estimated the odds to be a quarter of the occurrence of T4 items.

6 Four Melodic Tones Constituting a Pseudo-scale

Recognizing the four tone categories for tone-melody match is but the first step towards the understanding of the match mechanism. An immediate question that follows from such recognition is whether the two tones conflated as one category have their respective tone identities preserved in singing. And if so preserved, how? M. Chan (1987) has not addressed the first question, let alone the second. ① The uninitiated might then be led to think that the two conflated tones are neutralized in singing.

Cheung (2007) spelt it out clearly that "a salient characteristic of Cantonese-toned singing is that a rising tone is realized by adding a lower (by one step or two) grace note to a corresponding level tone (i. e. one with the same offset [as the rising tone])" ②, whereby answering both questions. Thus, T2 is the pre-rising counterpart of T1, the two constituting one category. Likewise, T5 is the pre-rising counterpart of T3, the two constituting one category. To capture the fact that these categories are posited for the sake of tone-melody match representation, they may be called melodic tones or "m-tones". The series of m-tones, sorted by pitch height, resembles a musical scale in the sense that it bears some resemblance to the series of notes in a musical scale. These ordered mtones may therefore be considered to constitute a "pseudo-scale" and in this sense can be referred to as "pseudo-notes" of the pseudo-scale. Mnemonic names conveying their relative position on the scale are assigned to these pseudo-notes to facilitate subsequent discussion. The pseudo-notes are presented in Table 9.

---

① Personal communication.

② The original Chinese text reads, "粤语歌唱一大特点，就是把升调处理为在相应的(即结束音高相同的)非升调前加个低二度或低三度的装饰音"。

Table 9

Offset in 5-point System	Level Tones (Numeric Sample)	Rising Tones, with Lower Grace Note (Numeric Sample)	Mnemonic Label of Pseudo-notes
5	T1(三 saam[1])	T2(九 gau[2])	尖 = SHARP
3	T3(四 sei[3])	T5(五 ng[5])	亢 = HIGH
2	T6(二 ji[6])		下 = LOW
1	T4(零 ling[4])		沉 = DEEP

To facilitate recognition, the pseudo-note labels will appear in the upper case throughout this paper as a matter of convention. The Chinese counterpart of these names 尖亢下沉 have the added advantage that each name also serves as an example of the (or one of two) lexical tone(s) associated with the pseudo-note it stands for; e. g. 尖 zim[1] is itself in T1, which belongs to SHARP.

A pseudo musical scale with four items having been posited, the question remains how on earth merely four pseudo-notes can accommodate an authentic song with a range typically spanning an interval of over a tenth and a permutation of ten different notes or so. It is the ultimate objective of this paper to posit that the secret of the tone-melody match mechanism for Cantonese-toned songs lies in two salient attributes of lexical tone systems in general. These attributes are ① tonal pitch space elasticity and ② tonal register transposability, to which we now turn.

7 Tonal Pitch Space Elasticity and Tonal Register Transposability

Lexical tones work within a pitch space. In the daily use of tones, the tonal pitch space exhibits notable elasticity. There are two types of elasticity. First, the entire tonal pitch range (tessitura) is elastic. Second, the pitch level gradations are also elastic. Y. R. Chao's tone-letters (CTL) have a system of five-point gradation of the tonal pitch range as their basis. The interval between 1 and 5 (representing tessitura) may be compressed or widened, as shown in Figure 4.

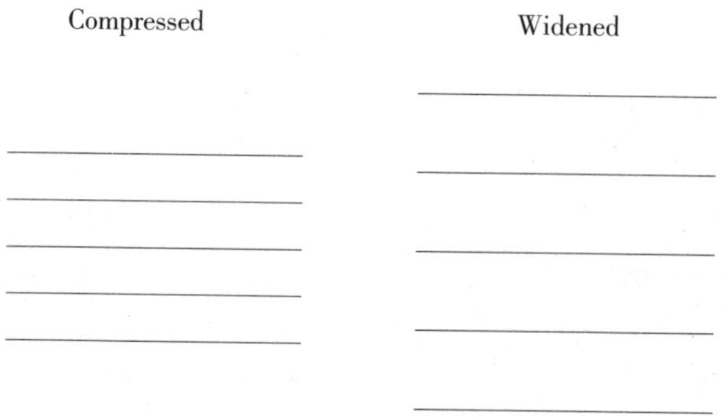

Compressed　　Widened

Figure 4

Compressing or widening of tessitura has a direct bearing on the interval between any two levels out of 1,2,3,4 and 5,as can be observed in Figure 4 shown above.

The second attribute is tonal register transposability. In the daily use of lexical tones, the "general pitch level of the tonal space" is movable upwards or downwards. To demonstrate it with the five-point system,the five bars of the system may as a whole be displaced upwards or downwards,as shown in Figure 5.

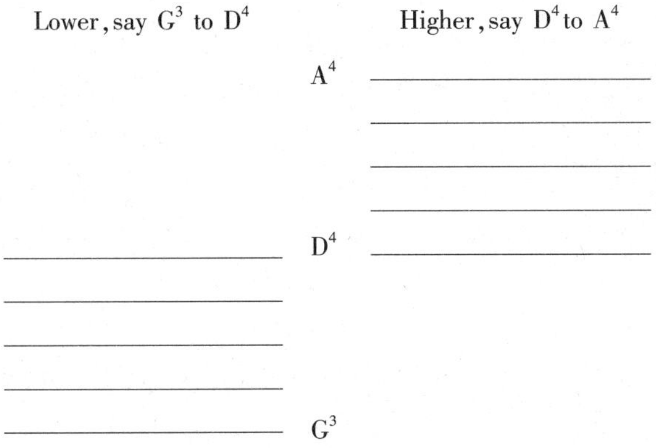

Lower, say G^3 to D^4 Higher, say D^4 to A^4

A^4

D^4

G^3

Figure 5

In the analysis of lexical tones,such difference is often referred to as a difference of "register". We borrow the musical term "transposing" to refer to such displacement of tonal space,hence "transposability". Interpersonal transposing of lexical tones is recognized in as early as Jones and Woo (1912),as shown in Figure 1 at the beginning of this paper. The language they look at is exactly Cantonese. One should not be misled into thinking that transposing merely reflects gender difference. People of the same gender have different general pitch range and the same person also displaces his/her pitch range upwards or downwards in different contexts. "Transposability" works independently of tonal tessitura elasticity. The interplay of the two is demonstrated in Figure 6.

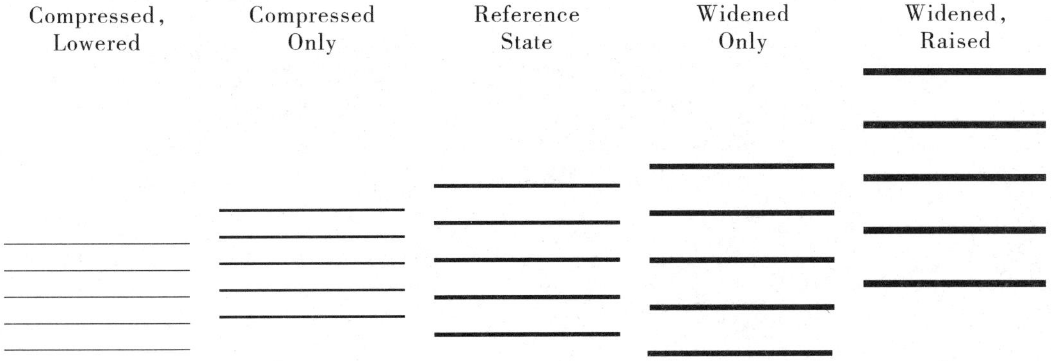

Compressed, Lowered Compressed Only Reference State Widened Only Widened, Raised

Figure 6

8 Typical Matching of Pseudo-notes with Melody

With the two attributes of lexical tone systems clearly spelt out, we are now in a much better position to dig into the very mechanism of tone-melody match for Cantonese. "Tone-melody match" should by now be understood to be the matching of pseudo-notes (in the pseudo-scale) with authentic musical notes in the melody. As we said earlier, the pseudo-notes "SHARP" and "DEEP" mark the top and bottom of a pseudo-scale.

When put against an authentic melody, the SHARP-DEEP range is typically of an interval of a perfect 5th, and a typical range is 2-5. Despite the typicality this particular interval "pitched" at this particular register is just one of many possibilities. The wide range of possibilities, however, does not preclude us from regarding the SHARP-DEEP range 2-5, in terms of both interval and register, as a point of departure to facilitate our exposition of the actual working of the tone-melody mechanism. Not only do we have a typical range of 2-5, which naturally maps SHARP to the note 2 and DEEP to the note 5, but within this range HIGH is also most typically mapped to the note 1 and LOW to the note 6, leaving a HIGH-LOW (as pseudo-notes) interval of a minor 3rd, as shown in Figure 7.

Perfect 5th {
2 SHARP 尖
1 HIGH 亢
7
6 LOW 下
5 DEEP 沉
}

Figure 7

Figure 7 actually shows a typical matching pattern. Recall that T1, T3, T6, T4 are representative of the m-tones/pseudo-notes "SHARP, HIGH, LOW, DEEP". The typicality of the mapping can be seen in the pronunciation ce1, saang3, si6, ho4 of the traditional Cantonese musical notes 尺上士合, which are exactly equivalent to the numerical notes 2, 1, 6, 5, as shown in Table 10.

Table 10

Cantonese Musical Note		Note	Pseudo-note	
Jyutping	Character		English	Chinese
ce1 (=车)	尺	2	SHARP	尖
saang3	上	1	HIGH	亢
si6	士	6	LOW	下
ho4 (=河)	合	5	DEEP	沉

9 Variability in the Matching of Pseudo-notes with Melody

Like the five-point system, the pseudo-scale "SHARP-HIGH-LOW-DEEP" also exhibits elasticity in general, and two kinds of elasticity in particular, which are comparable to (but not exactly the same as) the tessitura elasticity and gradation elasticity of lexical tones mentioned above. Compared with a typical tessitura of an interval of 5th, Figure 8 shows a widened tessitura of a 6th and a compressed tessitura of a 4th.

	6th	Note	4th	
6th	SHARP 尖	3		
	HIGH 亢	2		
		1	SHARP 尖	4th
		$\underset{\cdot}{7}$	HIGH 亢	
	LOW 下	$\underset{\cdot}{6}$	LOW 下	
	DEEP 沉	$\underset{\cdot}{5}$	DEEP 沉	

Figure 8

Recall that for the five-point system for lexical tone representation, the "compressing or widening of tessitura has a direct bearing on the interval between any two levels out of 1, 2, 3, 4 and 5" as mentioned above. At this juncture, it should be noted that there exists a significant difference between the gradations in the five-point system and the intervals between our posited pseudo-notes: the former are equi-distant by design while the latter are not necessarily so. Thus, while it still holds that compressing and widening of the SHARP-DEEP range has some bearing on the between-pseudo-note intervals, it does not follow that all the intervals between adjacent pseudo-notes must be affected (i. e. compressed or widened), as the effect may be carried by some but not all of the intervals. In Figure 8, in comparison with Figure 7, compression and widening are solely shouldered by the "HIGH-LOW" interval. While what we see in Figure 8 are legitimate mapping patterns, they are nevertheless not often utilized. In particular, compression of the SHARP-DEEP range to a 4th occurs infrequently and seems to be the farthest one can go as far as compression is concerned. Widening, on the other hand, is a different story, to which we now turn.

Given the typical mapping pattern as shown in Figure 7 and Table 10, how would a note 3 and a note $\underset{\cdot}{3}$ be interpreted? Tessitura elasticity without the equi-distant gradation interval requirement means that any note higher than the note 2 (which is the recognized corresponding note for SHARP) cannot but be interpreted as being mapped to SHARP, with the SHARP-HIGH interval temporarily increased to a 3rd. Likewise, any note lower than the note $\underset{\cdot}{5}$ (which is the recognized corresponding note for DEEP) cannot but be interpreted as being mapped to DEEP. This generalizable principle applicable to the two ends of the tessitura can be labelled as "extremity elasticity". The working of "extremity elasticity" can be captured by adding two extremity rows to the five-row representation in Figure 7 above, resulting in Table 11.

Table 11

Note	Pseudo-note	
Higher than 2	SHARP ↑	尖 ↑
2	SHARP	尖
1	HIGH	亢
$\underset{\cdot}{7}$		
$\underset{\cdot}{6}$	LOW	下
$\underset{\cdot}{5}$	DEEP	沉
Lower than $\underset{\cdot}{5}$	DEEP ↓	沉 ↓

Now let us go back to the mapping pattern for singsong per Chao (1930b) as presented in Table 7 above. Recall that the table was developed without the notion of four categories of m-tones or pseudo-notes (by virtue of conflating T1 and T2 and conflating T3 and T5) in mind. Seen in the light of the four pseudo-notes, with the said conflating duly incorporated, the mapping there would be simplified as mapping the pseudo-notes "SHARP, HIGH, LOW, DEEP" to 3, 1, $\underset{\cdot}{6}$, $\underset{\cdot}{5}$. Given that note 3 as SHARP ↑ is commonplace with note 2 mapped to SHARP recognized in the first place, one might be prepared, or even tempted, to interpret the note 3 in this vein. However, as the mapping pattern of Cantonese singsong is such that SHARP is mapped only to note 3 and never to note 2, it would be presumptuous to say that note 2 is recognized as the mapping note for SHARP in the first place. Thus, quite different from authentic Cantonese-toned songs which we shall turn to shortly, Cantonese singsong is subject to the following restrictions, which fact fails it as authentic singing:

(1) There is no elasticity:

a. SHARP is consistently mapped to a particular note rather than a range with the lowest possible note as threshold.

b. DEEP is consistently mapped to a particular note rather than a range with the highest possible note as threshold.

c. There is no compressing or widening of tessitura.

(2) There is no transposing, which topic we shall turn to shortly.

A comparison of the mapping for authentic Cantonese-toned songs (with the typical mapping pattern of 2, 1, $\underset{\cdot}{6}$, $\underset{\cdot}{5}$) and that for Cantonese singsong is shown in Table 12.

Table 12

Typical Mapping	Musical Note	Mapping for Singsong
SHARP 尖↑	Higher than 3	x
SHARP 尖↑	3	SHARP 尖
SHARP 尖	2	x
HIGH 亢	1	HIGH 亢
(Subject to interpretation①)	$\underset{\cdot}{7}$	x
LOW 下	$\underset{\cdot}{6}$	LOW 下
DEEP 沉	$\underset{\cdot}{5}$	DEEP 沉
DEEP 沉↓	Lower than $\underset{\cdot}{5}$	x

Transposability, the other major attribute of lexical tones contributing to Cantonese tone-melody match, works to vary the "register" or "general level of pitch range" of the pseudo-scale "SHARP-HIGH-LOW-DEEP". Recall that a person varies his/her pitch range by displacing it upwards or downwards at times. Cantonese-toned singing makes use of this commonplace variability of register by transposing the register intermittently within a song, such that the mapping of the pseudo-scale "SHARP-HIGH-LOW-DEEP" is able to reach a much wider range of musical notes than otherwise. As mentioned above, Cantonese singsong fails to qualify as authentic singing partly because it lacks transposability.

For reasons of Chinese musical style, although theoretically any register goes, the actual registers in common use are in fact limited. Thus, apart from the typical register associated with the typical mapping pattern mentioned above, there are two other commonly used registers. All three are referred to temporarily in terms of the SHARP-DEEP range in Table 13.

Table 13

		Register Type		
		2-$\underset{\cdot}{5}$	6-2	3-$\underset{\cdot}{6}$
SHARP↑	尖↑	Higher		
SHARP	尖	2	6	3
HIGH	亢	1	5	2
		$\underset{\cdot}{7}$	4	1
LOW	下	$\underset{\cdot}{6}$	3	$\underset{\cdot}{7}$
DEEP	沉	$\underset{\cdot}{5}$	2	$\underset{\cdot}{6}$
DEEP↓	沉↓	Lower		

① Unlike Cantonese singsongs, which have the four pseudo-notes rigidly mapped onto the same number of very specific musical notes, authentic Cantonese-toned songs has practically no limit as to what musical notes to use. The musical note on the empty row between HIGH and LOW, while often avoided (for Chinese music stylistic reasons), is nevertheless usable. When used, its mapping interpretation is "HIGH" sometimes and "LOW" at other times, depending on contexts.

These three registers are in common use in Cantonese-toned singing of all kinds, including Canto-pop and Cantonese operatic singing. It happens that they correspond to three functionally different tone-melody mapping patterns commonly in use in core Cantonese operatic music. Thus, the 2-5̣ register is labelled as "正线 zing[3]sin[3]", which can be glossed as "default"; the 6-2 register as "反线 faan[2]sin[3]" or "opposite", alternatively as "左撇 zo[2]pit[3]" or "6&3-prominent"; and the 3-6̣ register as "肉带左 juk[6]daai[3]zo[2]" or "default plus zo[2]pit[3]".

To enable us to visually grasp the relative height of different registers, the content of Table 13 can be organized in another way, such that the musical notes constitute one fixed series, with the mappings for various registers fitted against this fixed series, as shown in the left half of Table 14.

Table 14

	7̣-type	1-type	4-type	7-type	1 7̣-type	4/3-type	
2̇				SHARP 尖			2̇
1̇				HIGH 亢			1̇
7							7
6			SHARP 尖	LOW 下			6
5			HIGH 亢	DEEP 沉		SHARP 尖	5
4						HIGH 亢	4
3		SHARP 尖	LOW 下		SHARP 尖	LOW 下	3
2	SHARP 尖	HIGH 亢	DEEP 沉		HIGH 亢	DEEP 沉	2
1	HIGH 亢						1
7̣		LOW 下					7̣
6̣	LOW 下	DEEP 沉			LOW 下		6̣
5̣	DEEP 沉				DEEP 沉		5̣
4̣							4̣
3̣							3̣

In Table 14, the possibilities for "SHARP ↑" and "DEEP ↓" are taken for granted and are left unrepresented, both to drive home the principle that extremity elasticity has no boundary and to maximally simplify the representation. Another thing about Table 14 is that three more registers (on the right) are added to the three just introduced (on the left). In dealing with such a wider variety of registers, we need a more principled method to label the various register types. As the most usual structure of matching relations has a HIGH-LOW interval of a third, it would be convenient to make use of the single empty slot between HIGH and LOW as a register label. Thus, the "default" register type in Cantonese operatic music mentioned above can be re-labelled as the 7̣-type, etc. For a widened HIGH-LOW interval, we can use both notes in succession, e. g. 1 7̣-type, and for a compressed HIGH-LOW interval, we can make use of a slash, e. g. 4/3-type. As a matter of representational convention, if coloured representation is in use, colour temperature can be employed to signal the relative height of registers, namely the warmer the higher. Of the six register types presented in Table 14 above, it happens that all except the 1-type will appear in later illustrations in this paper.

A convention is adopted here whereby the range from the pseudo-note HIGH to the pseudo-note LOW is shadowed to facilitate visual capture of where a register lies relative to others. Represented in this fashion, it is easy to see that the 7̇-type and the 7-type are the farthest apart. It can also be seen that the 1-type "肉带左 juk^{6}daai^{3}zo^{2}" is closer to the 7̣-type "default" than to the 4-type "zo^{2}pit^{3}". The name "肉带左 juk^{6}daai^{3}zo^{2}" is now not so formidable, for its gloss "default plus zo^{2}pit^{3}" conveys the idea that it is close to "default" but subject to some influence from zo^{2}pit^{3}.

10 Song for Illustration: *The Bund*

It takes an authentic Cantonese-toned song to illustrate the actual working of tone-melody match for Cantonese. The author once used the fixed-tune song《妆台秋思》(zong^{1}toi^{4}cau^{1}si^{3}), the theme song of the Cantonese opera *The Flower Princess* (《帝女花》dai^{3}neoi^{2}faa^{1}) for illustration. While that song is arguably the most sung song in the history of Cantonese-toned singing, it nevertheless has the following drawbacks:

(1) Its popularity is in decline.

(2) It is no longer the best known song for the more active age group, say from 20 – 60 years of age.

(3) The fact it comes from Cantonese opera may lead some to think that it cannot represent Cantonese-toned singing in general.

Mindful of such drawbacks, we use the song *The Bund* (《上海滩》soeng^{6}hoi^{2}taan^{1}) in this paper instead.

The Bund was created in 1980, thus old enough to be a classic. It is in fact one of the long-lasting classics of Canto-pop songs. It was composed by Joseph Koo (顾家辉 Gu^{3} Gaa^{1}fai^{1}), generally held to be the top composer for Canto-pop. Its lyrics was written by James Wong (黄霑 Wong^{4} Zim^{1}), among the top lyricists for Canto-pop. The two together is generally held to be the best combination of composer and lyricist for Canto-pop. The singer is Frances Yip (叶丽仪 Jip^{6} Lai^{6}ji^{4}). There are some objective indications of the popularity of this song, which we will not go into here.

The lyrics of the song is shown in Table 15, which also shows the song's melody structure.

Table 15

<table>
<tr><th colspan="3">Melody Parts</th><th colspan="3">Lyrics</th></tr>
<tr><td rowspan="3">A</td><td>A1</td><td></td><td>1 浪奔，浪流。
万里滔滔江水永不休。
淘尽了世间事，
混作滔滔一片</td><td>3 是喜，是愁。
浪里分不清欢笑悲忧。
成功，失败；
浪里分不出有</td><td>6；9 又有喜，又有愁。
就算分不清欢笑悲忧。
仍愿翻百千浪，
在我心中起</td></tr>
<tr><td rowspan="2">A2</td><td>i（615）</td><td>2 潮流。</td><td></td><td></td></tr>
<tr><td>ii（651）</td><td></td><td>4 未有。</td><td>7；10 伏够。</td></tr>
<tr><td>B</td><td></td><td></td><td></td><td>5；8 爱你恨你，问君知否。
似大江一发不收。
转千弯，转千滩；
亦未平伏此中争斗。</td><td></td></tr>
</table>

The melody of the song has an AABA(BA) structure. The last quarter of A (coded as A2) has minor variation, hence A2i vs A2ii. The second BA is put in parentheses to signal that it is a repetition of the first BA, in terms of both melody and lyrics. The numbers 1-10 shows the order of lyrics parts. Those parts that are repeated have more than one numbers, hence "5; 8", "6; 9" and "7; 10". Towards the end of the song the last two lines of part 10 "仍愿翻百千浪，在我心中起伏够" are repeated. These two lines as repetition, which would be technically part 11, do not particularly concern us here and are not captured in Table 15. Also, as 8-10 are a repetition of 5-7, it suffices to account for tone-melody match up to just part 7.

There are numerous scores of the song made available on the web, mostly in numerical notation but some are in Western notation or both. Not all of these scores serve our purpose; nor are they all correct, as will be demonstrated shortly. Figure 9 is a reproduction of one that we consider to be helpful for our purpose. ①

① The URL is, as at 5 June, 2014, http://www.chaodikong.com/article/2005/1128/2568.html.

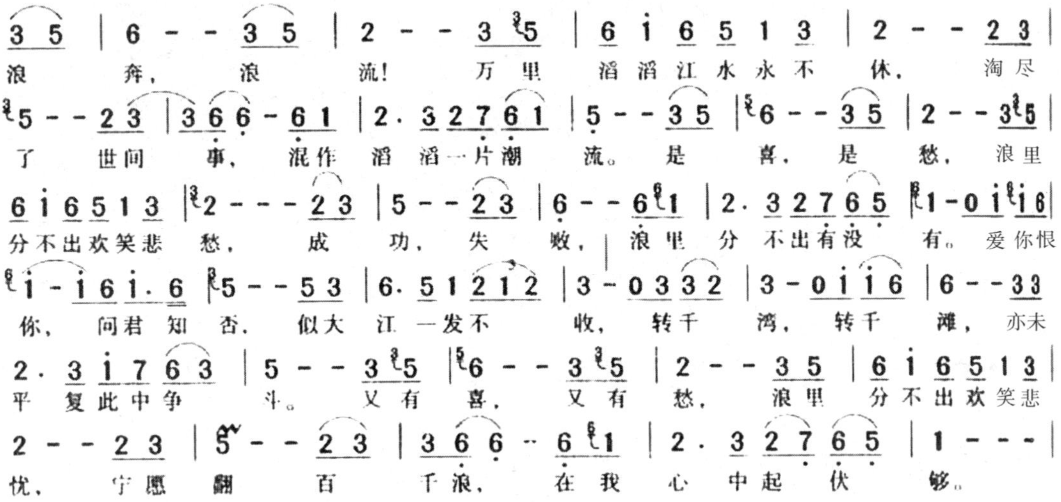

3 5 | 6 - - 3 5 | 2 - - 3 5 | 6 i 6 5 1 3 | 2 - - 2 3 |
浪 奔， 浪 流！ 万 里 滔 滔 江 水 永 不 休， 淘 尽

5 - - 2 3 | 3 6 6 - 6 1 | 2 · 3 2 7 6 1 | 5 - - 3 5 | 6 - - 3 5 | 2 - - 3 5 |
了 世 间 事， 混 作 滔 滔 一 片 潮 流。 是 喜， 是 愁， 浪 里

6 i 6 5 1 3 | 2 - - - 2 3 | 5 - - 2 3 | 6 - - 6 1 | 2 · 3 2 7 6 5 | 1 - 0 i i 6 |
分 不 出 欢 笑 悲 愁， 成 功， 失 败， 浪 里 分 不 出 有 没 有。 爱 你 恨

i - i 6 i · 6 | 5 - - 5 3 | 6 · 5 1 2 1 2 | 3 - 0 3 3 2 | 3 - 0 i i 6 | 6 - - 3 3 |
你， 问 君 知 否， 似 大 江 一 发 不 收， 转 千 湾， 转 千 滩， 亦 未

2 · 3 i 7 6 3 | 5 - - 3 5 | 6 - - 3 5 | 2 - - 3 5 | 6 i 6 5 1 3 |
平 复 此 中 争 斗。 又 有 喜， 又 有 愁， 浪 里 分 不 出 欢 笑 悲

2 - - 2 3 | 5 - - 2 3 | 3 6 6 - 6 1 | 2 · 3 2 7 6 5 | 1 - - - |
忧， 宁 愿 翻 百 千 浪， 在 我 心 中 起 伏 够。

Figure 9

11 Tone-Melody Match Mechanism: Tools for Illustration

By "tone-melody match" it is meant the matching of the four pseudo-notes (derived ultimately from the six distinct lexical tones) with the various musical notes (well more than four in number) which permute to form the melody of an authentic song. In the case of *The Bund*, the musical notes range from the highest i to the lowest 5, an interval of an 11th. It happens that the note 4 is not used and thus only ten musical notes are involved. The tone-melody match mechanism boils down to the very specific question of how the four pseudo-notes cope with the ten notes actually in use. We need representational tools aided with principled assumptions and conventions for the exposition. Let us start with the first ten morpho-syllables of the lyrics, not so much to illustrate the mechanism right away as to introduce such tools, assumptions and conventions, whereby laying down the foundation for subsequent exposition of the mechanism. Table 16 is a grid showing the ten morpho-syllables, their pseudo-note identity and the musical notes they are sung with.

Table 16

		3	5	6	3	5	2	3	5	6	i	6	5	
生 i	(SHARP)										滔			i
亿 7														7
五 6	SHARP			奔						滔		江	↓	6
六 5	HIGH		ong			ong			里				水	5
反 4														4

(continued)

		3	5	6	3	5	2	3	5	6	$\dot{1}$	6	5	
工 3	LOW	浪			浪			万						3
尺 2	DEEP						流							2
上 1														
乙 $\underset{\cdot}{7}$														
士 $\underset{\cdot}{6}$														
合 $\underset{\cdot}{5}$														
		long		ban	long		lau	maan	*lei*	tou	tou	gong	*seoi*	

The organization of the grid follows:

(1) The left-most column is the scale column, i. e. an ordered (from high to low) array of the range of musical notes as "types" employed in the song or song-part. The traditional Cantonese musical note equivalent is provided in the debut of scale column here but not in subsequent tables. This scale column can in principle be placed anywhere as convenient. As a matter of fact it reappears as the last column of the grid in Table 16.

(2) The second column arrays the four pseudo-notes "SHARP-HIGH-LOW-DEEP".

(3) The specific positioning of the four pseudo-notes in column two against column one shows the matching pattern of pseudo-notes with musical notes. Here it can be seen that they are matched to "6-5-3-2", i. e. the 6-2 type register as per Table 13 or, another way of putting it, the 4-type register as per Table 14 above.

(4) The top row is an array of the musical notes as "tokens" in temporal sequence making up the melody. The sequence of note tokens is exactly the same as that represented in the score shown in Figure 9. As musical rhythm has no direct bearing on tone-note correspondence, rhythm is not represented here. One can go back to the score to find the rhythmic status of the note in each cell on this row.

(5) The morpho-syllables, represented in Chinese characters, are placed in the same column as the note (on the top row) they were sung in. The specific cell a character occupies in the column in question is determined by the actual positioning of that note in the scale column. In this way the height of a character in the grid is directly tied to pitch height.

(6) The bottom row gives the Jyutping of each morpho-syllable, with tone number dropped except where the tone-note correspondence is not straight-forward and requires specific attention.

(7) The range from pseudo-notes HIGH to LOW is shaded, in line with Table 14 above. The

shading tells unequivocally not only which musical note is HIGH and which is LOW, but also what range is SHARP and what range is DEEP. The existence of this shading therefore renders the second column (with array of the four pseudo-notes to show default mapping) redundant, thus making it possible for doing away with this column in later presentations.

In our analysis the following assumptions are adopted:

(1) The duration of each musical note token has no bearing on tone-melody match. It follows from this assumption that the rhythm of the melody is considered irrelevant for the purpose of this paper.

(2) Despite the above assumption, a distinction is made between the main identity of a note and the grace note that precedes it, if any. It is the main identity that counts as the identity of a note. For example, "里 lei^5" is actually sung with a preceding grace note of 3, but it is what comes after this grace note, namely 5, that is taken to be the identity of the note.

(3) When two or more notes are sung to one syllable, it is the first main note (not grace note) that is responsible for tone-melody match.

Then, in our presentation, the following representational conventions are adopted:

(1) In line with assumptions 1 and 2, the duration of all the musical notes (with the exception of grace notes) is not represented.

(2) In line with assumption 2, the identity of grace notes is not represented.

(3) In line with assumption 3, a note other than the first (main) note sung to a syllable will be represented lexically as the latter part of a syllable transcribed in Jyutping in the appropriate cell, while the bottom cell will be left empty, e. g. "ong" as the latter part of "浪 long^6".

(4) In order to distinguish the rising version from the level version conflated as the same pseudo-note, the rising version is represented by italics in both Chinese characters and Jyutping. [It follows from this representational convention that all the six lexical tones are recoverable: the (correctly matched) pseudo-note identity puts them in the four m-tones while the plain vs italics distinction further subdivides an m-tone with two versions. The tone number is therefore dropped to save space unless when required for special reasons.]

On top of the above basic representational conventions, we shall come across some other conventions as we proceed.

12 Mechanism Illustration: First Cycle of Melody Part A

Our grid organization, analysis assumptions and basic representational conventions having been spelt out, we are now in a position to account for the tone-melody match mechanism illustrated with *The Bund*. Of the song-part presented in Table 16, matching for the first nine morpho-syllables (with the tenth item "水 seoi^{2}" disregarded) is fairly straightforward. Recall that rhythm is ignored in our presentation. The actual rhythm of this song would make it very different from singsong. However, as far as tone-melody correspondence is concerned, the first nine morpho-syllables do resemble a singsong. Of course there is a difference in register, but that alone does not make it less monotonous than singsong. What really makes the correspondence less monotonous is the fact that SHARP is matched to two different notes: to 6 in most instances but to $\dot{1}$ in one instance. There is no variation for the other pseudo-notes: HIGH is consistently matched to 5, LOW to 3, and DEEP to 2. SHARP's matching to $\dot{1}$ is of course by virtue of extremity elasticity. Thus, from the beginning item 浪 long^{6} to the item 江 gong^{1}, matching is straight forward.

There is only one rising-tone item from long^{6} to gong^{1}, namely 里 lei^{5}. On the score in Figure 9, the item is set to the note 5 with a preceding grace note 3. In singing, as pointed out above, a preceding lower grace note is imperative to realize the rise of a rising tone, with or without explicit marking on the score. Implementation in this way will apply to all rising-tone items in any Cantonese-toned singing. The tenth item 水 seoi^{2} is also in a rising tone. The above score is inconsistent in that for seoi^{2}, unlike for the earlier lei^{5}, the required preceding grace note 3 is not explicitly marked. As far as the actual implementation of rise is concerned, there is nothing special. However, for seoi^{2} there does exist another problem, to which we now turn.

While we are singing (or replaying a recording of) this part, if we stop immediately after seoi^{2}, this seoi^{2} will be heard as seoi^{5} by a native speaker. Why? It is because as far as the prevalent register is concerned the note 5 should be matched to HIGH, not to SHARP, where seoi^{2} belongs. So, relative to the string from the beginning to gong^{1}, the expected note for seoi^{2} would be 6 (or higher by virtue of extremity elasticity), not 5. As a matter of convention, a vertically downward arrow "↓" is placed in the cell for 6 to signal this expectancy: it should be 6 but is now displaced downwards. It looks as though seoi^{2} has violated tone-melody match, until we view the item in a wider perspective as in Table 17, which covers the first complete cycle of melody part A of the song. To facilitate reading, the scale column is placed near the middle part in this and subsequent grid tables.

Table 17 First Cycle of Melody Part A

3	5	6	3	5	2	3	5	6	1̇	6	5	1	3	2		2	3	5	2	3	6̣	6̣	1	2	3	2	7̣	6̣	1	5̣
									滔						1̇															
															7															
		奔						滔		江	↓				6															
	ong			ong			里				水				5			了	(↓)											
															4															
浪			浪			万							不		3		尽			间					滔					
					流						•			休	2	淘			世				(↓)	滔		一				
												永			1								作						iu	
															7̣												片			
															6̣						事	混						潮		
															5̣	↑														流
											seoi	*wing*	bat	jau		tou	zeon	*liu*	sai	gaan	si	wan	zok	tou		jat	pin^3	ciu^4		lau

Table 18 Second Cycle of Melody Part A

3	5	6	3	5	2	3	5	6	1̇	6	5	1	3	2		2	3	5	2	3	6̣	6̣	1	2	3	2	7̣	6̣	5̣	1
									不						1̇															
															7															
		喜						分		清	↓				6															
	i			i			里				欢				5			功	(↓)											
															4															
是			是			浪							悲		3		ng			at					不					
					愁						•			忧	2	成			失					分		出				
												笑			1								里							有
															7̣												有			
↑															6̣						败	浪						未		
															5̣	↑													i	
si		*hei*	si		sau	long	*leoi*	fan	bat	cing	fun	siu	bei	jau		sing		gung	sat		baai	long	*leoi*	fan	bat	ceot	*jau*^{5}	mei		*jau*

Table 19　Third Cycle of Melody Part A

3	5	6	3	5	2	3	5	6	1̇	6	5	1	3	2		2	3	5	2	3	6̣	6̣	1	2	3	2	7̣	6̣	5̣	1
									不						1̇															
															7															
		喜						分		清	↓				6															
	有			有			算				欢				5			翻												
															4				↓											
又			又			就							悲		3		愿			千					中					
					愁						•			忧	2	仍			百				↓	心		起				
												笑			1								我							够
															7̣												1̇			
															6̣						浪	在						伏		
															5̣	↑													uk	
jau	*jau*	*hei*	jau	*jau*	sau	zau	syun	fan	bat	cing	fun	siu	bei	jau		jing	jyun	faan	baak	cin	long	zoi	*ngo*	sam	zung	*hei*		fuk		gau

Now, relative to the three syllables that follow it, namely wing^{5} bat^{1} jau^{1}, seoi^{2} clearly qualifies as matching to SHARP. The fact that there are just two rising tones in Cantonese, T2 and T5, renders these two rising tones particularly readily recognizable in singing. Thus, given that the *wing* is T5, then the *seoi* that is pitched much higher must be T2. The string of items from seoi^{2} to jau^{1} constitute another matching group with a different matching pattern, one corresponding to 7̣-type melody as per Table 14. Wing^{5} is rightly matched to the note 1 and jau^{1} is matched to 2 by default. Bat^{1} and seoi^{2} are matched to 3 and 5 by virtue of extremity elasticity. Transposing, downwards, has occurred between gong^{1} and seoi^{1}. Before this point the register is the 4-type but after it the 7̣-type. The positioning of the downward arrow shows the default note for SHARP in the pre-transposing zone. As what seoi^{2} matched to is not the default note for SHARP after transposing, the default note is here marked by a dot to show, among other things, that the transposing is of a magnitude of four steps (from 6 to 2 for SHARP). As a matter of convention in register shading, the lower a register, the darker is the shading.

Wing^{5} is another rising tone. The treatment of this rising tone on the score above is like the seoi^{2} that precedes it: a preceding lower grace note (6̣ in this case) is not explicitly given but is required to be sung nevertheless.

Once we have come to grips with how transposing works, it should be easy for us to understand and interpret all the twists and turns triggered by transposing. Thus, between jau^{1} and tou^{4}, there is another transposing, this time reverting back to the 4-type register. An upward arrow captures the transposing. As tou^{4} is placed in the default position, a dot is not needed here. The distance between "↑" and the cell with "淘" shows the interval of transposing. Tou^{4} as DEEP is matched to 2 by default, whereas zeon[6] and liu[5] are rightly matched to 3 and 5. Needless to say, the rising of liu[5] is implemented by adding a lower grace note before 5. It is interesting that the grace note 3 is explicitly given on the score above. So, of the four rising tone items covered so far, two are with the grace note given while two are without. Such is the inconsistency. Bearing such inconsistency in mind in what follows we shall refrain from examining whether the grace note is explicitly given in the score.

Transposing takes place again after liu[5]. The newly arising register has the 1-type register matching for the upper half (comprising HIGH and SHARP) but the 7̣-type register matching for the lower half (comprising LOW and DEEP). The widened interval between HIGH and LOW qualifies the register as a 1 7̣-type, which is anomalous but still legitimate. We do not expect this kind of matching relation to cover a long string. Within this string the HIGH item sai[3] is rightly matched to 2, the LOW items si[6] and wan[6] rightly matched to 6̣, and the SHARP item gaan[1] matched to 3 by default. The arrow for sai[3] is put in parentheses to register the anomaly that its positioning applies to the upper half only.

Transposing takes place again after wan[6]. The transposing that takes place here is simply reverting from the anomalous 1 7̣-type register to the normal 7̣-type. The one-step downward displacement applies only to the upper half but not to the lower half, hence the arrow with parentheses again. ① Within the up-coming string, zok[3] is rightly matched to the note 1. The first tou[1] and jat[1] are matched to 2 and lau[4] to 5̣ by default. The second tou[1] is matched to 3 by virtue of extremity elasticity. Extremity elasticity applies so readily that it does not need any explanation. However, it is worth mentioning that the successive appearance of the same note in a melody is infrequent and so when there is a succession of SHARP or a succession of DEEP, more often than not at least one of the

① The string "sai[3] gaan[1] si[6] wan[6]" can have an alternative analysis as follows:

	2	3	5	2	3	6̣	6̣	1	2	3	2	7̣	6̣	1	5̣
1̇															
7															
6															
5			了	↓											
4															
3		尽			间					滔					
2	淘			世					滔		一				
1								作						iu	
7̣						↓						片			
6̣						事	混						潮		
5̣	↑														流
	tou	zeon	*liu*	sai	gaan	si	wan	zok	tou		jat	pin	ciu		lau

In this analysis, the anomalous augmented interval between HIGH and LOW is avoided. The cost is that the 1-type register applies to a string with as few as just two morpho-syllables, somewhat too short for a register to function convincingly.

SHARPs or DEEPs in succession applies extremity elasticity. Here within the string "tou^1 tou^1 jat^1" the middle item applies extremity elasticity, whereby fitting the local melody that exhibits a contour.

We have left pin^3 and ciu^4 unmentioned yet. Both items call for special attention. First, we look at pin^3. For the 7̣-type register, the note 1 matches HIGH and 6̣ matches LOW. What about 7̣, which is here sung to pin^3? In one sense, it could legitimately work for either HIGH or LOW and the Cantonese speaker resorts to other cues, say those from syntax and semantics, for disambiguation. However, given that 7̣ is a half tone from 1 but a full tone from 6̣, the HIGH interpretation takes precedence, other things being equal. So after all 7̣ as HIGH is not problematic.

Second, we look at ciu^4. T4 means DEEP and would be ideally matched to 5̣. On the other hand 6̣ would be ideally matched to LOW or T6. Now ciu^4, a DEEP item, is matched to 6̣. This is of course less than ideal, but is this matching simply wrong? Recall that an observation was made in the 1980s that "an intended T4 item is sometimes represented as if it was a T6 (in the sense of occupying a slot best suited to T6)" and the estimation of the odds to be a quarter of the occurrence of T4 items. The four pseudo-notes usually have unequivocal boundaries, with the exception of T6 being interpreted as T4 in singing at times. Thus, ideally LOW is T6 but LOW could be T4 by virtue of what I call "poetic license". As such, it is not operated indiscriminately. Some positions are considered more favourable for this license than other positions. Thus, when two T4 items are in succession, it is not unusual for the license to apply to one of them, more often than not the first item. So, when this is a succession of T4 items, apart from the application of extremity elasticity (when a T4 item is matched to a note lower than the default matching note), application of the said license (when a T4 item is matched to a note one-step higher than the default matching note) seems to be another way for a T4 cluster to fit a melody part with contour.

Supposing ciu^4 were replaced by a T6 item, say 浊 zuk^6, then the matching relation would be perfect. Not that the T4 to LOW matching is unavoidable; it is simply tolerated in practice. Why is this T4 as LOW relation tolerated in Cantonese-toned singing? We supply two pieces of information here. First, in a kind of traditional Cantonese *shuochang* called 板眼 baan^{2}ngaan^5, a T4 item is required to fill a LOW slot in some particular position, while the six tones are otherwise all clearly distinguishable (Cheung and Wong, 2008). Baan^{2}ngaan^5 has been incorporated into Cantonese operatic singing. Cantonese operatic singing in general permits, even more readily than in Canto-pop, the T4 to LOW matching, which may have come from baan^{2}ngaan^5 in the first place. Second, the undergraduate paper by 郑雅莹 (Cheng, 2004) observes the T4 as LOW phenomenon but characterizes it as failing tone-melody match. With these two things put together, we would like to make the following guess. T4 as LOW was extended from baan^{2}ngaan^5 to Cantonese operatic singing in general, which in turn influences Cantonese-toned singing in general. Canto-pop has been subject to this influence. However, as Canto-pop is moving farther away from Cantonese operatic singing, the T4 as LOW relation is gradually decreasing in acceptability. In the light of this guess, we would like to say that *The Bund* was created (in 1980) at a time when T4 as LOW is universally considered acceptable. So much for the T4 as LOW phenomenon.

Note that this first cycle of melody part A ends with "615", which is different from the other two cycles which end with "651". These last three notes are highlighted in Table 17 to attract attention.

Before we leave the current zone with the 7-type register, we would like to draw readers' attention to the fact that two notes in succession, 6 followed by 1, are sung to the syllable ciu^4. Following a convention introduced above, the second note 1 only takes the latter part, namely iu, of the syllable and does not participate in tone-melody match.

13 Mechanism Illustration: Second Cycle of Melody Part A

Lau^4 marks the end of the first cycle of A. Recall that the melody structure is AABA(BA). The second cycle of A follows. Table 18 above shows the grid for this cycle of A. The two cycles differ only in the last two notes. Cycle-1 ends with version A2i and cycle-2 with version A2ii. The grids for the two cycles, namely Tables 17 and 18 are juxtaposed above to facilitate comparison.

After lau^4 the lyrics is transposed back to the 4-type register. Thus, this second cycle of melody A begins with the 4-type register just as the first cycle is. Here is just the beginning. If we take an overview of the two grids, we can see that they are very similar. We therefore take advantage of the similarity to just concentrate on the differences.

For the first string with nine morpho-syllables, no account is needed here as the m-tone identity and positioning of all items are exactly the same. It is however worth mentioning that although both ban^1 in the first grid and the corresponding hei^2 in the second grid fall into the same m-tone or pseudo-note SHARP, they differ in that ban^1 is a level tone while hei^2 is a corresponding rising tone. This is a good example to demonstrate that T1 and T2 as a group (similar to T3 and T5 as a group) have exactly the same melodic potential.

In a similar fashion, the following string with four morpho-syllables for the two grids has the same positioning of items and again the difference lies in level vs rising: seoi^2 and wing^5 are rising whereas fun^1 and siu^3 are the corresponding level version. By the way, there is a typo in this part of the score presented: "愁" should read "忧".

A comparison of the next string comprising three notes promises to be interesting and even educational. We did not speak of this string in terms of how many "morpho-syllables", as this is exactly one difference between the two grids. In the first grid we have three (tou^4 zeon^6 liu^5); in the second grid, just two (sing^4 gung^1). In the second grid, two notes are sung to the syllable sing^4, where the note 3 only carries the latter part of sing^4 and as such does not participate in tone-melody match. Tou^4 and sing^4 are of the same tone as expected, but what happens to the liu^3-gung^1

pair, one being HIGH and the other SHARP? In order to account for the legitimacy of SHARP here, we have to compress the tessitura by compressing the HIGH-LOW interval to a semitone. A HIGH-LOW interval smaller than the norm, i. e. a 3rd, like one larger than the norm we encountered in the first grid, though somewhat anomalous, is still legitimate. As expected, this zone is short, in fact the shortest (in terms of number of notes) within the first two grids.

Recall that the four-item string "sai^{3} gaan^{1} si^{6} wan^{6}" in the first cycle that follows the part we just dealt with is of an anomalous register of the 1 $\underset{\cdot}{7}$-type: the lower half (LOW and DEEP) resembles the $\underset{\cdot}{7}$-type register but the upper half is one step higher. In the second cycle, the corresponding string "sat^{1} baai^{6} long^{6}" takes the normal, uncompressed $\underset{\cdot}{7}$-type register. Thus, although sat^{1} in the second cycle and sai^{3} in the first cycle are both sung with note 2, sat^{1} is SHARP but sai^{3} is HIGH. As the transposing is one from a compressed register (in the previous string) to a non-compressed register, the arrow is put in parentheses by convention. The second note sung to sat^{1}, as a rule, does not participate in tone-melody match. For the last two items in this string, "si^{6} wan^{6}" in the first grid and "baai^{6} long^{6}" in the second grid behave the same and call for no exposition.

The normal, uncompressed $\underset{\cdot}{7}$-type register for this string is no different from the remaining string in the second cycle of melody A. The two strings can be regarded as constituting one matching group, corresponding to two groups in the first cycle. The string from zok^{3} to pin^{3} (at the note $\underset{\cdot}{7}$) in the first cycle corresponds to the string from leoi^{5} to jau^{5} (at $\underset{\cdot}{7}$) in the second cycle. The two strings have exactly the same positioning of items. Further explanation is therefore not needed.

The item jau^{5} mentioned above marks the end of the melody part A1, which remains unchanged in all three cycles of A. The remaining portion of melody part A is variable, hence the differentiation A2i (for the first cycle) vs A2ii (for the second and third cycles). A2ii is made up of the string of notes "$\underset{\cdot}{6}\,\underset{\cdot}{5}1$". In this second cycle the corresponding lyrics is "mei^{6} jau^{5}". Here mei^{6} is rightly matched to $\underset{\cdot}{6}$ and jau^{5} to 1, in accordance with the $\underset{\cdot}{7}$-type register. The second note sung to mei^{6} does not participate in tone-melody match following our assumption.

14 Mechanism Illustration: Melody Part B

After the second cycle of melody part A comes melody part B, which is associated with just one set of lyrics. The grid for B is shown in Table 20.

Table 20

$\dot{1}$	$\dot{1}$	6	$\dot{1}$	6	$\dot{1}$	6	5	5	3	6	5	1	2	1	2	3		3	3	2	3	$\dot{1}$	$\dot{1}$	7	6	3	3	2	3	$\dot{1}$	7	6	3	5
					↓												$\dot{2}$																	
爱	你		你		君												$\dot{1}$					转	千							此				
																	7							in							中			
		根		问	•	知				江	↓						6					•			滩							争		
							* 否	似			一						5																	斗
																	4																	
									大							收	3	转	千		湾					亦	未		伏				ng	
											•		不		at		2			in		↑						平						
↑												发		a			1																	
																	$\underset{\cdot}{7}$																	
																	$\underset{\cdot}{6}$																	
																	$\underset{\cdot}{5}$																	
oi	*nei*	han	*nei*	man	gwan	zi	*fau*^{2}	*ci*	daai	gong	jat	faat	bat			sau		*zyun*	cin		waan	*zyun*	cin		taan	jik	mei	ping	fuk	*ci*	zung	zang		dau

Transposing occurs at the beginning of part B. The direction is upwards and the displacement is an octave, i. e. from the $\underset{\cdot}{7}$-type in the previous to the 7-type in the current zone. A register with such height should in principle be taxing on the singing. However, the highest note in this zone is just $\dot{1}$, which has been used before this zone and will be used after this zone. This is because there is no SHARP item within this zone. Oi^3 and nei^5 are rightly matched to the note $\dot{1}$ while han^6 and man^6, to 6. An octave's jump to an exceptionally high register marks this part of the song (comprising melody and lyrics) as the climax.

After man^6, matching relation is transposed to the 4-type register. No note 2 is used in the song but a row for note 2 is added to this grid to accommodate for the arrow needed to indicate the intended slot for SHARP (associated with gwan^1) in the previous register. In the upcoming zone, the item ci^5 is rightly matched to the note 5 and daai^6 to 3, while zi^1 and gong^1 are matched to 6 by default and gwan^1 to $\dot{1}$ by virtue of extremity elasticity. So far so good. However, fau^2 does pose a problem. It belongs to SHARP and should match the note 6 or higher, but it is sung with 5. Conversely, the note 5 matches HIGH, not SHARP. This second point dictates that the item, sung with 5, is heard as HIGH, not SHARP, in other words heard as T5, not T2, given the rising contour. Unlike handling the ambivalent slot between HIGH and LOW (which would be acceptable as either HIGH or LOW) or matching T4 to a LOW slot (which is supported by a time-honoured poetic license), matching T2 to a HIGH slot has no excuse and can be simply and sternly classified as mismatch in strict accordance with the matching requirement. To signal the "mismatch" status we borrow the convention in linguistics of signalling ill-formedness with a star (*) and put a star before the Chinese character "否" in the table. On the pragmatic plane, however, as fau^{5} happens to be an accidental gap in the Cantonese lexicon, the linguistic contexts give strong suggestion that the identity of this rising fau is fau^{2} rather than the fau^{5} in strict accordance with tone-melody match. After all, this mild mismatch has not barred the song from gaining immense popularity and becoming a Canto-pop classic.

After gong^{1} the register is transposed to the $\underset{\cdot}{7}$-type. Faat^{3} is rightly matched to the note 1. All the other items are SHARP. Among them bat^{1} is matched to 2 by default; sau^{1}, zyun^{2}, cin^{1} and waan^{1} to 3 by virtue of extremity elasticity; and jat^{1} to 5 by virtue of extremity elasticity in an even greater magnitude. The second note sung to cin^{1} does not participate in tone-melody match. Bat^{1} is the only item in the lyrics having three notes sung to it. The third note, just like the second note (for bat^{1} and for a number of other items in the lyrics), does not participate in the match.

After waan^{1} the register is transposed to the 4-type. Dau^{3} is rightly matched to note 5, and jik^{6}, mei^{6} and fuk^{6} to note 3. Ping^{4} is matched to 2 by default. All the other items in this string are SHARP. Among them taan^{1} and zang^{1} are matched to 6 by default, zyun^{2}, cin^{1} and ci^{2} to $\dot{1}$ by virtue of extremity elasticity, and zung^{1} to 7 (the note's only occurrence in this song) by virtue of extremity elasticity in a smaller magnitude. Now we have completed melody part B.

15 Mechanism Illustration: Third Cycle of Melody Part A

What follows melody part B is the third cycle of part A, the grid of which forms Table 19, placed together with the two earlier cycles of part A for easy comparison. The first thing you may have noticed is that unlike in the second cycle there is no arrow in the first column. The absence of an initial arrow indicates that there is no transposing at the beginning of this cycle of part A. The long stretch of 4-type register employed at the end of part B here continues with another long stretch of 4-type register at the beginning of this cycle of part A.

This first stretch of items basically resembles the corresponding stretches for the previous two cycles in positioning, the only difference being that whereas in the previous two cycles the two instances of note 5 serve as the second note sung to an item (long^{6} for cycle-1 and si^{6} for cycle-2), both instances of note 5 are now sung to an individual item jau^{5}. Jau^{5} is HIGH and is rightly matched to 5.

The second stretch of four items (fun^{1} siu^{3} bei^{1} jau^{1}) is a repeat of the corresponding stretch in the second cycle in both melody and lyrics.

The third stretch made up of the string of notes "2 3 5" has the same register and same positioning of lexical items as in the second cycle. Not unlike in the first stretch of items mentioned above, whereas note 3 is the second note sung to sing^{4} in cycle-2, this note 3 is now sung to an individual item jyun^{6}. Jyun^{6} is LOW and is here rightly matched to 3.

The stretch of the four items "baak^{3} cin^{1} long^{6} zoi^{6}" that follows resembles not the second cycle but the first cycle, in terms of both register and positioning of items. Like in the first cycle, at the end of this stretch the register reverts to the normal, non-widened 4-type till the very end of melody part A. The very last stretch in the third cycle of part A resembles the second cycle in terms of both melody and positioning of items, with the only difference that for the third cycle note 7̣ serves as the second note sung to hei^2.

Now we have completed the AABA cycle of the song. Afterwards the entire BA part (both melody and lyrics) is repeated, which does not call for further exposition.

16 An Overview of the Tone-melody Mapping Relations of the Entire Song

Table 21 gives an overview of the twists and turns of tone-melody mapping relations throughout the entire song, where only the first morpho-syllable is given to mark the beginning of every mapping group. The following things can be observed:

(1) The basic mapping pattern is the alternation of 4-type and 7̣-type registers, interleaved with relatively short excursions to some other registers.

(2) The highest and lowest registers are an octave apart.

(3) The highest register occurs at the beginning of B, which can be regarded as the climax of the song.

(4) All other registers are transitional in nature, which differ from the recurrent 4-type and 7̣-type registers in that they have the HIGH-LOW interval (a third by default) either widen to a fourth or compressed to a second.

Table 21

	A1					A2				B				A3				
$\dot{2}$											↓							
$\dot{1}$										爱	君		转					
7																		
6		↓					↓				·	↓	·		↓			
5		水		↓			欢		↓			一			欢			
4																	↓	
3	浪					是								又				
2		·	淘	世	↓		·	成	失			·	↑		·	仍	百	↓

(continued)

	A1					A2				B				A3				
1					作					↑								我
7̣																		
6̣						↑												
5̣			↑					↑								↑		
	long	*seoi*	tou	sai	zok	si	fun	sing	sat	oi	gwan	jat	*zyun*	jau	fun	jing	baak	*ngo*

17 Concluding Remarks

The foregoing is an attempt to explicate the Cantonese tone-melody match mechanism with the help of a set of concepts, terminology, expositional tools, analytical assumptions and representational conventions and demonstrated with the classic Canto-pop song *The Bund*. It is hoped that the long-time popularity of and hence the general familiarity with the song can greatly reduce the difficulty of such explication, which as far as I am aware of is the first attempt in this direction.

I conclude this paper with lyrics set to the melody of *The Bund* as shown in Table 22, which summarize the paper and give the gist of the mechanism of tone-melody match for Cantonese. To accommodate a larger amount of verbal content, the lyrics set to the repeat of the melody part BA and to the final repeat of the last quarter of A are not repeats as words. For this reason, B divides into B1 and B2 and A has a fourth cycle.

Table 22

	A1	A2 + B1	A3 + B2	A4 (final quarter of A repeated)
A	字会尖。字会沉。 任你几高，多高也归“尖”。 何谓“亢”? 怎么“下”? 待我哼出“尖亢下沉”。	极处尖；极处沉。 极致嗓音，高端算它“尖”。 随后：“亢”，再低：“下”； 仲更低，终归跌落“沉”处。	浪奔；浪流。 让四级音阶升降伸缩。 爬攀，跌堕。 像过山车高处骤然降。	浪奔；浪流。 粤音歌曲机制笃穿。 涟漪，四小步。 浪里翻，找“尖亢下沉”配。 //万阕歌，区区四字填晒。
B		听这“下亢”，绝顶高音。 似日出小鸟吱喳。 低音坍塌，高音冲天。 活像人肉音阶冲浪去。	喂！转调喇！拔尖冲顶。 降 key，即觉轻松。 此刻压低；彼刻飙高。 密密轮换，key 可枕住变。	

References

Chan, K. M. Marjorie 1987 Tone and melody in Cantonese. *Proceedings of the Thirteenth Annual Meeting*. Berkeley: Berkeley Linguistic Society.

Chao, Y. R. 1930a ə sistim əv "toun – letəz", lə mɛːtrə fɔnetik, 45: 24 – 27.

赵元任 1930b 《广西猺歌记音》(Phonetics of the Yao Folk-songs). Peiping: Academia Sinica.

Chao, Y. R. 1933 Tone and intonation in Chinese. *Bulletin of the Institute of History and Philology*, (4): 121 – 134.

Chao, Y. R. 1947 *Cantonese Primer*. Cambridge, Massachusetts: Harvard University Press.

张群显 2007 《粤语字调与旋律的配合初探》,《粤语研究》第 2 期, 第 8 ~ 12 页。

Cheung, Kwan Hin 2012 The mechanism of tone-melody match for tone preservation in Cantonese songs. Workshop on Innovations in Cantonese Linguistics, the Ohio State University, Columbus, Ohio, U. S. A., 16 – 17 March, 2012. Columbus, Ohio: The Ohio State University.

张群显、王胜焜 2008 《粤曲梆黄说唱字调乐调配合初探》,《粤语研究》第 3 期, 第 12 ~ 25 页。

郑雅莹 2004 《粤语流行曲拗音问题初探: 以 2000 年—2004 年粤语流行曲歌词为例》, UG dissertation, Hong Kong: Lingnan University. http://commons.ln.edu.hk/chi_diss/53/, as at 2 Nov., 2014.

Jones, D., and K. T. Woo 1912 *A Cantonese Phonetic Reader*. London: London University Press.

梁沛锦 1979 《粤剧剧目初编》, 香港: 学津书店。

梁沛锦 1982 《粤剧研究》, 香港: 龙门书店。

Yung, Bell 1983 Creative process in Cantonese opera Ⅰ: The role of linguistic tones. *Ethnomusicology*, 27: 29 – 47.

试谈现代粤语"阳入对转"中的音义关系
——以广州话单音节同义实词的语文工具书注音与释义为例

陈世安*

（台湾师范大学）

提　要：前人对古汉语字音韵尾的"对转"现象有不少研究，当中更不能忽视词汇中蕴含着的同义关系。本文综合相关研究观点，征之以现代粤语，基于广州话单音节同义实词的语文工具书注音与释义，归纳出三大类：收双唇鼻音韵尾-m 和双唇塞音韵尾-p 的共 16 组；收舌尖鼻音-n 和舌尖塞音-t 的共 21 组；收舌根鼻音韵尾-ŋ和舌根塞音韵尾-k 的共 18 组。通过分析归纳这 55 组单音节同义实词，进而把其中有规律的音义关系、方言佐证呈现出来。

关键词：阳入对转　广州话　音义关系　同义实词

1　引　言

根据韵尾的不同，上古汉语字音可分为阴声韵、阳声韵、入声韵三种。在李方桂（1980）的上古音系统中，阳声韵以＊-m、＊-n、＊-ŋ、＊-ŋw 收尾，阴声韵以＊-b、＊-d、＊-g、＊-gw 收尾，入声韵以＊-p、＊-t、＊-k、＊-kw 收尾。不过，李先生对构拟的具体音值并不十分肯定，他（1980：34）说："＊-p 跟＊-b，＊-d 跟＊-t，＊-g 跟＊-k 等并不一定含有清浊等的区别，但也不敢说一定没有区别。我们既然承认上古有四声，那么别的区别似乎是不重要的。"

尽管具体音值一时尚难断定，但是，与阴、阳、入相关的语言现象却是客观存在的，比如，谐声、假借、押韵、古注中的许多语音参差常常以阴、阳、入相对，尤其值得关注。我们来看一些例子，"斤"属阳声韵，以为声符的"近、靳、芹、欣"同此，但以为声符的"沂、祈、圻、颀"属于阴声韵。再如，《诗经·大雅·召旻》中"玷、贬、业"押韵。音读上的这些违拗，初看有些凌乱，但若从古音学的角度着眼，就会发现其间的规

＊　陈世安，台湾师范大学历史学系硕士研究生。本文于 2013 年 7 月 31 日前投稿于"第十八届国际粤方言研讨会香港语言学杰出学生论文奖"，同年 11 月 30 日内文调整后再次寄出，在 2013 年 12 月 7 日第十八届国际粤方言研讨会上宣读。为了《第十八届国际粤方言研讨会论文集》组稿，于 2014 年 5 月 31 日第三次微调内文后，再次寄出。后经有关单位及孙景涛老师对本文提出宝贵意见，于 2014 年 10 月和 12 月，先后经第四次和第五次修订，最终在 2015 年初获孙景涛老师帮忙整理而定稿完成，谨此致谢。

律。仍以上面所举为例，“斤、近、靳、芹、欣”与“沂、祈、圻、颀”分属文部和微部，“玷、贬、业”分属谈部和叶部，全部属于同一组别韵部之间的交替。字音之间的这种对应关系首先由清儒系统揭示，后来便有对转、旁转、通转、旁对转、旁纽、邻纽等名目的出现，可以阴阳对转统而称之。（参看孙景涛，2010：301～302）

李新魁（1994：90）也曾谈到这个问题，他说：“在汉语发展的过程中，出现过主元音相同而韵尾不同的字音相互转化的现象，前人称之为‘阴阳对转’。阴、阳对转是一种笼统的说法，具体分起来，应该是阴—阳—入对转。古人因为把入声韵母字合在阳声韵之内，所以称阴阳对转就概括了这三者的对转。”

根据我们的调查，“对转”语音变化不仅见于古代，现代方言中依然有所保留，主要集中在阳声韵尾与入声韵尾的交替上。本文试图将古音学中的“对转”理论应用于现代粤语的阳声韵和入声韵中，探寻“音转”与同义词之间的密切关系。我们将考察广州话的单音节实词的注音与释义，以论证其间存在的“声近义通”的同义现象，揭示“义由音生”的对应规律，说明现代广州话确实存在“阳入对转”现象。

除了“引言”之外，本文另分三小节：第二节，有关确定同义词以及音转理论与同义关系的若干研究；第三节，古音学“阳入对转”理论在广州话单音节同义实词简释中的实证；第四节，结语。

本文不少观点依据前贤时彦的研究，同时文献资料多所引用，为便于参考，均注明出处。

2　有关确定同义词以及音转理论与同义关系的若干研究

关于如何确定同义词的问题，学者们进行了很多研究。如，郭良夫（1985：49～50）指出：“两个或两个以上的词之间有同义关系，就成为一组同义词。……同义词，可以说有两种。一种是意义完全相同的，有的书上叫做等义词；一种是意义大致相同的，有的书上叫做近义词。”

周祖谟（2004：295）对同义词的性质和作用也作过解释：“语言里有很多发音不同而意义相同或意义非常相近的词，这种词称为‘同义词’。……同义词可以分为两类：一类是完全同义的词，一类是意义稍有差别的词。”

王力（1982：23～24）在分析同源字的过程中涉及同义词，他提出：“音义皆近的同义词，在原始时代本属一词。后来由于各种原因（如方言影响），语音分化了，但词义没有分化，或者只有细微的分别。这种同义词，在同源字中占很大的数量。”“所谓同义，是说这个词的某一意义和那个词的某一意义相同，不是说这个词的所有意义和那个词的所有意义都相同。”

符淮青（2004：101～102、107）以意义相同的程度为标准，将同义词分为“等义词”与“同义词”两类，前者是“概念义完全相等”，后者是“概念义有同，概念义和附属义有异的词”。

根据以上各家的说法，同义词可包括“等义词”、“同义词”、“近义词”，至于如何确定同义词，本文采用符淮青（2004）之说，即“从词的关系说，是基本义、常用义有相同或相近义项（一项或多项）的一组词，从义项的关系说，是概念义有很大的共同性，但又有某些差别，或者附属义有差别，或语法特点有差别的一组词”。我们将以此作为判定词与词之间是否同义的依据。

语言中的同义现象相当普遍，但是，这种现象是如何产生的呢？这是一个早在先秦时代即受学者关注的问题。到了清代，由于古音学的昌明，相关的理论实践得到了很大的发展。戴震、段玉裁、王念孙、孔广森、章炳麟等学者精研古音学，关注语音与意义的联系，发现了“声近义通”、“义由音生”的现象，在揭示同源分化的过程中提出了音转理论，并进一步发展出阴、阳、入对转的理论观念。

清代学者的理论建树对后代产生了很大影响，许多学者秉持音义相关、因声求义的正确理念，在阐释汉语语源流变方面取得了很好的成绩。比如王力（1982）精研同源词，获得了许多新的发现。他（1984：157）在讨论同源词研究方法时提到：“文字既是代表有声语言，同音的字就有同义的可能：不但同声符、不同意符的字可以同义；甚至意符、声符都不同，只要音同或音近，也还可能是同义的。”蒋绍愚（2005：156）也有类似的看法：“词是音义相结合而产生的，研究音义关系，是词汇研究中的一个重要问题。……在一种语言的基本词汇初步形成以后，在词义引申和新词滋生的过程中，一些（不是全部）意义有关的词往往会在语音上也有联系。”

音转理论在古汉语音义研究中的初步成功令人鼓舞。接下来我们自然会想到这一理论是否可以运用于现代方言中，已有学者对这一问题做了肯定回答。陆宗达、王宁（1994：399、402）在讨论训诂问题时曾有过这样的说明：“训诂学家所以用上古音系来讨论音转问题，是因为他们讨论的材料大多是先秦文献的书面语，在先秦文献里已经分化了的字词用上古音系也就是《诗经》音系来讨论它们的音转，自然是合理的。……尽管在汉语逐渐双音节化以后，单音节音变造词已经日趋减少，但直到今天，这种音转还间或发生，所以，按道理讲，讨论什么时候完成的字词分化，应当用什么时候的语音，才能全然准确。更严格些说，讨论哪一方言区的音转，应当用哪一方言的音系，才更为准确。然而汉语的各方言区既然同是一个母语发展来的，分别保留着不同时代的语言面貌，而汉语的语音分化造词大量发生还是在早期；所以，我们用一个或数个现代方言特别是保留古音较多的闽、粤方言来讨论汉字的音转，有时也能保证一定程度的准确性。”

在这里，陆、王二位先生的出发点是古汉语训诂，但他们明确表示在闽、粤方言中应该可以发现音转现象。这对我们的研究是一个很大的启发。总之，前贤时彦的研究使我们认识到，透过声音相近的语音规律，可以进而挖掘到词汇中的同义关系，当中所蕴含的因音转而保留其同义成分，或许也有某种结构性的制约原则。按照吴泽顺（2006：315 ~ 336）的研究，“音转的制约机制”分为“音义关系的机制”、“语言系统的制约性”与“声韵统一的制约”，并借此来检验音转的真实性和科学性。

3 古音学“阳入对转”理论在广州话单音节同义实词简释中的实证

汉语古音学中的“阳入对转”理论，在现代粤方言中是可以得到证实的，如詹伯慧（2002b：19）讨论广州话的阴阳对转时指出：“汉语韵母的阴声韵（元音收尾）、阳声韵（鼻音收尾）和入声韵（塞音收尾），出现过主要元音相同而韵尾不同的字音相互转化现象，前人称之为‘阴阳对转’。可以是‘阴—入’对转，也可以是‘阳—入’对转。广州话主要是‘阳—入’对转。”

陈伯煇（1998：84）同样关注这一问题，他说：“在粤方言中，对转主要出现在阳声韵与入声韵上，形成两个词彼此词性相同，词义相近。当中大多是‘遵古炮制’，本有其字的。”可见有音无文字的词语，在南方方言中是一个普遍而突出的现象。

李新魁等（1995：48）则将阴阳对转与语音的屈折相联系：屈折“指从一个词根出发，凭借语音形式的变换或衍生来表示不同的语法或词汇意义，创造新词。这些屈折现象是历时演变的结果，对于现代广州话这个共时语言体系来说，它们是凝固了的形式；其语法或词汇功能大多是可归纳的，但一般不能类推”。李新魁对阴阳对转也作了具体说明，指出这“是通过韵尾的变化来完成的屈折。就广州市区话内部而言，基本上只有阳声韵与入声韵之间的对转”。

广州话流行阳入对转有其特殊意义，这是由其强势方言的身份以及大量方言字的创制所决定的，张双庆（2002：394、395）对此有详细说明：“强势方言的一个表征是有自己的文言文学，有大批的方言字。所以研究粤方言特征词，可以考虑方言字的作用。在古汉语研究的过程中，摆脱文字的羁绊，曾是研究获得突破的一个重要因素。李如龙先生也说40年来汉语方言研究的重大突破，是‘跳出汉字的魔方’。但是作为一种强势方言，粤语有很完整的书面语系统，粤语口语词大多有书面形式，或用本字，或自造方言字，或借用同音字。加上广州和香港两大经济文化重心，有较多粤语出版物，方言字自然流行在粤方言区的各个角落。”

尽管相对于其他方言，粤语有书面形式的优势，直接促成方言字的流行，可是因欠缺规范，而且从广泛运用广州方言来写作的程度看，毕竟未获普遍的正式推广与重视，致使粤语方言字中存在形音义违拗的现象，因此，我们亟须全面调查这批材料，排列对比，条分缕析，力图在整理文字形音义的基础上，对阳入对转有进一步的了解。

本小节拟依照古音学阳入对转理论，基于粤语同义词的注音与释义而给出简要的分类。关于“阳入对转”的对应标准，我们依照张洪年（1972 /2007：4）的相关说明，即“鼻尾韵和塞尾韵相配，保存古韵，例如 a 行［aː m，aː n，aː ŋ］三者俱存，塞尾韵就有［aː p，aː t，aː k］；ɛ行只有［ɛŋ］，塞尾韵也只有［ɛk］。换言之收［-m］的就和同部位（homorganic）的［-p］相配。［-n］和［-t］，［-ŋ］和［-k］也是两两相配”。

另外需要说明的是，本文所谈的粤语是以广州话为代表的。因此，以下单音节同义实词字例的注音与释义，主要根据白宛如（1998）《广州方言词典》，并参考詹伯慧

(2002a)，黄谷甘（1993），李新魁（1994），李如龙、张双庆（1996）。在考察阳入配对中我们只关注单音节同义实词，虚词暂不在调查范围之内。下面的材料依据粤语发音部位而分为三大类，即-m/-p 类、-n/-t 类、-ŋ/-k 类，共包括55组单音节同义实词。

凡例说明：

（1）【】后面的读音、释义以白宛如（1998）为主，若为其他各家则另外注明，以斜线“/”隔开，或另作说明。

（2）引用文献的简称如下：

①《词典》：白宛如（1998）《广州方言词典》。

②《字典》：詹伯慧（2002a）《广州话正音字典》。

③《辨析》：黄谷甘（1993）《粤语词汇中“阳入对转”同义词的语义辨析》。

④《方言》：李新魁（1994）《广东的方言》。

⑤《派生词》：李如龙、张双庆（1996）《闽粤方言的“阳入对转”派生词》。

（3）音标右上角的数字为粤方言9个声调，包括：阴平55/53（1）、阴上35（2）、阴去33（3）、阳平21/11（4）、阳上13（5）、阳去22（6）、阴入55（7）、中入33（8）和阳入22（9）。声调系统根据詹伯慧（2002b）的“九声六调”：“即实际上广州话只有6个调位，七、八、九调可以看作是一、三、六调的变体。”

（4）送气符号一律改为 h。

-m/-p（16组）

1【吟】$\mathrm{ŋɐm}^{4}$喃喃，啰唆：唔知佢吟乜野。（《词典》297页）

【嚗】$\mathrm{ŋɐp}^{7}$胡诌，说：你嚗乜野！（《词典》431页）/詹作“噏”。（《字典》263页，《派生词》⑲）

2【冚】$\mathrm{khɐm}^{2}$ 以物遮盖：冚住啲菜。（《词典》297页）/李、詹均作“冚”。（《方言》91页；《字典》24页）

【笈】$\mathrm{khɐp}^{7}$（用器皿）覆盖，扣住：揾个杯笈住佢。（《词典》431页）/李作“盖”。（《方言》91页）

【磕】$\mathrm{khɐp}^{7}$盖（图章）：磕个印。（《词典》431页）/詹作“扱”。（《字典》204页）

【嗌】$\mathrm{khɐp}^{9}$压着，夹着：柜桶嗌住我件衫。（《词典》431页，《派生词》⑤）

3【点】tim^{2}蘸（流体物品）：沾酱油。（《词典》301页）

【玷】tim^{3}轻触：玷一玷都唔得。（《词典》302页）

【𫐗】tip^{7}小口品尝：𫐗下滋味。（《词典》434页）

4【拈】nim^{1}用两个手指夹取物件：个细路拈起野就食。（《词典》302页）

【捏】nip^{9}用拇指和其他手指去夹：捏一额汗。（《词典》434页）

5【揞】$\mathrm{ɐm}^{2}$用手掩、盖：揞实个嘴唔出声。（广韵感韵乌感切：手覆）（《词典》298页）/黄音作$\mathrm{ɔm}^{2}$(《辨析》115页)。詹音作am^{2}(《字典》221页)。

【罯】ɐp^{7}敷药于创处，热敷，冷敷：揾热毛巾罯头。（广韵合韵乌合切：覆盖也）（《词典》432 页）/黄音作ɔp^{7}（《辨析》115 页）。詹音作 ap^{7}，字作“罨”（《字典》494 页）。

6【淰】nɐm^{6}水湿透貌：件衫湿到淰，快啲换喇。（《词典》289 页）

【涩】nɐp^{9}潮，湿：件衫重涩嘅，唔好收自先别收。（《词典》428 页，《派生词》㉗）

7【扰】tɐm^{2}（用拳头）打，捶，砸：扰骨。（《词典》288 页）

【磍】tɐp^{9}捶打，擂（拳打）：磍骨。（《词典》427 页，《派生词》①）

8【闪】sim^{2}打闪：闪电。（《词典》304 页）

【摄】sip^{8}打闪：摄电。（《词典》435 页）

9【髧】tɐm^{3}耷拉，垂下来：髧条绳落来。（广韵感韵徒感切：发垂）（《词典》288 页）

【耷】tɐp^{7}耷拉，垂下：耷低头。（《词典》427 页，《派生词》⑬）

10【躐】lam^{3}迈，跨：躐门坎。（《词典》281 页）

【擸】lap^{8}大步走：三步擸埋两步走跨越。说明：白宛如无此字。形、义依据詹伯慧，字音詹作 laap，即白宛如的 lap。（《字典》231 页）

11【览】lam^{3}粗略地看。说明：白宛如无此字，故字形与字义据黄谷甘。（《辨析》11 页）

【䁁】lap^{8}粗略看（阅读），扫视：䁁一眼。（《词典》421 页，《派生词》⑥）

12【腌】jim^{1}/ jip^{8}用盐、糖、酒等渍制食品：腌黄瓜。说明：白宛如只有入声的“腌”（《词典》435 页）。/ 陈伯煇（1998：88）认为这个字本身具有阳入对转。故字形、字音与字义皆依据詹伯慧。（《字典》444 页，《派生词》⑪）

13【䁪】tsam^{2}眼睛很快地一闭一开：䁪眼。说明：字形与字义皆依据詹伯慧，字音是 dzaam，即白宛如的“tsam”，字形白宛如作“斬”。（《字典》487 页，《词典》281 页）

【眨】tsap^{8}（白宛如无此字）（眼睛）迅速地一闭一开：眨眼。说明：字形与字义皆依据詹伯慧，字音是 dzaap，即白宛如的 tsap。（《字典》485 页，《派生词》㉑）

14【㓨】tsham^{5}刺入肉中：㓨刺。（《词典》282 页）

【插】tshap^{9}刺入，穿入：插入。说明：字形与字义皆依据詹伯慧，字音是 tsaap，即白氏的 tshap。（《字典》224 页，《派生词》㉔）

15【谦】him^{3}/hip^{8}歉虚。（《词典》304 页）/ 对不住人的心情：道歉。另收“歉”，him^{3}音，释义为“收成不好”，用如“歉收”。（《字典》450 页）

16【扻】ham^{2}碰撞。（《词典》206 页）

【磕】ham^{2}/hap^{9}硬物相碰撞。（《词典》481 页）

-n/-t（21 组）

1【泍】pan⁶烂泥：一身。（《词典》306 页）

【坺】phat⁹量词。A. 泡，摊，用于稀烂之物：一坺酱糊。B. 锹，用于泥、土块之类：一坺泥。（《词典》436 页）

2【抆】mɐn₅²擦拭：抆屎纸。（《词典》322 页）

【抿】mɐn²抹：幅墙裂咗条罅，揾水泥抿返佢喇。（《词典》322 页）

【擜】mat⁸擦拭，抹掉：擜干净。（《词典》436 页）/詹作“抹”。（《字典》208 页）此组词的主要元音并不相配，有待考证。

3【摊】than¹平铺：摊开报纸。（《词典》310 页）

【笪】that⁸ A. 向四面张开：只猫冚只笪开来瞓。B.（展开）到尽头：开笪把遮喇。（《词典》438 页）

4【攒】tsan²积聚：攒钱。（《词典》313 页）/詹作聚在一起之义。（《字典》231 页）

【扎】tsat⁸ A. 缠，捆扎：扎纸花。B. 量词。束，把：一扎花。（《词典》438 页）/詹作捆在一起的东西之义。（《字典》202 页）

5【趱】tsan³颤动，跳动：激到佢趱趱跳。（《词典》313 页）

【扎】tsat⁸惊觉，惊跳：吓到我扎起来。（《词典》439 页）

6【问】mɐn⁶请人解答不明白或不知道的道理和事情：问价钱。（《词典》322 页）

【乜】mɐt⁷ A. 为什么，干吗（询问原因或目的）：乜你唔食呢？B. 疑问代词。什么：佢乜都唔知道。（《词典》444 页）

7【墩】tɐn¹突出的圆形部分，用于身体某些多肉处：面珠墩脸蛋儿。（《词典》324 页）

【凸】tɐt⁹ A. 鼓出：肥到凸起个肚。B. 露出：袜穿咗，凸出脚趾。（《词典》444 页，《派生词》㉘）

8【墩】tɐn²大力投放，放置：将包米墩喺处。（《词典》324 页）

【朏】tɐt⁷（把对象）重重地放下：将啲行李朏吽度喇。（《词典》442 页）

9【震】tsɐn³心惊，害怕：听日考试，我唔震。（《词典》326 页）

【踬】tsɐt⁹突然一惊：佢吓到踬一踬他吓了一跳。（《词典》445 页）

10【歆】hɐn⁶很想得到，渴望：佢歆生仔。（《词典》331 页）

【乞】hɐt⁷讨要，乞讨：随街乞饭。（《词典》448 页）

11【樽】tsøn¹瓶子：玻璃樽。（《词典》337 页）

【椊】tsøt⁷ A. 塞子：樽椊瓶塞。B. 塞，堵：椊住个樽。（《词典》454 页）

12【搴】khin²掀，揭：搴开被。（《词典》349 页）

【揭】khit⁸掀起：揭锅盖。（《字典》223 页，《派生词》⑱）

13【断】thyn⁵断绝，隔绝：断市货物脱销，缺货。（《词典》354 页）

【脱】thyt⁸解除，除下：脱市货物脱销，缺货。（《词典》463 页）

14【穿】tshyn¹以绳线贯穿物体使之连贯：穿珠仔。（《词典》356 页）

【撮】tshyt⁸用绳穿起（有小孔的东西）：将啲珠来撮起佢。（《词典》463 页）

15【尽】tsoen⁶A. 竭，完：取之不尽。B. 死亡：自尽。(《字典》296 页)
【卒】tsoet⁷ A. 完毕，结束：卒业。B. 死亡：生卒年。(《字典》20 页)
16【旱】hon⁵长时间不下雨或降雨量太少：旱灾。(《字典》406 页)
【喝】hot⁸饮：喝水。(《字典》20 页)
17【宽】fun¹阔大，范围广：马路很宽。(《字典》136 页)
【阔】fut⁸宽广：呢条路好阔。(《字典》146 页)
18【窜】tshyn²⁽³⁾逃跑，乱走：抱头鼠窜。(《字典》458 页)
【猝】tshyt⁸A. 匆忙：仓猝。B. 突然，立刻：猝不及防。(《字典》287 页)
19【研】ŋan⁴碾，指滚动摩擦：研药。(《字典》475 页)
【啮】ŋat⁹磨：啮牙睡觉磨牙。(《字典》253 页，《派生词》㉖)
20【辨】bin⁶分辨，辨别：辨明是非。(《字典》585 页)
【别】bit⁹区分：区别。(《字典》44 页)
21【溅】tsin³液体受冲击后四处射出去：飞溅。(《字典》144 页)
【泲】tsit⁷溅：被车子溅到满身泥。(《字典》102 页)
【揤】tsit⁷用手挤：揤牙膏。(《字典》208 页，《派生词》⑰)

-ŋ/-k (18 组)

1【逛】khuaŋ³/ khuak⁸到处游玩：逛街。(《词典》367 页) 游逛：逛街。(《词典》472 页) 此字为一字两音。
2【哽】khɐŋ²噎，卡(刺、骨在喉)：哽骨。(《词典》370 页)
【撠】khɐk⁷卡住，阻碍：揾块砖来撠住个车轮。(《词典》475 页，《派生词》㉚)
3【抨】phɛŋ¹用力砍杀：一刀抨过去。(《词典》373 页)
【劈】phɛk⁸ (用刀斧) 破开：劈柴。(《词典》476 页)
4【抨】phaŋ¹赶，打：抨佢出去。(广韵耕韵普耕切：掸也)(《词典》360 页)
【拍】phak⁹撵，赶：拍扯佢撵走他。(《词典》467 页)
5【揈】feŋ⁶晃动，甩动：洗完头，揈干头发。(《词典》380 页)
【擮】fek⁹用手巾、手帕类使劲挥动：唔好擮亲人别甩着人。(《词典》480 页)
6【啄】tœŋ¹/tœk⁸ (用尖嘴) 取食：鸡啄米。(《词典》390 页) / 黄、詹认为是白读/文读。(《辨析》117 页，《字典》252 页)
7【啄】tœŋ¹(锋利物) 砸落：把刀跌落来，啄亲我只脚。(《词典》390 页)
【剁】tœk⁸用刀向下砍：剁开两边。(《词典》487 页，《派生词》㉓)
8【仰】ŋɔŋ⁵仰头，脸、腹朝上：仰高头。(《词典》405 页) / 李、詹音ŋɔŋ⁴，字作"昂"。(《字典》407 页，《方言》91 页)
【顉】ŋɔk⁹仰头，抬头：顉高头。(《词典》496 页，《派生词》⑦)
9【靓】lɛŋ³漂亮好看：生得好靓。(《词典》375 页)
【叻】lɛk⁷能干，聪明，有本事：佢唱歌跳舞最叻。(《词典》476 页)
10【拎】leŋ¹A. 拿，持：拎住一本书。B. 提：拎唔起提不动。(《词典》382 页) / 李

音作 neŋ^{1}。(《方言》91 页)

【搦】nek^{7}提，拿：佢搦起皮箱就走咗。(《词典》481 页，《派生词》⑨)

11【椗】teŋ^{3}瓜果的蒂：苹果椗。(《词典》381 页)

【葝】tek^{7}物品上类似莲子的东西，供手拿的部分：茶壶葝茶壶盖的顶子。(《词典》480 页，《派生词》⑭)

12【绑】pɔŋ^{2}用绳、带等缠绕或捆扎：绑担架。(《字典》319 页)

【缚】pɔk^{8}捆绑：束缚。(《字典》325 页)

13【□】kaŋ^{3}较量，比武：□拳二人握拳，以腕相较力。此为有音无字。(《词典》364 页)

【格】kak^{8}抵挡：格拳二人用臂相击以较力。(《词典》469 页，《派生词》⑯)

14【捅】thong^{2}A. 戳，扎：用刀捅。B. 触动，碰：用胳膊肘捅了他一下。(《字典》216 页)

【豛】tok^{7} A. 刺，捅：豛一个窿。B. 用指头、棍棒轻击轻点：随笔点豛(《字典》18 页)。字形白作"斀"（斀：集韵烛韵株玉切，"刺也"）。(《词典》500 页)

15【盈】jieŋ^{4} A. 充满：热泪盈眶。B. 有余，多出：盈利。(《字典》495 页)

【溢】jat^{9} A. 充满：热情洋溢。B. 因充满而流出，泛滥：河水四溢。(《字典》116 页)(广韵质韵夷质切；上古为锡部)

16【框】kwaŋ^{1} A. 用来安装门窗的架子：门框。B. 镶在器物周围，起保护、支撑等作用的东西：镜框。(《字典》375 ~376 页)

17【啯】kwak^{7}圈儿：汽车兜了一个大圈。(《字典》263 页)

18【攻】koŋ^{1} 气味刺激鼻子，钻鼻子：攻鼻。(《词典》416 页)

【焗】kok^{9}闷，指空气不疏通，闷热。(《字典》343 页，《派生词》④)

在上述 ŋ－k 中的 14、15 最后两组相较于其余各组，语音对应似乎不齐（"捅"和"豛"声母有送气与否之别；"盈"和"溢"韵尾也有不同），但前者仍符合语音近似的同源原则，后者则由于历史音变的缘故反映不出对转现象，然从上古音仍可判断二者之间的同源关系。①

根据李如龙、张双庆（1996）的说法，"这种语词派生方式还可以追溯到中古汉语和上古汉语，看来应是汉语派生同源词的一条规律。……闽粤方言里这种'阳入对转'派生同源词的方式看来是源远流长的，《广韵》里的异读字有的就是阳声韵和入声韵与相应的入声韵并见，而且字义注释相同或相近。……所有的这些，都说明了'阳入对转'滋生新词可以追溯到上古汉语，它是早期的汉语词汇演生规律之一"。也许是观点的不同以及引

① 本文评审人指出："部分词例虽符合阳入对转的音理关系，唯词义相隔甚远，当中是否存在转化或派生关系，似可商榷。例如-n/-t 第 4 组 tsan^{2}—tsat^{8}，前者训'积聚'，后者训'捆扎、束'；同类第 10 组 hɐn^{6}—hɐt^{7}，前者训'很想得到'，后者训'讨要，乞讨'；同类第 16 组 hon^{5}—hot^{8}，前者训'雨量太少'，后者训'饮'；又如-ŋ/-k 第 9 组 lɛŋ^{3}—lɛk^{7}，前者训'漂亮好看'，后者训'能干，聪明，有本事'等，词与词之间的同义派生关系似乎皆不甚明显。"这些都是很有见地的意见，容以后进一步考察。

用文献的差异，李如龙、张双庆（1996）涉及泉州话、广州话各三十条实例，分别引用了《十五音》、《广韵》、《字林》、《前汉书·灌夫传》、《前汉书·惠帝纪》、《集韵》、《广州话方言词典》、《说文》、《周礼》、早期《切韵》（黄典诚《切韵综合研究》）、王力《同源字典》等。因此，跟李如龙、张双庆（1996）一文相比，只有10组是本文所没有的，包括李如龙、张双庆（1996）的第2组的n－p，第3组的ŋ－t，第8组、第9组的ŋ－k，第10组、第15组、第22组、第25组的m－p，第12组、第20组的n－t。

4 结　语

从以上将古音学中的音转理论运用于粤方言的实例中，可以看出阳声韵尾的-m、-n、-ŋ与入声韵尾的-p、-t、-k之间的确存在音转关系。联系单音节词的词义，可发现阳入对转关系与这些词义适成互为表里的关系，由此可进一步证明现代粤语单音节实词“音近义通”、“义由音生”的规律现象。正如齐佩瑢（1998：155）所说的那样：“语音与语义在起初配合时虽没有必然的因果关系，但后来在语言的演进过程中，因为词汇从同一语根孳生分化的缘故，音读相同相近者，其意义也往往相近相同，形成一个语族。”本文所考察的55组单音节同义实词，应该正是相同语根孳生分化的结果。

参考文献

白宛如　1998　《广州方言词典》，南京：江苏教育出版社。

陈伯煇　1998　《论粤方言词本字考释》，香港：中华书局有限公司。

符淮青　2004　《现代汉语词汇》，北京：北京大学出版社。

郭良夫　1985　《词汇》，北京：商务印书馆。

黄谷甘　1993　《粤语词汇中“阳入对转”同义词的语义辨析》，载于郑定欧主编《广州话研究与教学》，广州：中山大学出版社，第114～118页。

蒋绍愚　2005　《古汉语词汇纲要》，北京：商务印书馆。

李方桂　1980　《上古音研究》，北京：商务印书馆。

李如龙、张双庆　1996　《闽粤方言的“阳入对转”派生词》，载于《方言与音韵论集》，香港中文大学中国文化研究所吴多泰中国语文研究中心，第152～157页。

李新魁　1994　《广东的方言》，广州：广东人民出版社。

李新魁等　1995　《广州方言研究》，广州：广东人民出版社。

陆宗达、王宁　1994　《音转原理浅谈》，载于《训诂与训诂学》，太原：山西教育出版社。

齐佩瑢　1998　《语义和语音》，载于北京大学中国传统文化研究中心编　《北京大学百年国学文粹·语言文献卷》，北京：北京大学出版社，第152～157页。

孙景涛　2010　《元音交替与新词派生》，《语言科学》第3期，第301～310页。

王　力　1982　《同源字典》，北京：商务印书馆。

吴泽顺　2006　《汉语音转研究》，长沙：岳麓书社。

詹伯慧主编　2002a　《广州话正音字典》，广州：广东人民出版社。

詹伯慧主编　2002b　《广东粤方言概要》，广州：暨南大学出版社。

张洪年　2007　《香港粤语语法的研究》（增订版），香港：香港中文大学出版社。

张双庆　2002　《粤语的特征词》，载于李如龙主编　《汉语方言特征词研究》，厦门：厦门大学出版社，第390～414页。

周祖谟　2004　《周祖谟文字音韵训诂讲义》，天津：天津古籍出版社。

从短长到高低：广府片粤语入声的声学性质及演化路径*

沈瑞清

（香港科技大学）

提　要：本文从广府片粤语出发，探讨长短入声的声学性质及其演化路径。首先，根据声调声学描写的成果揭示广府片粤语入声的声学性质；然后，结合其他东南亚语言中类似的例子，指出长短入声音高分化的不平衡性："短高长低"模式远比"短长高低"常见；最后，从演化音法学的视角出发，尝试用 Ohala（1981）的听者过度改正（hypercorrection）模型解释这一模式的成因，并构拟了一条"从短长到高低"的演化路径。

关键词：粤语　长短元音　入声　演化音法学　过度改正

1　引　言

在大部分汉语方言里，中古清入类①如果仍然保留入声韵尾（p/t/k/ʔ）或者入声调，大都只对应一个调类。而在大部分粤语里，清入类却分化为两类，形成了以广府片粤语为典型的三个入声调。② 这种不管是历时演变还是共时表现都十分复杂的入声系统一直被视作粤语跟其他汉语方言的重要区别特征之一。

以往对粤语入声演变的研究主要是从中古音的框架出发，试图解释粤语入声调类的演变，而未见对微观音变的语音机制及其动因的研究。跟以往的研究相比，本文有三个新的出发点：一是根据声调声学描写的一些成果，揭示广府片粤语入声的声学性质；二是结合其他东南亚语言中类似的例子，指出长短入声音高分化的不对称性——"短高长低"模式

---

* 本文的撰写得到朱晓农老师的指导，在科大清水湾语言学讨论会报告内部讨论时，同门好友多有所指正，在第十八届国际粤方言研讨会报告时，蒙麦耘、孙景涛、张群显、张洪年等诸位先生赐教，又蒙 Phil Rose 与 Alexis Michaud 先生帮助，特此致谢。

① 汉语的"入声"至少有三种不同的含义：一种是历时层面的含义：对应早期汉语的"入声类"，可以翻译成 entering tone 或者 Ru tone。第二种和第三种是共时层面的含义。第二种指以塞音（包括喉塞音）收尾的声调，可以翻译成 stopped tone。第三种指以短时性跟其他声调区别的调类，可以翻译成 short tone。本文的"入声"单独使用时只用于第二种含义——共时层面的以塞音收尾的声调，如果要表达第一种历时意义，则加上"中古"、"类"等词来限定。

② 广府片粤语，又称为粤海片，主要分布在以广州为中心的珠江三角洲、粤中以及粤北部分地区。香港、澳门所通行的粤语基本上也属于粤海片。这种清入类的分化，除了粤语之外，还见于部分平话以及少量湘粤桂三省交界处的土话，另外，部分粤语的中古全浊入类也分化为两类，主要在广西境内（王莉宁，2011）。

远比“长高短低”模式常见；三是在演化音法学的视角下审视“短高长低”的自然语音模式，用听感的过度改正解释这一模式的成因，并构拟一条“从短长到高低”的演化路径。最后还附带讨论了粤语阴入分化的时间，以及其跟台语支语言入声相似性的成因究竟是底层、晚近影响还是平行演化的问题。

2 广府片粤语入声的声学性质

以广州粤语、香港粤语为代表的广府片粤语大概是研究最充分的粤语方言，前人对香港粤语的语音也有较充分的描写，[①] 所以我们用香港粤语作为例子来讨论广府片粤语入声的声学性质。

2.1 香港粤语的长短元音

广府片粤语的入声跟长短元音有密切的关联，要了解入声的声学性质，必须先从长短元音入手。Kao（1971：43－58）、李行德（1985）跟 Gordon（2002）都对长短元音在不同音节中的时长作了声学测量，数据如下：

表1　香港粤语长短元音的长度序列

音节类型	CVV	CVVN	CVVO	CVN	CVO
举例	ka:[②]	ka:m	ka:p	kɐm	kɐp
Kao（1971：43－58）	308	203	169	100	89
李行德（1985）[③]	345	238	162	104	77
Gordon（2002）	283	208	150	99	77
	长元音			短元音	

三家的数据不约而同地表现出“开音节长元音 > 鼻音尾长元音 > 塞音尾长元音 > 鼻音尾短元音 > 塞音尾短元音”这样由长到短的长度序列，也反映出了长短元音在时长上的显著差异。实验语音学的研究表明，粤语的长元音跟短元音除了音长方面的差异外，还有音

① 关于香港粤语声调的研究历史，请参看 Yim（2012：41－74）。

② 开尾韵音节只能出现长元音，没有长短元音的对立。

③ 李行德（1985）测量了广州、香港各三人，这里以“香港一”（见李行德，1985，表三）的数值为代表。

质的差异，[①] 这不仅体现在低元音［aː］［ɐ］的对立上，也体现在高元音中，只是语言学家仅凭借人耳很难分辨这些细微的音质差别，不过在元音声学图中则很明显：[②]

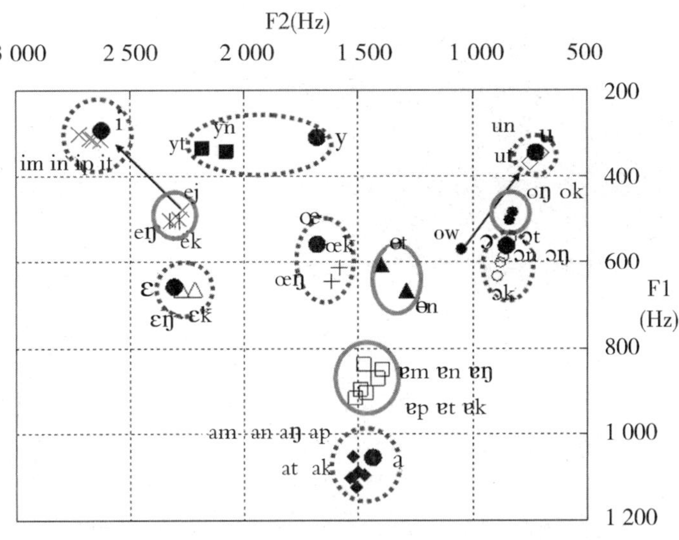

图 1　香港粤语声学元音图（转引自严至诚，2011：192）

图中实线圈里的是短元音，虚线圈里的是长元音，可以看到两者占据了不同的声学空间。以往对粤语的元音系统有不同的音位处理：有的处理侧重于元音音值的区别，而把元音长短放在次要的位置，因而得到较多的元音音位；有的处理则侧重元音长短的区别，因而有较少的元音音位。[③] 这反映了音位分析处理冗余语音信息的困境，“语音表达中的冗余信息对于分类来说是必要的”[④]，而音位分析中“只有一个特征被选来表达这种对立，这种选择是随意的，且根本不反映听感、语言学的实质”[⑤]。因此，我们对长短元音不做配对跟简化的音位分析，而是同意严至诚（2011）的看法，认为香港粤语一共有 11 个元

---

① 这跟英语的 tense-lax 元音很相似，所以 Yue（1972）认为 tense-lax 比 long-short 更合适粤语。本文仍然用 long-short，首先，因为如果将粤语 CVVN 与 CVN、CVVO 与 CVO 的长短元音的时长作对比（表 1），差不多是 2 倍，这跟其他典型长短元音语言的比例是一致的，见 Maddieson（2004：表 3）。而英语 tense-lax 元音的时长差别没有那么大（House 1961），关于时长与元音的关系，参看 Lehiste（1970：30－33），Rosner & Pickering（1994：199－203）。其次，大部分世界语言里的长短元音对立都伴随着细微音质差异，比如泰语（Abramson & Ren，1990）与红水河壮语（周学文，2012）的长短元音也有音质差异，所以音质差异并非 tense-lax 的特性。另外，tense-lax 有太多不同的含义（尤其是还用在跟发声态相关的对立上），而且暗含两两相配的意思，而 long-short 相对较少有附加含义，也不一定要两两相配。

② 金健、张梦翰（2013）对广州方言长短元音的声学分析及多元方差分析统计结果表明，广州方言长短元音的差异以音长为主，且大多伴有音质差异。同时，这种音质差异无法在长短元音搭配的框架里得到统一的解释。

③ 不同学者对音位的归并参看严至诚（2011），在此不再展开。

④ Redundancy in phonetic representation is essential to categorization.（Ohala & Ohala，1995）

⑤ Only one feature is chosen as expressing the contrast. This choice is arbitrary and often does not reflect the perceptual or linguistic reality.（Bybee，2001：42－43）

音，其中 7 个长元音［i/y/u/ɛ/œ/ɔ/a］（虚线圈）可以单独作为韵母，也可以与元音尾、鼻音尾、塞音尾结合，而 4 个短元音［e/o/ɵ/ɐ］（实线圈）不能单独作韵母，只能与元音尾、鼻音尾、塞音尾结合。

2.2 长短元音与调型的相位调整（phase realignment）

粤语的十一个长短元音都可以与响音尾（包括元音尾跟鼻音尾）、塞音尾相配。对于响音尾来说，长元音或短元音作为韵腹并不会对它的音长产生显著的影响，因为响音尾本身也是音长的负载单位之一。如果元音的音长较短，则响音尾会延长音长，从而补偿长短元音之间的音长差异。同时，元音的响音尾与音高的调型也会重新进行相位的调整（phase realignment）[①]，比如阳平调“蓝”［la:m］、“林”［lɐm］的对比：

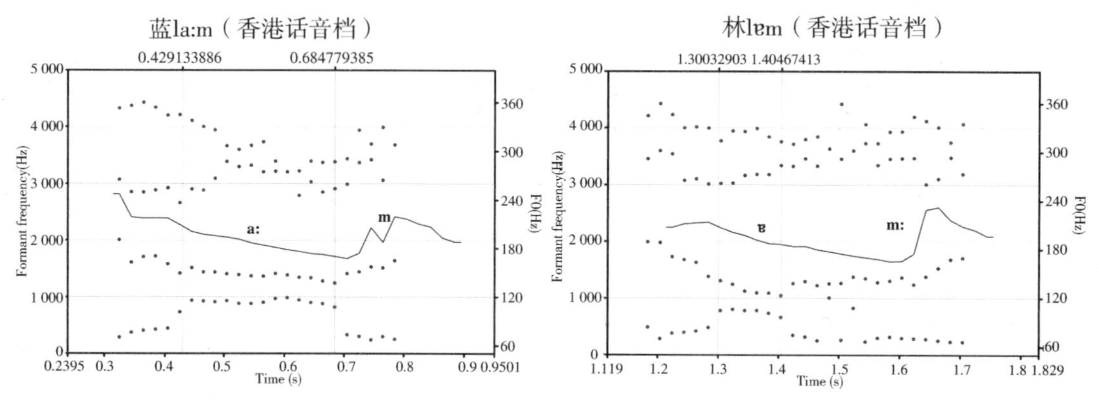

图 2 香港粤语[②]“蓝”［la:m］、“林”［lɐm］的声调曲线与元音起始（竖线标示）

图中虚线标示的是元音段，可以看到“蓝”的元音［a］比“林”的元音［ɐ］要长很多，但“林”的韵尾［m］也比“蓝”的韵尾［m］长很多。由于这种补偿作用，响音尾收尾的韵母总的声调时长并不会因为长短元音的不同而有太大差异，但对于塞音收尾的入声调来说，情况却很不一样。由于塞音尾不负载声调，因此长短元音的音长差异会直接反映在声调的时长上，下面是入声（上为阴入类，下为阳入类）部分例字的绝对时长图与等长图：[③]

① 这里采用的是 Roengpitya（2007）的术语。

② 本文香港粤语的材料都来自《现代汉语方言音库》的“香港话音档”，其他来源则另作说明。

③ 声调作图的方法根据朱晓农（2010：281～291）。

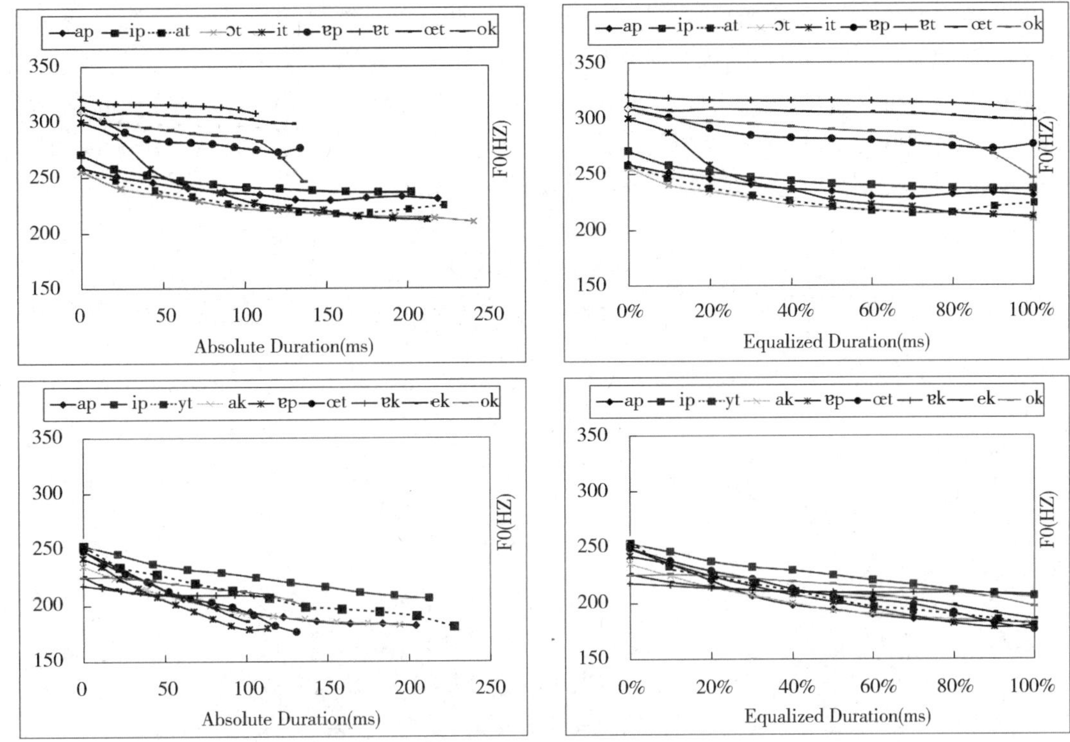

图 3 香港粤语入声部分例字的绝对时长图（左）与等长图（右）（上为阴入类，下为阳入类）

从图 3 左图中我们可以看到，阴入类跟阳入类都形成了长短两组，其中短阳入的分类完全与长短元音平行：一组对应 4 个短元音。长阳入一组则对应 7 个长元音。从图 3 右边的等长图上我们看到，跟阴入类分成有音高差别不同的两组不同，阳入类的两组没有明显的音高差别。

2.3 一个还是两个阳入

跟长短元音的音位分析类似，两组阳入的对立也可以有不同的音位分析：大多数学者的看法是把阳入类看作一个声调，而把差异归结为元音音质、音长的不同，而严至诚（Yim，2012）则把阳入类分成短阳入、长阳入两个声调，认为阳入类的差别跟阴入类的差别类似，都是不同的声调。究其根本原因，是因为在传统的音段/超音段两分框架里，音长正好处于一个两可的地位：

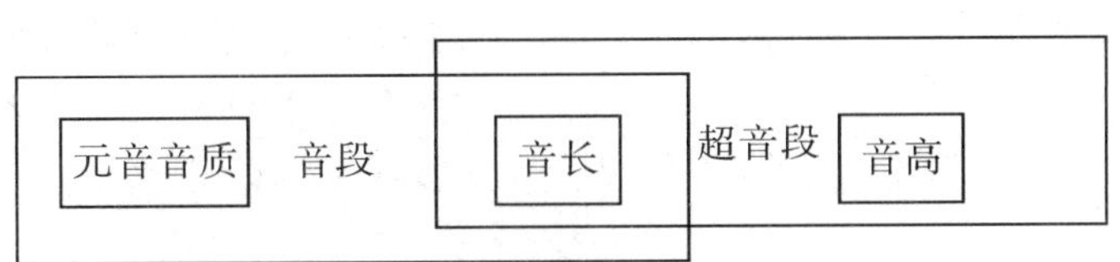

图 4 音段/超音段两分框架里音长的两可地位

音长既可以视作音段特征的一部分，也可以视作超音段特征的一部分。因此，音长的差异是否处理成声调有别，取决于对声调的定义。如果接受“声调＝音高”的说法，那么香港粤语只有三个入声，两组阳入的时长差异是元音的附加特征；如果接受声调多维说（朱晓农等，2010），即声调不仅包括音高，也包括时长等其他维度，那么香港粤语无疑有四个入声。表2是入声与长短元音的搭配关系及两种分析：

表2　香港粤语入声与长短元音的搭配及两种分析（左三个入声，右四个入声）

		上阴入	下阴入	阳入	上阴入	下阴入	短阳入	长阳入
短元音	ok/ɵt/ɐt/ɐk	+	-	+	+	-	+	-
	ek/ɐp	+	(+)	+	+	(+)	+	-
长元音	ip/yt/ut/œk/ɔt/at	-	+	+	-	+	-	+
	it/ɔk/ɛk/ap/ak	(+)	+	+	(+)	+	-	+

从表2我们看到，阳入类在与长短元音搭配时没有例外，所以可以有看作一类与看作互补的两类两种分析。而阴入类与长短元音相配却有一定数量的“例外”［图中（+）的部分］，所以必须分成上下阴入两类。[①] 可见，上下阴入跟阳入两类的区别的关键就在于这些“例外”，图5是香港粤语上下阴入部分例字的绝对时长与平均基频数据：

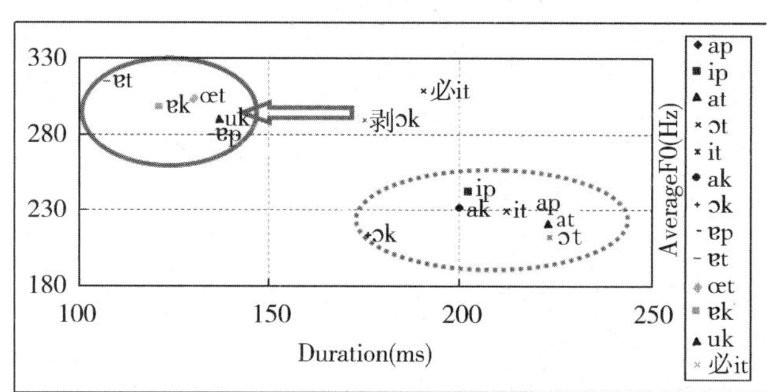

图5　香港粤语上下阴入部分例字的绝对时长（横轴）与平均基频（纵轴）

图5中的横轴是绝对时长，纵轴是平均基频。上阴入一般集中在左上角（实线圈），也就是说时长短、基频高；下阴入则集中在右下角（虚线圈），也就是说时长长、基频低；而“必”、“剥”两个字则在右上角，属于时长长（长元音）、基频高的“例外”。处于右上角的“必”、“剥”与左上角的上阴入有相近的基频，与下阴入则有相近的时长。说香港粤语的人把“必”、“剥”感知为上阴入而非下阴入，这说明从听感上来说，音高是比时长更重要的声学特性，可见上下阴入是以音高作为主要声学特性的，与阳入两类以时长

① Yue（1972：177）列出了上下阴入与长短元音相配的例外语素，其中上阴入与长元音相配的有13个，下阴入与短元音相配的有5个。

及元音音质作为主要声学特性不同。

我们在上文已经指出，香港粤语到底有三个还是四个入声调，取决于对声调的定义。我们更关心的是理解香港粤语阴入类跟阳入类的声学性质：上下阴入以音高作为主要声学特性，而阳入的长短两类没有音高区别，以时长及元音音质作为主要声学特性。

3 “短高长低”的入声模式

3.1 “短高长低”与“长高短低”

音高相同的长短入声如果产生音高分化，从逻辑上来说可以有两种不同的语音模式（sound pattern）：一种是“短高长低”，即时长较短的入声比时长较长的入声音高更高；另一种是“长高短低”，即时长较长的入声比时长较短的入声音高更高。

从图3左上的绝对时长图，我们可以看到香港粤语的阴入类呈现出“短高长低”的模式，王莉宁（2011）利用北京语言大学语言研究所“汉语方言地图集数据库”中61个粤语、39个平话以及20个湘粤桂土话调查点的材料，考察了古入声字“短元音与长元音短高长低分调”[①] 的音变现象，总结出7种不同的调值类型，除了部分平话（宾阳、罗城、上林）跟土话（嘉禾）浊入分调外，其他都符合“短高长低”的模式。

有意思的是，这种“短高长低”的模式并不是汉语方言的特色，而是普遍存在于东南亚语言中。下面我们举一些东南亚语言具有“短高长低”入声模式的例子。

3.1.1 扶平壮语的“短高长低”

第一种是扶平壮语，属于侗台语族的中部台语支。[②] 发音人为1979年生的男性，在广西德保县扶平乡长大。扶平壮语D2调的长短入声没有音高区别，而D1调有音高区别：

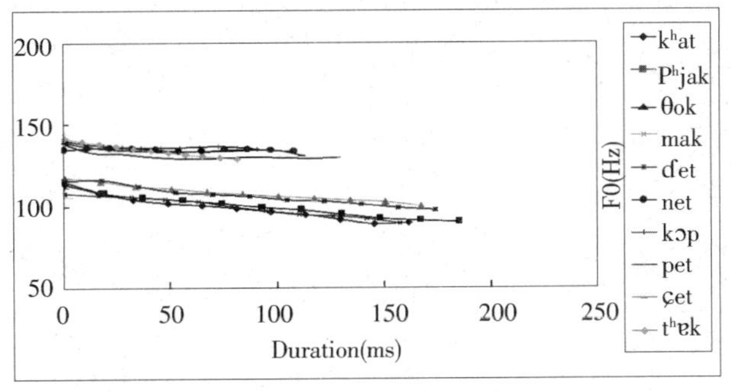

图6 扶平壮语D1长短入声的绝对时长图

① 原文用“高短元音与低长元音分调”的说法，这一说法容易引起“高短元音”比“低长元音”舌位更高的误解。其实，这里的高低是音高，属于声调的范围，与元音无关，所以这里采用了“短元音与长元音短高长低分调”的表述。

② 关于扶平壮语的概况及其声调声学的描写，参看Shen & Liao（2012）。

如图6所示，扶平壮语的D1呈现出跟粤语上下阴入非常相似的模式——“短高长低”。

3.1.2 PPN泰语方言的“短高长低”

下面我们来看属于侗台语族东南台语支的一种泰国南部方言的入声（Rose，1996），这种方言有六个入声调：

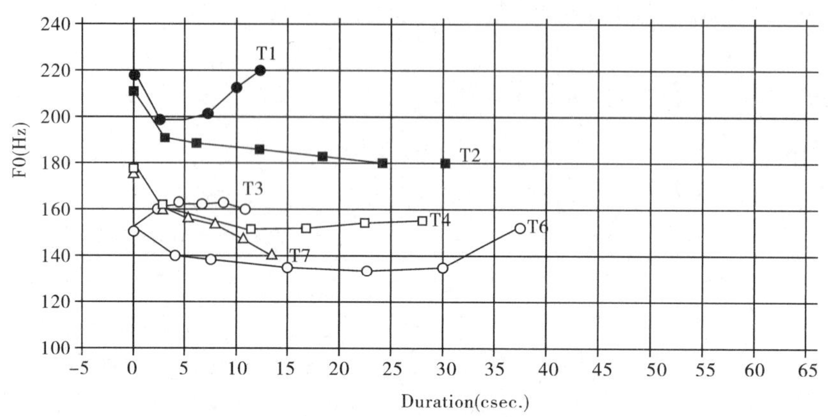

图7　PPN泰语入声的平均基频曲线（转引自Rose，1996）

从图7可以看到，六个入声两两相配分成三组（T1 – T2、T3 – T4、T7 – T6），这三组在早期应该各自具有相同的音高，后来逐渐产生分化。其中T3 – T4、T7 – T6的音高还比较接近，而T1的音高则明显高于T2，呈现“短高长低”的模式。

3.1.3 北中部越南语方言的“短高长低”

越南语属于南亚语族越芒语支，Honda的博士论文（2008）详细描写了北中部越南语方言的音系，发现河内越南语的两个入声Sac、Nang在这个方言里分别发生了进一步的分化：

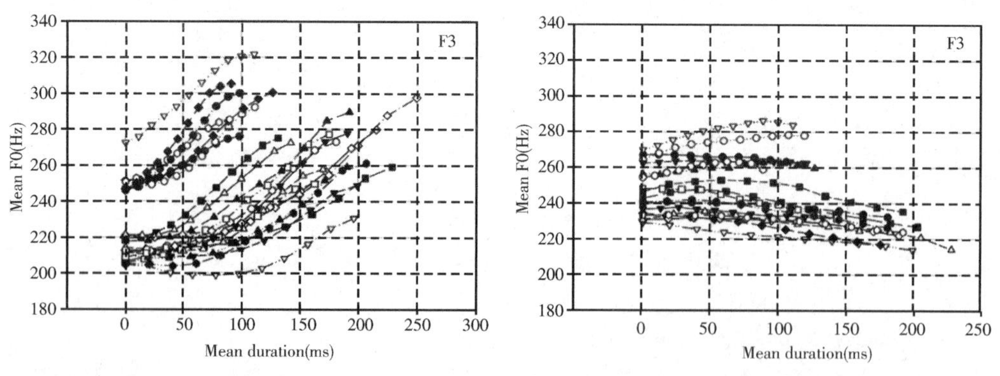

图8　越南语北中部方言入声的分化（转引自Honda，2008：114，123）

从图 8 中我们可以发现，左右两图中的短调都处在长调的上方，显然，该越南语方言入声的分化也遵循“短高长低”的原则。

3.2 自然语音模式（nature sound pattern）及其解释

如果长短入声的音高分化没有任何语音限制，那么“短高长低”与“长高短低”两种语音模式的分布应该具有对称性，即大致呈现相同的出现频率。

但是，我们在汉藏语族的汉语方言、侗台语族的台语支语言跟南亚语族的越南语方言里都发现了“短高长低”的入声模式，而“长高短低”的入声模式却非常罕见。[①] 可见这并非偶然，说明“短高长低”相对于“长高短低”来说是一种更自然的语音模式。

要解释自然语音模式最合理的办法是找到它的语音基础，并把它在实验室里用物理模型还原出来，这就是演化音法学[②]的目标。下面我们就从演化音法学的角度来看“短高长低”入声模式的语音基础及演化阶段。

4 “短高长低”入声模式的语音基础及演化阶段

4.1 “短高长低”的语音基础——发音

为什么不同语系不同方言在不同时期发生的长短入声音高分化都遵循“短高长低”模式？背后是什么语音机制在起作用？

如果我们把目光放到更大的范围，我们就会发现“短高长低”的模式不仅适用于入声，它对于平声也同样适用。跨语言的研究表明，平调中元音的时长跟平均基频有逆相关关系：当其他条件一致时，低调比高调的元音更长。尽管这条类型学共性由于一些反例而被质疑，但实际上还是成立的，相关的综述请看 Faytak & Yu（2011），在此不再赘述。

同时，“短高长低”的模式不仅在共时变异中有所体现，还有历时音变的证据。根据 Svantesson（1989，1991）对北部孟高棉语的声调起源研究，Hu 语的高低调来自长短元音：

① “长高短低”的语音模式在我们目前考察的语言中有泰语 D2 调疑似一例。其实，泰语的 D2L 与 D2S 有相似的基频范围，也不是严格的反例。而且，泰语入声的 D2S、D2L 一般认为对应非入声音节里的 High、Falling 调，Abramson（1962）描写的 High 调处在最高的基频区（约相当于五度制的 45），而在当代年轻人的泰语中这个 High 调已经逐渐降低，见 Thepboriruk（2010）。所以泰语入声的音高可能经历了较大的改变。

② 演化音法学是 Evolutionary Phonology 的译名（朱晓农，011），它把语言看作一个与生物有机体类似演化过程的复杂自我调整系统（adaptive system），也是根基于我们对声音发音和感知的物理实质的一个动态的、有概率性的演化系统（Ohala，1989；Blevins，2006）。

表3　来源于长短元音对立的 Hu 语高低调

Hu	Lamet	Gloss
jam（H）	jam	to die
jam（L）	jaːm	to cry

从表3中可以发现，Hu 语的高调对应 Lamet 语的短元音，而低调则对应长元音，这与我们上文总结的入声“短高低长”的模式完全一致。① 同样的情况也独立发生在新喀里多尼亚（New Caledonia）的南岛语，低调的［a］来自长［aa］（Rivierre，1993：163）。夏尔巴藏语（Sherpa）里非起首位置的音节根据韵母的长短分化出了高低调：短韵母高调、长韵母低调（Sun，2001：46）。另外，Gandour（1977）指出在部分泰语方言里长短元音发生了中和；在清莱方言（北部泰语）里，高平调的长元音变成了短元音；而在普吉方言（南部泰语）里，低、中平调里的短元音则变成了长元音。②

4.2　“短高长低”的语音基础——听感

有趣的是，平调中基频越高、时长越短的发音规律跟听感实验的结果却完全相反。Yu（2010）用300毫秒的［pa］音节合成了55、33、11、15、51五种声调，并对英语、粤语母语者进行听感测试，结果显示听感的长度序列为：非平调、高平调 > 中平调 > 低平调。

Gussenhoven & Zhou（2013）对荷兰语、汉语普通话母语者的测试进一步证实了这个规律，而这与上一节所指出的发音上高调更短、低调更长的规律正好相反。

同样，元音音高和元音长短的发音与听感也有类似的现象；一方面，在发音上存在“高元音比低元音更短”的跨语言现象；另一方面，在听感上时长相等的元音，往往是高元音听起来更长。

为什么听感跟发音之间会呈现出截然相反的规律呢？Gussenhoven（2007）用补偿听音（compensatory listening）机制来解释这一现象，他认为高元音听上去比低元音长，这是因为发音人知道高元音会发得比较短，所以有意识地在感知的时候给予补偿。Yu（2010）提出另一种解释，他认为说话人能意识到听感对不同高度音高的扭曲，为了把这种效应抵消，在发音时就会做出补偿来达到一致。也就是说，由于在感知低调时会导致时长缩短，所以说者有意识地把低调发得更长，以此来补偿自动缩短时长的听感效应；反过来，感知高调时会导致时长延长，说者就会有意识地把高调发得更短，从而抵消听感的加长效应。

Gussenhoven（2007）跟 Yu（2010）的解释都是从发音和听感的相互调适的角度出发的，唯一的不同是 Gussenhoven（2007）认为是听感迁就发音，而 Yu（2010）则认为是发

① Heike（2013：101）认为从元音长短到音高高低的演化方向较为少见，这是针对非塞音收尾韵说的，在第三节我们已经看到，对塞音收尾的入声来说，元音长短到音高高低的演化方向是极为自然的。当然，这跟入声的时长较短，增加了元音长短听辨的难度有关。

② 泰语方言的长短元音中和也发生在升调与降调中，由于升降调的时长牵涉到更多因素，暂时只考虑平调。

音迁就听感。其实，两者本质上是一样的，都是把发音和听感的不一致看作统一感知时长的归一化手段。

4.3 过度改正（hyper-correction）

在一般情况下，这种归一化手段会弥补高低调的时长差异。但是，在某些情况下，说话人有意识发出的时长差异也可能会被误解，重新分析为由于归一化手段而造成的时长差异，这就是 Ohala（1981）提出的过度改正效应。

我们认为，平调以及入声音高分化的“短高长低”就是由于过度改正而形成的。其具体过程可以用图 9 来表示：

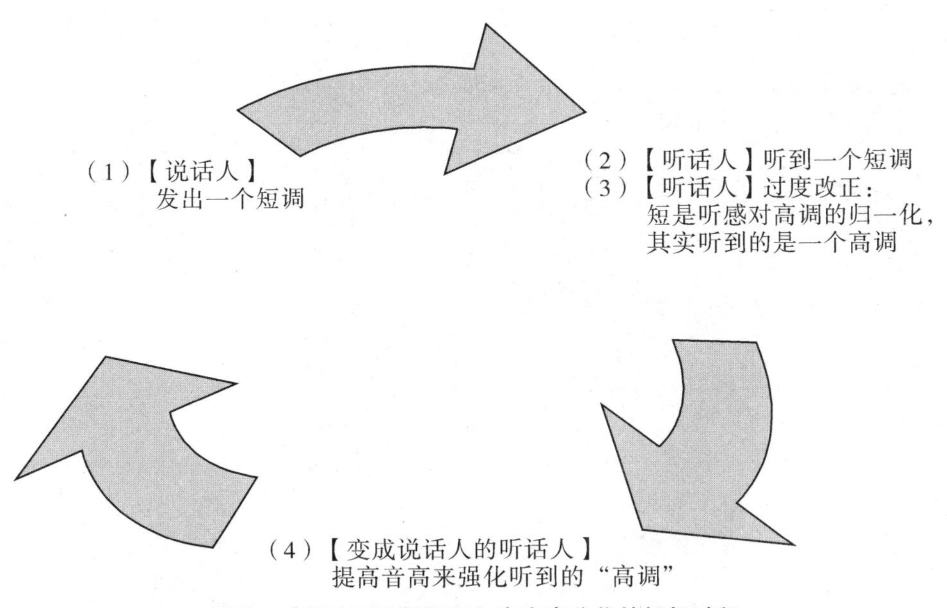

图 9　过度改正引起长短入声音高分化的假想过程

在图 9 过程（1）中说话人发了一个正常的短调，但是在过程（3）中听话人把听到的短调误解为是由于高调听得短的归一化手段而造成的短调。到过程（4），转变成说话人的听者就会提高音高，从而加强他所听到的“高调”，这样说话人所发出的短调的音高就会越来越高，形成“短高长低”的变异。

这种由于过度改正所导致的变异如果不断被加强（enhancement），并逐渐被语言社群所接受，就会成为演化的起因。那么这个演化又是如何逐渐完成的呢？下面，我们就根据长短入声的几个有代表性的共时模式来推测从短长到高低的演化阶段。

4.4 三个演化阶段

从第二节对香港粤语入声的声学描写可以看到，香港粤语的阳入类以时长为主要声学特性，音高不起作用，而香港粤语的上下阴入以音高为主要声学特性，两者分别代表了演化的起点与终点。

那么，演化的中间阶段如何呢？我们发现第三节介绍过的北中部越南语方言可以作为中间阶段的代表。Honda（2008：第6.3章）的研究表明，北中部越南语分化中的两类入声究竟是以音高还是时长作为主要声学特性在不同发音人中有不同的表现，有的发音人以音高为主要声学特性来区别两类入声，有的发音人则以时长为主要声学特性来区别两类入声。

结合粤语与北中部越南语方言的例子，我们可以把长短入声音高分化的过程重构为如表4所示的三个演化阶段：

表4　长短入声音高分化三个演化阶段的构想

阶段	例子	语音/音位表现	声调感知
1	香港粤语阳入类	长短入声有元音音质与时长的差异，没有音高区别	音高不起作用
2	北中部越南语入声	长短入声的元音音质、时长与音高都形成区别，音高区别较小	以音高还是时长作为主要声学特性在不同人群中有不同表现
3	香港粤语上下阴入	音高区别变大，并且在时长与音高的搭配中形成“例外”，形成了仅以音高区别的最小对立	以音高作为主要声学特性

表4中的第一阶段是起点，此时长短入声完全根据长短元音的时长来区别，音高不起作用。到了第二阶段，由于对长短对立的重新分析，“短高长低”的读音开始在语言社群中扩散，音高的差别也逐渐被感知，有些人群开始用音高代替时长来作为主要声学特性。到了第三阶段，音高区别变大，并且在时长跟音高的搭配中形成“例外”，形成了仅以音高区别的最小对立。

5　余　论

在上面讨论的基础上，本文最后附带讨论一个目前学界尚有争议的问题——粤语和壮语的入声都以元音长短分调，这反映的是古老的底层还是晚近的影响或平行演变？（麦耘，2009：224注1）

余蔼芹（Yue，1972：48）在比较了广州、台山、廉州三处阴入的分化之后，认为“阴入的分化在原始粤语里已经发生”，从原始粤语到现代粤语方言，阴入经历了以下三个阶段：

（1）音段跟声调区别共存（长短元音与上下阴入搭配一致）。

（2）声调区别作为音位区别（上下阴入以声调区别，不与长短元音一致）。

（3）根据新的音段情况重新指定调类（根据新的长短元音重新指派调类）。

我们对这个设想有两点疑问：第一，由于有了第三阶段重新制定调类的假设，所以这个解释无法得到材料的检验，无论我们把广州话、台山话、廉州话的哪一种阴入分布模式作为原始粤语的形式，都可以解释今天粤方言阴入分化的模式。第二，如果在第二阶段声调的音高区别已经固定，元音的长短已经不起什么作用了，那么第三阶段为什么会根据新的音段情况重新指派调类似乎缺乏合理的解释。

因此，我们同意王莉宁（2011）的看法，即粤语的“元音分调”（即本文的“音高分化”）有不同类型，“导致音变的关键因素应是音变发生时的实际音值，不能简单地归为‘古音’或‘今音’”。换句话说，长短入声（不管是阴入类还是阳入类）的音高分化是在粤语分支中各自独立发生的，根据的是当时长短元音的情况，所以在古音类的对应上会有所不同。

另外，有很多证据表明台语支语言长短入声的音高分化也是后起的，由于牵涉的问题较广，这里无法进一步论述。

根据本文的研究，长短入声演化为“短高长低”的模式是一种有自然语音基础的泛时音变，可以在任何时候独立地在具有长短入声的语言里发生。因此，粤语和台语支语言的相似性很可能是各自发生的平行演化。当然，我们不能排除语言接触会诱发音变的因素，语言演变的外部因素跟内部因素并非截然对立。

另外，粤语的长短元音与中古内外转的关系以及粤语和台语长短元音的相似性及其来源等，都是值得进一步讨论的相关问题。

参考文献

蔡荣男　2007　《傣语的声调格局和元音格局》，成都：四川大学出版社。

金健、张梦翰　2013　《广州方言长短元音统计分析》，《语言研究集刊》第 1 期，第 79 ~ 98 页。

李行德　1985　《广州话元音的音值及长短对立》，《方言》第 1 期，第 28 ~ 38 页。

麦　耘　2009　《从粤语的产生和发展看汉语方言形成的模式》，《方言》第 3 期，第 219 ~ 232 页。

王莉宁　2011　《粤语中的元音分调现象》，《中国语文》第 1 期，第 71 ~ 79 页。

严至诚　2011　《从普遍音节角度解决粤语语音描写与音系分析的纠葛》，《语言研究集刊》第 8 辑，第 191 ~ 207 页。

周学文　2010　《红水河壮语长短元音声学分析》，《中国语言学集刊》第 4 卷第 1 期，第 191 ~ 202 页。

朱晓农、焦磊、张偲偲　2010　《声调四维度》，载于潘悟云、沈钟伟编　《研究之乐：庆祝王士元先生七十五寿辰学术论文集》，上海：上海教育出版社，第 415 ~ 430 页。

朱晓农、严至诚　2009　《入声唯闭韵尾的共时变异和历时演化：香港粤语个案研究》，《南方语言学》第 1 期，第 34 ~ 44 页。

朱晓农　2009　《发声态的语言学功能》，《语言研究》第 3 期，第 1 ~ 19 页。

朱晓农　2010　《语音学》，北京：商务印书馆。

朱晓农　2011　《语言语音学和音法学：理论新框架》，《语言研究》第 1 期，第 64 ~ 87 页。

Abramson, A. S.　1963　The vowels and tones of standard Thai: Acoustical measurements and experiments. *American Anthropologist*, New Series, 65 (6): 1406 – 1407.

Abramson, A. S., & Ren, N.　1990　Distinctive vowel length: duration vs. spectrum in Thai. *Journal of Phonetics*, 18 (1): 79 – 92.

Alan, C. L.　2010　Tonal effects on perceived vowel duration. *Laboratory Phonology 10*, 4 (4): 151 – 168.

Blevins, J.　2004　*Evolutionary Phonology: The Emergence of Sound Patterns.* Cambridge: Cambridge University Press.

Blevins, J.　2006　A theoretical synopsis of Evolutionary Phonology. *Theoretical Linguistics*, 32: 117 – 166.

Blevins, J.　2008　Natural and unnatural sound patterns: a pocket field guide. In Willems, Klaas and Ludovic De Cuypere eds., *Naturalness and Iconicity in Language.* Amsterdam: John Benjamins Publishing Company. pp. 121 – 148.

Bybee, J.　2003　*Phonology and Language Use* (Vol. 94). Cambridge: Cambridge University Press.

Chao, Y. R.　1934　On the non-uniqueness of phonemic solutions of phonetic systems. *Bulletin of the Institute of History and Philology.* Academia Sinica, 4: 363 – 397.

Faytak, M., & Alan, C. L. Yu　2011　A typological study of the interaction between level tones and duration. In E. Zee ed., *Proceedings of the International Congress of the Phonetic Sciences XVII.* International Congress of the Phonetic Sciences.

http://home.uchicago.edu/~aclyu/papers/icphs2011_tone.pdf, accessed on Jan. 6, 2015.

Gandour, J.　1977　On the interaction between tone and vowel length: Evidence from Thai dialects. *Phonetica*, 34 (1): 54 – 65.

Gedney, W. J.　1972/1989　A checklist for determining tones in Tai dialects. In M. Estellie Smith ed., *Studies in Linguistics in Honor of George L. Trager.* The Hague: Mouton. pp. 423 – 437.

Gordon, M.　2002　A typology of contour tone restrictions. *Studies in Language*, 25 (3): 423 – 462.

Gussenhoven, C.　2007　A vowel height split explained: Compensatory listening and speaker control. *Laboratory Phonology 9.* pp. 145 – 172.

Gussenhoven, C., & Zhou, W.　2013　Revisiting pitch slope and height effects on perceived duration. *INTERSPEECH.* pp. 1365 – 1369.

Heike L – L.　2013　From long to short and from short to long: Perceptual motivations for changes in vocalic length. *Origins of Sound Change: Approaches to Phonologization.* Oxford:

Oxford University Press. pp. 98 – 111.

Honda, K. 2008 *Tone in the Lam River Speech of North-Central Vietnamese*. Ph. D. dissertation. Canberra: Australian National University.

House, A. S. 1961 On vowel duration in English. *The Journal of the Acoustical Society of America*, 33 (9): 1174 – 1178.

Kao, Diana L. 1971 *Structure of the Syllable in Cantonese*. Hague: Mouton.

Thepboriruk, K. 2010 Bangkok Thai tones revisited. *Journal of South East Asian Linguistic Society*, 3 (1): 86 – 105.

Lehiste, I. 1970 *Suprasegmentals*. Oxford, England: Massachusetts Institute of Technology.

Li, F. K. 1977 *A Handbook of Comparative Tai*. Honolulu: The University Press of Hawaii.

Maddieson, I. 2004 Timing and alignment: A case study of Lai. *Language and Linguistics*, 5 (4): 729 – 755.

Michaud, Alexis 2004 Final consonants and glottalization: New perspectives from Hanoi Vietnamese. *Phonetica*, 61 (2 – 3): 119 – 146.

Ohala, J. J. 1972 How to represent natural sound patterns. *Project on Linguistic Analysis 16*. Berkeley: Phonology Laboratory, University of California. pp. 40 – 57.

Ohala, J. J. 1981 The listener as a source of sound change. In C. S. Masek, R. A. Hendrick, & M. F. Miller eds., *Papers from the Parasession on Language and Behavior*. Chicago: Chicago Linguistic Society. pp. 178 – 203.

Ohala, J. J. 1989 Sound change is drawn from a pool of synchronic variation. In L. E. Breivik, & E. H. Jahr eds., *Language Change: Contributions to the Study of its Causes*. (Series: Trends in Linguistics, Studies and Monographs, No. 43) Berlin: Mouton de Gruyter. pp. 173 – 198.

Ohala, J. J., & Ohala, M. 1995 Speech perception and lexical representation: The role of vowel nasalization in Hindi and English. In B. Connell, & A. Arvaniti eds., *Phonology and Phonetic Evidence: Papers in Laboratory Phonology IV*. Cambridge: Cambridge University Press. pp. 41 – 60.

Rivierre, J. C. 1993 Tonogenesis in new Caledonia. Oceanic *Linguistics Special Publications*, 24: 155 – 173.

Roengpitya, R. 2007 The variations, quantification, and generalizations of Standard Thai tones. *Experimental Approaches to Phonology*. Oxford: Oxford University Press. pp. 270 – 301.

Rose, Phil. 1996 The realization of Stopped-syllable Tones in Hua Sai and Pakphanag Speech. In McCormack, P. & Russell, A. eds., *Proceedings of the 6th Australian International Conference on Speech Science and Technology*. Canberra: The Australian Speech Science and Technology Association. pp. 605 – 610.

Rosner, B. S., & Pickering, J. B. 1994 *Vowel Perception, & Production*. New York: Oxford University Press.

Shen Ruiqing, & Liao Hanbo 2012 Acoustic-tonetic Study of Pjang Zhuang: An undescribed Central Tai Variety. Paper presented at the 45th International conference on Sino-Tibetan Language and Linguistic. Singapore. October 26 – 28, 2012.

Sun, J. T. S. 2001 Variegated tonal development in Tibetan. The 34th International Conference on Sino-Tibetan Languages and Linguistics. Kunming: Yunnan University of Nationalities. October 24 – 28, 2001.

Svantesson, J. O. 1989 Tonogenetic mechanisms in northern Mon-Khmer. *Phonetica*, 46 (1 – 3): 60 – 79.

Svantesson, J. O. 1991 Hu-a language with unorthodox tonogenesis. In J. H. C. S. Davidson ed., *Austroasiatic Languages: Essays in Honour of H. L. Shorto*. London: SOAS. pp. 67 – 79.

Thepboriruk, K. 2010 Bangkok Thai Tones Revisited. *Journal of South East Asian Linguistic Society*, 3 (1): 86 – 105.

Yim, Chi Sing 2012 *A Phonetic Study of Syllabic Constituents in Hong Kong Cantones*. Ph. D. Thesis, Hong kong: Hong Kong University of Science and Technology.

Yu, A. C. L. 2010 Tonal effects on perceived vowel duration. In Fougeron, C., Kühnert, B., D' Imperio, M., Vallée, N. eds., *Laboratory Phonology 10*. Berlin: Mouton de Gruyter. pp. 151 – 168.

Yue Oi-Kan 1972 Interplay of Vocalic Segements and Tones in the Yueh Dialects. In Mantaro J. Hashimoto ed., *Genetic Relationship, Diffusion, and Typological Similarities of East and Southeast Asian Languages*. Tokyo: Japan Society for the Promotion of Sicience. pp. 47 – 59.

A Study of the Properties of Cantonese Sentence-final Particle *lu*³

Cindy Wan Yee LAU

(The Chinese University of Hong Kong)

Abstract: This study aims at investigating the semantic and pragmatic functions of the sentence-final particle *lu*³ in Hong Kong Cantonese. Cantonese is one of the major spoken dialects in Hong Kong, and sentence-final particle (hereafter SFPs) is one of the distinctive features of spoken Cantonese, which carries very special linguistic functions within an utterance. In the past years, researchers had limited discussion on the SFP *lu*³ (Fung, 2000; Leung, 2005). Some said that *lu*³ comes from *laa*³ while some claimed *lo*³. Leung gave an example on *lu*³ as below:

好嘢！做晒功课 lu³。 (Leung, 2005)

Yeah! (I) have done all the homework already.

Since there are not many studies focusing on the semantic functions of *lu*³, this paper attempts to examine the properties of *lu*³ by comparing it with other SFPs beginning with the same consonant l, mainly *laa*³ and *lo*³. Finally, a conclusion is made to show that there are two *lu*³ in Cantonese; one appears in declarative sentence while the other appears in imperative. *Lu*³ behaves like laa³ and also *lo*³, but it is not identical to any of them.

Key words: Cantonese sentence-final particles change of state suggestion

1 Introduction to Cantonese SFP *lu*³

Cantonese SFPs have been investigated for many years, many of them are not found in other Sinitic languages. In this paper, the semantic properties of *lu*³ are discussed. This SFP is found to be appeared in two distinct types of sentences and functions differently; lu_1^3 appears in declarative marking change of state, as in (1); while lu_2^3 appears in imperative, initiating a suggestion, as in (2). Even though *lu*³ is a frequently used SFP nowadays, neither any dictionaries nor corpuses involve descriptions of it. ① The only two descriptions on *lu*³ were found in Fung (2000) and Leung(2005); however, the semantic properties on *lu*³ were not accounted. ②

(1)我报咗名交咗钱 lu_1^3。 (memehk. com, 12/2/2013)

ngo⁵ bou³-zo²-meng² gaau¹-zo²-cin⁴ lu³.

I register-ASP pay-ASP SFP

I have registered and paid.

(2)I:(我)做紧功课 aa³。

zou⁶-gan² gung¹fo³ aa³.

do-ASP homework SFP

(I) am now doing homework.

R:咁唔阻你 lu_2^3。

gam² m⁴zo² nei⁵ lu³.

then not-disturb you SFP

It is better not to disturb you.

Even though *lu*³ is not found in previous literature, it is widely adopted by Cantonese speakers. They tend to use "lu" or "噜" to represent *lu*³ since it does not have a standard character. In this paper, the properties of *lu*³ are investigated by following the dissection and structural mapping model of SFPs as proposed by Li (2007). Since *lu*³ also begins with a consonant *l*, it is hypothesized that *lu*³ also shares the common properties of *l-family* members—change of state. In order to investigate whether *lu*³ is also a member of *l-family* and to examine its

---

① Dictionaries:
郑定欧 1997 《香港粤语词典》,南京:江苏教育出版社。
张励妍、倪列怀 1999 《港式广州话词典》,香港:万里书店。
赵嘉文 2010 《香港常用俗语小辞典》,香港:青春文化事业出版有限公司。
李荣主编 1998 《广州方言词典》,南京:江苏教育出版社。
吕叔湘 2010 《现代汉语八百词》,北京:商务印书馆。
麦耘、谭步云 2011 《实用广州话分类词典》,香港:商务印书馆。
欧阳觉亚、周无忌、饶秉才 2011 《广州话俗语词典》,香港:商务印书馆。
饶秉才 2012 《广州音字典》,广州:广东人民出版社。
饶秉才、欧阳觉亚、周无忌 2009 《广州话方言词典》(修订版),香港:商务印书馆。
詹伯慧 2013 《广州话正音字典》,广州:广东人民出版社。
Corpora:
香港二十世纪中期粤语语料库,http://ec-concord. ied. edu. hk/hkcc/introduction. html.
粤语审音配词字库,http://humanum. arts. cuhk. edu. hk/Lexis/lexi-can/.
粤拼,http://www. iso10646hk. net/jp/document/introduction. jsp.

② Fung (2000) and Leung (2005) have tried to account for the source of *lu*³. Fung (2000) proposed that *lu*³ is a variation of *lo*³ while Leung (2005) thought it comes from *laa*³ by undergoing "high-back labialization". Since this paper is not a phonetic study on *lu*³, the phonological derivation of *lu*³ is not the main focus here.

properties of *lu*^{3}, I tried to compare *lu*^{3} with two other family members: *laa*^{3} and *lo*^{3}. The "neutral" SFP *aa*^{3} is also used in certain examples as comparison.

As stated in previous studies (e. g. Leung, 2005), SFPs are usually found in casual speech and informal context, such as conversation between friends. *Lu*^{3} is also found in informal context. Fung (2000) said that *lo*^{3} possesses the most intensive emotions, and *laa*^{3} is less forceful. Here, it is believed that *lu*^{3} is the least forceful among the three. In other words, *lu*^{3} shows the most casual emotion. ①

2 Literature Review

2.1 The Common Properties of the *l-family Members*

Li (2007) and Fung (2000) investigated the internal structure of the SFPs, dissecting them into smaller meaningful units. Their studies have shown that *l-family* members generally have the common feature as change of state, indicating the completion or beginning of an event. Fung (2000) also described this property of *l* as epistemic modality, which marks realization of state and announcement on a new information. As Li (2007) claimed that *laa*^{3} is the most unmarked SFP, I will demonstrate the property of change of state using *laa*^{3}. As will be discussed later, *lu*^{3} also shares this property. Let us first take a look at the following examples:

(3) 佢做起功课 laa^3。(Fung, 2000)
keoi^5 zou^6 hei^2 gung^1 fo^3 laa^3.
s/he do-finish homework SFP
He/She has finished his/her homework (now).

(4) 佢走咗 laa^3。(Fung, 2000)
keoi^5 zau^2-zo^5 laa^3.
s/he go-ASP SFP
He/She has already gone.

In the examples above, when *laa*^{3} is attached to an utterance, a change of state must be involved. The *laa*^{3} can be paraphrased as "it is now the case that..." (Li, 2007). For example, (3) revealed that the speaker is announcing a piece of new information to the audience that somebody (he/she) has undergone a change from having not finished the homework to finally

① The examples used in this paper are drawn from previous studies, internet forums and natural conversations noticed by the author; the speakers are aging from 18 – 35. The phonetic transcription of Cantonese adopted in this paper is *Jyutping*, the romanization system proposed by the Linguistic Society of Hong Kong (LSHK).

finishing it. Such completion of an action is showing a change of state and therefore *laa*^{3} is compatible to this kind of sentence. Similarly, in example (4), the speaker is informing the audience that the person under discussion (he/she) has gone. Somebody was staying here, but he left a few minutes ago. As such, *laa*^{3} here indicates a change of state.

2.2 Structural Mapping Analysis of SFPs

Fung (2000) and Li (2007) adopt the structural mapping approach in the analysis of SFPs. Since a Cantonese syllable consists of an initial, a rhyme, a coda and a tone, Li (2007) stated that those components serve different functions in the meaning of an SFP. Use "*laa*^{3}" as an example:

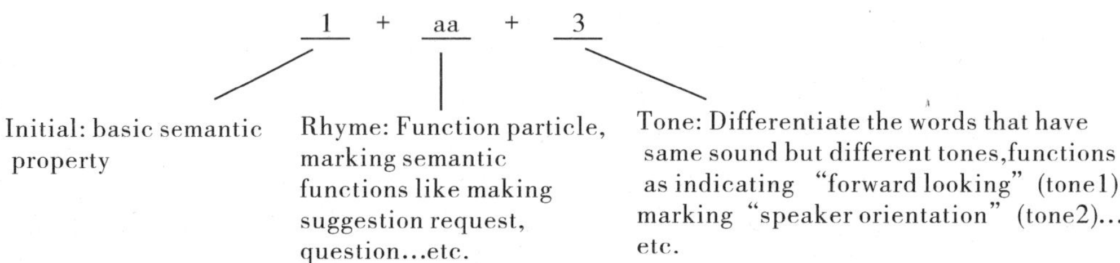

The SFP *laa*^{3} can be divided into three parts. The initial consonant "*l*" denotes the basic semantic property commonly shared by SFPs with the same initial consonant; here is "change of state". The vowel "*aa*" denotes the function of making suggestion, question and so on. The tone "3" is a default tone of all SFPs, which conveys a neutral attitude of the speaker.

Though *l-family* members seem to share some semantically similarities, each of them has its own meaning. To investigate the meaning of *lu*^{3}, the properties of *lu*^{3} will be compared and contrasted with those of *laa*^{3} and *lo*^{3} in the following section of this chapter.

3 Basic Semantic Properties of *lu*^{3}

There are mainly two functions of *lu*^{3}, indicating a change of physical state in declarative sentence, and marking suggestion in imperative. The discussion begins with the former one.

3.1 Change of State

All *l-family* members have the semantic properties as "change of state" (Li, 2007). Similar to *lo*^{3} and *laa*^{3}, *lu*^{3} can be attached to the predicate that involves a change of state and it can also indicate a current relevance.

(5) a. 落雨 laa^3。(Fang, 2003: 103)

lok^6 jyu^5 laa^3.

down rain SFP

It's raining now.

b. 落雨 lu^3。

lok^6 jyu^5 lu^3.

down rain SFP

It's raining now.

(6) a. 食咗饭 lo^3。(Cheung, 2007: 186)

sik^6-zo^2-faan^6 lo^3.

eat- ASP-meal SFP

I am done eating.

b. 食咗饭 lu^3。

sik^6-zo^2-faan^6 lu^3.

eat-ASP-meal SFP

I am done eating.

Both (5) a and (5) b indicate the event of raining is about to begin or just begin. In other words, the event has not yet been realized. (6) a and (6) b can both indicate the completion of an action, which is the completion of having a meal. *Lu*^{3} shares the common property of *l-family* which marks a change of state. Such property is closely related to the nature of the predicate of the sentence, which will be illustrated below.

Lu^3 can show its property of change of state in any kinds of predicates. Two predicates are discussed here: individual-level predicate and stage-level predicate (Ackerman & Webelhuth, 1998; Lyons, 1995; Saeed, 2003). "An *individual-level* predicate is true throughout the existence of an individual" (Ackerman & Webelhuth, 1998). For example, if John is "smart", this is a property that he has, regardless of the time that the statement is uttered. In other words, the event described does not have an end point. In contrast, a *stage-level predicate* requires an end point of an event to signal the change, see (7) – (9).

(7) a. 我系香港人 aa^3。

ngo^5 hai^6 Heong^1-gong^5-jan^4 aa^3.

I am Hong-Kong-person SFP

I am a Hong Kong resident.

b. *我系香港人 lu^3。

ngo^5 hai^6 Heong^1-gong^5-jan^4 lu^3.

I am Hong-Kong-person SFP

*I am a Hong Kong resident.

I have become a Hong Kong resident.

(8) a. 我识中文 aa³。
ngo⁵ sik¹ Zung¹man² aa³.
I know Chinese SFP
I know Chinese.
b. *我识中文 lu³。
ngo⁵ sik¹ Zung¹man² lu³.
I know Chinese SFP
*I know Chinese.
I have acquired Chinese.

(9) a. 小明去咗机铺打机 aa³。
Siu²ming⁴ heoi³-zo² gei¹pou² daa²gei¹ aa³.
Siu Ming go-ASP game-centre play-game SFP
Siu Ming has gone to the game centre.
b. 小明去咗机铺打机 lu³。
Siu²ming⁴ heoi³-zo² gei¹pou² daa² gei¹ lu³.
Siu Ming go-ASP game-centre play-game SFP
Siu Ming has gone to the game centre.

The above examples show the meaning difference between *aa*³ and *lu*³. However, when *lu*³ substitutes *aa*³, a different outcome may result. For (7)a, the speaker is a Hong Kong citizen throughout his life; however, speaker who utters (7)b may not be a Hong Kong resident before. After completing certain procedures, he becomes a Hong Kong resident now. Thus, a change must be involved. A similar example can be found in (8). Sentence (8)a means "I know Chinese" while (8)b means "I have acquired Chinese". A change of state has to be involved in the interpretation of (8)b. For example, the speaker is not a Chinese native speaker and he has recently completed some Chinese courses, and so he acquired Chinese at last. This reading is acceptable in only *lu*³ but not *aa*³. (7)b and (8)b are similar to (9), which is a typical example of stage-level predicate. Siu Ming shows a change of state from not going to the game centre to going there, so a change is resulted.

In short, no matter what kind of predicate *lu*³ is appended to, it necessarily shows a change of state in a declarative sentence.

Current Relevance

Besides indicating a change of state, *lu*³ can also depict current relevance. The event should be very close to the speech time, which means the action will be happened soon or just finished, or even occurred a long time ago but the result still holds at the moment of speaking. See the following examples (10) – (11):

(10) a. 我听日去日本 laa^3。

ngo^5 ting^{1}jat^6 heoi^3 Jat^{6}bun^2 laa^3.

I tomorrow go Japan SFP

I will go to Japan tomorrow.

b. 我听日去日本 lu^3。

ngo^5 ting^{1}jat^6 heoi^3 Jat^{6}bun^2 lu^3.

I tomorrow go Japan SFP

I will go to Japan tomorrow.

(11) a. 我十二年前就住喺度 laa^3。

ngo^5 sap^{6}ji^{6}nin^{4}cin^4 zau^6 zyu^6 hai^{2}dou^{6}laa^3.

I twelve-year-ago then live here SFP

I have lived here since twelve years ago.

b. 我十二年前就住喺度 lu^3。

ngo^5 sap^{6}ji^{6}nin^{4}cin^4 zau^6 zyu^6 hai^{2}dou^6 lu^3.

I twelve-year-ago then live here SFP

I have lived here since twelve years ago.

c. ??/*我十二年前就住喺度 lu^3,

ngo^5 sap^{6}ji^{6}nin^{4}cin^4 zau^6 zyu^6 hai^{2}dou^6 lu^3,

I twelve-year-ago then live here SFP

不过三年前搬咗去加拿大。

bat^{1}gwo^3 saam^{1}nin^{4}cin^4 bun^1-zo^2 heoi^3 Gaa^{1}naa^{4}daai^6.

but three-year-ago move-ASP go Canada

I lived here twelve years ago, but I moved to Canada three years ago.

(10) shows that an event is happening soon. The speaker is going to change the state from "not going to Japan" to "going to Japan". Therefore, both *laa*^{3} and *lu*^{3} are acceptable. (11) a and (11) b show that the speaker lived here since twelve years ago, and the speaker is still living here. Therefore, both *laa*^{3} and *lu*^{3} are also applicable. In (11) c, the speaker no longer lived here, and moved to Canada. Under this situation, *lu*^{3} is incompatible since the result no longer holds.

3.2 Suggestion

In fact, *laa*^{3}, *lo*^{3} and *lu*^{3} can also mark imperative; the only difference is that *laa*^{3} can be attached to a sentence denoting either a command (ordinary imperative) or a suggestion (inclusive imperative), while *lu*^{3} can only carry out the latter function. See the conversations below:

(12) 快啲做功课 laa^3/*lo^3/*lu^3。

faai^3 di^1 zou^6 gung^{1}fo^3 laa^3/lo^3/lu^3.

quickly do homework SFP

(You) do your homework!

(13) M: (In a telephone call…)

两点钟 *laa*³。

loeng⁵dim²zung¹ laa³.

two o'clock SFP

It's two o'clock now.

K: 喂,咁唔好倾 lu³,唔系听日又唔知醒。

wai³ gam² m⁴hou² king¹ lu³ m⁴hai⁶ ting¹jat⁶ jau⁶ m⁴ zi¹seng².

hey then not talk SFP, otherwise tomorrow again not awake

Hey, it's better not to continue; otherwise you will not be able to wake up in time tomorrow.

In (12), the speaker asked the addressee to do the homework. Such command is only compatible with *laa*³ but neither *lo*³ nor *lu*³, since they both cannot associate with command. The definition of inclusive imperative is that "one commits oneself to the action and seeks agreement from the addressee" (Huddleston & Pullum, 2002). (13) demonstrates that the suggestion marked by *lu*³ must involve both the speaker and the addressee. Even though the subject in K's reply is not overtly marked, we can still understand the implied subject should be "we". The context of (13) is that "M" and "K" were talking phone and "M" noticed that it was two o'clock already. "K" was afraid of not able to wake up in time so she suggested both she and "M" not continuing the call. As such, both parties are involved in the action. In this case we can see that *lu*³ is compatible to inclusive imperative.

The other criterion for the existence of *lu*³ is that the main verb in the imperative must be a non-stative verb.

(14) 我哋去睇戏 lu³。

ngo⁵dei⁶ heoi³ tai²hei³ lu³.

we go see film SFP

Let's go to see films, shall we?

(15) 食完饭唱 K lu³。

sik⁶jyun⁴faan⁶ coeng³ K lu³.

finish-ASP-meal sing karaoke SFP

(Let's) sing karaoke after the meal.

As for (14), imagine there are three people hanging around together, A, B and C. A uttered the above sentence in order to suggest B and C to go to watch movie with her. Therefore, all three of them go to the cinema finally. The main verb in the above sentence *heoi*³ is a non-stative verb, and so a suggestion is licensed. The same property is illustrated in (15). In this case, the speaker suggests go singing karaoke with the addressee after the meal. Even though the subject is covert, but we can still understand that it involves both the speaker and the hearer. Again, the non-stative verb *coeng*^{3} here licenses the use of *lu*^{3}.

4 Discussion

It is interesting to see that *lu*^{3} possesses properties that are not the same as any existing SFPs. In the beginning of this paper, we found that *lu*^{3} may be the variant of *laa*^{3} or *lo*^{3}. However, *lu*^{3} seems to comprise the properties found in those two. The following table helps summarize all functions found in *lu*^{3}:

Table 1 A Comparison of the Properties of *laa*^{3}, *lo*^{3} and *lu*^{3}

Properties	*laa*^{3}	*lo*^{3}	*lu*^{3}
Change of state	√	√	√
Suggestion	√#	√	

\# The suggestion use of *laa*^{3} here is regarded as imperative.

In short, there are four prominent functions that could be found in *lu*^{3}. For semantic functions, it can realize a change of state, and denote current relevance; in terms of sentence type, it exists in declarative or inclusive imperative. Here, I try to claim that there may be two senses of *lu*^{3} in Cantonese. The first lu_1^3 used in declarative sentence to show change of state, current relevance, and newsworthy; the second one, lu_2^3, used in suggestion. These two *lu*^{3} are in complementary distribution. When the predicate inside a sentence involves a stative verb, then the *lu*^{3} must be lu_1^3. See the examples below:

(16)我系香港人 lu_1^3。 [cf. (7)b]

ngo^5 hai^6 Hoeng^{1}gong^2 jan^4 lu^3.

I am HongKong person SFP

I have become a Hong Kong resident.

(17)我识中文 lu_1^3。 [cf. (8)b]

ngo^5 sik^1 Zung^{1}man^2 lu^3.

I know Chinese SFP

I have acquired Chinese.

“Hai^6” (am) and “sik^1” (know) are stative verbs. The lu_1^3 here marks a change of state that the speaker in (16) may not be a Hong Kong resident, but he is now; and in (17) the speaker changes the state from having no knowledge about Chinese to acquire it. This sentence also shows the noteworthy feature of lu_1^3 which assumes that the audience did not know this fact before. On the contrary, if the predicate involves a non-stative verb, the sentence can be ambiguous. The sentence can be a suggestion or a declarative statement. For example:

(18) 我哋去睇戏 lu_2^3。[cf. (14)]
ngo5 dei6 heoi3 tai2 hei3 lu3
we go see film SFP
We are going to see films. /Let's go to see films, shall we?

Imagine there are three people hanging around together, A, B and C. A uttered the above sentence which can be interpreted in two ways: first, A informed C that A would go to cinema with B. Thus, lu_1^3 is exemplified. The other interpretation is that A suggested all of them going to the cinema together. Then, the lu^3 is interpreted.

5 Conclusion

It can be concluded that lu^3 is a member of the *l-family* SFPs. It shares the common semantic properties and meanings with the other *l-family* members, which is showing change of state. Two senses of lu^3 can be found in Cantonese. One is an informative lu_1^3 used in declaratives which shows change of state. The other lu_2^3 can make suggestion. Lu_1^3 is compatible with stative and non-stative verbs; while lu_2^3 can only be compatible with non-stative verb. Unlike what the previous literature's claimed, lu^3 is not identical to any existed SFPs; rather, it is an *l-family* member which integrates different properties from other members.

This paper opens the door to the investigation on the SFP lu^3. It is hoped that this paper can contribute to the study on Cantonese linguistics and especially Cantonese sentence-final particles.

References

张洪年　2007　《香港粤语语法的研究》,香港:香港中文大学出版社。

方小燕　2003　《广州方言句末语气助词》,广州:暨南大学出版社。

Ackerman, F., and G. Webelhuth　1998　*A Theory of Predicates.* Stanford, CA: CSLI Publications.

Fung, Roxana Suk-Yee　2000　*Final Particles in Standard Cantonese: Semantic Extension and Pragmatic Inference.* Ph. D. dissertation, Columbus: Ohio State University.

Huddleston, R., and G. K. Pullum　2002　*The Cambridge Grammar of the English Language.* Cambridge: Cambridge University Press.

Leung, Chung-sum　2005　*A Study of the Utterance Particles in Cantonese as Spoken in*

Hong Kong. Hong Kong: City University of Hong Kong.

Li, B. , and R. Sybesma 2007 The dissection and structural mapping of Cantonese sentence final particles. *Lingua*,17(10): 1739 – 1783.

Lyons,John 1995 *Linguistic Semantics: An Introduction*. Cambridge: Cambridge University Press.

Saeed,J. I. 2003 *Semantics* (2nd edition). Malden,MA: Blackwell Publishers.

对外粤语教学与粤语语言学的互动：以量词的语法限制为例*

陈健荣

（香港中文大学、香港理工大学）

提　要：自20世纪以来，粤语研究多以内省（internal-reflection）、田野研究及问卷调查［如Francis and Matthews（2006）的连动句研究］、语料研究［如Chan（2002）的句末助词研究］等方法进行。前人研究颇有成效，但这种研究均是从母语使用者的角度去了解粤语。我们认为透过对外粤语教学，可以从一种全新的、非母语用户的视角去了解粤语，甚至发现一些前人未考虑到的地方。例如陈健荣、李兆麟（2014）对粤语学习者的语料进行偏误分析（error analysis，参考Corder，1967），发现目前粤语语法理论中忽略了语体（参考冯胜利，2011）的重要性。

以粤语［数量+名词］的句法为例，前人对粤语的［数+量+名］结构（如“一个人”、“一本书”）进行研究，了解到粤语的特点是：当数词为“一”时，数词可以省略（张洪年，1989、2007；周小兵，1997）。故此“我买咗一本书”（我买了一本书）可省略为“我买咗本书”。但是经过我们对粤语学习者的偏误分析，发现部分学习者即便熟悉了现有的语法规则，还是会误用量词，如并列式“*我今朝买咗本书、个苹果、抽提子……”（我今天早上买了一本书、一个苹果、一串葡萄……）。就语言本体而言，本文提出以下论点：①无定/指称不定的［ø+量+名］结构不能出现在多项名词并列式中；②这一现象可能与粤语的［ø+量+名］结构出现［数量“一”＞“不定量”］的演变有关；③［ø+量+名］结构发展出表“不定量”的功能，这为张洪年（1989）提出的量词“以单概双”的现象提供了解释。就方法论而言，本文从“对外粤语中量词的偏误分析”到“［ø+量+名］结构研究”，提出对外粤语教学有可能成为一种方言研究的新方法。

关键词：数词　量词　偏误分析　跨语言比较　对外粤语教学

1　粤语语言学的研究方法

传统方言研究中，研究人员多为母语使用者，故可以利用内省（internal-reflection）的方法，自行判别什么句子合法，什么句子通顺，然后对语言进行描写和分析。也有不少研究采用田野调查和问卷的方法，研究者先找来一些母语使用者进行调查，然后对搜集到的语料进行研究。例如Francis and Matthews（2006）邀请粤语的母语使用者参与问卷调查，

* 本文初稿曾在“第十八届国际粤方言研讨会”（香港科技大学，2013年12月）上宣读，得到与会者及匿名审稿人提出宝贵建议，在此表示衷心感谢。文中如有任何错误，均由作者负责。

让他们对不同结构的连动句按可接受度打分，从而得知哪些句子比较合语法，哪些比较难以接受。还有一种研究方法，就是研究者采集现成语料进行分析。例如 Chan（2002）从广东电视台的粤语电视剧中采集语料，分析多个句末助词的使用情况。

以上多种研究方法各有优点，但是这些研究都是从母语使用者的角度出发去理解该语言/方言。刘丹青（2006）注意到方言与其他语言的比较，甚至是类型学方面的研究的重要性。透过语言之间的比较，我们可以从另一角度了解所研究的语言/方言。例如 Liu and Peyraube（1994）从古汉语的语料中构拟出［动词 > 介词 > 连词］的语法化路径。吴福祥（2002）则从类型学的角度，进一步找出汉语的 SVO 语序，为语法化［动词 > 介词 > 连词］提供了条件。

我们同意刘丹青（2006）的见解，并且认为将粤语与其他语言进行比较，可以为对外汉语教学提供不少有价值的参考数据。粤语的二语学习者来自多个国家，他们在语言背景、阅历、文化等方面各有差异。他们在学习过程中出现的偏误往往天马行空，这是以粤语为母语的研究者不一定能轻易想到的。以陈健荣、李兆麟（2014）为例，传统的粤语研究不常提及粤语的词汇和句法的正式度，以至正式和俗常的语言成分能否同现于一个句子/语篇中等问题（在汉语中也有相关问题出现，参考冯胜利，2011）。例如“煮”和“烹调”，两者的意思相近（表“to cook”义），但后者的正式度比前者高，所以即使“煮饭”符合语法，但“*烹调饭”就不能接受了。陈、李透过对粤语学习者进行偏误分析（error analysis①），发现部分学生虽然能依照教科书上的语法规则，但因忽略粤语的语体（register-style）与语法的关系，因此写出来的文章仍然让母语使用者难以接受。这些问题母语使用者不一定能轻易想到，但透过研究学习粤语的外国学生的偏误，诸如语体语法等现象便会浮现。

本节比较了多种研究粤语的方法，并提出对外粤语教学的重要性。以下将以量词的用法为例，从粤语学习者对量词的误用角度探讨前人粤语量词研究的有余与不足之处。本文的研究流程如下：

第一步：以现有的语言本体理论指导教学内容，带进语言课堂。

第二步：学生在学习过程中难免会出现偏误，粤语研究者便可进行分析。

第三步：如果现有的语言本体理论足可纠正偏误，教师便可对症下药。如果偏误是现有的语言本体理论所不能纠正的，研究者就需要拿偏误与现有理论进行对比，从而完善现有理论，甚至提出新理论。这样，无论是粤语研究还是粤语教学均可改进。

因篇幅有限，本文只集中讨论第二步和第三步。

---

① Corder（1967）把语言学习者的错误分为两类：偏误（error）和错误（mistake）。前者是学生因缺乏某种语言知识而犯的，后者则是因大意而造成的无心之失。本文的重点在“偏误”而非“错误”。

2　前人的量词研究

2.1　[数 + 量 + 名] 结构与 [指示 + 量 + 名] 结构

张洪年(1989, 2007), Matthews and Yip(1994)指出在粤语中,以数词修饰名词时必须加入量词,成为 [数 + 量 + 名] 结构。例如要强调名词"狗"的数量,就应该用"两只狗"而不是"* 两狗"。另外,当名词是有指称/有定[①]时,除了指示词"呢,吖"(这,那)外,亦必须使用量词,组成 [指示 + 量 + 名] 结构。例如"呢只狗"(这只狗)可说,但"* 呢狗"不可说,这一点跟普通话不同。

2.2　有定与无定

张洪年(1989)注意到 [量 + 名] 的结构有"有定"和"无定"之分。相当于英语的 definite/indefinite。同时,张氏把"无定"称为"指称不定",又把"有定"分为"定称有指"(远指近指清楚标明)和"定称无指"(远指近指不明)两种情况。比较以下例句:

(1) 呢本书几好睇。(这书挺好看。)[②]

(2) 我买咗两本书。(我买了两本书。)

(3) 我买咗本书。(我买了一本书。)/(我买了这/那本书。)

(1)的"呢本书"和(3)的"本书"均为有定,可是前者明确表明是近指而非远指,后者则是远指近指不明,严谨而言,把(3)翻译为"我买了这/那本书"并不完全恰当,周小兵(1997: 46)指出粤语的这种结构"既不等同于北京话的'这',也不等同于'那',而是等于两者的总和"。(2)中的"两本书"属无定,注意(3)的"本书"亦可以理解为无定,这个时候句子的意思是"我买了一本书"。单韵鸣(2007)认为,像(3)的 [量 + 名] 结构什么时候理解为无定,什么时候理解为定称无指,需要从具体语境来判断。

张洪年(1989)指出,无定/指称不定的名词组一般只出现在宾语位置;而周小兵(1997)则留意到有定的名词组在谓语前出现的频率比在谓语后出现的频率高,因为"有定的词语是旧信息,倾向于在句子的前半部出现;表示无定的词语是新信息,倾向于在句子后半部出现"(周小兵, 1997: 46)。单韵鸣(2007)则引述赵元任(1979)的看法,指出汉语中主语多属有定,宾语多属无定。本文的目标旨在列出 [量 + 名] 结构的各种可能,故此有关有定/无定在句法上的特点的解释暂且不作讨论。

① 周小兵(1997)、单韵鸣(2007)用"有定"(definite)一词,而张洪年(1989)则把"有定"视为"有指称",具体情况可参考"2.2　有定与无定"。

② 本文所有粤语例句均附有普通话翻译,并以括号标注。

2.3 [ø +量+名] 结构

张洪年（1989）指出，定称无指的名词组多采用 [ø+量+名][①] 结构 [参考例句（3）]。另一方面，当数词为“一”时，粤语的 [数+量+名] 结构可省略为 [ø+量+名] 结构。故例句（3）（表“我买了一本书”义时）可以视为（3”）的省略式：

（3”）我买咗一本书。（我买了一本书。）

总结以上的前人研究，粤语 [量+名] 的结构有以下三种情况：

情况1：[数+量+名] 结构属无定/指称不定的名词组，多出现在宾语位置。

情况2：[指示+量+名] 属有定/定称有指的名词组，可作主语或宾语。

情况3：[ø +量+名] 有两种可能：（ⅰ）属无定/指称不定的名词组，出现在宾语位置，是 [一+量+名] 的省略式；（ⅱ）属有定/定称无指的名词组，可作主语或宾语。[②]

3 偏误分析：粤语学习者对 [ø +量+名] 结构的运用

从上一节中我们可以看到三种 [量+名] 结构的区别。事实上这些语法规则在对外粤语的教科书上也有所反映。但仍有学生在按照这些规则的情况下造出一些不合语法的句子。本节将利用偏误分析[③]，把这些不合语法的句子列出来，以便讨论。

3.1 材料搜集

我们搜集并分析了20个粤语二语学习者的约100篇口头演讲。这些学生于2010—2012年间在香港中文大学学习粤语。学生背景可参考表1：

表1

学生数目	学习了多久?	国籍
7名	5个学期[④]	日本，澳大利亚，孟加拉国
9名	1个学期	法国，墨西哥，日本，泰国，黎巴嫩
4名	2个学期	日本，泰国

① 为强调量词前不带数词或指示词，本文一律用 [ø+量+名] 表示。ø并不等同于句法学的空语类（empty category）。

② 注意无定/指称不定的 [ø +量+名] 和有定/定称无指的 [ø +量+名] 是同形异质的结构，因此情况3(i)和情况3(ii) 需要分开处理。这里感谢匿名审稿人的提醒。

③ 偏误分析（error analysis）由Corder（1967）提出，原意是要分析二语学习者在学习过程中出现的偏误，与语言习得者的偏误进行对比，以论证二语学习与语言习得在本质上其实没有太大分别。后来不少研究对外汉语的学者开始使用偏误分析以了解学生的问题，从而对症下药。

④ 一个学期约十三个星期。

我们邀请这些学生每星期或每两个星期在课上进行一次口头演讲。演讲题目由授课老师提前一周提供给学生。我们以这些演讲为研究对象，有两个原因：①所有学生均有充足的准备时间，因不小心而造成的语法、生词运用上的错误便可减少；②在课堂上的演讲并非考试的一部分，故学生的表现不会受考试带来的心理压力影响。另外，学生发音的准确度亦非本文研究的对象，故不会就此进行讨论。

搜集学生语料以后，我们让粤语母语使用者对语料进行分析，把不合语法的部分找出来，然后再向学生确认他们所说句子的原意，避免误解。

3.2 不合语法的例句

我们搜集到的不合语法的句子，与量词相关的有两类，例句如下：

（4） ＊我钟意喺洪都拉斯住，吖度喺墨西哥南面，而家等我同你哋介绍个国家。
（我喜欢在洪都拉斯住，那儿在墨西哥南面，现在让我来给你们介绍这个国家。）
（学生 HWG，墨西哥人，2011 年 3 月；题目：你喜欢在哪儿住?）

（5） ＊请你拎件批，件饼，啲梳打，啲饼干……嚟我哋嘅生日会。
（请你拿一个馅饼，一个蛋糕，一些汽水，一些饼干……来我们的生日会。）
（学生 MDY，美国人，2011 年 2 月；题目：最开心的生日会）

根据我们的初步分析，（4）的“＊等我同你哋介绍个国家”改为“等我同你哋介绍（下）呢个国家”会更合语法。本文第二节已经从前人的研究得知，定称有指的名词组应加上指示词“呢/吖”（这/那），即［指示＋量＋名］形式。而学生 HWG 则采用了［ø＋量＋名］形式，故可接受程度较低。

然而，（5）的偏误则不容易解释。根据学生 MDY 的原意，并列式中所有名词（馅饼、蛋糕、汽水、饼干）均为无定/指称不定的。按照前人的研究，由于每一个名词组的数词均为“一”，这些名词组可采用［数＋量＋名］或［ø＋量＋名］。但是（5）使用［ø＋量＋名］却不合语法，改为［数＋量＋名］时则较易接受：

（5）a　请你拎一件批，一件饼，一啲梳打，一啲饼干……嚟我哋嘅生日会。

总结以上两种偏误，（4）的出现证明该学生尚未掌握前人已清楚列明的语法。本文不再就此进行后续讨论。（5）的出现则是前人研究所未谈及的，第二节中提到的情况 3 并不能解释为什么（5）a 较（5）容易接受。针对这个问题，我们将于第四节中重新讨论第二节所提［量＋名］结构的三种情况。

4 ［ø+量+名］的语法限制

4.1 ［ø+量+名］与并列式的冲突

回顾前人研究所使用的例句，涉及［量+名］结构的名词组大多并非并列式。故本节将测试第二节的三项［量+名］结构语法规则是否适用于并列式。重看（5）和（5）a两句：

（5）＊请你拎件批，件饼，啲梳打，啲饼干……嚟我哋嘅生日会。
（5）a　请你拎一件批，一件饼，一啲梳打，一啲饼干……嚟我哋嘅生日会。

第三节已经谈过，（5）a的并列式中每一个名词组都是［数+量+名］，比（5）的［ø+量+名］结构合语法。可见以［数+量+名］组成并列式是符合粤语语法的，因此情况1无须修改。

（5）b　请你拎呢件批，呢件饼，呢啲梳打，吓啲饼干……嚟我哋嘅生日会。
（请你拿这个馅饼，这个蛋糕，这些汽水，那些饼干……来我们的生日会。）
（6）呢件批，呢件饼，呢啲梳打，吓啲饼干都几平。
（这个馅饼，这个蛋糕，这些汽水，那些饼干都挺便宜。）

以上两句中，并列的名词组属有定/定称有指。（5）b的并列式处宾语位置，（6）的并列式处主语位置，两句都符合语法。可见以［指示+量+名］组成并列式是符合粤语语法的，因此情况2也无须修改。

目前我们已知名词并列式中，名词可使用［数+量+名］结构而不可以使用［ø+量+名］结构。从以下两句我们更发现并列式中就算有部分名词组使用［数+量+名］结构，其余使用［ø+量+名］结构，句子仍然不合语法：

（5）c　＊请你拎一件批，件饼，啲梳打，啲饼干……嚟我哋嘅生日会。
（5）d　＊请你拎件批，件饼，一啲梳打，一啲饼干……嚟我哋嘅生日会。

另外，如果把动词放进每一个并列成分（就是说把名词并列式变成谓词并列式），句子便可接受：

（5）e　请你拎件批，拎件饼，拎啲梳打，拎啲饼干……嚟我哋嘅生日会。

如果并列成分仍然是名词，不用数词和量词也合语法：

（5）f　请你拎批，饼，梳打，饼干……嚟我哋嘅生日会。

然而，如果并列成分只有两项，则是可以使用［ø＋量＋名］结构的：

（5）g　请你拎件批，件饼嚟我哋嘅生日会。

从（5）、（5）c、（5）d 三个不合语法的句子中，可见情况 3（i），即当［ø＋量＋名］属无定/指称不定时，不适用于多项①并列句，故需要作出修改。

至于情况 3（ii），即当［ø＋量＋名］属定称无指，处宾语位置时，并不存在并列式的语法限制：

（7）我想买本书、支笔同埋叠纸。（我想买这/那本书，这/那支笔和这/那叠纸。）

定称无指的［ø＋量＋名］处主语位置时，包含并列式的句子仍然符合语法：

（8）本书、支笔同埋叠纸都几贵。（这/那本书，这/那支笔和这/那叠纸都挺贵。）②

可见情况 3（ii），即当［ø＋量＋名］属定称无指时，无论处于主语还是宾语位置，均可以使用并列句，故没有必要作出修改。

本节测试结果总结如下：

表 2

	单项式	并列式
情况 1： ［数＋量＋名］作宾语	+	+
情况 2： ［指示＋量＋名］作主语	+	+
情况 2： ［指示＋量＋名］作宾语	+	+
情况 3（i）： ［ø＋量＋名］属指称不定	+	+（两项）/ –（多项）
情况 3（ii）： ［ø＋量＋名］属定称无指，处主语位置	+	+
情况 3（ii）： ［ø＋量＋名］属定称无指，处宾语位置	+	+

注：“+”代表合语法，“–”代表不合语法。

① 本文的“多项”指多于两项。

② 单韵鸣（2007）指出：当说话人认为“对方应该知道”所指的事物时（例如回指或情景有所指时）才会倾向于使用［ø＋量＋名］结构。否则就会使用［指示＋量＋名］或其他形式。故（7）和（8）为合法句的前提是：说话人认为“对方应该知道”各个［ø＋量＋名］结构所指的是哪些事物。

综上所述，我们认为不管是否并列式，对第二节的［量＋名］情况1和情况2均没有影响，无须修改。而情况3则应修改为：①

情况3'：［ø＋量＋名］有两种可能：（i）属无定/指称不定的名词组，出现在宾语位置，是［一＋量＋名］的省略式。但是，如果句子涉及多项名词并列式，则不能使用［ø＋量＋名］结构；（ii）属有定/定称无指的名词组，可作主语或宾语。

4.2 现象分析

事实上，数词"一"的省略在粤语中并不罕见。比如动宾结构"食一个包"＞"食个包"、重叠结构"试一试"＞"试试"等等。这就解释了为什么［ø＋量＋名］并列式不可接受，而［动＋量＋名］并列式则可。参考4.1的（5）和（5）e：

（5）＊请你拎件批，件饼，啲梳打，啲饼干……嚟我哋嘅生日会。

（5）e　请你拎件批，拎件饼，拎啲梳打，拎啲饼干……嚟我哋嘅生日会。

由于（5）的"件饼"、"啲梳打"、"啲饼干"并非直接后置于动词，故数词"一"不能省略。而（5）e的"件饼"、"啲梳打"、"啲饼干"直接后置于动词"拎"，故符合语法。

不过，"并列式中每一个［ø＋量＋名］都必须紧靠在动词后"的论点仍然存在着一些问题。首先，这不能解释为什么只有两项［ø＋量＋名］并列式时，句子仍然符合语法。参考4.1的（5）g：

（5）g　请你拎件批，件饼嚟我哋嘅生日会。

（5）g的"件饼"并非直接后置于动词，可是其数词"一"可以省略。可见动宾结构内数词"一"容易被省略，不一定可以解释本文所观察到的［ø＋量＋名］排斥多项并列式的现象。

再者，多项［指示＋量＋名］结构并列时，并不需要每一个结构都紧靠在动词后。参考4.1的（5）b：

（5）b　请你拎呢件批，呢件饼，呢啲梳打，吖啲饼干……嚟我哋嘅生日会。
（请你拿这个馅饼，这个蛋糕，这些汽水，那些饼干……来我们的生日会。）

（5）b的"呢件批"直接后置于动词"拎"，可是其他并列成分"呢件饼"、"呢啲梳打"、"吖啲饼干"则不然。可见，句子是否合语法，与［量＋名］结构是否直接后置于动词没有必然关系。

目前，从句子结构的角度尚未能找出指称不定的［ø＋量＋名］结构的多项并列式不

---

① 本文在第十八届粤方言研讨会上发表时，曾有学者建议对量词的每个分类都分别进行研究。目前我们发现，按照张洪年（2007）的分类，本文第四节的论点涵盖类词（个、件……），容器量词（碗、碟……）和部分量词（啲）的并列式。因篇幅有限，具体分析将另文讨论。

合语法的原因。不过，我们从语义的角度出发，认为这种现象可能与［量＋名］结构及其所表达的数量有关。参考表3的句子：

表3

	单项式	多项并列式
情况1：［数＋量＋名］作宾语	（9）a　我想买一本书。（我想买一本书。）	（9）b　我想买一本书，一本字典，一支笔。（我想买一本书，一本字典，一支笔。）
情况2：［指示＋量＋名］作主语	（10）a　呢本书系中国出嘅。（这本书是中国生产的。）	（10）b　呢本书，呢本字典，呢支笔都系中国出嘅。（这本书，这本字典，这支笔都是中国生产的。）
情况2：［指示＋量＋名］作宾语	（11）a　我想买呢本书。（我想买这本书。）	（11）b　我想买呢本书，呢本字典，呢支笔。（我想买这本书，这本字典，这支笔。）
情况3（i）：［ø＋量＋名］属指称不定	（12）a　我想买本书。（我想买一本书。）	（12）b　＊我想买本书，本字典，支笔。（我想买一本书，一本字典，一支笔。）
情况3（ii）：［ø＋量＋名］属定称无指，处主语位置	（13）a　本书系中国出嘅。（这/那本书是中国生产的。）	（13）b　本书，本字典，支笔都系中国出嘅。（这/那本书，这/那本字典，这/那支笔都是中国生产的。）
情况3（ii）：［ø＋量＋名］属定称无指，处宾语位置	（14）a　我想买本书。（我想买这/那本书。）	（14）b　我想买本书，本字典，支笔。（我想买这/那本书，这/那本字典，这/那支笔。）

我们认为，指称不定的［ø＋量＋名］结构与其他［量＋名］结构的分别，在于其所表达的数量：（9）a的宾语“书”受数词“一”修饰，其数量只能理解为“一”。（10）a、（11）a的主/宾语“书”受指示词“呢”（这）修饰，其数量也只能理解为“一”。（13）a、（14）a的主/宾语“书”属定称无指，按照单韵鸣（2007：274），说话人判断对方应该知道句子所指的是什么事物，有可能是回指实际交际中刚提到过的事物，说话人也有可能利用眼神或手势等方式确保对方能辨认所指对象。也就是说，在（13）a、（14）a两句中，说话人所说的“书”是有所指的，我们进一步强调，这两句的“书”的数量只能理解为“一”。（12）a的表层结构虽然与（14）a相同（“我想买本书”），可是（12）a的“书”所指的是哪一本书并不明确，甚至数量也可能不是“一”。所以，在指称不定的［ø＋量＋名］结构中，所指事物的数量可以是客观的“一”，也可以是不定量的。

由此可见，指称不定的［ø＋量＋名］结构［即情况3(i)］与其他［量＋名］结构在表量方面不尽相同。我们推论，这正是导致指称不定的［ø＋量＋名］结构排斥多项并列式的原因。参考（9）b、（10）b、（11）b、（13）b 和（14）b，各［量＋名］结构的数量都是客观的“一”，在交际过程中受话人能准确理解说话人所指事物的数量。然而，当数量不确的［ø＋量＋名］结构并列起来时，受话人就难以判断说话人所指的事物的数量。［倘若说话人不打算把事物的数量交代清楚，使用光杆名词的手段便可。例如（12）b 可改为“我想买书、字典、笔”］这样就可以理解，为什么在多项指称不定的［ø＋量＋名］结构并列的句子中，并列成分越多，句子越难接受：

（15）a　我琴日买咗盒鸡蛋。（我昨天买了一盒鸡蛋。）

（15）b　我琴日买咗盒鸡蛋同袋面粉。（我昨天买了一盒鸡蛋和一包面粉。）

（15）c　＊我琴日买咗盒鸡蛋、袋面粉同盒牛奶。（我昨天买了一盒鸡蛋、一包面粉和一盒牛奶。）

（15）d　＊＊我琴日买咗盒鸡蛋、袋面粉、罐奶茶同盒牛奶。（我昨天买了一盒鸡蛋、一包面粉、一罐奶茶和一盒牛奶。）

4.3　客观“数量一”和“不定量”的关系

上一节我们论证了在指称不定的［ø＋量＋名］结构中，所指事物的数量可以是客观的“一”，亦可以是“不定量”。现在我们进一步指出，客观数量“一”可以发展出“不定量”的概念，而这一现象是符合世界语言共性的。首先，［客观＞主观］这个演变过程符合语言演变理论。Traugott（1989：34－35）提出语义演变的三种普遍趋势（universal tendency），其中一种是“主观化”：

> …meanings become increasingly based in the speaker's subjective beliefs and attitudes …

例如，英语的“probably”本来表“有可能”（plausibly）义，属于客观描述。经过演变后，表达说话人较主观的评价（speaker's evaluation of evidence，例如：She is probably going to be promoted.）。［量＋名］结构在发生演变前也只是表达客观的数量“一”，演变后该结构所表达的数量是相对主观的“不定量”。我们调查过一些粤语的母语使用者，他们都认为“饮杯茶先啦”（先喝杯茶吧）并不一定是指“喝一杯茶”，喝一小口、半杯，或者两杯都可以。

要论证［量＋名］结构由“一”演变成“不定量”，除了主观化外，还需要探究人类对“量”概念的处理手段。参考以下引文：

> Greenberg（1978）对人类语言数词系统普遍特征的考察，“零”从来就不是任何自然语言数目系统中的计数成分，当指称一个包含“零”个成员的空集合时，自然语言不用数词结构，而只用否定结构。在任何语言中，“零”都对应于“没有”，而从“一”到无穷大都是“有”……“一”引入“有”的观念，是“有”的起点。由于量是一个相对的概念，单个实体在“零”无法充任其参照点的情况下，不能引入量观念，故“一”不是

"量"的起点。"二"才是量的起点…… 当然，数目"一"也可被看作一种量，但这种量概念不是它本身带来的，而是以"二"或大于二的数目作为潜在的参照点时才出现的。（张敏，2001：32）

根据上文，"一"并不一定是客观的数量，"一"可以是与"二"相对的量（客观数量），也可以是与"无"相对的"有"（主观数量）。

Heine and Kuteva（2002）参考了大量语言，整理出若干常见的语法化过程，其中"一"概念可发展出"只有"（only）义，如 Nama 语的 *gui*，Lezgian 语的 *sa* 等。也有一些语言从"一"发展成为单数标记，如 Akatek 语的 *jun*。还有一种情况，数词"一"可发展出数量不定的"一些"（some）义，如 Basque 语的 *bat*［参考（16）］，Tamil 语的 *oru*，Lezgian 语的 *sa*［参考（17）］等。

（16） hogei　　bat
Twenty　　one
about twenty

（17） sa　sumud　ktab
One　how, many　book
some books

总括以上论证，可知世界上不少语言演变有以下趋势：①［客观 > 主观］；②［客观数量 > 主观数量］。所以，粤语中表客观数量"一"的［ø + 量 + 名］结构有条件发展出表非客观的"不定量"的功能。

4.4　有关量词"以单概双"的现象

确定了粤语［ø + 量 + 名］结构所指事物的数量可以使用"不定量"后，还可以解释为什么量词出现"以单概双"的现象。张洪年（1989：772）注意到一些带［ø + 量 + 名］结构的句子，表面上数量虽然是"一"，但实指数目是"二"：

（18） 企到只脚好瘆。（站得脚都累坏了。）

（19） 因住，整亲只眼。（小心，别伤了眼睛。）

以上两句的量词都是"只"，表示所修饰的名词是单数。然而，两句的名词"脚"和"眼"的数量并不是"一"，而是"二"。

我们认为，正是因为［ø + 量 + 名］结构从客观数量"一"发展出"不定量"义，粤语才有条件出现"以单概双"的现象。

诚然，本文只观察到无定/指称不定的［ø + 量 + 名］结构与"不定量"的密切关系，而以单概双的现象则可见于有定和无定的［ø + 量 + 名］结构。为什么有定的结构也可以表"不定量"义呢？这一点尚待进一步研究。

5 结　论

本文从对外粤语教学出发，先对外国学生的语言偏误进行分析，发现无定/指称不定的［ø＋量＋名］结构排斥多项名词并列式。进一步发现这一现象与粤语［ø＋量＋名］结构的［一＞不定量］演变过程有关。通过共时比较，发现这种演变过程也可见于其他语言，从而为本文的论点提供了旁证。

本文的研究反映了透过对外语言教学可以发现一些传统研究方法所忽略的地方，可以让我们对语言有更全面、深入的认识。以［ø＋量＋名］结构为例，当我们了解了指称不定的［ø＋量＋名］结构不能出现在多项名词并列式后，便可以完善量名结构的语法规则（参考4.1中从情况3修改成情况3'的内容）。还可以解答一些前人未能解释的现象（参考4.4有关量词“以单概双”的现象）。

参考文献

陈健荣、李兆麟　2014　《粤语二语学习者的语体偏误分析》，载于吴伟平、李兆麟编　《语言学与华语二语教学：语用能力培养的理论与实践》，香港：商务印书局，第225～236页。

单韵鸣　2007　《粤语有定的“量＋名”结构》，载于张洪年、张双庆、陈雄根主编《第十届国际粤方言研讨会论文集》，北京：中国社会科学出版社，第271～276页。

冯胜利　2011　《语体语法及其文学功能》，《当代修辞学》第4期，第1～13页。

刘丹青　2006　《汉语方言语法调查研究的三种模式》，《中国方言学报》第1期，第87～106页。

张洪年　1989　《粤语量词用法的研究》，载于“中央”研究院编　《第二届国际汉学会议论文集》，台北：“中央”研究院，第752～774页。

张洪年　2007　《香港粤语语法的研究》（增订版），香港：香港中文大学出版社。

张　敏　2001　《汉语方言重叠式语义模式的研究》，《中国语文研究》第1期，第24～42页。

赵元任著，吕叔湘译　1979　《汉语口语语法》，北京：商务印书馆。

周小兵　1997　《广州话量词的定指功能》，《方言》第1期，第45～47页。

Chan, Marjorie K. M.　2002　Gender-related use of sentence-final particles in Cantonese. In Marlis Hellinger and Hadumod Bussmann eds., *Gender Across Languages: The Linguistics Representation of Women and Men*, Vol. 2. Philadelphia: John Benjamins. pp. 57－72.

Corder, S. P.　1967　The significance of learners' errors. *International Review of Applied Linguistics*, 5: 161－169.

Francis, Elaine J., and Stephen Matthews　2006　Categoriality and object extraction in Cantonese serial verb constructions. *Natural Language and Linguistic Theory*, 24 (3): 751－801.

Greenberg, Joseph H. 1978 Diachrony, synchrony and language universals. In Joseph H. Greenberg, Charles A. Ferguson, and Edith A. Moravcsik eds., *Universals of Human Language, Vol. 1: Method and Theory*. Stanford: Stanford University. pp. 61 – 92.

Heine, Bernd, and Tania Kuteva 2002 *World Lexicon of Grammaticalization*. Cambridge: Cambridge University Press.

Liu, Jian, and Alain Peyraube 1994 History of some coordinative conjunctions in Chinese. *Journal of Chinese Linguistics*, 22: 179 – 201.

Matthews, Stephen, and Virginia Yip 1994 *Cantonese: A Comprehensive Grammar*. London and New York: Routledge.

Traugott, Elizabeth C. 1989 On the rise of epistemic meanings in English: an example of subjectification in semantic change. *Language*, 65 (1): 31 – 55.

粤语句末助词“嘅 ge^2”的两种功能和交互主观化现象

饭田真纪

（日本北海道大学）

提　要：本文首先对粤语句末助词 ge^2（短而急升的 ge^2）的功能加以分析，并指出它具有“表反预期”与“反驳”两种不同的功能。至于这两种功能的演变关系，本文认为是从“表反预期”用法中经过中间用法进而发展出“反驳”用法。而推动这一演变的契机是说话者在形成预期时，是否受到他人的暗示所影响。最后指出，ge^2 的功能扩张（语义变化）方向是由“对事”变为“对人”，因此可以视为一种交互主观化现象。

关键词：句末助词　反预期　反驳　语义变化　交互主观化

1　问题的提出

1.1　本文的研究对象

本文要讨论的是粤语①的句末助词“嘅”［kɛ˧˥］。为方便起见，以下将其写作“ge^2”（数字 2 代表阴上调˧˥）。

以往研究普遍显示，具有这一语音形式（即［kɛ˧˥］）的句末助词其实有两个。由于在音长和调型上，两者有细微的差异，即一个是短而急升的 ge^2，而另外一个是长而缓升的 ge^2（以下分别称为“短的 ge^2”与“长的 ge^2”），因此，以往研究中，有的把两者当作不同的句末助词来处理（梁仲森，1992），有的则把两者当作同一个句末助词，从中分出不同的用法（Kwok，1984；Law，1990；Matthews and Yip，1994：349；Fung，2000：158 等）。

无论是哪一种说法，以往研究都承认“短的 ge^2”与“长的 ge^2”，两者无论是在形态上还是功能上都是有区别的。

我们也认为有充足的理由把上述两者作严格区分。

① 本文所说的“粤语”是指广州、香港等珠江三角洲地区通行的粤方言。

而本文要讨论的重点是"短的 ge^2"。如下列例句（1）、（2）：[①]

（1） H：喂，你喺边呀？
（喂，你在哪里呀？）
女：我咪喺天星码头啰！
（我不就在天星码头吗！）
H：我都喺天星码头喎！我唔见你 ge^2！
（我也在天星码头耶！我怎么看不见你呢？）　　（《森》：229～230）

（2） 速递员：收包裹呀！呢度签收吖唔该！放响出面啲箱！！
（收包裹了！这里签收啊谢谢！放在外面的箱子！！）
罗拔图：到啦到啦！批货到啦！
（到了，到了！货到了！）
文哥：哗！咁重 ge^2？乜嘢衫嚟㗎？
（哇！怎么这么重？什么衣服呀？）　　（《903》：225）

由于本文只讨论"短的 ge^2"，并不打算讨论"长的 ge^2"。因此，在以下各节中，将以 ge^2 这一名称来代表"短的 ge^2"，以避免烦冗。

1.2　以往研究回顾

关于 ge^2 的功能，从以往的研究分析中，可以看出如下两个特征。

第一，不少学者都着眼于 ge^2 跟"为什么"问句的密切关系，认为 ge^2 具有问原因的功能。Kwok（1984：73）很早就指出，ge^2 可以出现在特指疑问句中，但仅限于一些含有疑问之义的字句，例如"点解"（为什么）、"做乜"（干吗）等（以下称为"为什么"问句）。Kwok（1984）还指出，ge^2 除了用于"为什么"问句句末之外，还可以出现在陈述句句末，使之变作问"为什么"之用，而在这两种情况下，ge^2 都表达说话者的困惑之感（"puzzled on the part of the speaker"，Kwok，1984：73）。除了 Kwok（1984）之外，梁仲森（1992：97～98）、李新魁等（1995：512）、Fung（2000：160）、方小燕（2003：75，89～91）也都提到 ge^2 有问原因的疑问功能。以下是梁仲森（1992：97）的例句：

（3） 阿康呀，你买乜鬼嘢 zek^1？去到咁晏 ge^2？（"问原因"，梁仲森，1992：97）
（阿康呀，你买什么呀？怎么去了这么久？）

第二，还有一些研究试着从说话者表达的语气或功能方面加以解释。如上所述，Kwok（1984）提到，在两种句法环境下，ge^2 都表达说话者的困惑之感。Matthews and Yip（1994：349）也继承这个说法，指出 ge^2 表达对事态的困惑。

另外值得一提的是梁仲森（1992）的分析。在过去的文献中，梁仲森（1992）对 ge^2

① 本文使用的语料来自以粤语书写的小说或剧本等资料以及网络上以粤语写的文章。所有例句都经母语人士确认或修改过。

的分析最为详细。除了上述"问原因"功能之外，梁仲森（1992）还区分出了另外两种功能，即"埋怨"以及"辩白"，分别表示"对人对事感到不合理而产生埋怨的情绪"（梁仲森，1992：97）以及"这个语气助词所出现的句子，是说话者提出的理由、事实、证据，为自己或句中出现的'佢'的行为、责任辩白"（梁仲森，1992：98）。

梁仲森（1992）指出的两种功能分别如下：

（4）我对袜唔见咗 ge^2。（"埋怨"，梁仲森，1992：98）
（怎么我的袜子不见了?!）

（5）［被怀疑是在偷懒，没有帮她妈妈。］①
我边有蛇王呀？阿妈话自己做 ge^2。（"辩白"，梁仲森，1992：98）
（我哪有偷懒呢？妈妈说自己要做的。）

以上前人的分析都值得参考，不过，仍有以下几点不足之处。

第一，关于"问原因"功能。正如以往研究所说，ge^2 可以出现于"为什么"问句。然而，在我们看来，这种问句里，问原因的功能应该是由"为什么"义之疑问词的词汇意义带出来的。虽然在陈述句句末，ge^2 也可以独自出现，使整个句子带上类似"问原因"的意思［如例（3）］，但针对这个情形，我们也可以设想另一种解释方法。即 ge^2 以出现在陈述句为常态，它的核心功能是表示对陈述事态的某种态度，而不是使整个句子变成疑问句。至于 ge^2 跟"为什么"义疑问词共现的特殊情形，则需另做处理。（事实上，这就是我们要采取的处理方式。请参看2.2。）

再者，关于疑问功能，我们要指出另一个问题。按照前人的说法，ge^2 可以出现在陈述句句末，使整个句子带上"问原因"的意思，如例（3），但这些句子能否算作疑问句，仍有些保留。

例如，ge^2 多用于自言自语、本不期待对方回答的情况，如下所示：

（6）喂！三叔！三～～～～～～～叔～～～～～～～～！喂！有反应 ge^2？
（喂！三叔！三～～～～～～～叔～～～～～～～～！喂！怎么没反应?）（《八王子01》：340）

因为说话者知道对方（＝三叔）没有听到自己的声音，所以"冇反应 ge^2?"这一句话应该理解成说话者的自言自语，决不是说话者为了得到什么回答而说。

由此可见，ge^2 的语义中缺乏要求对方回答的成分。从这个语义特点来看，我们认为，与其说 ge^2 具有把陈述句变成"为什么"问句的功能，不如说 ge^2 出现在陈述句句末，表示说话者对陈述事态的某种态度。

第二，关于 ge^2 表达的语气或功能，以往研究中也有几点值得商榷。可以概括为以下两点：

① 梁仲森（1992：98）未提供这个例句的上下文。在此只能自行补充。

其一，单靠语气，很难解释不同功能之间的区别。例如，梁仲森（1992：97～98）把“埋怨”的 ge^2 从“问原因”的 ge^2 中独立出来，可是在我们看来，这两者是不能明确区分的。比如，梁文所说的表达“埋怨”的例句（4），亦可以视为具有“问原因”的功能，两者的界限不甚清晰。如果在句末打上问号，例句（4）就会变成“问原因”的例句，如下：①

（7）我对袜唔见咗 ge^2？［由例句（4）改变而成］
（为什么我的袜子不见了？）

鉴于这一事实，我们没有足够的理由把“埋怨”独立出来。因此，把“埋怨”用法放进“问原因”用法中，合并成同一个用法，较为合理。

其二，梁仲森（1992：98）所说的“辩白”功能应该怎么处理呢？他举了以下例句：

（8）你自己整 ge^2，佢都冇行过埋去。
（你自己弄的，他根本没有靠近。）

（9）我买俾佢 ge^2。边个话攞你 ga。
（我买给他的。谁说要拿你的。）

其实，以往的研究很少提到“辩白”功能。而这一功能与上述“埋怨”功能不同，其很难与“问原因”功能合并在一起。因为从定义上来看，“问原因”和“辩白”［或者“提出理由、事实、证据”（梁仲森，1992：98）］是完全相反的功能。

因此，我们可以确定 ge^2 至少有两个不同的功能。

那么，接下来要问的是，“问原因”和“辩白”这两种功能之间究竟有什么联系呢？换句话说，为什么 ge^2 会有两种看起来完全相反的功能呢？

我们在上文回顾以往研究，整理出了本文主要探讨的问题：

第一，厘清两种 ge^2 的本质功能。我们认为前人所说的“问原因”与“辩白”等解释或标签有必要重新检讨，所以本文要提出一个更具说服力的解释。第二，本文还要进一步探讨两种功能之间的联系和演变关系。

2　关于第一种 ge^2

2.1　功能分析

在以下两节，我们要讨论第一个问题，即厘清两种 ge^2 的本质功能。

首先来看第一种 ge^2，也就是所谓“问原因”用法。如上所述，我们不能认同 ge^2 本身具有“问原因”功能的这个说法。那么应该怎么来定义呢？

① 事实上，梁文的所有“问原因”例句句末都打上了问号。

我们回顾过去的文献，并结合上述讨论来看，ge² 出现的句类应该是以陈述句作为基础的。而出现在"为什么"问句的情形，则可以以扩张用法来解释。也就是说，ge² 作为一个句末助词（语气助词），它的功能是表示说话者在说话时对陈述内容（命题）的一种态度。那么，具体来说是什么样的态度呢？

我们认为，ge² 表达说话者把命题表示的事态认定为"违反预期"的事态。也就是说，当前的事态并不是本来被预期会实现的事态，即说话者的心目中有另一个被预期会实现的事态，然而眼前的事实把这一预期彻底否定了。也就是，说话者的预期受到了否定。下面，举个例子来说明一下：

（10）H：喂，你喺边呀？
　　　（喂？你在哪里呀？）
　　女：我咪喺天星码头啰！
　　　（我不就在天星码头吗！）
　　H：我都喺天星码头喎！我唔见你 ge²！
　　　（我也在天星码头耶！我怎么看不见你呢？）
　　　　　　　　　　　　　　　　　　　　　　［同（1）］

在一般情况下，如果两个人同时在同一个地方，应该可以看到彼此（除非那个地方太大或者聚集了很多人）。所以，例句（10）中的说话者（＝H）也按照这个思路去推测，预期只要一到天星码头就一定能看见对方。这是说话者预期的事态。可是现实中，自己已经在天星码头了，却看不见对方（＝女）。说话者这才恍然发现自己的预期被彻底否定了。换言之，"我唔见你"是个违反说话者预期的事情。

由于预期中的事是一种缺省值（default value），反预期的事则被认为是种偏离常规的异常事态，因此，ge² 总会带来"事情不应该这样，怎么会这样？"等含义。这就是 ge² 会带上"问原因"或"困惑"语气的根源。再来看看另一个实例：

（11）喂！三叔！三～～～～～～叔～～～～～～～！喂！冇反应 ge²？
　　（喂！三叔！三～～～～～～叔～～～～～～～！喂！怎么没反应？）
　　　　　　　　　　　　　　　　　　　　　　　　［同（6）］

在一般情况下，如果你跟人打招呼，对方必定会回应。而例句（11）的说话者也这么期待。但没料到，叫了几声，对方（＝三叔）始终没有回应。显而易见，对说话者来说，"（对方）冇反应"是种违反预期的事态。

在以下情况，说话者知道包裹里的货品都是衣服，所以预期这包裹应该会很轻。因此，对他来说，"（包裹）咁重"是件反预期的事情。

（12）速递员：收包裹呀！呢度签收吖唔该！放响出面啲箱！！
　　　　（收包裹了！这里签收啊谢谢！放在外面的箱子！！）

罗拔图：到啦到啦！批货到啦！
（到了，到了！货到了！）
文哥：哗！咁重 ge^2？乜野衫嚟㗎？
（哇！怎么这么重？什么衣服呀？）
［同（2）］

由此可见，ge^2 表达的对命题的态度，具体来说，就是说话者认定当前事态是违反预期的。其语义特点如下：把目前的反预期事态与本该实现的合乎预期的事态对比着看。

只是，这里要补充一点。虽然我们说 ge^2 把目前的反预期事态与合乎预期事态对比着看，但这并不等于说，使用 ge^2 的说话者在事前实际上形成了某种预期。而是当他用上 ge^2 时，在语言表达上选择了以这种模式来表达对当前事态的态度。

比如在下列例句中，说话者可能事先没有明确形成预期。（或者，最多只能说，预期一切如常，包括对方的外貌。）

（13）蒋生：好耐冇见!!（好久不见!）
罗拔图：蒋生!!（蒋先生!）
蒋生：剪咗条辫 ge^2？（怎么剪辫子了?）
罗拔图：系啊!!（是啊!） （《903》：291～292）

因此，就 ge^2 的功能来说，必须澄清这一点，即说话者一旦使用 ge^2，命题就带上违反预期的印记，从而激活本应实现的预期中事态之存在。

这一点，若跟另外一个与预期（expectation）有关的句末助词比较起来，或许显得更为清晰。

例如，粤语里有一个句末助词 wo^4，根据前人研究，是表达“unexpected”（Kwok，1984：68）、“意想不到”（梁仲森，1992：115）或“出乎意料、吃惊、惊奇等”（方小燕，2003：162）意思。例如：

（14）雪姑七友变晒老鼠 wo^4。（Kwok，1984：68～69）
［白雪公主的七个小矮人（居然）变成老鼠耶。］
（15）一个仙都唔使 wo^4。（Kwok，1984：68～69）
（连一毛钱都不用付耶。）

这里不打算讨论 wo^4 的详细语义特点。从前人研究的描写和例子，可以估计 wo^4 大概表示说话者正在把新发现的事态编入自己的信息库里。与 ge^2 不同，wo^4 不涉及本应实现的事态，它只表达当前事态意外地发生。换句话说，同样是表达意外事态，说话者的描写方式是有所区别的。如果就说话者对意外事态出现的感受方式作个比喻，wo^4 就是“从无生有”的“出现”模式，而 ge^2 则是“非此（而彼）”的“否定”模式。

2.2 跟“为什么”问句的共现

上一节讨论到 ge² 所附着的句子是以陈述句为主，而它的功能是“表反预期”。

然而，如上所述，不少学者曾指出，ge² 不仅可以出现在陈述句句末，还可以出现在“为什么”问句句末。如下：

（16）点解你识讲日文 ge²？（为什么你会讲日语？）
（17）做乜染咗头发 ge²？（干吗染头发？）

这个事实，乍看之下，与上述句法分布特征有所冲突，其实不然。

首先，“为什么”问句跟其他类型的问句，性质有所不同。“为什么”问句的句式意义是询问已确定的事态（=P）和导致它发生的原因事态（=Q）之间的联系，换言之，它同时涉及两个事态（P 和 Q）。而其他类型的疑问句则只涉及一个事件。譬如，在“几时”（什么时候）、“边个”（谁）等其他疑问词构成的特指问句中，说话者针对一个事态 P 中的不确定因素 X，作出询问。而在是非问句中，说话者则是针对某一个事态 P 的真假作出询问。无论是哪一种，这些问句中的事态 P 都含有不确定因素，亦即事态 P 在说话者心目中尚未成为确定事态。

既然是不确定事态，就无谓谈论该事态是否合乎说话者的预期。所以，ge² 不能出现在这些类型的疑问句中。如 Fung（2000：168）的例句所示：

（18）*边度后面有条河 ge²？（哪里后面有条河？）
（19）*后面系唔系有条河 ge²？（后面是不是有条河？）

相较之下，“为什么”问句可以同时涉及两个事态，即当前事态 P 与原因事态 Q。其中，当前事态 P 本身不存在任何不确定因素。以（16）为例，事态 P“你识讲日文”是已被证实为真的确定事态，说话者对它的成立毫无疑问。不确定的是，导致事态 P 发生的另外一个事态 Q 到底是什么。也就是说，在“为什么”问句中，当前事态 P 是已证实为真的事态，不存在任何不确定因素，因此，说话者可以表达违反预期。

由此可见，虽然 ge² 以出现在陈述句句末为常态，但当它出现在“为什么”问句句末时也并不构成例外。

由于“为什么”问句与 ge² 的相容性较大，所以导致产生了以下特殊情况：当“点解”出现的时候，事态内容本身不需要出现。如下列例句所示：

（20）阿烦：我有做吓间 design 公司。
（我已不在那家设计公司了。）
阿水：吓？点解 ge²？个老板呃你呀？
（啊？为什么？老板骗你啊？）　　（《落雨》：282）

在这个例句中，说话者没有说出他认为违反预期的具体事态内容，即“（对方）有做

� 公司”，只表达对目前事态是违反预期的。又如：

（21）LuLu：有冇睇戏呀？
（有没有看电影？）
Robert：呢排冇，好忙。
（最近没有，很忙。）
LuLu：点解 ge^2？
（为什么？）　　（《玩》：22）

在这个例句中，说话者没有提到违反她预期的具体事态内容，即“（对方）很忙”，只表达这个事态违反了她的预期。

3　关于第二种 ge^2

3.1　与第一种 ge^2 的区别

上一节所举的例句都代表 ge^2 的其中一个功能，即“表反预期”。我们暂且把用作这一种功能的例子简称为 A 用法。

然而，在第一节提到，ge^2 还有一个功能，即前人所说的“辩白”功能。如下：

（22）[被怀疑是在偷懒，没有帮她妈妈。]
我边有蛇王呀？阿妈话自己做 ge^2。
（我哪有偷懒呢？妈妈说自己要做的。）
[同（5）]

（23）[患者被怀疑是失忆，于是医生逐个问她身边人的身份。]
蚌：呢个系我老公杜国滔啰！
（这个是我老公杜国滔！）
医生：咁呢位又系……
（那这位是……）
蚌：佢？！佢咪系我家姐百合啰……
（她？她不就是我姐姐百合嘛……）
医生：咁呢位……
（那这位……）
蚌：啤！我都唔识佢 ge^2！
（哎！我又不认识她！）　　（《诱惑·完》：92）

（24）吖晚闷得济畀佢哋拉咗去睇歌剧，你知啦，我都唔啱呢啲嘢 ge^2。
（那天晚上太无聊，被他们拉去看歌剧，你知道的，我老不适合这些东西。）
（*John*：160）

与A用法不同的地方是，在这些例句中，ge^2 所附着的命题无法视为“违反说话者预期”的事态。正如梁仲森（1992：98）所说，这种 ge^2“所出现的句子，是说话者提出的理由、事实、证据”。于是，我们把用作这一种功能的例子暂且叫作“B用法”。

若从信息性质的角度来看A用法与B用法，我们可以指出两种用法之间存在着以下差异。在A用法中，ge^2 所附着的命题内容代表违反说话者预期的事态，所以，它通常是说话者在说话时当场发现或意识到的信息。例如：

（25）速递员：收包裹呀！呢度签收吖唔该！放响出面啲箱！！
（收包裹了！这里签收啊谢谢！放在外面的箱子！！）
罗拔图：到啦到啦！批货到啦！
（到了，到了！货到了！）
文哥：哗！咁重 ge^2？乜嘢衫嚟㗎？
（哇！怎么这么重？什么衣服呀？）（《903》：225）
［同（2）］

这句话的语境显示，“咁重”这一事实，是说话者当场才发现的。

与A用法相比，在B用法中，ge^2 所附着的命题内容代表“说话者提出的理由、事实、证据”。所以，对说话者来说，这一信息不会是在说话时当场才发现或意识到的，而是早在说话之前就已经知道了。例句（24）最能说明这一点。说话者既然使用“你知啦”来要求对方确认后面要表达的内容，他/她自己对该事态应该是十分熟悉的，决不可能是当场获悉的信息。

此外，B用法的 ge^2 句中经常出现语气副词“都”，例如（23）、（24）。[①]

3.2 功能分析

上述B用法，梁仲森（1992：98）称之为“辩白”。然而，若再仔细观察，我们就会发现“辩白”这一标签并不能完全涵盖所有实例。例如，以下例句（26）、（27）中的 ge^2，按照上述标准（即说话者对命题内容的知悉度），显然是B用法。可是要把这些例句中的功能说成“辩白”，却又显得不甚贴切。因为，按照一般理解，“辩白”这一行为，是在被人怀疑或受到批评等时，为了辩护自己或自己以外的某人的立场而被诱发出来的。可是，在以下情况中，说话者或他人的立场并未受到威胁或误会，不需要作辩白。

（26）A：哎吔！我又肥咗啦！
（哎呀！我又胖了！）
丁：你边度肥啫？
（你哪里胖啊？）

① 梁仲森（1992）在讨论“埋怨”用法时，也提到这一用法多数与“都”或“又”共现。可是，我们在上文说过不认同区分出“埋怨”用法。

希：系喇……

（对啦……）

A：我琦晚又锯扒！

（我昨天晚上又吃牛扒！）

希：怕咩啫，你食极都唔肥 ge²！

（怕什么？你怎么吃也不会胖的！）　　（《男上》：86）

（27）阿敏：不如我哋去第二度食 lo³。走 lo³。

（要不我们到别的地方吃吧。走吧。）

阿杰：点解呀？又系你话嚟呢度食 ge²。

（为什么？是你说要来这里吃的。）　　（《电影》：194）

可见，“辩白”这一说法恐怕有过于片面之嫌。

那么应该怎么来定义呢？

其实，属于B用法的上述例句［（22）~（24）、（26）、（27）］中，都有一个共通点，即说话者在他人言行中看到某种主张或见解，对此感到不以为然，因此要进行反驳。而 ge² 所附着的命题（=P）则是用来反驳的理据。

譬如例（27），说话者（阿杰）从对方（阿敏）的言行中得知阿敏主张应该到别的地方吃饭，对此感到不以为然，所以要以命题P作为理据来纠正她的错误。又如例（24），说话者从“佢哋”的行动（带“我”去看歌剧）中看到他们认为说话者喜欢看歌剧，其实不然，所以说话者要以命题P作为理据来纠正他们的错误。由于反驳是一种有可能跟别人产生摩擦的行为，所以B用法的 ge² 总会带有不满/埋怨等负面情绪。

鉴于这种语义特征，我们把B用法的 ge² 视为具有“反驳”功能。

4　两种 ge² 之间的联系

4.1　具体演变过程

那么，接下来的问题是，到底 ge² 的A用法（“表反预期”）跟B用法（“反驳”）之间有什么联系？假如两者之间有联系，到底是哪个用法先出现的呢？中间是不是有过渡的用法呢？

乍看之下，A用法与B用法之间的差别相当大。ge² 所附着的命题P在A用法中是违反说话者预期的事态本身［例（28）］，而在B用法中则是说话者用来反驳的理据［例（29）］。

（28）文哥：哗！咁重 ge²？乜嘢衫嚟㗎？（A用法，表反预期）

（哇！怎么这么重？什么衣服呀？）

［同（2）］

（29）我边有蛇王呀？阿妈话自己做 ge²。（B用法，反驳）

(我哪有偷懒呢？妈妈说自己要做的。)

[同(5)]

然而，这些都是A用法和B用法的典型例子。如果再仔细观察，我们就能找到一些位于两者中间的用法。[①]也就是说，在这一中间用法中，ge^2 所附着的命题P既能看成是说话者感到违反预期的事态，也能看成是用来反驳他人的理据。例如：

(30) 罗拔图：咁你间铺到底卖咩㗎？

(那么你这间店到底卖什么呀？)

琳琳：咪之前电话同你讲过啦！卖衫啰！

(之前电话里跟你讲过啦！卖衣服啊！)

罗拔图：咁啲衫呢？唔见 ge^2！

(那么衣服呢？没看到呀！)　　(《903》：164)

(31) 想借问一下，dl 完之后要点开？我 unzip 完 double click sv4. exe 都有反应 ge^2。(想请问一下，下载完之后要怎么打开？我解压完 double click sv4. exe 都没有反应。)　　(《网》)

首先看(30)，说话者听到眼前这间店是卖衣服的，因而推论里面应该有很多衣服，可是事实违反了他/她的预期，店里一件衣服也见不到(=P)。从这个角度来说，他/她纯粹要表达事态P的意外性。亦即，A用法(表反预期)。但从另一个角度来看，也可以这样理解：说话者是要把P作为理据来指出对方给她的解释(即这家店是卖衣服的)是不正确的，换言之，是要反驳对方。这样一来，在例(30)中可以看到B用法(反驳)的萌芽。

同样，例(31)中，ge^2 既能理解为表示眼前事实"没反应"是个违反说话者预期的事态，也可以理解为表示他/她要用这一事态作为理据来主张教他/她操作的某人(可能是听话者)的指示是不正确的。

我们认为，从这些中间用法中产生B用法诠释的契机在于，说话者的预期是否受到他人暗示的影响。在一般情况下，说话者是自己形成预期的。例如(28)，因为包裹里只有衣服，所以应该很轻，而在这一推论过程中，说话者并未受到他人的影响。但有时候，说

---

① 其实，本文初稿原本没有设定中间用法(A/B用法)，是一位匿名评审员的启示让我们发现了中间用法的存在和语义特征，在此深表感谢。该评审员指出，除了本文所说的"表反预期"用法和"反驳"用法以外，还应该分出另一种用法("非议")，并提供了以下例句：

(a)(仲话重视人哋 tim^1，系鬼！)我送畀佢对袜都唔见佢着 ge^2！

[(还说重视人家，鬼话！)我送他的袜子都没见他穿过！]

(b)外面啲人话老板系大好人，其实佢一啲都唔关心啲员工 ge^2！

(外面的人都说老板是大好人，其实他一点儿都不关心员工！)

虽然这些例句中的 ge^2 似乎自成一类，但经过多番考虑，我们还是没有将"非议"单独列为一类。我们采取的方法是把这一类的用法定位于"表反预期"与"反驳"之间的过渡阶段。实际上，上列"非议"例句，按照我们的分类，可以看成是中间用法(A/B用法)，又或者是"反驳"用法。[视乎语境而定。如果说话者对事态(下线部分)感到意外的含义还很浓厚，则可看成是中间用法。]

这样，我们的处理与这位评审员给予的启示并不矛盾。

话者的预期也会受到他人意见或暗示的影响。在这种情况下，说话者一旦发现事实不是预期中的那样，在感到“事情不应该这样”之余，还可能会把矛头指向这个他人，指责这个他人的意见/看法是不正确的。例（30）、（31）可算是这种情况。

由此可见，当说话者形成错误预期，而原因或责任是在他人身上时，较易产生反驳他人的含义（implicature）。这种含义当初可能像例（30）在特定语境中才会产生。然而，随着长期使用，这种含义本身受到了前景化作用，最终成为 ge^2 的另一个功能，从而产生了B用法。

为了更明确地显示从A用法到B用法的连续性，下面我们把各种用法按发展的顺序排列。

首先看A用法的 ge^2。如上所述，这个 ge^2 表反预期，可以概括为（32）。

（32）A用法：Pge^2（P为命题内容，“～”代表否定）

在说话者预期Q实现的情况下 　　事态P（＝～Q）实现　（表反预期）

在A用法（表反预期）中，命题P代表的是预期Q的否定～Q。例如（33），说话者预期Q“三叔会回应”，然而现实是～Q“有反应”。

（33）喂！三叔！三～～～～～～叔～～～～～～～！喂！有反应 ge^2？

［同（6）］

接下来看A/B用法（中间用法）的 ge^2。与A用法不同，这一用法的特点是说话者形成预期时，受到了他人暗示的影响。亦即因为他人暗示Q，所以说话者也预期Q会实现。另外一点不同之处就是中间用法具有反驳功能，亦即主张与Q对立的命题～Q。如下：

（34）A/B用法：Pge^2

在他人暗示Q的情况下　⇒　在说话者预期Q实现的情况下 　　事态P（＝～Q）实现（表反预期） 　　　　＋ 　　主张命题P（＝～Q）　（反驳）　（含义）

（35）咁哋衫呢？唔见 ge^2！

［同（30）］

例如在（35）中，他人暗示Q“店里有很多衣服”，所以说话者也预期Q，然而现实是～Q“（一件衣服都）见不到”，所以是个反预期的事态。而从另一个角度看，则可以理解为说话者以主张～Q来指出Q是错的，也就是在进行反驳。因此，在A/B这一用法中，命题P代表的，既是预期Q的否定～Q，也是用来否定他人主张Q的理据～Q。

最后我们来看B用法的 ge^2。与A/B用法不同，这一用法跟预期无关，只有反驳他人的功能，亦即在他人暗示Q的情况下，主张否定Q的命题～Q。如下：

(36) B 用法：Pge²

在他人暗示 Q 的情况下 　　主张命题 P（= ~Q）　　（反驳）

(37) 我边有蛇王呀？阿妈话自己做 ge²。
　　（我哪有偷懒呢？妈妈说自己要做的。）

［同（5）］

例如在（37）中，有人暗示 Q“我有义务帮妈妈”，然而现实是 ~ Q“妈妈说自己要做”。而在这一用法中，命题 P 代表的是用来否定他人主张 Q 的理据 ~ Q。

由此可见，虽然典型的 A 用法例子和 B 用法例子之间差异相当大［例如（28）和（29）］，但是 A 用法变为 B 用法的推移是具有连续性的。

4.2 交互主观化

上面讨论到，ge² 的“反驳”用法是从“表反预期”用法经过中间用法演变出来的。而引起这个演变的契机在于说话者形成预期时是否受到他人暗示的影响。因为说话者感觉到他人的干扰，才会产生对他人进行反驳的动机。

由此可见，从“表反预期”到“反驳”这一演变过程中，表示说话者与别人产生交互关系的发展趋势越来越明显。也就是说，“表反预期”是一种对命题的表态，所以它的功能是针对事态的。而“反驳”则是一种与他人的语言交际活动，所以它的功能是针对人的。

鉴于这种性质，我们可以把 ge² 的功能扩张视为交互主观化（inter-subjectification）的一种体现。①如下所示：

(38)

［A 用法］对事（说话者对命题内容表态）　　（表反预期）

↓ 交互主观化　inter-subjectification

［B 用法］对人（说话者与他人产生交互关系）　　（反驳）

5 结　语

以上分析显示，句末助词 ge² 有两种功能，分别用于“表反预期”和“反驳”用法。在“表反预期”用法中，说话者感到命题表示的事态是反预期的；在“反驳”用法中，

① 根据 Traugott（2010：35），交互主观化现象是指语言形式的语义越来越指向听话者的发展机制，例如变为顾虑听话者面子的语义。所以，严格来说，ge² 的演变现象，不完全合乎这个定义，因为说话者的反驳对象不一定等同于听话者，如例（24）。而且“反驳”又是缺乏礼貌的语言交际活动。可是，在 ge² 的整个演变过程中，交互意义的增强是无可否认的。因此，这里所说的交互主观化应该按广义去理解。

说话者用命题表示的事态作为理据进行反驳。

至于两种功能的演变关系，本文认为是“表反预期”用法经过中间用法的过渡最终发展出了“反驳”用法。而这一演变过程代表由“对事”变为“对人”的功能扩张，可以算是一种交互主观化现象。

最后我们要补充的是，本文提出有关 ge^2 演变过程的分析，毕竟只是根据共时语言事实所作出的一种推论结果。最为理想的方法是能找到历史资料来作印证。只是，目前粤语作为地方方言，书面资料不足，且 ge^2 又是一个跟语调有密切关系的形式，因此很难在历史文献中找到证明。①在种种条件限制下，我们目前只能根据共时的语言事实推论演变过程。基于这一研究意义，我们相信本文的分析对于澄清句末助词的功能扩张（语义变化）这一课题能作出一定的贡献。

参考文献

方小燕　2003　《广州方言句末语气助词》，广州：暨南大学出版社。

李新魁等　1995　《广州方言研究》，广州：广东人民出版社。

梁仲森　1992　《香港粤语语助词的研究》，香港理工大学硕士学位论文。

张洪年　2009　《Cantonese Made Easy：早期粤语中的语气助词》，《中国语言学集刊》第2卷第2期，第131～167页。

Fung，Roxana Suk Yee　2000　*Final Particles in Standard Cantonese：Semantic Extension and Pragmatic Inference*. Ph. D. Dissertation，Department of East Asian Languages and Literatures，Columbus：The Ohio State University.

Kwok，Helen　1984　*Sentence Particles in Cantonese*. Centre of Asian Studies. Hong Kong：University of Hong Kong.

Law，Sam-Po　1990　*The Syntax and Phonology of Cantonese Sentence-final Particles*. Doctoral dissertation，Boston：Boston University.

Matthews，Stephen and Yip，Virginia　1994　*Cantonese：A Comprehensive Grammar*. London　and New York：Routledge.

Traugott，Elizabeth C.　2010　（Inter）subjectivity and（inter）subjectification：A reassessment. In Kristin Davidse，Lieven Vandelanotte，and Hubert Cuyckens eds.，*Subjectification，Intersubjectification and Grammaticalization*. Berlin：Mouton De Gruyter. pp. 29－71.

例句出处：

没有记载出处的例句是由作者自撰，并经过数名粤语母语合作者（均为广州人）确认

① 张洪年（2009）以 *Cantonese Made Easy* 为资料，对早期粤语的句末助词作出探讨，是这一方面仅有的研究成果。可是，根据他的归纳，这本书里似乎没有出现 ge^2 的例子。

的例子。

出处后的数字代表原文所在的页码。为了统一汉字写法，文中有些例句采用了与原文不同的写法。

《网》：在网络上检索到的例句，并作了适当修改。

《森》：《森之爱情》　森美　2007　香港：青春文化。

《903》：《903 巴治奥广播剧剧本》　林海峰、小克　2002　香港：商台制作有限公司。

《落雨》：《落雨路》　少爷占　2007　香港：青春文化。

《玩》：《郑振初剧本集：〈咪玩嘢〉、〈玩反转〉》　郑振初　1999　香港：国际演艺评论家协会。

《八王子 01》：《八王子（上集）》（广播剧小说）　少爷占、王贻兴　2005　香港：青春文化。

《诱惑·完》：《诱惑年月日（完结篇）》　郑丹瑞原著　李灏编剧　1998　香港：商台制作有限公司。

John：*John and Mary*　邓蔼霖　1988　香港：博益出版集团有限公司。

《男上》：《男上女下》（广播剧小说）　林海峰、卓韵芝　2003　香港：商台制作有限公司。

《电影》：《香港电影的广东语》　陈敏仪　1995　东京：キネマ旬报社。

论粤方言异体字的规范

侯兴泉、吴南开

（暨南大学汉语方言研究中心/中文系）

提　要：由于缺乏相应的规范，粤方言字一直都存在用字混乱的情况，其中异体字问题最为突出。众多的异体字给粤方言的信息化处理以及日常的使用和教学带来了诸多不便。异体字的规范是提高粤方言信息处理速度与效率的重要途径，对粤语教学等社会应用也有重要的意义。论文讨论了粤方言异体字的四种形成原因，据此确定了八项规范原则——通用性、示意性、示音性、传承性、简易性、系统性、区别性、操作性，并在此基础上提出先平行处理后加权的操作方法，最后运用这些规范原则和方法对五组较为典型的异体字组进行举例分析。

关键词：粤方言字　异体字　规范

1　引　言

粤方言跟其他汉语方言相比，除了在语音、词汇、语法上独具特色外，更重要的一点是有大量的方言自造字。这些方言自造字跟通用汉字一起搭配使用的结果是粤方言区的人们基本可以做到“我手写我口”，因此粤方言区尤其是港澳地区存在大量用方言字记录的文本资料，对这些文献资料进行整理与分析具有十分重要的研究价值和应用价值。但是由于粤方言字属于方言用字，一直以来都缺乏必要的规范，因此粤方言区内的方言用字使用情况较为混乱，韦树关（1997）、周无忌（2003）、詹伯慧（2003，2008）、郭敏珊（2008）对此都有相关的论述。归纳起来，粤方言用字比较明显的问题有异体字众多、繁体字和简体字并用、一字多词、一字多音、一字多义、有字无码（无相应的计算机编码）、有音无字等，其中以异体字使用问题最为突出。

粤方言异体字指的是粤方言字中那些读音和意义相同而字形不同的字。关于粤方言异体字是否需要规范这个问题，学界有不同的看法。有的学者认为粤方言字属于方言用字，非官方规定的正式用字，没有规范的必要。有的学者认识到粤方言异体字规范的重要性，但因有非学术层面的担心而一直没有行动。还有部分学者积极主张要对粤方言用字进行规范，如周无忌（2003）就曾呼吁“粤方言用字应予以规范”并提出四点意见；韦树关（1997）针对粤语的用字问题也曾提出五点规范意见；郭敏珊（2008）也讨论过粤方言字的规范问题；邓景滨（2004）提出要对粤方言字进行优化处理，主要是针对粤方言异体字进行整理和规范；侯兴泉等（2014）从信息处理的角度强调了粤方言字规范的重要性，并探讨了粤方言字规范的主要内容。我们认为粤方言异体字的规范是提高粤方言信息化处理效率的重要途径，在提高粤方言文语转换、机器翻译效率方面具有重要的意义，同时粤方言异体字的规范对粤语的教学等应用也有重要的意义。因此，本文延续侯兴泉等（2014）的基本观点，重点讨论粤方言异体字的规范问题。

对粤方言字的收集与整理是粤方言异体字得以规范的前提，张群显、包睿舜（2002）在《用汉字写粤语》（*The Representation of Cantonese with Chinese Characters*）一书中根据以往的研究文献收集了1 095个粤方言字，对每个字的音、义、码、普英对译、出处都做了详细的说明，为粤方言异体字的规范奠定了坚实的基础。本文在此基础上补充收集了2002年之后在广东地区出版发行的报纸杂志、粤语教材、相声粤曲等口传文化艺术台本中的600余用字，并建成粤方言字库，借此讨论粤方言异体字的规范问题。

2 粤方言异体字的成因

粤方言异体字跟通用汉字的异体字一样，也分“严格异体字”和“非严格异体字”两类。严格异体字指的是粤方言中音义全同、记词职能完全一样、仅仅字形不同的一些字样，它们在任何语境下都能互相替代而不影响意义表达，如表“切开、割开”义的“鎅”和“𠝹”。非严格异体字通常指的是一些在使用职能上存在涵盖关系和交叉关系的通假字、分化字，如“煲”和“𤆵”在动词义“煮、烧”上构成异体字，又如“攋”和“䀞”在“扫视、浏览”义上构成异体字。粤方言字中还有一种情况值得注意，即那些意义相同但由于读音有细微的区别（多是由于没有规范而导致的异读）而形成的异形字，如同表“婴儿吃的软饭”义而声母接近的“𩟔 ngam^{1}［ŋɐm^{55}］”和“𠿭 mam^{1}［mɐm^{55}］”，同表“推或击打”义而韵母接近的“嘔 beu^{6}［pɛu^{22}］”和“骠 biu^{6}［piu^{22}］”，同表“坠下、垂下”义而声调接近的“㗻 doe^{6}［tœ^{22}］”和“涹 doe^{4}［tœ^{21}］”等，这类字也可以看作是粤方言的非严格异体字。

形成粤方言异体字的原因有很多，主要体现在以下四个方面：

（1）造字理据不同而导致的异体字。除了一部分反切注音字外，粤方言字的造字法基本上没有超出六书的范畴。由于造字时不同的人使用的造字理据不同，因此会导致异体字的产生。如“不正、歪斜”义的“歪”和“呗”，前者是会意造字，后者是形声造字；又如表男阴的“𡳞”和“𨳊”，前者是象形兼会意造字，后者是形声造字；表女阴的“肦”和“女”则是形声造字和指示造字的不同。同样是形声字，由于大家所用的形旁或义旁不同，也会出现异体字，如“分支河道”义的“滘”和“漖”（声旁不同），又如“浪费”义的“嘥”和“𣳼”（形旁不同），再如“翘起”义的“趷”和“趌”（声旁和形旁皆不同）。

（2）假借音同或音近的通用汉字也是造成粤方言异体字众多的一个主要原因。粤语中有许多不同于其他方言的特色词，这些特色词多没有相应的汉字可以记录。粤人在记录这些词语的时候除了自造字外，还经常假借音同或音近的通用汉字来记录。如用“呢”或

"哩"来记录粤语的近指代词，用"晒"或"嗺"来表示兼表"全部"和"完成"义的动态助词等。有些粤方言字民间很早就有相应的写法，如蛋、卵以前多写作"𥻘"或"𤘿"，但是由于这两个字不好写，字库也不容易找到，现在很多人习惯写成跟通用汉字同音的"春"。粤方言中还有很多音译外来词，在翻译这些外来词的时候也常借用音同或音近但字形不同的汉字来记录。如用"臣"或"神"来记录英文词 fashion 中的 shion 音节。

(3) 繁简并用导致的异体字。目前粤方言区用字的状况是港澳地区和海外社区使用繁体字，而广东地区则是繁简体字并用。改革开放后，穗港澳地区人员商旅事务往来频繁，粤方言区人们的用字经常会发生繁简体字混用的情况。由于繁简体字的混用而造成的一些异体字，甚至在一些粤语教材中也经常能看到。例如表判定的系动词"系"和"係"，表远指的代词"吓"和"嗰"，表"拿、持"义的"捞"和"攞"等等。严格说来，繁简体字不应看作是异体字。但由于粤方言字的繁简对应并不像通用汉字那样有系统的对应关系，多数粤方言字都处于有繁无简或有简无繁的状态，因此对于有繁简对应且在日常使用中经常混用的繁简体字，我们暂时也先把它们处理为异体字。

(4) 本字和自造字或假借字并用产生的异体字。粤方言有一部分字其实是有本字的，由于时间久远（读音通常会出现一定程度的变异），多数人已经不知道其来源了，因此有人另造字体或假借通用汉字来记录它，这样也会造成异体字。如"无"和"冇"、"来"和"嚟"、"脸"和"烩"、"重"和"仲"等等。在本字和自造字并用的异体字中，有一类是粤人在本字的基础上添加类符（多加口字旁）而造成的，如"添"和"嚈"、"弊"和"嘝"等。

3 粤方言异体字的规范原则和操作方法

3.1 粤方言异体字的规范原则

粤方言字作为通用汉字的从属系统，其异体字的规范也应参考通用汉字的相关规范（详见《语言文字规范手册》最新版，2014）。王宁（1991）曾提出有关汉字优化的五项原则：①有利于形成和保持严密的文字系统；②尽量保持和维护汉字的表义示源功能；③最大限度地减少笔画；④字符之间有足够的区别度；⑤尽可能估计字符的社会流通程度。这五项原则可视为通用汉字规范的指导性原则。邓景滨（2004）将其概括为系统性原则、示意性原则、简易性原则、区别性原则、认受性原则，并根据粤方言字的实际增加了表音性、传承性、操作性和美观性四项标准。其中表音性指一个方言字的表音准确程度，即其表音功能的有无强弱；传承性指一个方言字的历史传承，即该字是否本字或古字；操作性指字的编码是否适合电脑的输入和操作；美观性指字的笔画结构的匀称程度。周无忌（2003）就粤方言字的规范也提出过几点意见：①尽可能做到一个词用一个书写形式，一个字表示一个词或词素；②优化字向通用汉字靠拢，凡是通用汉字有相应同义且与粤方言同音的，不另用方言字；③规范后用字要以常用字为主，同时要照顾古字；④对于有音无字者，应当予以定形，可以用近音字、同音字替代，或者干脆新造一字，新造字可以六书方法进行。周先生的意见除了第四点跟异体字规范没有太多关系外，其余三点都可作为异体字规范的相关原则，其中第一点意见可视为区别性原则，第二点意见可视为通用字优先原则，第三点可归结为常用字优先原则。

我们认为邓景滨（2004）关于粤方言字优化的九项原则大部分都是适用于异体字的整理和规范的。美观性由于主观性较大，而且欠缺美观性的汉字多是由于违背了汉字的系统性原则而导致的，故予以取消。董月凯、邓景滨（2011）把表音性改为示音性，更为准确了，我们认同示音性的提法。认受性原则这一提法容易引起误解，我们将其改为通用性原则。总结起来，适用于粤方言异体字整理的原则共有八项，分别为通用性、示意性、示音性、传承性、简易性、系统性、区别性、操作性。

3.2 规范粤方言异体字的操作方法

有了八项原则进行总体的规范指导，接下来最关键的问题就是如何运用这些原则对具体的异体字组进行操作。邓景滨（2004）在九项优化原则的基础上提出分级加权的方法。他根据重要性原则把九项原则进行排序，分别为表音性、示意性、认受性、传承性、简易性、系统性、区别性、操作性、美观性，并在此基础上拟定了一个优化量表，将九项原则分成三个层级，配以不同的加权指数：①表音性、示意性为第一层级，加权指数为3；②认受性、传承性、简易性为第二层级，加权指数为2；③系统性、区别性、操作性、美观性为第三层级，加权指数为1。在优化整理粤方言异体字的过程中，可以先在第一层级中比较，若优劣明显，则可定论；若优劣不明显，则进入第二层级进行比较以定优劣，若是在第二层级中仍无法分出优劣，则进入第三层级。以此类推，最终以总分最多者为优。

分级加权法的优点是层级主次分明，可减少具体的操作步骤。缺点有二：一是层级的确立建立在假设之上，为何要分为三个层级，缺乏深入详细的论证。二是分值的选定很容易加入研究者的主观因素。以对粤方言“撳”、“揿”、“扲”、“撚”这四个异体字的分析为例，邓先生认为它们在第一层级上就分出胜负了，四字都具备示意性，故得分相同；“撚”字的表音性最强（得3分），“扲”次之（得2分），其余两字各得1分。这里有关示音性的分值明显有主观判断在里面，声旁“今 gam^{1} [kɐm^{55}]”和“禁 gam^{3} [kɐm^{33}]”跟表“压、撳”义的 gam^{6} [kɐm^{22}] 都是声母和韵母同而声调异，为何分值有别？而声旁“恩 ian^{1} [iɐn^{55}]”的示音性明显要比“钦 iam^{1} [iɐm^{55}] /ham^{1} [hɐm^{55}]”差，但是两者的分值却是一样的。

为了尽可能地减少研究者主观因素的加入，我们不赞成一开始就分级加权而提倡先平行处理后加权的方法。具体来说，就是实际操作的时候先不对异体字整理的各项原则进行分级加权，姑且认为它们是一样重要的（譬如都用一个“√”表示，或都是1分），进行异体字整理的时候首先看哪个汉字符合的原则更多，多者作为推荐用字。平行处理可能会出现几个异体字符合的原则一样多的情况，我们建议这个时候再对某一原则进行具体的加权。假如两个异体字符合的原则数目是一样的，但在某一原则如理据性或示音性上程度有别（譬如程度更高者用两个“√”表示），那么程度强者为推荐用字。如果是某两个原则之间存在差异（如A字符合C原则，B字符合D原则），则参考侯兴泉等（2014）提出的几点权衡意见：①对于使用频率接近的异体字，应优先考虑来源可征的字形；如果来源皆不可考，应优先考虑民众乐于接受的字形。②对于使用频率相差较大的异体字，应优先采用使用频率较高的字形。③对于同时有自造字和借用字的异体字，除非借用字使用频率非常高，一般情况下优先使用自造字。如果运用以上方法仍然难以取舍，将由规范小组组织小范围的抽样，选择其中一个认可度相对较高的字暂时作为推荐用字。过若干年后重新观察该异体字组的实际使用情况，若无变化则保持原状，若变化甚大则需重新挑选推荐用字。

平行处理还可能会出现某字虽然符合的原则总数不如另外一个异体字，但其通用性特别高，这时候就会出现选择出来的推荐字跟一般人的实际选择互相矛盾的情况，要是真有这种情况则可以考虑采用类似邓先生的分级加权法来处理。从目前我们收集和整理的粤方言异体字的情况来看，暂时还没有碰到这样的用例。

4　粤方言异体字规范例析

有了异体字的规范原则和具体的操作方法，我们就可以对每一组具体的异体字进行整理和规范了。下面我们将用列表的方式对几组较为典型的异体字组进行规范整理，选出推荐用字。在考察方言字通用性的时候，主要考察目前市面上通用的粤方言字词典、粤方言教科书、我们自建的100万字的广州话方言语料库，以及对应方言字在谷歌或百度上的出现频率。理据性方面主要参考《说文解字》、《广韵》、《集韵》和《康熙字典》等古代字书或韵书，尽量符合音义皆通的原则。其余几项标准详见王宁（1991）和邓景滨（2004）的说明。

4.1　“撳 gam^{6}［kɐm^{22}］”组异体字

粤方言表示“按、压”义的常见异体字有“撳”、“揿”、“搇”、“扲”和“揼”。其中“揼”是训读字，不大符合通用性、示音性、传承性、区别性等原则；“扲”字则不符合通用性、传承性和区别性原则（常作表“掏出”义读音为 ngam^{4}的方言字）；“搇”和“揿”字都不符合传承性。“撳”字除了示音性稍弱一点外，基本都符合异体字整理的八项原则，因此我们建议这一组的异体字的推荐用字为“撳”。在香港和澳门，一些人习惯用“揿”字，但在网络上，“撳”字的使用占了压倒性的优势。我们以“撳制”和“揿制”这组粤方言特色词组为检索词，通过谷歌搜索观察“撳”和“揿”这两个粤方言字在网络上的出现频率，截至2014年5月27日10点30分，“撳制”（含相应的繁体）约有8 770 000条结果；“揿制”约有89 400条结果。这个例子充分表明，在网络普及化的今天，研究字词的通用性不再是个难题，制定规范的时候一定要充分考虑老百姓的实际应用，否则专家选出的某些推荐用字可能会跟老百姓用双手“选”出的用字相差甚远。

表 1 “揿”组异体字规范整理表

异体字	通用性	示意性	示音性	传承性	简易性	操作性	区别性	系统性	推荐字
摁		√			√	√		√	
揿	√	√	√	√	√	√	√	√	揿
扲		√	√√		√	√		√	
搇		√	√		√	√	√	√	
㩒		√	√√		√	√	√	√	

4.2 “趷 gat^{6} [kɐt^{22}]”组异体字

粤方言中表“翘起、起身”义的常见异体字有“趷”、“趌”、“𧺟”和“跀”。“趷”、“趌”、“𧺟”在汉典、百度百科以及《广州话正音字典》中都被认为是粤方言字，而“跀”在汉典及《广州话正音字典》、《现代汉语词典》中则被视为“刖”的异体字。由于“跀”在通用性、示音性、传承性以及系统性方面都比较差，故推荐用字可以先排除此字。“𧺟”在通用性方面不如“趷”和“趌”。“趷”和“趌”基本上都符合除传承性以外的七项规范原则，不同的是“趷”的通用性要比“趌”强，“趷”字是目前市面流行的各类粤方言字词典以及教科书里面的常用字，故其在网络上的使用频率也要高于“趌”；但是“趌”的示音性要强于“趷”。这种情况下我们可根据“对于使用频率相差较大的异体字，应优先采用使用频率较高的字形”的取舍原则把“趷”作为该组异体字的推荐用字。

表 2 “趷”组异体字规范整理表

异体字	通用性	示意性	示音性	传承性	简易性	操作性	区别性	系统性	推荐字
趷	√√	√	√		√	√	√	√	趷
𧺟		√	√		√	√	√	√	
趌	√	√	√√		√	√	√	√	
跀		√			√	√	√		

4.3 “仲 zung^{6} [tsoŋ^{22}]”组异体字

表 3 “仲”组异体字规范整理表

异体字	通用性	示意性	示音性	传承性	简易性	操作性	区别性	系统性	推荐字
仲	√		√		√	√	√	√	仲
重			√	√	√	√		√	

粤方言中表示“还、再次”义的常用异体字是“重”和“仲”。这两字在示音性、简易性、操作性以及系统性方面都差不多，不同的是“重”是本字，但使用频率较低，“仲”虽是假借字，但是使用频率很高。另外“仲”字的区别性也要比“重”字高一些，譬如粤方言若是要表达“还来”意的时候，若是用“重”字，就有“还来”和“重新来”两种意思，用“仲”字就不会出现这样的歧义。综合起来，这组异体字的推荐用字应为“仲”。

4.4 “晒 saai^{3} [sai^{33}]”组异体字

表 4 “晒”组异体字规范整理表

异体字	通用性	示意性	示音性	传承性	简易性	操作性	区别性	系统性	推荐字
哂		√	√√		√	√	√√	√	
晒	√		√√		√√	√√	√	√	晒
嗮		√	√		√	√			

粤方言兼表“全部”和“完成”义的动态助词的常见异体字有“哂”、“晒”和“嗮”。其中“嗮”字在粤方言中多作为表“浪费”义的用字，故其区别性和系统性较差，而且通用性也不高。“晒”字在网络上的使用频率要远高于“哂”（估计跟“哂”字在电脑上输入没有“晒”方便有关），但由于“晒”字是假借字，故其区别性相对于自造字“哂”来说就差些（动态助词“晒”跟“晒”的本义与用法相差甚远，一般不会引起歧义）。“晒”字的简易性相对“哂”字来说稍微占优，但是“哂”字由于有“口”字旁作为类符，提示该字为口语常用自造字，故具备一定程度的示意性。由于两字各有优劣较难取舍，我们暂时根据通用性优先的取舍原则把“晒”字作为推荐字。

4.5 “噫 ji^{1} [i^{55}]”组异体字

表 5 “噫”组异体字规范整理表

异体字	通用性	示意性	示音性	传承性	简易性	操作性	区别性	系统性	推荐字
㖂		√	√		√		√	√	
齸		√	√				√	√	
噫（𠼮）		√	√	√			√	√	噫（𠼮）
齮		√	√				√	√	

粤方言表示“咧嘴、张开嘴笑”义的常见异体字有“㖂”、“噫（𠼮）”、“齸”、“齮”。这四个字在操作性和通用性方面都不是很好（“㖂”、“齸”和“噫”虽然都有 unicode 码，但由于其在 CKJ 字符集的扩展区，故一般的输入法也难以录入）。“齸”、和“齮”在传承性和简易性方面不如“㖂”和“噫（𠼮）”。“㖂”在简易性方面比“噫”好，但其传承性

不如“嚟”，因此在第一次整理的时候我们可以同时选出“㖭”和“嚟”作为推荐用字。不过“嚟”字对应的简体字“㗅”也符合简易性原则，加上“嚟”字为本字（见《集韵》），根据“对于使用频率接近的异体字，应优先考虑来源可征的字形”的整理意见，也应该优先立“嚟（㗅）”为推荐用字。《广州话正音字典》正是把“嚟（㗅）”看作正体，把“䶗”看作其异体字。

5 结 论

粤方言相比其他汉语方言而言，一个突出的特点是有比较系统的方言字以及以这些方言字为载体的文本资料。但由于缺乏必要的规范，粤方言一直都存在用字混乱的情况。在所有的用字问题中，异体字问题是最为突出的。众多的异体字给粤方言的信息化处理以及日常的教学和使用带来了诸多不便。因此，有必要对粤方言的异体字进行规范。本文重点讨论了粤方言异体字的规范原则和具体操作方法等问题，认为粤方言异体字的规范是提高粤方言信息化处理速度和效率的重要途径，对粤语的教学等应用也有重要的意义。

粤方言异体字的成因主要有四点：一是造字理据不同而导致的异体字；二是假借音同或音近的通用汉字造成的异体字；三是繁简并用造成的异体字；四是本字和自造字或假借字并用产生的异体字。根据粤方言异体字的成因以及前贤的意见我们确定了八项规范原则，即通用性、示意性、示音性、传承性、简易性、系统性、区别性、操作性，并在此基础上提出先平行处理后加权的操作方法，最后运用这些规范原则和方法对五组较为典型的异体字组进行举例分析。

粤方言异体字的整理和规范是一项繁重而富有意义的工作。本文重在原则和方法层面的讨论，在附录里面列举了我们初步整理出来的常用粤方言异体字对照表。希望我们的工作能进一步推动粤方言字的研究和应用。

附录：常见粤方言异体字音形义对照表（征求意见版）

字音（粤拼）	推荐字	异体字	字义
(ng)aak1	呃	詎（讵）阨	欺骗
(ng)aap3	押	壓 㗒 抏	按压、捆扎
(ng)aau1	撹	挍摷	抓，挠
(ng)aau3	詏	唷拗	争论，辩论
(ng)ai1	呃	嗚（呐）	恳求、哀求
(ng)ai3	翳	曀	湿热难耐的，心情压抑
(ng)am4	揞	捦拎	掏出，拉出
(ng)ap1	噏	喰 囉 嗗	说话

（续上表）

字音（粤拼）	推荐字	异体字	字义
(ng)ang^{2}	�béi	痩	撞伤
(ng)ap^{6}	砐	咠扱	点头
(ng)ung^{2}	挐	拢 攏 噏 搴	推
(ng)ok^{6}	頟（颚）	咢	抬，仰
bai^{6}	嘥	獘	糟糕，不好的，堕落的
bei^{2}	畀	俾比	给
beng^{3}	竮	啲	躲，藏
bo^{3}	噃	嚩	语气词，表示提醒，有时带有劝告意味
bou^{1}	煲	缶 爆	煮，饭罐/锅
bok^{1}	攴	撲	击打，敲打
buk^{6}	伏	蹼（卧）噗（卟）	伏倒，趴倒
caam^{5}	劖	劖	刺破，刺穿
caang^{1}	鐺（铛）	鎗	炒菜锅
caau^{1}	觘	犞觧	用角撞，牛～人
caau^{3}	摷	嘨吵	搜寻，搜查
cai^{3}	摕	𢯎	击打
cat^{6}	閂	屮	男性器官
ceoi^{4}	嚍	唷	气味
ceon^{1}	春	麯檎	蛋，卵
ci^{1}	黐	糍	粘，黏附
ci^{2}	欼	扯	用嘴或手把东西撕开或扯开
cik^{1}	摵	敊	拉起，提起
cing^{4}	埕	鋥	量词，坛或罐
cou^{5}	撸	搯	节约，节省
cok^{3}	剒	勸	用力拉扯
dak^{6}	杙	桊	木桩
dam^{6}	跌	蹗	跺脚
dam^{4}，tam^{4}	氹	凼躭	～～转
dam^{3}	髧	缐嚓	下垂，放下，掉下
dam^{2}	扰	搽	击打，捶打，扔下
dan^{3}	扽	撴震	重重地往下放，通过震动使其减少空间
dap^{1}	聕	嗒	低（头）

（续上表）

字音（粤拼）	推荐字	异体字	字义
dap^{6}	湁	搭揼哋㖸	打湿，敲打
dat^{1}	咄	嗟	反驳，指责
dat^{1}	揬	咄	塞，坐
deng^{6}	埞	矴	地方，阻~
deoi^{2}	搥	㨃（㧞）㩀（㧢）掛（𢭃）𢭏捽懟	戳，刺，伸出
deoi^{3}	腿	嚉	肿胀，形容词
dau^{3}	鬥（斗）	鬬	拼合、对准
dau^{3}	窦	荳㖈	巢，窝
dau^{3}	逗	𠹌（吽）挍	逗，抚摸
dim^{6}	掂	啱𠹻	垂直的，好了，用手指捡起，动词完成体标记
diu^{2}	屌	閅	性交，骂人话
duk^{1}	督	笃𧀂	一泡尿的“泡”，量词
duk^{1}	豚	启𡲰𠮨笃	底部，尽头
duk^{1}	㧻	擉（㩳）豛	戳，刺
faak^{3}	拃	𢴪	鞭打，甩，拂
fing^{6}	揈	拼𧞕	摇晃，摆动，丢掉
gaa^{3}	㗎	嘎嚗（噶）	“嘅啊”的合音
gaai^{3}	鎅（锞）	剘摵	用刀或剪裁开、锯开
gaan^{3}	间	㮙 撊（搁）	有间隔地划分
gaang^{3}	浭	踁挭	涉、蹚过
gaau^{3}	滘	漖	河流的分岔口，多用于地名
gam^{2}	噉	咁	那，那么
gam^{6}	撳	揿搇扲撍	按、压
gang^{2}	哽	梗	当然
gap^{6}	眍	眏眣（嗑）	盯着看，偷看
gau^{1}	㞗	鸠閄	男性器官
gau^{6}	嚿（咱）	㕮嗒	团、块，量词
gat^{6}	趷	趌趌趷𨀤（𧼮）	起身，翘起
geng^{6}	撽	儆嚐𢢔	看住，防备，留意
git^{6}	滐	㗬	浓、稠

（续上表）

字音（粤拼）	推荐字	异体字	字义
gui^{6}	攰	癐噲（哙）蹶（跻）	累，筋疲力尽
gwaa^{3}	啩	啩	疑问语气词，表推测
haa^{1}	蝦（虾）	嘏廝	欺负
haau^{4}	姣	姣	妖媚
hai^{1}	閪	閪女屌	女性器官
hau^{1}	睺	睺	看住，盯紧
ham^{6}	冚	唅嘁冚	所有，全部，整个
ham^{6}	冚	唅峉	盖，关紧
ham^{2}	揿	揿	敲击，撞击
hang^{4}	揯	揯	绷紧，快速转动
hing^{3}	熒	燛（烘）	热，形容词
hong$^{6/2}$	项	檺	未下蛋的母鸡
jaang^{3}	蹲	躍（躍）踭蹔（蹬）	用脚蹭、踢、踩
jaap^{3}	厴	揞	折起，卷起
jai^{5}	曳	吟	淘气，差劲
jan^{6}	屻	峹峹	尖锐的
ji^{1}	囈（呓）	齕齸咦	咧嘴，张开嘴笑
jik^{1}	膱	膉	油脂食物变坏的味道
jim^{2}	靨	黶黶（黡）	痂，伤口愈合后血凝结成的硬壳
juk^{1}	哪	逌鬱（郁）	动
jyn^{5}	蘧（莚）	薾（菸）	菜茎
kak^{1}	搉	趷㨇喀	卡，绊
kam^{1}	啉	昖	持久、耐用
kam^{2}	冚	唅掹蠒唫㩒	盖
kap^{6}	㧡	啞齡（龄）扱	咬
kap^{1}	擨（掇）	扱	盖，按
ke^{1}	椰	屙	婴儿屎，烂屎
kiu^{2}	巧	噏篙（笳）	巧合，碰巧
laa^{2}	揦	擸揸	用手抓
laai^{6}	攋	嚹	放下，丢下，遗漏
laang^{1}	氄	冷	毛线
laap^{3}	擸	妠	收集，聚拢，抓取

（续上表）

字音（粤拼）	推荐字	异体字	字义
laap^{3}	䁽	擸𥄫	扫视，浏览
lai^{2}	𢡎	𡃍（𠯿）	训斥，诽谤，扭伤
lai^{6}	矋	𥌃覼	怒视
lam^{1}	菻	冧	花蕾，花骨朵
lam^{3}	冧	𡋿𣿛	倒塌
lei^{4}，lai^{4}	嚟	𡅏来	来，到
lek^{1}	叻	呖𡅅（唠）	聪明，有能力
leng^{1}	𫢗（𫢶）	𠾵篓	小年轻，偏贬义
leoi^{1}	𨁋	𨃀	突然倒下或跌倒
leon^{1}	嶙	啱𩞄（饹）	咀嚼、吮吸骨头
lip^{1}	𨋢（𫐎）	𡅼	电梯
lo^{3}	燶（㶸）	氌（氇）	烟熏味
long^{2}	哴	㨴𣻹㖫	漱（口）
luk^{6}	渌（渌）	熝（炉）㷻	用热水或蒸汽烫
man^{3}	呡	𠍳𡢃（㜷）㗂	边缘，结束，最后时刻
mak$^{6/2}$	𤺥	𦢊瘼	痦子，突起的痣
mang^{1}	掹	掤擝	拔出
mau^{1}	踎	蹘蹀	蹲，待着
me^{2}	孭	㖡歪	歪
me^{1}	孭	揹𡥧（孭）㜷	背
mei^{6}	沬	沕	潜（水）
mei^{1}	蜫	蝞	塘~，蜻蜓
mei^{1}	瞇	咪瞶（眎）	眯，闭
mui$^{2/4}$	燘	㖄酶	烂，熟
naa^{1}	揇	嗱瘩	和，跟
naa^{1}	㾞	瘩	伤疤
naa^{2}	乸	毑	母，母性
naat^{3}	焫	爇炼	热，烫
nam^{4}	腍	煁焓淰	软，透，烂熟，柔弱
nang^{3}	𧙚	紧𠹌揇	连接，联系，包括
nap^{6}	粒	湆粒涊	粘，不平滑，缓慢
nau^{1}	嬲	獳嬲	生气

（续上表）

字音（粤拼）	推荐字	异体字	字义
n/li^{1}	呢	哩	这
nin^{1}	脌	犁奶	乳房，奶
ning^{1}	拧	擰搵擰	拿，带
nung^{1}	燶（炆）	黷黰	用手扭或摩擦
paang^{1}	捹	嘭揼搒	驱赶，追捕
pai^{1}	刿	剘	用刀削，剥
pau^{3}	婄	婷	松软；泡，不结实
pok^{1}	朴	皺	有勇气，大胆
pung^{1}	埲	埲埲	像尘土一样随风扬起
saai^{1}	嘥	揌漇	浪费
saai^{3}	晒	哂嘥	结构助词，表全部完成
saang^{2}	揝	碜啱	冲，擦，责骂
saap^{3}	烚	嚶躍烚叼	不成词语素，争论，反对。如~气
saap^{6}	焗	烿熬	在热水里煮
saau^{4}	睄	瞞	眼光掠过，匆匆一看
sek^{3}	啱（嚼）	鍚（鍚）	喜欢，疼爱，亲吻
sin^{3}	剷	刬	阉
sin^{3}	蹁	瑞碥砭	滑落，滑倒
sip^{3}	攝	褌片妾	（席子）底下，垫，塞（片状物）
taai^{1}	呔	袪	领带，是英语 tie 的音译词
taai^{5}	舦	艜	船舵
taan^{3}	嘆（叹）	賧鏫	享受，赚钱
tam^{3}	氹	氹諃（谭）言凼	愚弄，哄骗，劝诱，讨好
tan^{3}	趰	迺	移动，转移，后退
tap^{1}	佮	黏嗱	对准，拼合
tau^{2}	唞	蚪嘇敨敨	休息
waa^{2}	搲	揓	抓，手指或爪抓
wat^{1}	煀	爩	用烟熏
wo^{5}	喎（㖞）	㗻（㖞）咊	语气词，表示转告别人的意见
zaam^{2}	嚒（嘶）	嘶（嘶）	眨眼
zaang^{1}	睜（睁）	睜（睁）	欠
zaang^{1}	踭	腈（静）	脚跟

（续上表）

字音（粤拼）	推荐字	异体字	字义
zai^{3}	啸	[illegible]嚌（哜）	做或干，愿意
zai^{6}	滞	嚌	动态助词，太过的标记
zat^{1}	揑	[illegible]	塞，挤
ze^{1}	啫	脽	语气词，表示不过如此
zi^{1}	[illegible]	[illegible]螆	虱子，寄生虫，疥虫
zit^{1}	[illegible]（[illegible]）	瀄乳[illegible]	挤出
zo^{2}	咗	[illegible]	完结，结束
zoe^{1}	脽	啫	小孩子的阳物
zong^{1}	睵	[illegible]	偷看，偷窥

参考文献

邓景滨　2004　《粤方言字的优化》，《澳门研究》第 24 期，第 192 ~ 203 页。

董月凯、邓景滨　2011　《优化汉字：汉字统一的必由之路》，第六届海峡两岸现代汉语问题学术研讨会论文，澳门理工学院。

郭敏珊　2008　《谈谈粤语方言字在使用中的问题》，《广东工业大学学报》（社会科学版）第 4 期，第 71 ~ 73 页。

侯兴泉、彭志峰、钟奇、彭小川　2014　《面向中文信息处理的粤方言字规范刍议》，《语言教学与研究》第 4 期，第 107 ~ 112 页。

王　宁　1991　《汉字的优化与简化》，《中国社会科学》第 1 期，第 69 ~ 80 页。

韦树关　1997　《粤语方言字刍议》，《广西民族学院学报》（哲学社会科学版）第 2 期，第 109 ~ 121 页。

魏　励编　2014　《语言文字规范手册》，北京：商务印书馆国际有限公司。

詹伯慧　2003　《关于方言词的用字问题——以粤方言为例》，载于《漫步语坛的第三个脚印：汉语方言与语言应用论集》，广州：暨南大学出版社，第 90 ~ 106 页。

詹伯慧　2008　《粤语研究与粤语应用》，《学术研究》第 10 期，第 127 ~ 131 页。

周无忌　2003　《粤方言用字应予以规范》，载于《第六届国际粤方言研讨会论文集》，澳门：澳门中国语文学会，第 7 ~ 9 页。

Cheung Kwan-hin，Robert S. Bauer　2002　The representation of Cantonese with Chinese characters. *Journal of Chinese Linguistics*，Monograph Series Number 18.

香港粤语亲属称谓与拟亲属称谓的变调规律

黄炳蔚[1]　李深红[2]　左霭云[3]

（1 东华学院；2、3 香港公开大学）

提　要：香港粤语亲属称谓的变调，以高升变调为主，其次为高平变调，低变调则较少。高升变调的音节，原调多是阳去调，而阳平调较少；低变调主要出现于叠音词的第一个音节，或者一些双音节拟亲属称谓词的第二个音节。粤语亲属称谓词以双音节为主，可以分为叠词与非叠词两种。前者以变调的称谓词为主，而后者较少变调，要变调的话，通常位于第二个音节。亲属称谓的变调跟字调、字义、词的结构有关，情况复杂，具体规律还有待进一步探析。

关键词：亲属称谓　拟亲属称谓　变调

1　香港粤语的声调

香港粤语有九种声调，本文用粤拼标示声调，简化为1~6调号。入声以音高、调值论，可归入1，3，6三个调号。其韵母的塞音已表明入声，不必另以7，8，9调号标示（见表1）。粤语的阴平可分为高降（53）和高平（55）两种，现时香港年轻人大多只念高平调，还有念高平和高降二调的，多属于自由变体（free variation）。

表1　香港粤语的声调

调名	调值	粤拼调号	调名	调值	粤拼调号
阴平	55/53	1	阴入	55	1
阴上	25/35	2			
阴去	33	3	中入	33	3
阳平	21/11	4			
阳上	13/23	5			
阳去	22	6	阳入	22	6

阴入也称为上阴入，中入也称为下阴入。有些粤音系统在标调时会以双/单个数字表示入声韵腹的长/短，例如袁家骅等（1983），就以韵腹长短来区分上阴入和下阴入，见

(1)。这种是概括划分两种阴入的方法，本文的研究并无区分这种特征的必要，因此不打算讨论这些细节。

(1) 上阴入：5　　下阴入：33　　阳入：22/2

变调的调值

粤语有三种变调，均可以出现于舒声和入声中，分别为：①高平变调（调值55）；②高升变调（调值25）；③低变调（调值21，11）。它们的调值分别跟阴平、阴上、阳平相若，因此本文以粤拼调号1，2，4表示。①

粤语的入声变调有两种，高平变调的调值跟阴入相若，而高升变调跟阴上声相若（见表2的"→"位置）。粤语本有三种入声，即粤拼调号1，3，6。高升变调的入声，黄大方（1989）称之为"新入声"，即"第十调"。李新魁等（1995）、麦耘（2000）描述的声调系统，也包括新入声。本文采用粤拼系统，把新入声标注为2号声调，跟阴上声无异。

表2　香港粤语入声的调值

调名	调值	粤拼调号
阴入	55	1
→	25	2
中入	33	3
—	—	—
—	—	—
阳入	22	6

2　香港粤语的亲属称谓语

前人的研究收集了丰富的变调词例（例如 Bauer & Benedict，1997），当中以名词为最多，也包括一些亲属称谓语的例子。在日常交际中经常用到亲属称谓语，但过往的研究只是简单道出其变调规律，而对低变调规律的说明稍嫌简略，更少提及拟亲属称谓语的变调。因此，本文打算在这方面作初步的探析。

麦耘（2000）认为，名词变调可以划分为四类：①名词性标志；②小称标志；③特指

① 高华年（1980）、袁家骅等（1983）认为，高平变调比阴平调略高，而高升变调比阴上调稍微提高一点。可是，现时香港粤语的高平变调跟阴平调实难以分辨，调值均可标注为55。高升变调与阴上调也相若，因此调值都可标注为25。

标志等；④音译外来词的变调。亲属称谓的变调，属于小称标志。

2.1 亲属称谓

就构词法来说，香港粤语只有少量单音节亲属称谓语（如“仔”、“女”、“侄”等），而大多数是双音节词。虽然有一些三音节称谓语，但主要是在双音节词的基础上发展而来的，对变调规律的影响较少，因此本文主要还是集中研究双音节词。[①]有一部分“拟亲属称谓语”（见 2.2）本身就是三音节的，如“伯爷公”等有特定的变调形式，本文会在 3.2.2.4 节讨论这种现象。

双音节亲属称谓语可分为叠词类和非叠词类两种，后者还可细分为附加类（前缀“阿”、后缀“仔”）和复合类（联合、偏正）。

2.1.1 叠词类亲属称谓

叠词类称谓语有表示亲昵的作用，源于儿语，故划分为小称标志（麦耘，2000），词例有爸爸、妈妈、哥哥、姐姐、叔叔、姨姨、婆婆等。

2.1.2 非叠词类亲属称谓

大多数亲属称谓词都是非叠词类的，而且大部分不能变调，当中能够变调的词例，例如家姐、三姨，是复合类的偏正结构；又如阿姨、姨仔，是附加类的前缀、后缀类别。当中，“仔”属于小称标志，但变调词例并不多。

2.2 拟亲属称谓

拟亲属称谓是指以亲属的称谓语称呼没有血缘关系的人，把他们当作亲属般对待。从词语结构模式概括分类，可以分为直接用亲属称谓语和“姓/名 + 亲属称谓”结构两种。

2.2.1 直接用亲属称谓语

我们可以直接用亲属称谓语称呼别人，以表示亲昵，例如我们用“哥哥”称呼比自己年长的男子，以“姐姐”称呼比自己年长的女子。我们还可用“细佬”或“弟弟”（di^{4} di^{2}）称呼足以作为自己幼儿的男孩，可用“妹妹”（$mui^{6\text{-}4}$ $mui^{6\text{-}2}$）[②]称呼足以作为自己幼女的女孩，这样听起来颇为亲切。在家庭中，家长往往从幼儿的角度去称呼各成员，因此父母也会把长子称为哥哥，把长女称为姐姐。如家里聘用了女佣，则会从幼儿角度称她为“姐姐”。这种称谓让小孩觉得女佣也颇亲近，感到大家都是一家人。

“姐姐”的变调作用相对复杂一点。这种叠词主要是“低变调 + 高平变调”（如“$ze^{2\text{-}4}$

---

① 三音节亲属称谓语，例如“堂阿哥、堂细佬、表姨妈、表姨丈”等，其结构均是以双音节词为基础，再在前面加“堂”、“表”之类的修饰语。有些三音节称谓语加了表示排名的修饰语，例如“大、三、四”等，形成了“大表哥、三表弟、四表妹”等称谓。另有一些三、四音节的称谓语，如“三兄妹、两母子、兄弟姐妹”，属于组合称谓语，指涉多个人，只用于背称。其实上述粤语称谓语，如果出现变调，并不会因为多或少了“堂、表、大、三”等字而有所影响，因此本文不打算详列这些细节。不过，有一种三音节称谓语，其结构跟上述情形不同，例如“表妹夫”，是在“表妹”的基础上再加语素“夫”。这对变调有一定影响，其相关讨论见于本文的 3.2.2.4 节部分。

② 本文的标调方式是先标原调，再标变调，两者以“-”分隔。“6-4”是指调号 6 为原调，而调号 4 是变调。“6-2”指调号 6 为原调，而调号 2 是变调。

$ze^{2\text{-}1}$”）的形式，用法多是敬称，有亲昵意味。就一些观察所得，例如有些电视节目会邀请一些女性长者做节目嘉宾，主持人身为后辈，多称呼她们为“姐姐”（$ze^{2\text{-}4}$ $ze^{2\text{-}1}$），既表示尊敬又显得亲切。近日笔者听到有低变调叠词“姐姐”（$ze^{2\text{-}4}$ $ze^{2\text{-}4}$）的用法，作为女佣的背称，以“ze^{4} ze^{4}”清楚表明是“女佣”，有别于亲属“姐姐”（$ze^{2\text{-}4}$ $ze^{2\text{-}1}$），这种似是蔑称，有关系较疏远的意味。

2.2.2 “姓/名 + 亲属称谓”结构

香港人常用“姓/名 + 亲属称谓”结构作拟亲属称谓。刚才提及的“姐姐”，前面就可以加一个工作类别名称，例如“工人姐姐$_{\text{女佣}}$”，或者加上名字，例如“Maria 姐姐”等。这类多音节称谓语属于词组结构。另外，有些组合是合成词，以两音节为主，例如表 3 的“蓉姐、陈伯”等，这些大多是用来称呼长辈的用语。它们还可以加前缀，例如“阿蓉姐”、“阿陈伯”。名字方面，可以单音节或双音节。单音节的姓或名，有时用变调，例如表 3 的“陈”字和“棠”字，但通常用原调，例如“强”字。亲属称谓部分大多是单音节，但也可以是双音节，如“婆婆”（po^{4} $po^{4\text{-}2}$）、“姨姨”（$ji^{4\text{-}1}$ $ji^{4\text{-}1}$）等。

表 3 “姓/名 + 亲属称谓”结构的词例

姓/名	亲属称谓（单音节）	注
蓉	姐	“姐”（$ze^{2\text{-}1}$）高平变调，但也可用原调（ze^{2}）
强	哥	没变调
棠	哥	“棠”（$tong^{4\text{-}2}$）高升变调
陈	伯	“陈”（$can^{4\text{-}2}$）高升变调

2.2.3 变调的别义作用

拟亲属称谓除了表亲昵义外，也可表蔑称义，两者都属小称变调。小称表示“小、少”之义，所以可引申出“微小、次要、轻视”之义（詹伯慧，2002）。如表 4 所示：

表 4 蔑称义的拟亲属称谓词例

亲属称谓	后缀	注
姐（$ze^{2\text{-}1}$）	仔	年轻女艺员，一般地位不高
妹（$mui^{6\text{-}1}$）	仔	婢女
伯父（fu^{6-2}）		老头儿

在拟亲属称谓中，变调的语素往往有别义作用。例如“姐”（ze^{2}）读原调（阴上）时，有“姐姐”的意义，大都是敬称。“姐”读高平变调时，则有别义作用，是拟亲属称谓，是对“女士”的一种称呼，可以敬称长辈或有相当地位的女士，例如“Liza 姐”是对艺人 Liza（汪明荃）的尊称。另一个尊称是“阿姐”（$ze^{2\text{-}1}$）。但“阿姐”也有贬称的

用法，如有网民用“榴梿阿姐”或“榴梿姐”来称呼一名女士，因为她在港铁车厢中吃榴梿，实有对其不顾公德行为之不满。也有网民用“厚多士姐”① 来指一名女士因维护在车厢内进食的幼子，而与旁边的女乘客对骂，当中的“姐”均有贬义，表达出香港人对一些不顾公德之人的不满。

“仔”是小称后缀，含“微小、年轻”等意义，词根“姐”（ze$^{2-1}$）加上“仔”之后，意义上“姐”的地位就降低了。例如，电视台的所谓“姐仔”是指“年轻女艺员”，地位较低，远不及“阿姐”的崇高地位。

“妹”原调读阳去（调号6），是“妹妹”的本义；读高升变调（调号2），例如“阿妹”(mui$^{6-2}$)，也是“妹妹”之意。高平变调（调号1）有别义作用，读作“妹”(mui$^{6-1}$)，多有贬义，例如“妹仔”是“婢女”之义；“肥妹仔”是“肥胖的女孩”。

“伯父”一词，若“父”（fu^{6}）读原调时，本义是“父亲的哥哥”；但若读阴上变调，读成“伯父”（fu$^{6-2}$），则是“老头儿”之意，是对年长男子的蔑称。

3 分析

从声调来说，粤语变调以高升变调出现的机会较多，其次是高平变调（张励妍，1986），而低变调出现的情况很少。变调本质上属于口语现象，随着口语音势力的扩展，语素变调已渗透到书面语层次了。（麦耘，2000）

3.1 低变调

过往的研究认为（如 Matthews & Yip，2011；麦耘，2000），低变调只限于叠音的亲属称谓语的第一个音节，例如表5的叠音词。以下亲属称谓，口语使用上都用变调，但书面语用读书音的话，仍可念原调（Matthews & Yip，2011）。

表5 叠音亲属称谓语第一音节有低变调的词例

叠音亲属称谓语	读音
姐姐	ze$^{2-4}$ ze$^{2-1}$
弟弟	dai$^{6-4}$ dai$^{6-2}$
妹妹	mui$^{6-4}$ mui$^{6-2}$
爸爸	baa$^{1-4}$ baa^{1}
妈妈	maa$^{1-4}$ maa^{1}

3.1.1 非叠音词类的低变调

上述概括似有不足之处。其实，低变调还可以出现于非叠音词的第二个音节，例如：

① “厚多士”是“好多事”之谐音，是指某人多管闲事之意。

“阿爸”（aa^{3} baa$^{1-4}$）中的“爸”读低变调（阳平）；
“大姐”（daai^{6} ze$^{2-4}$）中的“姐”读低变调（阳平）；
“叻哥”（lek^{1} go$^{1-4}$）中的“哥”可读阴平原调或低变调；
“菊姐”（guk^{1} ze$^{2-4}$）中的“姐”可读高平变调或低变调；①
“梅姐”（mui$^{4-1}$ ze$^{2-4}$）中的“姐”可读高平变调或低变调。

“阿爸、大姐”是亲属称谓。“叻哥、菊姐、梅姐”均是拟亲属称谓，以下再多举一些例子：

（2）~哥（go$^{1-4}$）：辉哥、标哥、嘉哥
（3）~姐（ze$^{2-4}$）：心姐、卿姐、姗姐、英姐、明（ming$^{4-1}$）姐

以上（2）、（3）例都是双音节词，结构都是从名字中取个单字（通常是最后一个字），再加“姐/哥”。如果名字取用两个字，“姐”就不可以使用低变调，例如（4）a，而必须用原调或高平变调，如（4）b。“哥”字情况相若，名字如有两个字，“哥”不可以低变调，如（5）a，而必须用原调，如（5）b。

（4）a. ＊雪心姐（syut^{3} sam^{1} ze$^{2-4}$）
　　b. 雪心姐（syut^{3} sam^{1} ze^{2}/ze$^{2-1}$）
（5）a. ＊明辉哥（ming^{4} fai^{1} go$^{1-4}$）
　　b. 明辉哥（ming^{4} fai^{1} go^{1}）

这类结构有另一个限制，就是名字一般要读阴平或阴入声（粤拼调号1）才行。例如（6）和（7），“才”和“明”都是阳平声，两者均不可以跟低变调的“哥/姐”配搭，见（6）a和（7）a，它们只可跟高平调的“哥/姐”搭配，如（6）b和（7）b所示。“明”字作名字称谓，容许读高平变调，但必须变调后，才可以跟低变调的“姐”搭配，如(7)b。“才”字作名字称谓并不容许高平变调，因此它不能跟低变调的“哥/姐”搭配。

（6）a. ＊才哥（coi^{4} go$^{1-4}$）
　　b. 才哥（coi^{4}go^{1}）
（7）a. ＊明姐（ming^{4} ze$^{1-4}$）
　　b. 明姐（ming^{4} ze$^{2-1}$）/（ming^{4} ze^{2}）
（8）a. Ming^{1}姐（ming^{1} ze^{1}）
　　b. Ming^{1}姐（ming^{1}ze^{4}）

① “姐”如读原调阴上，也可以指中国女佣“马姐”（maa^{5} ze^{2}），她们身穿白衣黑裤，多来自广东顺德。例如，有一出电影《桃姐》，讲述的就是一名叫“桃姐”的女佣。这个词的结构就是“名字+‘姐’”的形式。名字多数取单字，但变调的情况不多。以“桃”字为例，人们多数读原调阳平声，但也有人读高升变调［tou$^{4-2}$］。其他阳平声的字多数不能变调，如“明姐”（ming^{4} ze^{2}）中的“明”就不可以。这种变调现象似乎只适用于个别单字，很难归纳出一些类推规则作解释。

另一种涉及低变调的结构是“~爸”。其能产性不高，也必须是双音节词，现在似只有“组爸（baa$^{1-4}$）”一词可用，它指“大学迎新营中负责带组的师兄”，负责照料其组员（即“组仔”、“组女”）。迎新营还有“组妈”一词，指“负责照料其组员的师姐”，但“妈”不容许变调。“妈”（maa^{1}）如果低变调为“maa^{4}”，就会跟“嫲”（maa^{4}，即祖母）字相混，引起误解，故不可行。

3.1.2 拟亲属称谓语的低变调或受外来语影响

低变调可出现于非叠音类双音节拟亲属称谓词的第二个音节，而香港一些地名，如“铜锣湾”、“长沙湾”等三音节词，“湾”可读 waan$^{1-4}$低变调。这类低变调在香港并不常用，但在四邑方言中，低变调是十分普遍的。了解四邑的变调情况，也许会有助于我们了解香港粤语的低变调。①据甘于恩（2010），四邑话早期的变调有低调和升调两种类型，当这两种类型使用过后，由于语义引申的需要，新义须考虑改用高变调，但它还在发展中，能产性还比较低。例如，亲属称谓“大姨”（ji^{22}）读本调，“阿姨”（ji^{11}）（母亲的妹妹）读低变调。②以“姨”称呼年轻女性，读高平变调（ji^{55}），这类拟亲属称谓词，是借入广州话词汇的较新用法。另一种变调是低变调后再变作升调，从 11 变为 115，用在序数词之后，表示亲昵，如“二姨”（ji^{115}）。若探究声调的对应关系，广州话 ji$^{11\text{或}21}$（即粤拼的第 4 声调），对应于四邑（开平）话的 ji^{22}；广州话 ji$^{55\text{或}53}$（即粤拼的第 1 声调），对应于四邑（开平）话的 ji^{33}。而四邑话“妈妈”、“爸爸”、“哥哥”的第二音节读高平变调 55（即粤拼的第 1 声调），是借入了广州话词汇，并标明是新词。从“呔”（taai^{55}）（即粤拼第 1 声调）一类的外来词例，可推断高平调是一种借入的“新变调”。

甘于恩（2010）认为，四邑方言固有词的词义引申，大多采用低调和升调的变调形式，只有在低调变调和升调变调都用过之后，才可能采用高调变调，这种变调往往是借入了外来新词。换个角度看香港粤语，其变调并没有四邑话那么丰富，但也有一个共同点。香港粤语主要用高平和高升变调，低变调（双音节词的第二个音节）是较新的变调形式，很可能也是引入外来语，有标示外来名词的作用。③ 香港粤语的亲属称谓有少量如“爹哋”（daddy）、“妈咪”（mommy）等音译外来亲属称谓语词。④其英语源词的第一个音节是重音，转译为粤语时多用阴平调，第二个音节并非重音，多数转译为粤语阳平调，例如表 6 的“哋”和“咪”，就是阳平调。

---

① 感谢匿名审稿者指出，广东四邑话有普遍的低变调现象。本文尝试参考这方面的资料作分析，但难免存在一些问题，这概由本人负责。

② 本文是用调值标示四邑话声调的，标示香港粤语声调则主要用粤拼调号。

③ 本文在第十八届国际粤方言研讨会（2013 年 12 月 7—8 日，香港）宣读时，惠蒙姚玉敏博士等学者对粤语亲属称谓的低变调现象提出意见，本人谨致谢忱。

④ 粤语还会直接用英语词“Uncle”、“Auntie”作称谓，年轻人尤为常用。这类词算作夹杂入粤语的英语词，不是音译外来词。

表 6　外来语亲属称谓词

称谓词	声调
爹哋（de^{1} di^{4}）	1 + 4
妈咪（maa^{1} mi^{4}）	1 + 4

这种“声调 1 + 4”的称谓词在日常生活中经常用到，但现时只限于对父母的称谓。香港年轻人很喜欢使用英语称谓或外来语称谓，同侪之间尤爱用英文名字称呼，感觉亲近；甚至用外来语称呼父母，也习以为常。这种“声调 1 + 4”的称谓形式，或会影响到拟亲属称谓词，从而衍生出更多的“声调 1 + 4”词语。综合上述的双音节亲属称谓和拟亲属称谓，其第二音节有低变调的组合，都只限于很亲近的家庭成员，并且是用于对长辈的称呼，前者是对父母的称谓，后者则有“哥、姐、爸”，把非亲属如亲人一样称呼，有表示亲近的作用。

3.2　亲属称谓变调的构词分析

以上部分讨论了低变调的问题，以下再回到亲属称谓的构词分析。香港粤语有六个单音节亲属称谓词，见表 7。

表 7　单音节亲属称谓词

称谓	声韵	原调	变调	词义
女	neoi	5	2	女儿
妹	mui	6	2	妹妹
侄	zat	6	2	侄儿
仔	zai	2	—	儿子
孙	syun	1	—	孙子
息（sak^{1}）	sak	1	—	曾孙

单音节亲属称谓词“仔”、“孙”、“息”（sak^{1}）可独立使用，也可以出现于句（9）的句构中。“女”（$neoi^{5}$）、“妹”（mui^{6}）、“侄”（zat^{6}）如读原调（书面读音），就不可以单独用于口语的称谓词，见（10）a。它们只能被视为语素，必须跟另一语素组成合成词，才可以独立使用，例如“女婿”、“妹夫”、“侄女”，正如（11）a ~ c 所示，要高升变调才可以独立使用，详见（10）b。

（9）我有一个______。［词例：<u>仔</u>（zai^{2}）、<u>孙</u>（$syun^{1}$）、<u>息</u>（sak^{1}）］

（10）a. * 我有一个______。［词例：<u>女</u>（$neoi^{5}$）、<u>妹</u>（mui^{6}）、<u>侄</u>（zat^{6}）］

　　　b. 我有一个______。［词例：<u>女</u>（$neoi^{5\text{-}2}$）、<u>妹</u>（$mui^{6\text{-}2}$）、<u>侄</u>（$zat^{6\text{-}2}$）］

（11）a. 我有一个<u>女</u>婿（<u>neoi</u>^{5} sai^{3}）。

b. 我有一个妹夫（mui[6] fu[1]）。

c. 我有一个侄女（zat[6] neoi[5-2]）。

3.2.1 叠词类亲属称谓

香港粤语的单音节亲属称谓语并不多，大多数是双音节的。双音节可以分为叠词类和非叠词类两种。后者可再细分为附加类（前缀“阿”、后缀“仔”）和复合类（联合、偏正）。

3.2.1.1 变调：调号前4后1

表8列出叠词类亲属称谓有变调的词例。以下各词，其原调大都是阴平调的，只是“姐姐”不同，属于阴上调。它们的变调模式一样，调号前4后1（见表8）。口语一般常用的是变调，读原调的是书面读音。

表8　叠词类亲属称谓变调：调号前4后1

称谓	声韵	原调	变调
爸爸	baa baa	1 1	4 1
妈妈	maa maa	1 1	4 1
哥哥	go go	1 1	4 1
姐姐	ze ze	2 2	4 1
公公	gung gung	1 1	4 1

3.2.1.2 变调：调号前4后2

另一种变调模式是调号前4后2，详见表9。表9的词中，“奶奶”、“仔仔”、“女女”都不能读原调，而只能读变调。其他词一般是原调、变调均可使用，原调是书面读音，变调是口语读音，也是较常用的读音。这类词的特色是，原调多数是4～6号的阳声调。唯一例外的是“仔仔”，原调是阴上调，第二音节不需作高升变调。

表9　叠词类亲属称谓变调：调号前4后2

称谓	声韵	原调①	变调	词义
婆婆	po po	4 4	4 2	外婆
奶奶	naai naai	* 5 5	4 2	婆婆
弟弟	dai dai	6 6	4 2	弟弟
妹妹	mui mui	6 6	4 2	妹妹
仔仔	zai zai	* 2 2	4 2	儿子
女女	neoi neoi	* 5 5	4 2	女儿
爷爷	je je	4 4	4 2	祖父

① 在表9中，加*表示不合语法。此符号的标注含义也适用于表10～表12。

比较表 8 和表 9 可知，只要原调不是阴平，叠词大多会采用调号前 4 后 2 的模式。唯一不符合此规律的称谓语是“姐姐”，它是由原调［ze^{2} ze^{2}］变调为［ze^{4} ze^{1}］。其原因可能是，“姐”作为双音节词（非叠音类）的后一音节，例如“阿姐”，是读［ze^{1}］的，叠音词的后一音节读［ze^{1}］，正与这种模式相契合。

3.2.1.3　其他规律

此外，有两个叠词称谓语与上述两种变调模式稍有不同（见表 10）。“太太”、“姨姨”的第一音节变调，并不是 4 号声调，而分别是 3 号和 1 号声调，不过第二音节跟上述 3.2.1.1 和 3.2.1.2 所说的模式一样，都是变调为 2 号或 1 号声调。这里第二音节的声调和 3.2.2.1 附加式“阿 –”的一样，如“阿太”（taai$^{3\text{-}2}$）、“阿姨”（ji$^{4\text{-}1}$）。两种模式似是相关的。

表 10　叠词类亲属称谓变调：其他模式

称谓	声韵	原调	变调	词义
太太	taai taai	*3 3	3 2	太太
姨姨	ji ji	*4 4	1 1	阿姨

另有四个叠音称谓语不能变调，分别为“叔叔”（suk^{1} suk^{1}）、“婶婶”（sam^{2} sam^{2}）、“嫲嫲”（maa^{4} maa^{4}）、“伯伯”（baak^{3} baak^{3}），数量并不多。当中，“叔”和“婶”分别是高平调和高升调，难有空间变调并升为更高的声调。

叠词类亲属称谓语源于儿语（motherese）。香港儿语的叠词，如“船船”（syun^{4} syun$^{4\text{-}2}$）、“牛牛”（ngau^{4} ngau$^{4\text{-}2}$）、“面面”（min$^{6\text{-}1}$ min$^{6\text{-}1}$）、“毛毛”（mou^{4} mou$^{4\text{-}1}$）等，其变调规律是，如果第二个音节是高升变调，调号则用前 4 后 2 式；如果第二个音节是高平变调，调号则用前 4 后 1 式或前 1 后 1 式。当中也有一些不变调的例子，如“菜菜”（coi^{3} coi^{3}）、“饭饭”（faan^{3} faan^{3}）等，但总体上双音节词的第二个音节一般有较高的音调（pitch）。此变调规律与上述叠词亲属称谓相似。据 Jurafsky（1996），变调是小称的一种手段，与儿语有语义或语用关联。婴孩较喜欢提高音调，成年人与他们沟通、玩耍，也常提高音调，这是儿语的特色。影响所及，以音调高低变化区别词义的声调语言（tonal language），如粤语，其双音节词的第二个音节也多数会提高声调（高平调或高升调）。儿语让儿童认识身边的人和物，如“船船”、“牛牛”，而语用方面则有助于亲属与儿童的关系更为亲昵。儿语尤常用叠词类亲属称谓词，两者有密切的关联。

3.2.2　非叠词类亲属称谓

非叠词类可再分为附加式和复合式，各有两个细类，下文将列出这四个细类的变调词例。

3.2.2.1　附加式：前缀“阿 –”

表 11 列出的附加式的称谓语，都必须读变调。词根部分有三种变调：①高平变调，有“阿姐”、“阿姨”两例。②高升变调比较多，例如“妹”、“女”、“太”、“大”和

“二”。③低变调，只有“爸”和“姐”。“姐”比较特别，低变调的“阿姐”只表示“姐姐”，高平变调的“阿姐”，有区别词义的作用，常用于拟亲属称谓。

表 11　附加式：前缀“阿 -”

称谓	声韵	原调	变调	词义
阿爸	aa baa	*3 1	3 4	爸爸
阿姨	aa ji	*3 4	3 1	阿姨
阿姐	aa je	*3 2	3 4	姐姐
阿姐	aa je	*3 2	3 1	对女士的称谓，只用于拟亲属称谓
阿妹	aa mui	*3 6	3 2	妹妹
阿女	aa neoi	*3 5	3 2	女儿
阿太	aa taai	*3 3	3 2	对已婚女士的称谓
阿大	aa daai	*3 6	3 2	老大
阿二	aa ji	*3 6	3 2	老二

其实有不少前附加式的“阿 -”亲属称谓语并不能变调，如“阿妈”、“阿叔”、“阿婶”、“阿仔”、“阿嫲”、“阿爷”、“阿哥”等。“妈”、“叔”、“哥”都是粤拼调号 1，调值 55，其实已没有空间变调并读为更高调值的读音了。“妈”、“哥”若要变调，就只能低变调，读阳平，但常见的是用于叠词的第一个音节，详见 3. 2. 1. 1 节。

3. 2. 2. 2　附加式：后缀“ - 仔”

加后缀“ - 仔”的亲属称谓语不多，高平变调的很少，详见表 12。有很多称谓语并不变调，例如“叔仔”、“姑仔”、“舅仔”、“老婆仔”、“老公仔”等。反而是拟亲属称谓要用变调，例如“妹仔”、“姐仔”。

表 12　附加式：后缀“ - 仔”的亲属称谓

称谓	声韵	原调	变调	词义
姨仔	ji zai	*4 2	1 2	小姨
妹仔	mui zai	*6 2	1 2	婢女
姐仔	ze zai	*2 2	1 2	地位低微的年轻女艺员

3. 2. 2. 3　复合式亲属称谓：联合式

复合式亲属称谓有联合式和偏正式两种。联合式的词例较少，多数是背称，变调例子也较少，例如“兄妹”（ $mui^{6\text{-}2}$ ）、“姊妹”（$mui^{6\text{-}2}$）中的“妹”字，作为双音节词的最后一个音节，一般可以变调。可是也有不变的情况，例如“弟妹”是两个同辈的合称，“妹”必须读原调。“父子”、“母女”、“叔侄”、“甥舅”、“婆媳”等都是不同辈之合称，但只有“母女”一词的“女”读变调。其实，“女”在双音节词（多音节词也是）的最后一个音节都读高升变调，多音节词如“三仔一女”（联合式）、“外甥女”（偏正式）也是这样，这与词的结构并无关系。

3.2.2.4　复合式亲属称谓：偏正式

偏正式是复合式亲属称谓的主要形式，词例较多，其实大多不变调，但相对之下，变调词例还是比联合式的多。变调大多出现于双音节词的后一音节，因此表 13 ~ 表 15 均以后一音节的单字为基础，列出相关词例。

表 13　偏正式亲属称谓词例（一）

~弟（dai$^{6-2}$）	~妹（mui$^{6-2}$）	~姐（ze$^{2-1}$）	~姨（ji$^{4-1}$）
表弟	表妹	姑姐	三姨、四姨……
堂弟	堂妹	家姐	细姨
	细妹		

表 14 的“父”字在“伯父”、“叔父”等词中必须读原调，才表示亲属称谓语。变调的“伯父”(fu$^{6-2}$)、“叔父”(fu$^{6-2}$)，有别义作用，都是拟亲属称谓语，也都倾向于蔑称，前者指“老头儿”，后者指“叔父（fu$^{6-2}$）辈”，估计与自己叔父的年纪和辈分相若。

表 14　偏正式亲属称谓词例（二）

~父（fu$^{6-2}$）	~丈（zoeng$^{6-2}$）	~母（mou$^{5-2}$）	~女（neoi$^{5-2}$）
岳父	岳丈	岳母	侄女
外父	姨丈	外母	外甥女
	姑丈		孙女
			大女、细女……

表 15 的“爷”(je$^{4-1}$）比较特别。不变调的“爷”(je^{4}）是祖父的意思，也可作为拟亲属称谓语，例如“财爷”是称呼财政司司长一职的。“伯爷”(je$^{4-1}$）是亲属称谓，指“老父”的意思。“伯爷(je$^{4-1}$）公”、“伯爷(je$^{4-1}$）婆”，都是拟亲属称谓，指老伯伯和老妇，也可以作为老夫、老妻之间的称呼。

表 15　偏正式亲属称谓词例（三）

~奶（naai$^{5-1}$）	~婆（po$^{4-2}$）
姑奶（丈夫的姐姐）	家婆（婆婆）
少奶	大婆（大老婆）
二奶（小老婆）	细婆（小老婆）
	两公婆（两夫妻）
	老太婆（老妇）
	伯爷（je$^{4-1}$）婆（老妇）

大致上，不论是高平变调还是高升变调，其原调多是阳声调（即粤拼调号4～6）。复合式亲属称谓的变调主要出现于最后一个词根上。

高升变调的字较多，计有：弟、妹、丈、父、母、婆、女。

高平变调的字较少，计有：姐、姨、奶、爷。

以“妹”字为例，变调主要出现于最后一个音节/词根上，如（12）a，当“妹”出现于词的其他位置，如（12）b，就只能读原调。当然这个概括并不能完全适用于其他字。以（13）的“爷”为例，（13）a符合前述原则，但是（13）b的“爷”字并不在最后一个音节之上，却依然变调。这也许跟别义作用有关，也跟语素的组合关系有关。“伯爷”本身就必须读变调［baak^{3} je$^{4\text{-}1}$］，才有“老父”或“年长”的含义，其意义不是指老伯伯，所以“爷”不能读原调［je^{4}］。语素“爷”跟“婆”不可能先结合成词，而必须是语素“伯”跟“爷”结合，再加上“婆”字。（12）b的“表妹夫”，词语结构跟（13）b的一样，语素“表”和“妹”先结合，最后再加上“夫”。“妹”却不可以读变调，相信这是跟“妹夫”的语素组合关系有关。“妹夫”的“妹”不可变调，在“妹”字前加“表”或“二”、“三”等表示排行的语素，“妹”字均不可以读变调。即使“表妹”一词变调，但“妹”字跟“妹夫”的“妹”字叠合，结果还是采用了不变调的读法。这种语素组合的关系，影响到三音节词“表妹夫”的读音。类似的词例还有亲属称谓“表弟”和“表弟妇”，前者的“弟”须用高升变调，后者则要读原调（阳去）。另一个类似例子是“老太”和“老太婆”。前者的“太”读高升变调，后者的“太”必须用原调（阴去）。

（12）a. 表妹（mui$^{6\text{-}2}$）

b. 表妹（mui^{6}）夫

（13）a. 伯爷（je$^{4\text{-}1}$）

b. 伯爷（je$^{4\text{-}1}$）婆/公

4 总 结

香港粤语亲属称谓的变调模式，是高升变调（调值25）比高平变调（调值55）多。这与粤语一般变调规律一致。高升变调的音节，原调多数是阳去，例如“弟”、“妹”、“丈”、“父”；原调属阳平调的相对较少，如“爷”、“婆”。低变调（调值21）主要出现于叠音词的第一个音节，但也出现于一些双音节拟亲属称谓词的第二个音节，而语素只限于“姐”、“哥”、“爸”；其第一个音节通常是阴平或阴入调，本身不是这些声调的字，就要用高平变调来符合这个限制。而从构词法的角度看，香港粤语有六个单音节亲属称谓，有三个须变调才能独立使用。亲属称谓词以双音节为主，可以分类为叠词与非叠词两种。前者以变调的称谓词为主，而后者较少变调，要变调的话，位置通常在第二个音节。不过，上述概括只是大致的情况，实际情况要复杂得多，正如李新魁等（1995）所讲，变调是以词为单位的，其用法不能类推到其他近似的词语。就以本文所研究的亲属称谓为例，多数阳平调的语素，如“姨”、“婆”、“爷”均可变调，可是“嫲”字也是阳平调，意义上与“婆”接近，有老妇的含义，却不可以变调。可见，粤语的变调规律是颇为复杂的，亲属称谓的变调与字调、字义、词的结构有关，但具体规律还有待进一步探析。

参考文献

甘于恩　2010　《广东四邑方言语法研究》，广州：暨南大学出版社。

高华年　1980　《广州方言研究》，香港：商务印书馆。

黄大方　1989　《论广州话的变调兼评诸家之说》，《汕头大学学报》（人文社会科学版）第4期，第89~97页。

李新魁等　1995　《广州方言研究》，广州：广东人民出版社。

麦　耘　2000　《广州话的声调系统与语素变调》，《开篇》第20期，第1~21页。

袁家骅等　1983　《汉语方言概要》（第二版），北京：文字改革出版社。

詹伯慧主编　2002　《广东粤方言概要》，广州：暨南大学出版社。

张励妍　1986　《广州话高升变调规律初探》，《语文杂志》第13期，第41~48页。

Bauer, R. S., Benedict, P. K.　1997　*Modern Cantonese Phonology*. Berlin: Mouton de Gruyter.

Jurafsky, D.　1996　Universal tendencies in the semantics of the diminutive. *Language*, 72 (4): 533-578.

Matthews, S. and Yip, V.　2011　*Cantonese: A Comprehensive Grammar*. 2nd edition. London: Routledge.

粤语及普通话量词通用分类体系初探

黄阡薇　李　辉

（香港大学）

提　要：量词是汉藏语系中独有且争议较大的词类。关于其中、英文命名，界定以及分类等问题在汉语言学界一直众说纷纭。本文主要探讨以下几个问题：①汉语量词的定义及其中、英文名称；②对现有汉语量词分类系统详加分析，指出其在分类指标、覆盖面和排他性方面存在的问题；③对我们建立的粤语及普通话儿童语料库中所见量词进行对比分析和归类，根据归类结果建立一个粤普双语共享的量词分类体系；④建构的新体系将汉语量词分为两大类八小类：名量词（个体量词、集合量词、度量衡量词、不定量词、借用量词）及动量词（专用动量词、借用动量词、同源动量词）。该体系成功地对粤普双语语料库中的量词进行了编码与分类，重码率低，覆盖面广，为我们进一步研究儿童早期量词习得提供了有效的分析工具，有助于解决长久以来关于量词分类的争议。

关键词：量词分类　普通话　粤语　广东话　语料库

人类语言一般可二分为量词型语言（classifier language）和非量词型语言（non-classifier language）。汉语是典型的量词型语言，但量词却是现代汉语中最后一个独立出来的词类，同时也是一个争议较大的词类（何杰，2000）。对于量词的命名及分类等问题，语言学界更是众说纷纭。我们在2007年成功建立了儿童粤语语料库，并对香港儿童量词的习得进行了大量的实证研究（Tse，Li & Leung，2007）。2011年起，我们又在同一平台上建立了北京和新加坡学前儿童普通话语料库。为了展开普通话和粤语习得的跨语言比较分析，我们必须建立一个粤普双语共享的量词分类体系，本文主要汇报这一方面的理论探索成果。

1　汉语量词的定义

量词往往是数词后头的黏着词，在汉语中最常见的使用环境是“数词—量词—名词”结构，即数量结构，如“一张纸”。这一结构当中的量词就是“名量词”，指的是在名词词组中与数词配合，用以指示参照物形状或种类的语素。大多数情况下，名量词放在数词或指示代词之后、名词之前。但在一定的语言或处境语境之下，名词也可以不出现。其中，语言语境（linguistic context）往往指在前面提到的事物，即前指（antecedent），如“这张（纸）”。而处境语境（situational context）指当事双方在特定情境下无须使用名词或指示代词也能清楚地明白数量结构所指示的事物，如粤语“架车坏咗”。另外一个常见的量词使用环境就是“动词—数词—量词”结构，即动量结构。这一结构当中的量词就是“动量词”，用来指示动词词组表达的动作的数量，如“唱一次”（朱德熙，2008）。

所以，现代汉语量词基本上可以分为两大类：一大类是名量词，和数词、指示代词等一起指示事物（名词充当）的数量（quantity）；另一大类是动量词，和数词一起指示动作（动词充当）的次数（frequency）。值得大家留意的是，下面的例子里并没有名量词及动量词：“重五斤”（重：形容词；五：数词；斤：名词）、“高四寸”（高：形容词；四：数词；寸：名词），当中，“斤”及“寸”并不是量词，而是名词。又如“走了五天”（走：动词；五：数词；天：名词）”、“睡了两小时”（睡：动词；两：数词；小时：名词），当中，“五天”并不是“走”的次数、“两小时”并不是“睡”的次数，所以它们不是动量词，而是名词。

我们认为现代汉语中没有形量词，因为汉语没有表示性质（形容词充当）的数量（指有量可数）和次数的说法。常见的情况是将“数词 + 名量词”短语放在形容词后面，作为形容词的补语。例如，“轻（一）些”（一：数词；些：名量词），“长（一）点儿（一：数词；点儿：名量词）”，“矮（一）点儿（一：数词；点儿：名量词）”等。在此，“些”和“点”并不是在修饰形容词所指性质的数量和次数，而是在补充说明被指示物（名词）的属性差别，所以应当归入名量词的范畴。所以，在以下例子中，“些”和“点”都是名量词，它们所组成的“一些/点儿”短语是形容词的补语：“快一些/一点儿”，“留神一些/点儿”，“大声一些/点儿”，“小声一些/点儿”，“高一些/点儿”，“胖一些/点儿”。在这里，普通话的“一些”及“一点儿”，即粤语的“一啲”，其中的“一”有时候可以省略，而意义不变。

2 汉语量词的命名

量词往往是数词后头的黏着词，跟数词组合成数量值修饰名词或动作，如“一张纸”、“唱一次”；跟指示词组合成指量结构来指示特定的对象或动作，如“这张（纸）”、“这次”（朱德熙，2008）。而在各词类中，量词的异名最多，有单位词、副名词、助名词、辅名词、称数词、数位词、助量词、别词、类词、陪衬词、计标等共 16 种名称（何杰，2000），名称的丰富性折射出量词性质的复杂性，对此不同的学者有不同的观点。本文遵从绝大多数语言学家的意见，采用“量词”这一国际广泛接受的名称。

量词的中文名称易定，但英文名却较难取舍。国际语言学界通用的英文名称是 classifier，绝大多数研究中国语言的学者也使用这一名称来指代普通话和粤语中的量词（Erbaugh，2002；Matthews & Yip，2011；Tse，Li & Leung，2007）。但是，也有一些大师坚持用 measure word 来指代量词，如赵元任（1968）和张洪年（2010）等。其实，汉语量词的英文名称如何取舍，端赖于我们对量词的定位及其性质的界定。

一般而言，量词是用来界定某一词类（名词和动词）可数的单位或次数的词。崔健（2010）认为，范畴化（categorization）和个体化（individuation）是量词的两大主要功能。

范畴化功能主要关注名词和量词之间的选择关系，把量词看作名词的语义分类（semantic categorization）手段，如“一张纸”、“一叠纸”。据此，我们认为，在名量词尤其是个体量词当中，量词的范畴化功能相当突出，此时使用“classifier”一词是实至名归的。但是，因为传统语法把不具有范畴化功能的度量衡等“单位词”（measure word）划入量词范畴，如“一里路”，这样就令“classifier”无法涵盖“量词”的所有范畴，也令我们无法科学地对量词的形态、句法及属性进行充分的研究与认识。在这种情况下，一些学者坚持使用“measure word”一词也是有其道理的。另外，动量词组合中的量词其实也是用来指示动作数量的单位词，并不具备范畴化功能，因此也不能称之为“classifier”。所以，对于这一类量词，我们倾向于支持赵元任、张洪年的意见，采用“measure word / measure”一词。虽然“classifier”未能全面准确地反映及涵盖汉语量词的复杂性，但由于国际语言学界的主流是使用“classifier”一词来指代世界各地语言中的“量词”（Aikhenvald，2000；Yamamoto，2005），因此为了方便语言学界比较及研究世界各地语言中的“量词”，我们建议采用“Chinese classifier”（CL）这一词作为汉语量词的英文名称，以解决长久以来的混淆及分歧。

3　现代汉语量词分类的问题

3.1　普通话和粤语可否共享同一个量词分类法？

根据周小兵（1997）的研究分析，普通话和粤语中的名量词之间有四大差别：①相同名词使用不同的量词搭配，如普通话的“一根针”粤语说成“一眼针”；②使用不同的“数—量—名”结构表示相同的意思，如普通话的“五分钟”时间，即粤语的“一个字”；③名词和量词搭配的范围不同，如粤语“一部车、一部洗衣机”，普通话说“一辆车、一台洗衣机”；④量词的定指功能，粤语量词还有数词及指示代词功能，如普通话说“那一辆车停了”，但粤语可以说成“架车停咗”（周小兵，1997；Matthews & Yip，2011）。而在普通话和粤语的动量词中，其“动词”与“动量词”之间的用语搭配有点不同，但“动—数—量”结构没有改变，如普通话“睡一觉”，粤语说成“瞓一觉”；普通话“念一遍”，粤语是“读一次”；普通话“歇一歇”，粤语是“唞一唞”。虽然普通话和粤语量词有上述语义、功能及搭配上的不同，但除了有少数名量词使用不同的“数—量—名”结构表示相同的意思之外，大体在分类的层面上仍可共享一个以文法为本的量词分类系统。下文主要是探讨建立一个粤普共享量词分类系统，以便我们展开后续的粤普儿童量词的对比研究。

3.2　量词可细分为几大类？

在现代汉语量词的分类问题上，各个学者因其采取的角度不同、观点不一而争论不休，在此列出较具代表性的分类学说。吕叔湘（1999）在《现代汉语八百词》中提出九大分类：个体量词（根、粒）、集合量词（排、包）、容器量词（杯、篮）、临时量词（身、桌子）、度量量词（米、斤）、自主量词（区、星期）、复合量词（人次、秒立方）、部分量词（些、片、层）、动量词（遍、下）。而朱德熙（2008）在《语法讲义》中将名量词分七大类：①个体量词（一本书）；②集合量词（两套家具）；③度量词（三斗米）；④不定量词（一些饮料）；⑤临时量词，临时借用名词来充当量词（一身泥）；⑥准量词（两县人）；⑦动量词。他将动量词又分为三类：①专用动量词（看一次）；②借用名词（看一眼）；③重复量词（看一看）。而《现代汉语使用手册》（2009）则将量词分为六大类：①名量词（个、条）；②动量词（遍、阵）；③不定量词（些、点儿）；④复合量词（公斤）；⑤借用量词（一口猪、画一笔）；⑥准量词（三站路）。

中国量词研究专家何杰（2000）把现代汉语量词分成四大类：①名量词；②动量词；③兼职量词；④复合量词。第一大类的名量词再细分成七小类：①个体量词（位、棵）；②集合量词［定量词（双）、不定量词（群）］；③部分量词（段）；④专职量词（张、匹）；⑤借用量词/容载量词（杯）；⑥临时量词（脸）；⑦度量衡量词［市制单位（斤）、公制单位（厘米）、外来单位（磅）、古代单位（樽）］。第二大类的动量词，分为：①专用动量词（趟）；②借用动量词（切一刀）、借用动词（睡一觉）。第三大类的兼职量词（一把刀，拉他一把）则没有子集，而第四大类的复合量词再分成两类：①组合类（场次）；②选择型（部集）。

我们在早期研究粤语量词时，借鉴了西方学者对汉语量词分类的方法（Tse，Li & Leung，2007；Matthews & Yip，2000、2011；Aikhenvald，2000；Killingley，1983；Yamamoto，2005），将粤语量词分为动量词（Verb Classifier）和名量词（Noun Classifier）两大类，动量词是修饰动作出现的次数，没有子类（sub-category）；而名量词修饰的是名词数量，有两个大子类：类量词（Sortal Classifier）和度量词（Mensural Classifier）。类量词分为两类：①生物（Animate），即人类（Human）与动物（Animal）。②非生物（Inanimate），包括有形名量词（Concrete）及无形名量词（Abstract）。而有形名量词再细分功能（Function）和形状（Shape）。当中形状名量词细分为一维（1-Dimension）、二维（2-Dimensions）和三维（3-Dimensions）。度量词指示有关事物、动作或属性的程度或数量，又可细分为：①集合量词（Collective Classifier）；②容器量词（Containment）；③度量衡量词（Measurement Classifier）。动量词则是修饰动作出现的次数（Tse，Li & Leung，2007）。

但是以上种种分类法运用于实际语料库分类量词时会出现困难，如“一团烟”及“一桌子书”。若用朱德熙（2008）之说“团”为名量词、“桌”为临时量词；以吕叔湘（1999）之说“团”为部分量词、“桌”为临时量词；以何杰（2000）之说“团”为不定量词、“桌”为临时量词；以《现代汉语使用手册》之说“团”为名量词、“桌”为借用量词；但若以西方学派之说“团”则应为无形名量词，还是三维有形名量词（Concrete-3D）？而“桌”应为有形名量词中的二维，还是三维，抑或是度量词中的容器量词？莫衷一是。

由此可见，量词本身的多样性及兼容性，令其分类问题变得相当复杂。而各家分类标准不一，又令分类系统更加繁复多变。有的以语义功能（Semantic Function）分类，有的以语法功能（Syntactic Function）分类，有的则将语义和语法混为一体来分类；有的按照同一标准一分到底，有的则在同一分类系统中运用不同标准和角度，令本来就复杂的量词分类系统更加纷繁重复。本研究旨在寻求并建立一种可以贯彻始终、打通粤普的标准来对量词进行分类的更加简明、科学的量词分类体系，以有助于汉语语言研究。

4　粤语及普通话量词通用分类系统

因此，根据上述分析，我们将在朱德熙（2008：45～48）量词分类的基础上，根据现代汉语里量词的语法特征，将其分为两大类八小类，具体分类如下（见图1）：

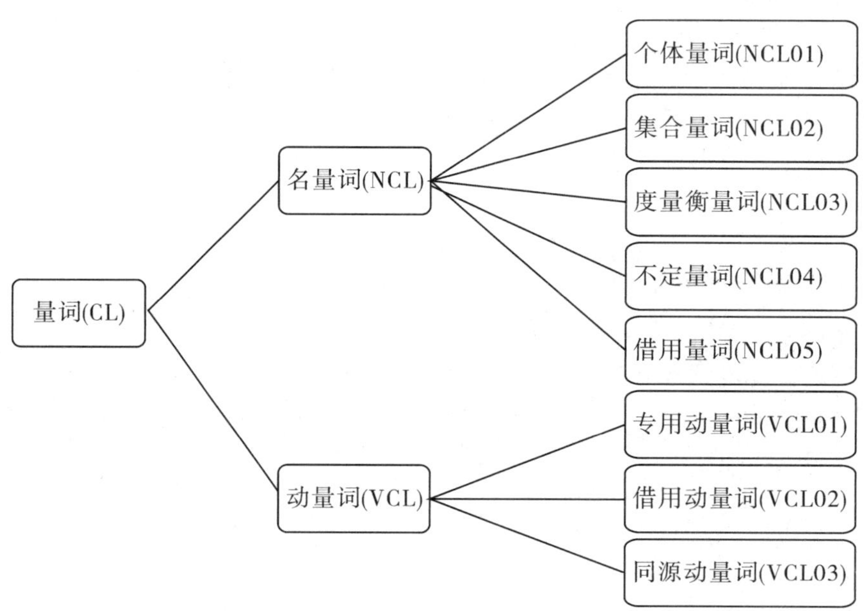

图1　粤语及普通话量词通用分类体系

4.1　名量词（Noun Classifier，NCL）

4.1.1　个体量词（Individual Classifier）

个体量词即表示个体事物数量的名量词（代码 NCL01 类）。其语法特点是：①数词＋NCL01＋名词，表示事物（名词充当）的数量。数词可以是“一”或其他数词。②NCL01 表示单数，个数名词有自己特定的 NCL01（个体量词）。③NCL01＋名词之前，也可以是指代词。④如果有语言或处境语境，名词可以不出现。“个”是 NCL01 类中用得最广泛的一个，也是普通话和粤语中的“通用量词”（General Classifier）。普通话例子：本（书）；张（床）；匹（马）等。粤语例子：嚿（番枧）；堆（嘢）；只（雀仔）等。

4.1.2　集合量词（Collective Classifier）

集合量词是指示集合事物数量的名量词（代码 NCL02 类）。其语法特点是：①数词＋

NCL02＋名词。NCL02 表示成组或成群，数词可以是“一”或其他数词。②NCL02＋名词之前也可以是指代词。③如果有语言或处境语境，名词可以不出现。④数词＋NCL02＋名词，表示事物（名词充当）有多少个成组事物或多少个成群事物。⑤NCL02 类，不可跟不可数名词（Uncountable Noun）组合。这也使得 NCL02 类与 NCL01 类不同。普通话例子：窝（小猫）；双（筷子）；批（货）等。粤语例子：班（马骝）；叠（纸）等。

4.1.3 度量衡量词（Measurement Classifier）

度量衡量词是表示度量衡的名量词（代码 NCL03 类）。传统上，度量衡是度（计量长度）、量（计量体积）、衡（计量轻重）的统称。现代对度量衡的广泛定义为任何表示物理量（如温度、时间）的公制单位。但本系统中只指传统上的度量衡，并不包括其他公制单位。

其语法特点是：①在某些情况下，度量衡的名量词有其同形的名词。例如“两斤共有三十二两”一句中，“斤”和“两”是名词。又例如“这把刀长三尺”句中的“尺”也是名词。②NCL03 类与 NCL01 及 NCL02 类有别，主要在于 NCL03 类有其同形的名词，而 NCL01 和 NCL02 类并没有同形的名词。③数词＋NCL03＋名词：NCL03 表示度量衡的单位，数词可以是“一”或其他数词。④NCL03＋名词之前，也可以是指代词。⑤如果有语言或处境语境，名词也可以不出现。⑥数词＋NCL03＋名词，表示事物（名词充当）在那个度量衡方面有多少个数量单位。普通话例子：尺（布）；斤（肉）；里（路）；公斤（菜）等。粤语例子：尺（布）；斤（肉）；里（路）；公斤（菜）等。

4.1.4 不定量词／“点儿、些”量词（Indefinite Classifier）

不定量词即表示不定数量的“些”和“点儿”的名量词（代码 NCL04 类）。其语法特点是：①数词＋NCL04＋名词。NCL04 表示不定数，量指不便说清的数目或无法说清的数目。②数词只有一个可能，就是“一”。③NCL04＋名词之前，也可以是指代词。④如果有语言语境或处境语境，名词可以不出现。

4.1.5 借用量词（Temporary Noun Classifier）

这类名量词，在其他场合，有其同形的名词（代码 NCL05 类），所以被称为“借用量词”或“临时量词”。其语法特点是：①在其他场合，有同形的名词，例如：碗、书架、桌子、脸、脚、星期、小时等。②数词＋部分 NCL05＋名词，表示事物（名词充当）的数量，数词可以是“一”或其他数词，例如：三碗饭。③数词＋部分 NCL05＋名词，数词只可以是“一”，也可转换为“满”，而意义不变，如“一头汗”即“满头汗”。④NCL05 类与 NCL01、NCL02 和 NCL04 类都不同，因为 NCL05 类在其他场合有同形的名词，而其他三类没有同形的名词。NCL05 类与 NCL03 类在其他场合都有同形的名词，但 NCL03 类是度量衡单位，而 NCL05 类不是度量衡单位，所以两者又有区别。

4.2 动量词（Verbal Classifier，VCL）

动量词放在动词之后，用来指示动作的数量，最常见的语法组合是“动词＋数词＋动量词”。其中的动量词表示动作（由动词充当）的次数。如果动词后面有数词和某词，而且并不表示动作的次数，则那个词并非动量词，而可能是名词或名量词。例如，“走了五天”（走：动词；五：数词；天：名词），“读了五本书”（读：动词；五：数词；本：名量词）。另外，动作次数多少与动作时间长短并无必然关系。即使次数只有一次，也可能占用很长时间，例如“去了一趟北京”：“趟”是补充说明动作次数多少而非动作时间长短；还有,“去了一趟北京”的“趟”是说明“去”的次数而非“北京”这个地方。又如“读了一回圣经”：此“回”视为动量词，而非名量词。因为我们只有“一本圣经”而没有“一回圣经”，所以这个“回”是用来补充说明“读”的次数的。但若是“读了一回章回小说”，其中的“一回”则表示阅读“章回小说”的一章，所以它在此是名量词，但这种说法在现代标准汉语中已经很少用了。

4.2.1 专用动量词（Specified Verb Classifier）

视不同动词而采用不同的动量词（代码 VCL01 类）（或称专用的动量词），但有些动量词可跟多个动词组合。其语法特点：①不及物动词 + 数词 + VCL01 + 没有名词的宾语。数词是“一”或是其他数词。②不及物动词 + 数词 + VCL01 + 没有名词的宾语。表示动作（由动词充当）重复的次数。③不及物动词 + 数词 + VCL01 + 名词宾语。数词是“一”或其他数词。值得注意的是：动词 + 数词 + 名量词 + 名词宾语。数词是“一”或其他数词。动量词跟名量词两者有分别，例如：在“他唱了两次歌”中用的是 VCL01 类量词“次”，表示动作（唱）的次数；在“他唱了三首歌”中用的是 NCL01 类量词“首”，表示事物（歌）的数量。④及物动词 + 数词 + VCL01 + 没有名词的宾语，表示及物动作（由动词充当）重复的次数。及物动词后面之所以没有名词宾语，是因为由语言语境或处境语境提供了，名词可以不出现。普通话例子：不带宾语：（哭两）回；（休息四）次；（醉三）次等。带宾语：（去四）趟（澳门）；（看一）次（电影）；（叫一）声（哥哥）等。粤语例子：不带宾语：（喊两）次；（休息四）次；（醉三）次等。带宾语：（去四）趟（澳门）；（看一）次电影；（叫一）声（哥哥）等。

4.2.2 借用动量词（Temporary Verb Classifier）

这类动量词的语法特点是有其同形的名词（代码 VCL02 类）。其常见语法组合有：动词 + 数词 + VCL02。数词可以是“一”或其他数词，或表示动作（由动词充当）重复了数词说的次数。普通话例子：（切三）刀；（抽四）鞭；（看一）眼；（踢两）脚等。粤语例子：（切三）刀；（抽四）鞭；（睇一）眼；（踢两）脚等。

4.2.3 同源动量词（Cognate Verb Classifier）

同源动量词即动量词跟动词同形，代码 VCL03 类。其语法特点是：①动词 + 数词 + VCL03。数词“一”可以省略，而意义不变。②动词 + “一” + VCL03，表示动作（由动词充当）只重复一次，而且往往表示该动作时间短。普通话例子：（看一）看 =（看）看；（想一）想 =（想）想等。粤语例子：（睇一）睇 =（睇）睇；（谂一）谂 =（谂）谂等。

5　分类系统注意事项

5.1　名量词和动量词的区分

本分类系统具有高度的排他性，基本可以杜绝分类重叠现象。NCL01、NCL02、NCL03、NCL04、NCL05 五者之间有排他性，即没有重叠的现象。VCL01、VCL02 和 VCL03 三者之间有排他性，即没有重叠的现象。

但是，部分量词因其有同形名量词和同形动量词，所以在实际分类过程中要根据语序及句法特征来划分。除了以下所述的兼类量词（即有同形名量词和同形动量词）以外，名量词和动量词两者之间皆具有排他性，没有重叠的现象。

表 1　同形名量词与动量词的区分

	同形名量词	同形动量词
把	一把刀	拉他一把
场	一场芭蕾舞	大哭一场
阵	一阵风	说了一阵
面	三面镜子	见一面
顿	一顿饭	打他一顿
次	三次考试	减价三次

上述这些同形名量词和同形动量词在表面上好像有重叠，但我们可以从它们的语法功能上分辨：表示事物（由名词充当）的数量是名量词；表示动作（由动词充当）的次数则是动量词。而离合词若拆分为词组，有些用到名量词，有些用到动量词，两者也容易分辨。如果是“动词 + 数词 + 量词 + 其他成分”，我们倾向于分析为“动词 + 数词 + 名量词 + 名词”结构，如下面例子所示：

（1）睡了一回觉（回：名量词，觉：名词）
（2）离了两次婚（次：名量词，婚：名词）
（3）鞠了三个躬（个：名量词，躬：名词）
（4）救了四条命（条：名量词，命：名词）

如果只是“动词 + （体貌词） + 数词 + 量词”，则可分析为“动词 + （体貌词） + 数词 + 动量词”，例如：

（5）睡了一觉（觉：动量词，备用名词作动量词）
（6）告了两状（状：动量词，备用名词作动量词）

(7) 鞠了三躬（躬：动量词，备用名词作动量词）

(8) 救了我一命（命：动量词，备用名词作动量词）

如上文“睡了一回觉”，因其为离合词分拆的词组，故在此不可与前文“去了一趟北京”及“读了一回圣经”相提并论。而“离了两次婚”跟“看了他两次”不一样，前者的“两次”是在补充说明结婚的次数，所以它是名量词；而后者是在补充“看”的次数，所以它是动量词。正如“救了我一命”，虽然短语中加了代名词“我”，但是“一命”在此还是在补充说明“救”这个动作，所以它是动量词。

当然，有时我们会看到“及物动词 + 一些/点儿”，后面没有名词宾语，那是因为有语言或处境语境的关系提供，所以名词不必出现。在这种情况下，“些/点儿”还是名量词。例如：“他虽然喜欢吃饭，但今天只吃了一些/点儿。”其中，“只吃了一些/点儿”后面虽然没有名词，但其实是有“饭”的，只是承前语境省略了，所以“一些/点儿”仍算是名量词。在这种情况下，数词“一”也可以省略，而意义不变。

5.2 通用量词“个”与同形结构助词“个”的区分

名量词“个”有其同形的结构助词，但它们不是名量词，其结构是“动词 + 结构助词‘个’+ 补语”，详见下文：

(1) 同形结构助词“个”可放在并列的数量值组，那并列数量值组是补语，表示概数。例如“得等个两三天”（等：动词；两三天：补语；个：结构助词）。

(2) 同形结构助词“个”，放在形容词前面。那形容词是补语。例如“玩个痛快”（玩：动词；痛快：补语；个：结构助词）。

(3) 同形结构助词“个”，放在动词的否定形式前。否定词 + 动词构成的词组是补语。例如“说个没完”（说：动词；没完：补语；个：结构助词；没：副词；完：动词）、“笑个不停”（笑：动词；不停：补语；个：结构助词；不：副词；停：动词）等。

总而言之，我们认为普通话和粤语可以分为两大类八小类，共享图 1 所示的分类体系。运用这一体系对我们现有两个语料库量词语料进行分析后发现，NCL01、NCL02、NCL03、NCL04、NCL05 五者之间没有重叠现象，VCL01、VCL02、VCL03 三者之间也没有重叠现象，所以用这种方法来分类是清晰和明确的。表 2、表 3 是我们据此分类体系对粤语及普通话儿童语料库中量词进行分类的结果。我们将会在后续量词研究工作中进一步完善和细化这一分类系统，以彻底解决量词的分类问题。

表 2　粤普儿童语料库中名量词分类词汇表

名量词	编码	语料库中的量词	
		北京	香港
个体量词	NCL01	个、块、只、种、回、层、份、条、片、棵、台、根、张、件、朵、套、道、锅、顿、下、句、声、把、间、架、副、幅、幢、辆	个、架、只、张、间、支、道、嚿、把、条、朵、样、部、块、包、枝、格、层、杯、粒、棵、座、份、顶、种、截、片、句、本、位、首、颗
集合量词	NCL02	对、排、堆、帮、段、把	嚿、对、份、套、家、堆、叠、包、批、班、种
度量衡量词	NCL03	块、度、分钟	蚊、分钟、度、磅、斤、楼、毫、鸡、年
不定量词	NCL04	些、点、点儿	啲、些、点
借用量词	NCL05	瓶、杯、家、碗、车、包、盘、箱、锅、身、盒、锤	杯、盒、樽、碗、地、煲、碟、盘、口、针、兜、瓶、袋、餐、罐

表 3　粤普儿童语料库中动量词分类词汇表

动量词	编码	语料库中的量词	
		北京	香港
专用动量词	VCL01	次、遍、圈、会（儿）、一下	次、顿、（一）阵、一下
借用动量词	VCL02	觉、口、碗、刀、眼、声	啖、针、眼
同源动量词	VCL03	看、开、听、等、煮、问、照、尝、弄、找、热、试、加、打、动、炒、洗、停、推、量、摸、瞧、换	看、等、量、写、碌、煲、揸、渌、剪、做、借、洗、玩、打

参考文献

崔　健　2010　《量词的功能差异和词类地位》,《汉语学习》第 6 期，第 69 ~ 81 页。

何　杰　2001　《现代汉语量词研究》，北京：民族出版社。

吕叔湘　1999　《现代汉语八百词》（增订本），北京：商务印书馆。

张洪年　2010　《香港粤语语法的研究》，香港：香港中文大学。

中国社会科学院语言研究所《中国语文》编辑部编　2009　《现代汉语使用手册》，北京：北京出版社。

周小兵　1997　《广州话量词的定指功能》，《方言》第 1 期，第 45 ~ 47 页。

朱德熙　2008　《语法讲义》，香港：商务印书馆。

Aikhenvald, Aleksandra TUr, evna 2000 *Classifiers: A Typology of Noun Categorization Devices*. Oxford: Oxford University Press.

Chao, Yuen Ren 1968 *A Grammar of Spoken Chinese.* Berkeley: University of California Press.

Erbaugh, Mary. S. 2002 Classifiers are for specification: Complementary functions for sortal and general classifiers in Cantonese and Mandarin. *Cahiers de Linguistique, Asie Orientale*, 31 (1): 33 -69.

Killingley, Siew-Yue 1983 *Cantonese Classifiers: Syntax and Semantics.* Newcastle upon Tyne: Grevatt & Grevatt.

Matthews, Stephen and Yip, Virginia 2011 *Cantonese: A Comprehensive Grammar.* London, New York: Routledge.

Tse, ShekKam., Li, Hui, & Leung, Shing On 2007 The Acquisition of Cantonese Classifiers by Preschool Children in Hong Kong. *Journal of Child Language*, 34 (2): 495 -517.

Yamamoto, Kasumi 2005 *The Acquisition of Numeral Classifiers: The Case of Japanese Children.* Berlin: Mouton de Gruyter.

Yip, Virginia and Matthews, Stephen 2000 *Basic Cantonese: A Grammar and Workbook.* New York: Routledge.

从老中青的差异看广州方言词类的演变情况

林茵茵

（香港理工大学）

提　要：本文以裨治文的《中文读本》（1841）为基础，在考察19世纪词汇演变情况的基础上，尝试延展广州方言词汇历时研究的跨度，探讨17世纪至今约三百年的广州方言的演变规律与特点。本文调查了老中青三派语言使用者的实际使用情况，对《中文读本》中几个主要词类进行了比较详细的分析，透过纵向比较，特写几十年间广州方言词汇的演变及原因。研究结果显示，词汇演变主要受社会文化生活、词汇系统的竞争与发展、语言接触的影响。

关键词：广州方言　词汇系统演变　基本词汇

词汇是语言三要素中最活跃的部分，它总处于不断的变动之中。这个复杂又多面的系统，对社会生活有着最敏锐的反映。半个多世纪以来，社会经济、文化快速发展，广播、影视等媒体的影响力急剧增强，使方言变化的速度明显加快。当中的变化可以通过比较历史文献之间的差异、比较语言使用者之间的差异等方法呈现出来。

从历史文献的角度出发的，闽方言的有李如龙、徐睿渊（2007），林寒生（2001）等。李如龙、徐睿渊调查了《翻译英华厦腔语汇》、《厦英大词典》、《英华口才集》三本教会厦门话语料，结果显示厦门方言常用基本词的变化不大，一般词汇则有半数发生了变化。林寒生以三本福州话地方历史文献《闽都别记》、《闽小记》、《闽杂记》为调查对象，结果反映"绝大部分口语词具有相对的稳定性及长期的延续性"，其中"核心词汇的变动小，一般词汇的变动大"。广州话方面，有黄小娅（2000）、赵恩挺（2003）；上海话则有胡明扬（1978）等。

以语言使用者为调查对象的，主要是考察老中青三派之间词汇的变化情况。如苏晓青、佟秋妹、王海燕的《徐州方言词汇60年来的变化》，郑见见的《流失中的厦门方言词汇》，陈章太的《四代同堂的语言生活》等。苏晓青、佟秋妹、王海燕（2004）从《徐州方言词典》、《江苏省和上海市方言概况》中筛选出282个词，调查老中青三派的差异，结果显示新老派之间的词汇使用情况有很大的差别。郑见见（2007）从《厦门方言研究》、《闽南方言大词典》中选出1 469个词，调查祖孙三代的使用情况，结果显示"大约有一半的厦门方言词汇已经或正在流失"。

本文综合了上述的调查方法，以历史文献裨治文的《中文读本》(以下简称《读本》)［E. C. Bridgman（1841）：*Chinese Chrestomathy in the Canton Dialect.* Macao：S. Wells

Williams］为根据，从一般词汇与常用基本词汇的角度出发，以老中青三派为调查对象，调查了分属三个年代于香港土生土长的男性，尝试将历史文献以及语言使用者的情况作一个纵向的比较，特写几十年来广州话词汇的演变。考察范围包括名词、动词、形容词、量词、代词五类，合共4 477个词。

一般认为，“基本词汇是在历史变迁中比较稳定的，在各种地域和社会集团中普遍使用的并具有派生能力的词。……有些基本词汇是共同语和方言共有的，例如天、地、山、水……粤语区：嘢（东西）、遮（伞）、脷（舌头）、樽（瓶）、送（菜肴）……”（李如龙，2001：103）。而本文的“常用基本词汇”，指的是在《读本》中出现并重现于下面三本文献中的词汇，包括屈大均《广东新语》（1687）、包尔滕《散语四十章》（1877）、孔仲南《广东俗语考》（1933）①；不属于本文所定义的“常用基本词汇”，均视作“一般词汇”。简言之，在这四本粤语文献中重复出现的词汇为“常用基本词汇”，这些词汇的变化比较稳定，并且普遍使用。

本文的调查对象有三位，分别出生在1940年、1956年、1970年，三人之间相差约15年，调查对象本身及其配偶的籍贯均属粤海片（广府片）的南海、番禺、顺德。三人的教育程度都在中五以上。三位调查对象的资料如下表所示：

出生地（籍贯）	姓名	性别	出生年份	文化程度
香港（番禺）	何多梁	男	1940	大专
香港（顺德）	胡泽荣	男	1956	中五
香港（番禺）	张志勤	男	1970	博士

本文所使用的《读本》是当时最早出版的外国人学中文课本，（游汝杰，2004：232）由“在华实用知识传播会”资助。书中保留了大量丰富的清代广州话方言词汇资料，裨治文在引言中指出：除了马礼逊（Robert Morrison）博士的《字汇》以外，暂时没有这种方言的著作供学生使用。② 换言之，《读本》应是当时广州地区第一本供外国人学习中文的书籍。《读本》全书分为十七章，内容包罗万象，涵盖天文地理、商业贸易、生活日用、人体医学、朝廷制度等等。与同期的教科书相比，此书提供了比较丰富的社会文化知识，在内容、取材上略超过一般的纯教科书。书中的对话部分以粤语口语编写，其他的说明文字，除粤语外，夹杂白话文及文言文。内容每页分三栏，第一栏是英文句子，第二栏是中文句子，第三栏是罗马字母拼音。有需要时，编者还会在页底加上解释。裨治文采用这种编排模式，反映了他的编写目的：①协助外国人学习中文；②协助中国人学习英语；③通

① 构思本文时，原打算只用地方文献作为考察对比的材料，即屈大均《广东新语》（1687）、招子庸《粤讴》（1828）及孔仲南《广东俗语考》（1933）。但因《粤讴》是情歌，内容比较集中，所用词汇也多有重复，在词汇量方面有明显的不足，因此最后改用与《粤讴》年代相近的《散语四十章》。

② 此句的原文为：“But，except a small vocabulary published by Dr. Morrison in 1829，no work of any note has yet been provided for the students in this dialect.”见《读本》引言，第 i 页。

过罗马字母来表达中文。《读本》原稿由马礼逊审定，商业贸易两章（第五、第六）由罗伯聃（Robert Thom）编纂，自然历史及索引部分由卫三畏（Samuel Wells Williams）编纂。[①]

调查结果显示：①现代广州话常用基本词汇的变动小，一般词汇的变化大。②各类词汇以名词的变化最快、最大，代词的变化最慢、最小。③老中青之间的差异，即使是变化最大的名词，老青之间的差距也少于25%。而广州方言词汇发生变化，主要是由于社会文化生活的改变、词汇系统的竞争发展以及语言接触引起的。

1 《读本》中词汇使用的整体情况

根据本文的研究结果，《读本》中的整体情况是：一般词汇变化大而迅速，常用基本词汇的变化小而缓慢。老中青之间的差异，无论是一般词汇还是常用基本词汇，总体趋势是保留率与年龄成正比，年纪越大，保留率越高；丢失率与年龄成反比，年纪越小，丢失率越高。各词类以名词变化最快，代词最慢。我们在下文会把《读本》的一般词汇与常用基本词汇的使用情况进行列表比较，逐一探讨。

1.1 老中青的整体情况

《读本》中词汇分布的总体情况是：一般词汇的丢失速度和变化速度快，保留率低；常用基本词汇的保存率高，丢失速度和变化速度慢。

《读本》中的一般词汇共有 4 477 个，常用基本词汇有 701 个，占总词量的 15.7%。老中青三派词汇的整体使用情况，主要划分为老中青相同和老中青不同两大类。具体情况如下表所示：

A 老中青相同	A1	不再使用	→	已经死亡	
	A2	仍然使用	→	生命力强	
	A3	词义词形有变化	→	变化中	
B 老中青不同	B1	老中派（老/老中/中）使用	→	变化中	（失去活力）
	B2	青派（老青/中青/青）使用	→	变化中	（仍有存活力）
	B3	词义词形有变化	→	变化中	

老中青相同的，分三类："A1 不再使用"，是已经死亡的词；"A2 仍然使用"，是生命力较强的词；"A3 词义词形有变化"，是处于变化阶段的词。老中青不同的，全都是处于变化阶段的词，也分三类：一是只有"B1 老中派（老/老中/中）使用"的词，是已经失

① 详见《读本·前言》。

去活力的词；二是“B2 青派（老青/中青/青）使用”的词，仍有一定的存活力；三是“B3 词义词形有变化的词”。

《读本》中的词汇根据上述的方法划分后，情况如下表所示：

			一般词汇		（小结）	常用基本词汇		（小结）
A 老中青相同	A1	不再使用	1 533	（34.2%）	1 533（34.2%）	61	（8.7%）	61（8.7%）
	A2	仍然使用	1 649	（36.8%）	1 649（36.8%）	511	（72.9%）	511（72.9%）
	A3	词义词形有变化	61	（1.4%）		14	（2.0%）	
B 老中青不同	B1	老中派使用	1 071	（23.9%）		91	（13.0%）	
	B2	青派使用	128	（2.9%）		17	（2.4%）	
	B3	词义词形有变化	35	（0.8%）	1 295（29%）	7	（1.0%）	129（18.4%）
		总数	4 477	（100.0%）		701	（100.0%）	

先谈一般词汇。从上面的资料可见，《读本》的一般词汇中，“A1 不再使用”的有 1 533条，占34.2%；“A2 仍然使用”的有1 649 条，占36.8%；A3 及 B 类“变化中”的有1 295 条，占29%。大体上，“不再使用”、“仍然使用”、“变化中”各占1/3。其中，已经失去活力的词汇（即“B1 老中派使用”的），有1 071 条，占23.9%。如果我们把已经死亡以及濒临死亡的词相加，即“A1 不再使用”的词加上“B1 老中派使用”的词，从《读本》至今的170 年间，占总数超过五成，合共58.1%。

然而，常用基本词汇的情况与一般词汇的并不相同。《读本》中的常用基本词汇，不再使用的只有61 条，占8.7%；仍然使用的占大多数，有511 条，占72.9%；变化中的词有129 条，只占18.4%。如果我们把“A1 不再使用”的词与只有“B1 老中派使用”的词相加，已经死亡以及濒临死亡的词只有21.7%。表示常用基本词汇的使用率、稳定性都比一般词汇要高。

从丢失的速度和存留的情况来看，一般词汇的丢失速度较快，数量多；常用基本词汇的丢失速度较慢，数量少。在丢失比率上，一般词汇几乎是常用基本词汇的四倍。至于存留的情况，常用基本词汇的保留率是一般词汇的一倍。除此以外，一般词汇失去活力的速度也较常用基本词汇迅速，所有变化中的词汇，一般词汇的变化比例是常用基本词汇的一倍半以上，情况简列如下表所示：

类别\比例\使用情况	不再使用	仍然使用	变化中
一般词汇：常用基本词汇	3.9：1	0.5：1	1.6：1

1.2 老中青的差异

一般词汇与常用基本词汇在老中青三派中的使用情况，总体的趋势相同：丢失率与年龄成反比，保留率与年龄成正比。就是年纪越大，丢失越少，保留越多；年纪越小，丢失越多，保留越少。主要的差异在于老中之间、中青之间的差距，一般词汇比常用基本词汇大一倍。

一般词汇在老中青三派语言使用者中的存留情况，如下表所示：

派别\数量\使用情况	不再使用		仍然使用		词义词形有变化		总数	
老派	1 626	(36.3%)	2 783	(62.2%)	68	(1.5%)	4 477	(100.0%)
中派	2 385	(53.3%)	2 010	(44.9%)	82	(1.8%)	4 477	(100.0%)
青派	2 614	(58.4%)	1 779	(39.7%)	84	(1.9%)	4 477	(100.0%)

从上表可见，在一般词汇中，年纪越大，保留得越好，年纪越小，保留得越差，而词义词形有变化的三派都少于2%。三派中以青派的丢失率最高，占58.4%；中派次之，占53.3%；老派丢失的最少，占36.3%。保留率则相反，老派保留得最好，占62.2%；中派次之，占44.9%；青派保留得较差，只有39.7%。整体上，中派与青派的情况较为接近。

至于常用基本词汇在老中青三派中的存留情况，如下表所示：

派别\数量\使用情况	不再使用		仍然使用		词义词形有变化		总数	
老派	68	(9.7%)	617	(88.0%)	16	(2.3%)	701	(100.0%)
中派	129	(18.4%)	554	(79.0%)	18	(2.6%)	701	(100.0%)
青派	152	(21.7%)	529	(75.5%)	20	(2.9%)	701	(100.0%)

在常用基本词汇中，老中青三派保留率是年纪大的保留得多，年纪小的丢失得多，词义词形有变化的，则三派都少于3%。就丢失率而言，三派的丢失率都不算高：老派的丢失率少于10%，中派的少于20%，青派的则刚超过20%。就保存率来说，三派的保存率都比较高，老派的保存率几乎是90%，中派的接近80%，青派的也超过75%。由此可见，在常用基本词汇中，也是中派与青派的存留情况较为接近。

一般词汇与常用基本词汇在三派中的使用比例，简列如下：

派别\比例\使用情况	不再使用	仍然使用	词义词形有变化
老派	3.7:1	0.7:1	0.7:1
中派	2.9:1	0.6:1	0.7:1
青派	2.7:1	0.5:1	0.7:1

从上表的资料可以看到，老中青三派的丢失率，大致是一般词汇丢失约 3 个，常用基本词汇丢失 1 个。保存率大体是一般词汇保留 2 个，常用基本词汇保留 3 个。词义词形有变化的也算接近，大约是一般词汇 2 个词有变化，常用基本词汇则有 3 个词有变化。

整体上，一般词汇和常用基本词汇的使用与丢失的趋势相近；唯老派与中青两派的差距较大，中派与青派则较为接近。详细情况如下表所示：

派别\数量\使用情况	一般词汇				常用基本词汇			
	不再使用		仍然使用		不再使用		仍然使用	
老派	1 626	(36.3%)	2 783	(62.2%)	68	(9.7%)	617	(88.0%)
青派	2 614	(58.4%)	1 779	(39.7%)	152	(21.7%)	529	(75.5%)
差距	988	(22.1%)	1 004	(22.5%)	84	(12.0%)	88	(12.5%)
老派	1 626	(36.3%)	2 783	(62.2%)	68	(9.7%)	617	(88.0%)
中派	2 385	(53.3%)	2 010	(44.9%)	129	(18.4%)	554	(79.0%)
差距	759	(17.0%)	773	(17.3%)	61	(8.7%)	63	(9.0%)
中派	2 385	(53.3%)	2 010	(44.9%)	129	(18.4%)	554	(79.0%)
青派	2 614	(58.4%)	1 779	(39.7%)	152	(21.7%)	529	(75.5%)
差距	229	(5.1%)	231	(5.2%)	23	(3.3%)	25	(3.5%)

先看“不再使用”的情况。在一般词汇中，老青的差距是 22.1%，老中的差距大约为 17.0%，中青的差距大约是 5.1%；而在常用基本词汇中，老青的差距为 12.0%，老中的差距是 8.7%，中青的差距是 3.3%。由此可见，一般词汇的丢失率大概是常用基本词汇的一倍：老青之间的差距，在一般词汇中是 22.1%，在常用基本词汇中是 12.0%，两者的差距接近一倍；老中之间的差距，在一般词汇中是 17.0%，在常用基本词汇中是 8.7%，差距也大约是一倍；中青之间的差距，在一般词汇中是 5.1%，在常用基本词汇中是 3.3%，差距也接近一倍。这种情况也出现在“仍然使用”的词汇中。简言之，一般词汇与常用基本词汇相比，老中或中青差距比例都大概是 2：1。

除此以外，老派与中青两派的差距明显较大，中派与青派则比较接近。老中之间的差距若是 3 个，则中青之间的差距只是 1 个，比例大约是 3：1。不论一般词汇、常用基本词汇、不再使用的词和仍然使用的词，大致都是这种情况。由此可见，虽然三派之间都相差 15 年，但老中之间的 15 年所发生的变化大于中青之间的 15 年。

这里有历史的原因。1941—1945 年，日军占领香港，香港人称之为“三年零八个月”。当时的香港，“人口从 160 万降至 60 万……大约有 17 万人无家可归……市场百物奇缺，价格昂贵”（黄鸿钊，2004：207）。老派调查对象当时也被迫离开香港，回乡避难。到现在，老派仍对当时的生活有一定的印象。1945 年底，华人陆续返港，香港人口骤增至百万，房屋、粮食、各类物资严重短缺。而老派也随家人返港，与农民、渔民为邻，生活艰苦。因这段历史的缘故，老派的生活经验比中、青两派丰富。中、青两派是在香港战后至 1991 年五十年间，人口增长最快的两个阶段出生的。青派大约在 1971—1981 年阶段出生，是人口增长最快的时期；中派在 1951—1961 年阶段出生，人口增长速度次之。而中派出生之时，正值香港工业化的高潮时期；青派出生后，香港金融业的规模不断扩大，香港迅速崛起成为国际大城市。（黄鸿钊，2004：287、299）虽然发展速度快，但两派生活经验比较相近，加上生活比较安定，因此差距比较小。

1.3 小　结

总的来说，《读本》的老中青调查再一次证明，一般词汇经常变动，常用基本词汇则比较稳固。一般词汇丢失、变化的速度较为迅速，保存的比例较低；常用基本词汇的丢失、变化速度较为缓慢，保存比例较高。

结合老中青的整体情况与个别差距，我们可以把这种变动与保留速度用比较具体的数字来呈现：在丢失率上，一般词汇与常用基本词汇至少接近 3∶1；在存留率上比较接近 1∶2。

至于老中青的差距方面，主要是由于时局变化引起的社会动荡，令老与中青的差距较大；而经济起飞带来了生活的稳定，令中与青之间的差距较小。

2. 《读本》中各词类的情况

《读本》中名词、动词、形容词、量词、代词五类的总体情况是：名词词量大，但常用基本词汇少；量词、代词的词量小，但常用基本词汇多。各词类按一般词汇、常用基本词汇来划分，两大类别的丢失率、保存率的异动情况相近。丢失的情况从大至小是名词、动词、形容词、量词、代词。

2.1 各词类的整体情况

整体来说，名词的词量大，但常用基本词汇所占的比例少。量词、代词的词量小，但常用基本词汇所占的比例大。其中量词、代词超过六成是常用基本词汇，保存的机会相对较高。

各词类在一般词汇与常用基本词汇中的分布情况如下表所示：

词类\数量\类别	一般词汇	常用基本词汇
名词	3 647（100.0%）	452（12.4%）
动词	560（100.0%）	151（27.0%）
形容词	194（100.0%）	49（25.3%）
量词	42（100.0%）	28（66.7%）
代词	34（100.0%）	21（61.8%）
总数	4 477（100.0%）	701（15.7%）

按词量由大至小排列分别是：名词（3 647）、动词（560）、形容词（194）、量词（42）、代词（34）。按常用基本词汇所占比例从大至小排列是：量词（66.7%）、代词（61.8%）、动词（27.0%）、形容词（25.3%）、名词（12.4%）。然而《读本》中各词类的变化并不同步，但各词类在一般词汇和常用基本词汇中的变动情况大致相同。其中“不再使用”的词，按变化情况从大到小的是：名词、动词、形容词、量词、代词。

不再使用的词的具体情况见下面的简表：

类别\百分比\词类	名词	动词	形容词	量词	代词
一般词汇	1 402（38.4%）	110（19.6%）	20（10.3%）	1（2.4%）	0（0.0%）
常用基本词汇	51（11.3%）	8（5.3%）	2（4.1%）	0（0.0%）	0（0.0%）

“不再使用”的一般词汇中，各词类的异动情况顺序为名词（38.4%）、动词（19.6%）、形容词（10.3%）、量词（2.4%）、代词（0.0%）。常用基本词汇的情况则为名词（11.3%）、动词（5.3%）、形容词（4.1%）、量词（0.0%）、代词（0.0%）。当中以名词的变化最大，反映了在各个词类中，名词是最为活跃的词类，它的变化最为迅速，反应最为敏感，这一点与林寒生（2001）的研究相同。而动词和形容词与名词的关系相对比较密切，所以其变化速度紧随其后。在名词、动词、形容词这三类词中，一般词汇的丢失速度较快，丢失数量多；常用基本词汇的丢失速度较慢，丢失数量少。

至于“仍然使用”的词，一般词汇按保存比例从大到小为：代词、量词、形容词、动词、名词。常用基本词汇按保存比例从大到小为：代词、量词、动词、形容词、名词。简列如下表：

类别\词类\保存情况	大————				→小
一般词汇	代词 88.2%	量词 69.0%	形容词 61.9%	动词 54.8%	名词 31.9%
常用基本词汇	代词 85.7%	量词 82.1%	动词 82.1%	形容词 81.6%	名词 67.5%

从上表可见，一般词汇和常用基本词汇保存比例的大小只在“形容词”、“动词”两项稍有不同。由于常用基本词汇中的“形容词”和“动词”的差距只有0.5%，因此，我

们可以概括地说，一般词汇和常用基本词汇中各词类的“仍然使用”情况接近，变动从大至小排列是：代词、量词、动词、形容词、名词。其中代词与量词是最为稳定的词类。

代词、量词的词量虽然少，但大多是常用基本词汇，这一先天条件是两种词的保存率比较高的一个原因。而上面的数据同时表明，固有的代词、量词在大多数情况下都能够发挥其语法功能：代词一般都能代替新产生的名词、动词、形容词，使语言简洁、经济；而固有的量词绝大部分都能用作新产生的人、事物、动作的单位。因此，代词、量词的变化最小，变化速度也相对缓慢。

简言之，名词的变化最迅速，它对时代的变化与发展、新旧事物的出现与消亡最为敏感，使用情况也较为波动。动词和形容词与名词的关系相对比较密切，所以其变化速度紧居其后。量词、代词则是变化最缓慢、稳定程度较高的一类。

2.2　各词类的变化情况

2.2.1　名词的变化情况

老中青三派之间使用情况不相同的词[①]，应是最能反映时代的变化以及派与派之间的差异的词。这种变化与差异，可以从老中青使用情况不相同的词中显示。老中青之间不同的词中，变化最大的是“3：展现社会生活的词”。具体情况如下表所示：

类别\比例	一般词汇						常用基本词汇					
	老中青相同		老中青不同		总数		老中青相同		老中青不同		总数	
3 房屋	47.8%	64	+52.2%	70	100.0%	134	50.0%	4	+50.0%	4	100.0%	8
3 文化娱乐	50.0%	11	+50.0%	11	100.0%	22	50.0%	1	+50.0%	1	100.0%	2
3 国家地区	50.0%	5	+50.0%	5	100.0%	10	100.0%	1	0.0%	0	100.0%	1
3 器具日常用具	50.4%	132	49.6%	130	100.0%	262	77.8%	21	22.2%	6	100.0%	27
3 工具材料	52.9%	250	47.1%	223	100.0%	473	64.0%	16	36.0%	9	100.0%	25
3 服饰	55.0%	55	45.0%	45	100.0%	100	66.7%	16	33.3%	8	100.0%	24
1 矿物自然物	63.6%	14	36.4%	8	100.0%	22	100.0%	2	0.0%	0	100.0%	2
2 人品	63.9%	122	36.1%	69	100.0%	191	60.6%	20	39.4%	13	100.0%	33
2 亲属称呼	63.9%	131	36.1%	74	100.0%	205	92.9%	26	7.1%	2	100.0%	28
3 其他	66.7%	34	33.3%	17	100.0%	51	83.3%	10	16.7%	2	100.0%	12
1 时间节令	71.4%	10	28.6%	4	100.0%	14	75.0%	6	25.0%	2	100.0%	8
3 商业邮电交通	75.3%	134	24.7%	44	100.0%	178	76.9%	10	23.1%	3	100.0%	13

① 老中青不同有三类，分别是老中派使用、青派使用、词义词形有变化；老中青相同也有三类，包括不再使用、仍然使用、词义词形有变化。见本文 1.1。

（续上表）

类别＼比例	一般词汇						常用基本词汇					
	老中青相同		老中青不同		总数		老中青相同		老中青不同		总数	
2 生理病理	79.6%	78	20.4%	20	100.0%	98	100.0%	1	0.0%	0	100.0%	1
1 植物	80.3%	478	19.7%	117	100.0%	595	83.9%	94	16.1%	18	100.0%	112
3 饮食	83.7%	128	16.3%	25	100.0%	153	93.7%	15	6.3%	1	100.0%	16
1 动物	84.8%	701	15.2%	126	100.0%	827	83.7%	82	16.3%	16	100.0%	98
2 人体	85.5%	247	14.5%	42	100.0%	289	88.6%	31	11.4%	4	100.0%	35
1 方位	90.0%	9	10.0%	1	100.0%	10	66.7%	2	33.3%	1	100.0%	3
1 天象地理	90.0%	9	10.0%	1	100.0%	10	100.0%	4	0.0%	0	100.0%	4
总数	71.7%	2 612	28.3%	1 032	100.0%	3 644	80.1%	362	19.9%	90	100.0%	452

注：1：反映自然世界的词；2：体现人及人际关系的词；3：展现社会生活的词；+：老中青不同的百分比≥50%。

从上表可见，名词中变化最大的是“3：展现社会生活的词”。一般词汇中以“房屋”、“文化娱乐”、“国家地区”三类在老中青之间差别最大。常用基本词汇则以“房屋”、“文化娱乐”两类的差异最大。其中“房屋”、“文化娱乐”重见于一般词汇与常用基本词汇，反映了在几十年之间，变化最大的就是“房屋”与“文化娱乐”两类。

以房屋为例，老派曾住老式宅院，也认识许多与旧式建筑有关的词汇，如头门（principal outer gate）、二门（front gate）、大楼（floors）、小楼（祀神或旁奉祖先于其上）、土库（楼下房）、洗身房（bathroom）、板帘（blinds）、窗压（bars in the windows）、灶窟（ash-hole of the furnace）等等，这些词汇，中青派都不认识。

除了个人原因以外，主要是居住环境的改变令老中青对房屋的词汇有不同的认识。战后香港人口急剧增长，市区的人口密度大，木屋区（木屋指用铁皮、木板搭建而成的屋子）越来越多，在20世纪50年代初有30万人居于木屋区，60年代增加至80万人。由于50年代木屋区几次发生火灾，数万居民无家可归，迫使政府注意木屋区的情况，兴建“徙置屋”安置受灾居民。之后政府开始营建公共房屋（廉租房）来解决木屋区居民住房的问题，例如70年代的“十年建屋计划”、“新市镇发展计划”，目的就是解决180万缺房人口的住房问题。（黄钊鸿，2004：303～305）政府政策使社会生活发生了巨大的变化，使市民的居住环境发生改变，从而令老派与中青派在房屋的词汇上有显著的差异。

其次是文化方面，例如“番字”（foreign letters），现代称之为“字母”，只有老派认识。事实上《读本》中还有许多与“番”有关的词，例如番斜纹布（foreign dimity）、番人（foreigners）、番桅（masts in foreign vessel）、番国（foreign countries）、番船（foreign ships）、番舶（foreign ships）、番铜（foreign copper）、番钱（foreign coins）、番碱（soaps come from foreign countries）、番茄（tomatoes）等等。现在老中青仍然使用的是番碱（肥皂，现代一般写作“番枧”）、番茄（西红柿），其他大多数都已经丢失，或个别为老派认识。由“番”字组成的词逐渐丢失，主要是因为人们知识面扩宽，与外国的交流增加，对外国事物的认识逐渐加深，从而使语言使用者的态度逐渐改变，不再用带贬义的“番”来指称外国的事物。

2.2.2 动词的变化情况

动词中，老中青最大的差异在文化娱乐、生理病理两类；在常用基本词汇中，文化娱乐的差异也最大，情况如下表所示：

类别＼比例	一般词汇						常用基本词汇					
	老中青相同		老中青不同		总数		老中青相同		老中青不同		总数	
文化娱乐	33.3%	1	66.7%	2	100.0%	3	0.0%	0	100.0%	1	100.0%	1
生理病理	68.1%	81	31.9%	38	100.0%	119	83.3%	5	16.7%	1	100.0%	6
日常操作	71.6%	156	28.4%	62	100.0%	218	82.1%	55	17.9%	12	100.0%	67
其他	76.2%	16	23.8%	5	100.0%	21	50.0%	1	50.0%	1	100.0%	2
交际事务人事	79.3%	69	20.7%	18	100.0%	87	91.7%	22	8.3%	2	100.0%	24
愿望判断	83.3%	5	16.7%	1	100.0%	6	100.0%	3	0.0%	0	100.0%	3
肢体动作	84.6%	55	15.4%	10	100.0%	65	100.0%	29	0.0%	0	100.0%	29
五官动作	87.0%	20	13.0%	3	100.0%	23	100.0%	6	0.0%	0	100.0%	6
感受思维	100.0%	17	0.0%	0	100.0%	17	100.0%	12	0.0%	0	100.0%	12
自然变化	100.0%	1	0.0%	0	100.0%	1	100.0%	1	0.0%	0	100.0%	1
总数	75.2%	421	24.8%	139	100.0%	560	88.7%	134	11.3%	17	100.0%	151

不论是在名词还是动词中，老中青差异最大的都是文化娱乐一类。可见在这170年间文化娱乐有相当大的变化。例如：

（1）你念得过吖簿书唔念得呢？（1841：1.2）（你能不能读那本书？/Are you able to rehearse those volumes?）

（2）东家你要我念过你听呀？（1841：5.8）（老板，你要我念给你听吗？/Do you sir, wish me to read it to you?）

上面两个例子，现代广州话一般用“读”，可见“念”受书面语影响而发生改变。

然而现代广州话仍有用“念”（一般写作“唸”）组成的词，如“唸经”、“唸南无”（念经）、“唸口簧”（读顺口溜）等说法。“唸经”、“唸南无”除本义以外，已由“念经”的低沉声音引申为说话唠叨，声音低微难辨；而“唸口簧”本指读顺口溜，现在比喻死板地背诵，流利而没有感情地唸。如：“你读书系唸口簧嘅，知唔知讲啲乜啫？”（你读书就像是读顺口溜，知不知道说的是啥？）（麦耘、谭步云，2011：220）《实用广州话分类词典》（修订版）（以下简称《分类词典》）、《广州话方言词典》（以下简称《方言词典》）均指“唸口簧”用法同“读口簧”（饶秉才、欧阳觉亚、周无忌，2009：179）。可见，“念”曾在广州话口语中使用，有“朗诵”（rehearse）、“读”（read）的意思，但这两个义项现在已经被书面语“读”取代，而由“念”组成的词，其本义仍可使用，但较多用引申义。可见，动词“念”的完全更替仍未完成，“念”与“读”仍然处于竞争的状态。

2.2.3 形容词的变化情况

形容词中，老中青最大的差异在形状情况与生理感觉两类，但其中只有一般词汇的形状情况一类大于30%。具体差异如下表所示：

类别\比例	一般词汇						常用基本词汇					
	老中青相同		老中青不同		总数		老中青相同		老中青不同		总数	
形状情况	68.3%	84	31.7%	39	100.0%	123	91.4%	32	8.6%	3	100.0%	35
生理感觉	77.8%	14	22.2%	4	100.0%	18	85.7%	6	14.3%	1	100.0%	7
形貌体态	81.8%	27	18.2%	6	100.0%	33	100.0%	3	0.0%	0	100.0%	3
性质	87.5%	7	12.5%	1	100.0%	8	100.0%	2	0.0%	0	100.0%	2
心理感受	100.0%	1	0.0%	0	100.0%	2	0.0%	0	0.0%	0	100.0%	0
品性行为	100.0%	11	0.0%	0	100.0%	11	100.0%	2	0.0%	0	100.0%	2
总数	74.2%	144	25.8%	50	100.0%	194	91.8%	45	8.2%	4	100.0%	49

根据上表的资料，一般词汇和常用基本词汇中，老中青之间的差异最大的是“形状情况”以及“生理感觉”。在常用基本词汇中，“形状情况”的例子如下：

（3）眼水淋淋漓。（1841：2.8）（泪水淋漓。/The tears flow down in streams.）

现代广州话已没有“淋淋漓”的说法，近似的说法是“喊到乜嘢噉”。至于“生理感觉”，例子如下：

（4）先日我都食夜餐，整得我成夜都瞓唔着，惮惮恷恷咁。（1841：5.10）（前一阵子，我很晚用餐，害我整晚都睡不着，心神不安。/Formerly, I was accustomed to eat an evening meal, and then was unable to sleep, and was restless and disturb all night long.）

“生理感觉”在一般词汇中的例子有：

（5）近日都系带静咯。（1841：3.1）（近日身体很衰弱。/Of late he has been rather _eehle.① and infirm.）

例（4）的“惮惮恷恷”，只有中派听过，大意是身体不舒服。这个词，现代广州话已经不再使用，但现代有同音字“惮憸（腌尖）”（jim[1] tsim[1]），是挑剔的意思，“惮憸”

① 《读本》原文是微型胶卷，胶卷上的英文翻译部分较为模糊，未能显示该字。

可能是由于身体不舒服而令人觉得事事挑剔。

例（5）的“带静”（tai[3] tsaŋ[1]），只有老派听过，意思是身体不舒服。这个词现代广州话已经不再使用，是濒临死亡的词。

2.2.4 **量词的变化情况**

量词是表示事物或动作的单位词，就老中青三派的使用情况来看，量词在使用上的差异大多是由书面语造成的。先看具体的数据：

类别\比例	一般词汇						常用基本词汇					
	老中青相同		老中青不同		总数		老中青相同		老中青不同		总数	
物量词	74.4%	29	25.6%	10	100.0%	39	84.6%	22	15.4%	4	100.0%	26
动量词	50.0%	1	50.0%	1	100.0%	2	100.0%	1	0.0%	0	100.0%	1
时量词	100.0%	1	0.0%	0	100.0%	1	100.0%	1	0.0%	0	100.0%	1
总数	73.8%	31	26.2%	11	100.0%	42	85.7%	24	14.3%	4	100.0%	28

老中青不同的情况以物量词为最，一般词汇是25.6%，常用基本词汇是15.4%；其次是动量词。一般词汇中，三派中使用有差异的如“堂”、“簿”、“打臣”、“烟治”，具体情况如下：

堂

（6）一堂漆圈手椅（1841：5.3）（一套上漆圈手椅/a set of lacquered arm-chairs）

在老派中“一堂”就是“一套”，中青两派都没有听过这种说法。根据《读本》中的英文解说，“一堂”也就是“一套”（a set），与老派的认知相同。现代广州话的“堂”用于眉毛、鼻涕、梯子、蚊帐等，如一堂眉（一对眉）、吖堂鼻涕（那两行鼻涕）、一堂梯（一把梯子）、一堂蚊帐（一顶蚊帐）等，但“一堂”已经没有“一套”的意思。而用“一套”取代“一堂”应是受了书面语的影响。

簿

（7）三簿大字书起咯。（1841：1.2）（从三部大字书开始。/With the three volumes in the large character.）

老派、中派指“书”的量词就是“簿”，读pou[6]；青派则认为“书”应用“部”（也读pou[6]），两者是词形的差异，青派改用“部”代替“簿”应是受了书面语的影响。此外，《方言词典》、《分类词典》已没有收“簿”作量词；《方言词典》指“簿”是“本子”，读pou[2]。可见，写作“簿pou[6]”的量词已经濒临死亡，取而代之的是词形与书面语相同的“部”。

至于“打臣”、“烟治”是英国度量衡的单位，“打臣”是dozen（打）的音译，“烟治”是 inch（英寸）的音译，例子如下：

打臣

（8）每打臣一个八承本。（1841：6.6）（每打一块八成本。/Each dozen stood me in $1.80 prime cost.）

烟治

（9）我的货都够三十三个烟治。（1841：6.6）（我的货也够三十三英寸。/My goods are all full thirty three and a half inches wide.）

“打臣”、“烟治”两个音译词，只有老派听过，中青两派都不认识。“打臣”现代广州话用“打”（ta^1），用法与书面语相同。“烟治”《读本》读作 jin^1tsi^6，《分类词典》写作“烟子”，读作 jin^1tsi^2（麦耘、谭步云，2011：339），读 tsi^2 应是变调。现代广州话已用“寸”来代替“烟治”。简而言之，这两个音译词最后由书面语的说法胜出。

一般词汇中，动量词“回”的使用，在老派以及中青派中也有差异，例如：

回

（10）勤力学多几回啰。（1841：1.1）（用功多学几次。/Then study assiduously，often repeating what you learn.）

（11）一日饮几回。（1841：5.11）（一天喝几次。/Several times a day.）

（12）呢回唔怕。（1841：6.5）（这次不怕。/On this occasion you have no cause to fear.）

“回”老派指以前有“呢一回”（这一次）的说法，但只限于这种搭配。例子可见（10）~（12）中的“回”，是广州话中濒临死亡的量词，《方言词典》、《分类词典》已不收“回”作量词。现代广州话已改用与书面语相同的“次”，又或是用“匀”、“轮”来表示“次”；按语感以“次”的使用频率为高。

至于常用基本词汇中，量词有变异的例子有“件”、“乘”、“管”，例句如下：

件

（13）戴件雨帽遮雨。（1841：5.4）（戴顶雨帽挡雨。/Put on a rain-hat to shelter from the rain.）

（14）你试吓个件帽。（1841：5.5 09）（你试一下那顶帽子。/Just try on that bonnet and see if it will suit you.）

（15）要几件干平果。（1841：5.7）（要几块干苹果。/We want some dried apples.）

（16）多食几件肥腻。（1841：5.12）（多吃几件油腻的。/I eat a few bit of fat or oily food.）

例（13）、（14）以“件”搭配名词“帽”，现在已经不再使用，现代广州话“帽”的量词是“顶”，与书面语相同。可见，“顶”的搭配对象在这170年间有的不变，有的已经改变，是一种不变中有变、变中有不变的情况。例（15）、（16）的“件”用于食物

（一般是小块的）（麦耘、谭步云，2011：336），现代广州话仍然使用这种搭配。广州话量词“件”的其他用法与书面语相同，如一件事、两件衫、三件行李。

乘

（17）抬乘轿去拜会。（1841：5.3）（抬一顶轿子去拜会。/He has gone in a sedan to repay visits.）

例（17）的“乘”只有老派听过，但现代广州话不再使用，《方言词典》和《分类词典》也都没有收作量词，可见“乘”是濒临死亡的量词。至于“轿”现代广州话用的量词是“顶”，与书面语相同。

管

（18）穿管针联衣服。（1841：5.5）（穿一根针来缝衣服。/Thread a needle and sew this garment.）

例（18）的“管”，老派指“管”是以前的说法。现代广州话“针”的量词是“眼”或“枝”，《方言词典》和《分类词典》已没有收“管”作量词。换句话说，“管”也是濒临死亡的量词。

总的来说，量词在三派中的变化明显受书面语的影响，上面所举的八个量词，七个都受书面语影响，用了书面语的说法。“一堂（椅）”改用“一套（椅）”，“一簿（书）”改用“一部（书）”，“一打臣”改用“一打”，“一烟治”改用“一寸”，“一回”改用“一次”，“一件（帽）”改用“一顶（帽）”，“一乘（轿）”改用“一顶（轿）”，剩下的“一管（针）”的“管”则已退出了量词的舞台。当中“堂”、“簿”、“打臣”、“烟治”、“回”已是濒临死亡的量词，只有老派听过，但也不再使用。

结果显示书面语与口语的竞争在量词中特别明显。这表明了一个具体的事实：从《读本》至今的170年间，书面语不断冲击广州话口语，并以各种方式传播四方，继而影响口语，使广州话口语与书面语呈现逐渐靠拢的趋势。

2.2.5 代词的变化情况

代词的老中青差异并不明显，三派之间只有指示代词的用法有差异，具体情况如下表所示：

类别\比例	老中青相同		老中青不同		总数		老中青相同		老中青不同		总数	
人称代词	100.0%	7	0.0%	0	7	100.0%	100.0%	6	0.0%	0	6	100.0%
疑问代词	100.0%	12	0.0%	0	12	100.0%	100.0%	10	0.0%	0	10	100.0%
指示代词	93.3%	14	6.7%	1	15	100.0%	80.0%	4	20.0%	1	5	100.0%
总数	97.1%	33	2.9%	1	34	100.0%	95.2%	20	4.8%	1	21	100.0%

从上表可见，三派之间的差异在指示代词中，具体的例子是处所指示代词“处”。根

据《广州方言研究》,“处所指示代词除了近指和远指外，还有一种不分远近的中性指，表示无须分别或分不出远近的处所（不是指不远不近)”，“这种中性指只用于照应”（李新魁等，1995：469)。“中性指并没有出现新的指示代词，而‘中性指’的意思，是说该词组（如佢度）所指示的处所，不是指距离的远近，而是由‘佢’的位置决定的，所以可远可近，是为中性指”（张双庆，2009：349)。

现代广州话远指一般用“吓度”、“吓处”（那儿)，近指用“呢度”、“呢处”（这儿)，中性指用“度”、“处”（这儿)，“度”、“处”前面可加上名词或代名词，如“佢度”、“佢处”（他那儿)。无论远指、近指、中性指，“度”都较常用。《读本》的情况与现代广州话不同，《读本》只用“处”，不用“度”，近指用“呢处”，远指在《读本》中没有例子，中性指用“处”。用“处”不用“度”这种情况也见于同类型的调查。（黄小娅，2000：26)

《读本》中的例子：

(19) 各样颜色都齐呢处。(1841：6.6)（各种颜色都在这儿。/All sorts of colors are here mixed together.)

(20) 已经拧定喺呢处嚟嘑。（1841：5.8）（我已经预先拿好放在这儿了。/I have already brought it, and here it is.)

(21) 春季折枝驳口处包坭。(1841：9.2)（在春季折枝的驳口那儿包泥。/The scions are cut out in spring, and earth is bound about the place where they are inserted.)

(22) 有的新过喺处。(1841：5.6)（有些新的在这儿。/There are some new ones.)

例（19)、(20）是近指，例（21)、(22）是中性指。这两种用法现在广州话仍然使用，然而《读本》中有中性指的用法，现代广州话已经不再使用，例如：

(23) 挤番枝盐羹处。（1841：5.3）（把盐匙放回去。/Put the salt spoon back in its place.)

例（23）的说法现代广州话已经不用。上文提过“‘中性指’……该词组所指示的处所……由‘佢’的位置决定”，这里要放的东西是“盐羹”，但放的位置又由“盐羹”决定，便造成指代不明的情况。因此，例（23）的情况，在现代广州话中所放的东西不可以是“盐羹”，而必须是其他物品。

3 结语:《读本》中的词汇演变情况及原因

根据上文的分析，《读本》中的老中青使用情况有以下特点：①现代广州方言常用基本词汇的变动小，一般词汇的变化大。②变化情况从大至小的排列是名词、动词、形容词、量词、代词。③老中青之间的差距，即使是变化最大的名词，老青之间的差距也少于25%，显示广州话的保留情况良好。广州方言词汇发生变化，主要是由社会文化生活的改变、词汇系统的竞争发展以及语言接触引起的。

3.1 《读本》中的词汇演变情况

3.1.1 常用基本词汇变化小，一般词汇变化大

“汉语的基本词汇，它们一直从先秦使用到现在。常用词语具有较大的稳固性，产生以后被人们普遍使用，其中有不少一直延续到现代汉语中，成了现代汉语的基本词汇。非常用词语变化较快，有些用了一个时期以后就不再使用或意义完全改变了”（蒋绍愚，2005：273）。《读本》的老中青使用情况，再一次证明了这种情况：常用基本词的变化比较稳定，一般词汇比较变动。本文的结果经量化后，比例如下：

类别\比例\使用情况	不再使用	仍然使用
一般词汇：常用基本词汇	3.9：1	0.5：1

在丢失率上，一般词汇与常用基本词汇相比，至少是3：1。在存留率上，比较接近1：2。影响词汇的因素有很多，词汇的变化虽然不一定可以绝对地用数学的概念来表述，但至少可用这个比较具体的方式来说明一般词汇变化大的“大”以及常用基本词汇变化小的“小”所指的内涵是什么。

上面的数据显示在那170年间，一般词汇与常用基本词汇的不再使用率的比例，保守地说是3：1，即一般词汇丢失3个，常用基本词汇丢失1个；仍然使用的比例是1：2，即一般词汇保留1个，常用基本词汇保留2个。

然而，这个一般词汇与常用基本词汇的变化趋势，在各词类之间仍有一些差异。按一般词汇与常用基本词汇的差距大小来排列是名词、动词、形容词、量词、代词，而在代词中，一般词汇与常用基本词汇几乎已没有差异。

此外，在各词类的小类之中，一般词汇丢失的小类多，常用基本词汇丢失的小类少。也就是说，常用基本词汇确保了老中青之间，在日常沟通上无论是量和类都比较稳定，有利于沟通顺利进行。

3.1.2 名词丢失最迅速，代词丢失最缓慢

“名词是变化最快的一类，因为它跟社会的发展、物质文明和精神文明的进步关系最为直接。”“从数量上看，形容词在历史上发生过新旧更替的可能要略少于名词。”（汪维辉，2000：23、324）本文的基本情况也是如此。如前所说，在《读本》中词汇丢失的情况从大至小的排列是名词、动词、形容词、量词、代词，无论在一般词汇或是常用基本词汇中，都是类似的情况。在各词类中，名词最为活跃，它的变化最为迅速，反应最为敏感，而动词和形容词与名词的关系相对较为密切，所以其变化速度紧随其后。量词、代词则丢失得最缓慢，这表示固有的量词、代词一般已能服务新出现的词，较不容易丢失。

除此之外，各词类的整体情况大致是年龄越大，保留越多；年龄越小，保留越少。但年龄因素的影响在名词、动词中较为明显，在量词、代词中比较小。换句话说，年龄这一

因素也同样说明了名词、动词的变化较为迅速，量词、代词较为稳定。

3.1.3 广州方言中老青的存留与丢失的差距在25%之内

老中青三派在《读本》中的使用差距上，与厦门方言的情况不相同。郑见见调查了祖孙三代的使用情况，结果显示“有大约一半的厦门方言词汇已经或正在……流失”（郑见见，2007：4）。然而，广州方言中老青的差距，无论在整体情况还是五类词汇的情况中，差距都在25%之内，具体情况如下表：

词类\老青差距	一般词汇				常用基本词汇			
	不再使用		仍然使用		不再使用		仍然使用	
整体	988	(22.1%)	1 004	(22.5%)	84	(12.0%)	88	(12.5%)
名词	837	(23.0%)	853	(23.4%)	70	(15.5%)	72	(15.9%)
动词	105	(18.8%)	106	(18.9%)	11	(7.3%)	12	(8.0%)
形容词	37	(19.1%)	36	(18.6%)	1	(2.0%)	1	(2.1%)
量词	8	(19.0%)	8	(19.1%)	1	(3.6%)	2	(7.1%)
代词	1	(2.9%)	1	(3.0%)	1	(4.8%)	1	(4.8%)

综合上表的资料可见，广州方言即使是变化最快的名词，在一般词汇中，老青的整体差距约为22%（不再使用是22.1%，仍然使用是22.5%），而差距在20%左右的占多数（不再使用：名词23.0%、动词18.8%、形容词19.1%、量词19.0%；仍然使用：名词23.4%、动词18.9%、形容词18.6%、量词19.1%）。在常用基本词汇中，除名词外，老青的差距主要在10%以下（不再使用：动词7.3%、形容词2.0%、量词3.6%、代词4.8%；仍然使用：动词8.0%、形容词2.1%、量词7.1%、代词4.8%）。由此可见，广州话的保留情况仍然良好。其中一个主要原因是，在香港，广州话代替了普通话，在口语、书面语、文艺语中全面覆盖，可演说、授课。换方音可表达白话文、文言文（参看李如龙，2012）；然而自香港回归以后，普通话开始进入香港社会，这种“保存良好”的情况可能会逐渐改变。

3.2 影响词汇演变的因素

3.2.1 语言的外部因素：社会文化生活的改变

总体来说，《读本》中老派与中青两派的距离明显较远，中派与青派则比较接近。由此可见，虽然三派之间的差距都是十五年，但老中之间所发生的变化大于中青之间的变化。

老派与中青之间所发生的重要历史事件是日军占领香港，当时许多香港市民被迫离开香港避难。及后华人陆续返港，香港人口骤增至百万，房屋、粮食、各类物资严重短缺。这段历史使香港的生活发生了极大的变化，当时的香港百废待兴，人民生活、经济结构都经历着重大的改变。然而，由于中青两派在香港战后出生，生活比较安定，生活经验也比较相近，因此差距较小。

除此以外，旧事物消亡也令相关的词语退出历史舞台。战后香港人口急剧增长，木屋区越来越多。政府也兴建了“徙置屋”，同时开始营建公共房屋（廉租房）来解决住房问题。政府政策使社会生活发生了巨大的变化，使市民的居住环境发生了改变，也因此令老派与中青两派在房屋的词汇上有显著的差异。

至于在文化方面，《读本》中还有许多与“番”有关的词，例如“番字”（英文字母）、番斜纹布（西洋麻纱）、番人（外国人）等等，大多数都已经丢失。一方面是因为人们知识面的扩阔，另一方面是英国统治香港的其中一个目的是加强欧亚的贸易联系，香港与外国的交流增加，对外国事物的认识也因而逐步加深，继而使语言使用者的态度发生改变。到现在，虽然已经较少使用带有贬义的“番”来指称外国的事物，但仍然保留了一些与“番”字组合成词的词汇，如“番瓜”（南瓜）、“番鬼荔枝”（番荔枝）、“番鬼佬”（老外）、“番薯”等（饶秉才、欧阳觉亚、周无忌，2009：56）。

3.2.2 语言的内部因素：词汇系统的竞争与发展

在语言演变的过程中，除了外部因素以外，内部因素才是语言发展与演变的最基本动因。（徐睿渊，2008）其中近义词的竞争、口语书面语的竞争在《读本》中有相当多的例子。

近义词是任何一个语言词汇中，意义相同或基本相同而材料构造却不相同的词。（参看刘叔新，1987：导论）以副词为例，广州方言的“上头”、“下头”在指排行方面已被“对上”、“对落”取代；在指上边、下边方面则被比较概括化的“上便”、“下便”取代。

书面语与口语的竞争，使老中青之间的差异非常明显。“口语总是‘短兵相接’，一发即逝，难以慢条斯理地推敲；书面语则可以精雕细刻，进行科学和艺术的加工……特别是在现代社会里，人们交往频繁，信息爆炸，出版物泛滥，书面语的普及以及传输到口语比以往任何时代都迅速。”（李如龙，2004：194）从老中青的使用差异中，可见保存率最高的量词，也明显受到书面语的影响，例如“一堂（椅）”改用“一套（椅）”、“一簿（书）”改用“一部（书）”、“一回”改用“一次”等等。时量词也同时受着书面语的影响，如“点钟”（钟头）已有向普通话靠拢的趋势。

由此可见，香港在口语的语用方面虽然全面由广州方言覆盖，但从《读本》至今的170年间，书面语仍保留着巨大的撞击力，不断冲击着广州话口语，使得书面语和口语逐渐靠拢。

3.2.3 语言的内部因素：语言接触引起的词汇变化

一般来说，方言与通语、周边方言、外语都有所接触。除了与通语的接触外，广州方言因外语接触也起了不少变化。例如，英国的度量衡“打臣”（打）与“烟治”（寸），在词义系统里起了补缺的作用。此外，房屋类词汇中的“土库”（楼下房），只有老派听过，可能是受印尼语、马来西亚语的影响。

参考文献

胡明扬　1978　《上海话一百年来的若干变化》，《中国语文》第3期，第199～205页。

黄鸿钊　2004　《香港近代史》，香港：学津书店。

黄小娅　2000　《近两百年来广州方言词汇和方言用字的演变》，暨南大学博士学位论文。

蒋绍愚　2005　《近代汉语研究概要》，北京：北京大学出版社。

李如龙、徐睿渊　2007　《厦门方言词汇一百多年来的变化——对三本教会厦门话语料的考察》，《厦门大学学报》第1期，第84～91页。

李如龙　2001　《汉语方言学》，北京：高等教育出版社。

李如龙　2004　《汉语应用研究》，北京：中国传媒大学出版社。

李如龙　2012　《试论粤语的特征》（未发表论文）。

李新魁等　1995　《广州方言研究》，广州：广东人民出版社。

林寒生　2001　《福州方言词汇二三百年来的历史演变》，第七届闽方言国际研讨会论文。

刘叔新　1987　《现代汉语同义词词典》，天津：天津人民出版社。

麦耘、谭步云　2011　《实用广州话分类词典》，香港：商务印书馆。

饶秉才、欧阳觉亚、周无忌　2009　《广州话方言词典》（修订版），香港：商务印书馆。

苏晓青、佟秋妹、王海燕　2004　《徐州方言词汇60年来的变化——徐州方言向普通话靠拢的趋势考察之二》，《江苏师范大学学报》第3期，第61～64页。

汪维辉　2000　《东汉—隋常用词演变研究》，南京：南京大学出版社。

徐睿渊　2008　《厦门方言一百多年来语音系统和词汇系统的演变——对三本教会语料的考察》，厦门大学博士学位论文。

游汝杰　2004　《汉语方言学教程》，上海：上海教育出版社。

张双庆　2009　《香港粤语的代词》，载于李如龙、张双庆主编　《代词》，广州：暨南大学出版社，第345～360页。

赵恩挺　2003　《广州话百年来的词汇变迁》，台湾师范大学博士学位论文。

郑见见　2007　《流失中的厦门方言词汇——以一家祖孙三代方言词汇的使用情况为例》，厦门大学学士学位论文。

粤语句末语气助词“定喇”刍议*

颜耀良

（美国国防语言学院）

提　要：“定（$diŋ^{35}$）喇”是粤方言中的一个句末语气助词，而“吧”则是普通话中语义上和使用上较为接近“定喇”的一个句末语气助词，两者都有很多值得探讨的地方。本文拟讨论“定喇”的语义含义、句子特点以及与“吧”的主要不同。第一节讨论“定喇”的语义和句法特点，第二节讨论此二句末语气助词的不同。

关键词：语气助词　定喇　吧

1　“定喇”的语义和句法特点

“定喇”是粤方言中的一个语气助词，它通常接于陈述句句末，表示一种推测的语气，适合于各种形式的陈述句，包括肯定、否定以及不同谓语形式的陈述句。其核心情态语义大致相当于普通话的“很可能”或“大概……吧”。例如：

（1）我谂，佢哋梗系赚到盘满钵满定喇。（网上②）
（2）你未去过西贡浪茄定喇。（网上）
（3）你梗系好饿定喇。（网上）
（4）咁你梗系北京人定喇！（网上）
（5）佢琴日头又痛定喇。

例（1）和例（2）的“定喇”接在动词性谓语陈述句的后面，表示推测，增加该二陈述句的存疑度。而例（3）、例（4）和例（5）则接在形容词性谓语陈述句、名词性谓语句以及主谓谓语陈述句的后面，表示说话人的推测。其中，例（2）是否定陈述句，其他各句则都是肯定陈述句。

---

*　谨此感谢审稿人提出的宝贵意见，文中错漏之处概由本人负责。

②　标有“网上”的句子都是网上摘录下来、未经过改动的句子。

此类句子有一个突出的特点就是“推测人”通常是第一人称，而且此人称一般在句子里采取隐含或无标记的形式，即代词“我/我哋”无须出现，如以上例（2）至例（5）四句，虽然说话人“我”没有出现，但我们都可以毫不困难地理解为推测者是说话人“我”。然而，推测者“我”也可采取有标记的形式出现，如例（1）的“我谂”。此外，推测者也可以是其他人称，不过如果是其他人称，推测者一定要采取有标记的形式，而且往往需要用间接引语的形式。如：

（6）a. 佢讲你梗系北京人定喇！

b. 佢讲佢谂你梗系系北京人定喇！

另外，也可以使用直接引语的形式。不过，使用直接引语的形式时，如果说话人是推测者，引语内的推测者通常需要用第一人称，它既可以采取无标记的形式，如（7）a，也可以采取有标记的形式，如（7）b。但如果推测者是别的人称，则需要采取明示的形式，而且不能再使用“定喇”，如（8）a～b。例如：

（7）a. 张三讲：“琴日你头又痛定喇。”

b. 张三讲：“我谂琴日你头又痛定喇。”

（8）a. 张三讲：“李四谂你琴日头又痛喇。”

b. *张三讲：“李四谂你琴日头又痛定喇。”

此类句子还有一个特点就是推测的内容通常是一个子句，这个子句跟“我谂”和“定喇”不在一个句法层次上，前者处于低层次，而后者处于高层次。例如：

（9）我谂［佢琴日头又痛］定喇。

2 “定喇”句与普通话“吧”字句的不同

较之于普通话的所有句末语气助词，“定喇”无论是从功能、语义或是句法上讲，都与“吧”最为接近。跟“定喇”一样，普通话的“吧”也可以接在各种谓语形式的陈述句后，表示说话人的推测。比如第一节中的例（1）到例（5）这五个句子我们就可以把它们转换成带“吧”的普通话句子，见例（10）～（14），转换以后，它们的意思还是比较接近的。

（10）我想，他们一定赚了很多钱吧。（佢哋梗系赚到盘满钵满定喇。）

（11）你没去过西贡浪茄吧。（你未去过西贡浪茄定喇。）

（12）你一定很饿（了）吧。（你梗系好饿定喇。）

（13）那你一定是北京人吧！（咁你一定系北京人定喇！）

（14）他昨天头又疼（了）吧。（佢琴日头又痛定喇。）

尽管粤语的“定喇”和普通话的“吧”有很多相似的地方，但二者之间还是有好些不一样的地方，下面我们有选择地讨论一下这些不同。

2.1 句法上的不同

跟“定喇”只能接在陈述句的后面不同，“吧”除了可以用于陈述句以外，还可以用于疑问句、祈使句以及感叹句。例如：

（15）疑问句：

a. 难道我的话就不算数？我现在问你，我的裁决已经下了，你出不出钱吧？（当代\应用文\中国农民调查23）

b. 粤语：……＊你出唔出钱定喇？

（16）祈使句：

a. 看到我，他起初一愣，随即笑了：“不急，暂时还没角色，你慢慢等吧！”（当代\史传\中国北漂艺人生存实录4）

b. 粤语：……＊你慢慢等定喇！

（17）感叹句：

a. 佩特娜·柯特恳求她。“我这么屈辱地来，可见我多么爱他吧。”

b. 粤语：……＊可见我几甘爱佢定喇！

2.2 “定喇”和“吧”在“三域”使用上的不同

“定喇”和“吧”也可以放到“三域”的框架内来对比考察，在这一方面我们也觉得它们有明显的不同。“定喇”的使用主要集中于“知域”方面，而“行域”和“言域”方面的使用都比较有限，而“吧”在“行域”、“知域”和“言域”方面的使用都极为普遍。在“行域”方面，用于“行域”的“吧”字句，转换成带“定喇”的粤语句子时，一般的情况是，要么它们变成“知域”的句子，要么就是变得难以接受。

（18）a. 你怕（担心）赶不上汽车吧。

b. 你怕（担心）赶唔到汽车定喇。

c. 你怕（担心）赶唔到汽车。

按照肖治野的分析，例（18）a 的“吧”属于“行域”用法（肖治野，2010：131），如果我们把“吧”换成“定喇”，变成例（18）b 的粤语句，那么由于“定喇”的出现，例（18）b 就变为“知域”的用法了。但是如果再把例（18）b 的“定喇”去掉，该句就又可以分析为“行域”用法的句子了［例（18）c］。又如：

（19）a. “住好久啦？”“快一年了吧。”（礼平《小站的黄昏》）

b. 粤语：“＊就快一年定喇。”

肖治野（2010：128）认为例（19）a“快一年了吧”的“吧”表示不确定语气，属于“行域”的用法。我们同意其看法，因为它是说话人就自己（在那儿）居住了多长时间而回答对方的问话，他应该清楚地知道自己已经住了多长时间，不需要推测。但是，如果例（19）a换上了粤语表示推测的“知域”用法的“定喇”，就不合适了［例（19）b］。因此“定喇”具有把“行域”句转变成“知域”句的功能，但这种转换具有局限性，它只能部分转换，而不可全部转换。

在“言域”方面，很多常用的、典型的“言域”用法，如命令、请求、催促、应允、建议、劝止、承诺、拒绝等，“吧”字句都可以胜任，而“定喇”句则无能为力。例如：

（20） a. 坐下吧！→＊坐低定喇。（命令）（但可用“啦^{55}”）
　　b. 你先说个价吧！→＊你先畀个价定喇。（请求）（可用“啦^{55}”）
　　c. 快点吧！→＊快啲定喇。（催促）（可用“啦^{55}”）
　　d. 就这样吧！→＊就噉定喇。（应允）（可用“啦^{55}”）
（21） a. 三点出发吧！→＊三点出发定喇。（建议，征求意见）（可用“咧^{21}”）
　　b. 别抽烟了吧！→＊无食烟定喇。（劝止）
（22） a. 我全都包了吧！→＊我冚唪呤包晒定喇。（承诺/建议）（可用“喇^{33}”）
　　b. 不了吧！→＊毋喇定喇。（拒绝）（可用“喇啩”）

以上8例［例（20）~（22）］“吧”字句都是“言域”的句子，把它们转换成“定喇”句以后就变得难以被接受了，要让这些句子合法化就必须放弃“定喇”而代之以其他语气助词，像“啦^{55}、咧^{21}、喇^{33}、喇啩”等。可见，“定喇”的使用域比普通话的“吧”窄得多，它跟很多“言域”的用法是不匹配的。

2.3 “定喇”句和“吧”字句在主观性方面的不同

“吧”和“定喇”都有一个共同点就是明显地带有说话人推测的主观性，但二者有一个明显不同的地方就是“吧”比“定（diŋ^{2}）喇”具有更明显的交互主观性。例如：

（23） a. 追得上他那物价，追不上他那粮价啊！我现在这么说的都录下来了吧？我说这就是实际情况。（当代\口语\1982年北京话调查资料11）
　　＊b. 粤语：我宜家讲嘅都录咗落来定喇。

例（23）b是例（23）a的“吧”字句转换成粤语的“定喇”句后的句子，转换后的例（23）b是不能用于例（23）a这种语境的，因为二者在主观性和交互主观性方面有所不同。例（23）b的“定喇”虽然也表示说话人的主观推测，但这种推测是说话人内心独自的推测，这种推测是独立于听话人的态度、反应或情感的。虽然例（23）a的“吧”也是说话人的主观推测，但它是以问话的形式或询问听话人的形式进行的，它期待着听话人的互动，所以是一种带有交互主观性的推测。

又如上文例（20）~（22）中“言域”的各种用法也反映了说话人对听话人不同的态度

或情感。例（20）a～c 要是没有“吧”，也是表示“命令/请求/催促”，但加上“吧”以后更缓和了说话人说话的语气，听话人也可以感觉到说话人亲切的情感和态度。同样例（21）a～b 中的“吧”也缓和了说话语气，让听话人感到说话人客气的情感和态度。如果将“吧”去掉，该二例就变成语气生硬的“命令”，而不是语气温和的“建议”和“劝止”了。

相比之下，“定喇”是缺乏这些功能的，之所以这样，与“定喇”主要用于“知域”有密切关系。“定喇”的推测主要是说话人自己的推测，在“知域”方面的使用一般不必涉及对听话人或第三者的情感和态度，而“吧”的使用则常常涉及，因此，它带有比“定喇”明显得多的交互主观性。

3 结 语

“定喇”是粤方言中的一个句末语气助词，而“吧”是普通话所有的句末语气助词中在语义和使用上最为接近“定喇”的。虽然二者具有很多相同的地方，但本文着重讨论了二者的不同。与普通话的“吧”可以用于多种句式不同，粤语的“定喇”只能用于陈述句。其次“定喇”主要用于“知域”，而“吧”则可广泛用于“三域”的场合。虽然“定喇”句和“吧”字句都蕴含着说话人推测的主观性，但是与“定喇”不同，“吧”的使用还常常带有比“定喇”明显得多的交互主观性。此外“吧”的语义较多，而“定喇”的语义较单一，所以，“吧”具有粤语中多个语气助词的功能和作用，而“定喇”的用法只相当于“吧”的用法的一部分，并且这些用法主要集中在“知域”的场合。因此要把“吧”字句转换成粤语的句子，除了需要使用“定喇”以外，还需要使用粤语的其他语气助词。

参考文献

Traugott, Elizabeth Closs　2010　(Inter) subjectivity and (inter) subjectification: a reassessment. In Davidse Kristin, Lieven Vandelanotte and Hubert Cuyckens eds., *Subjectification, Intersubjectification and Grammaticalization.* Berlin: Mouton de Gruyter. pp. 29－71.

肖治野　2010　《现代汉语语气词语的行、知、言三域研究》，浙江大学博士学位论文。

肖治野、沈家煊　2009　《“了^2”的行、知、言三域》，《中国语文》第 6 期，第 518～527 页。

广州话韵腹［ɐ］的两个来源

尤　盛

（香港理工大学）

提　要：现代广州话存在短韵腹［ɐ］，这个音素一般被认为不是古代汉语的原有特征，而是后来在粤地区演化出来的，是古韵腹［ɐ］化的结果。本文利用中古音韵腹属性的划分，尝试解释现代广州话韵腹［ɐ］化的路径和成因。

关键词：广州话　韵腹［ɐ］　中古音　高韵腹型摄　壮侗语

1　引　言

现代粤方言的广府片和香山片有部分韵腹为短、低、央元音 ɐ[①]，与长、低、央元音 aː（严式为 äː）形成一套 aː～ɐ 的长短配对（詹伯慧，1990），这个配对被认为不是古代汉语的原有特征，而是后来在粤地区演化出来的结果，是古韵腹 ɐ 化的音变。

现代广州话韵腹为 ɐ 的有中古的止、蟹、流、深、咸、臻、曾、梗八摄，而当中的止、流、深、臻、曾五摄为中古高韵腹型摄，而蟹、咸、梗三摄为中古低韵腹型摄，但由于蟹、梗摄后来出现了高韵腹化，因此，除了咸摄外，韵腹 ɐ 化都出现在高韵腹型摄，这是讨论韵腹 ɐ 化音变的一个重要线索。但 ɐ 是一个低元音，所以有这样的问题：韵腹如何由高元音发展至低元音，音系经历过什么改变？另外，唯一的例外——从来不属于高韵腹的咸摄，其 ɐ 化仅形成于几十年前，而且来源明显与其他各摄不同。

由于以上提及的八摄的 ɐ 化或多或少有不同，而且音变的历时也相当长，是由中古时期开始，到现代才完成的，故本文将会以中古音为起点，逐摄去讨论它们的 ɐ 化过程，并且列出一些重要的音变步骤，希望能有系统地分析韵腹 ɐ 化的路径和成因。

2　韵腹自然类对立

罗常培（1933）率先从现代语言学理论的角度，提出韵腹属性假说，去解释中国传统

① 以国标音标表示，下同。

音韵学的“内外转”概念（见图1），虚线以上为“内转”，虚线以下为“外转”，及韵腹e以短音为“内转”，长音为“外转”，这一反《四声等子》对“内外转”为有无真正二等的描述，以及“内外”各八转的划分。

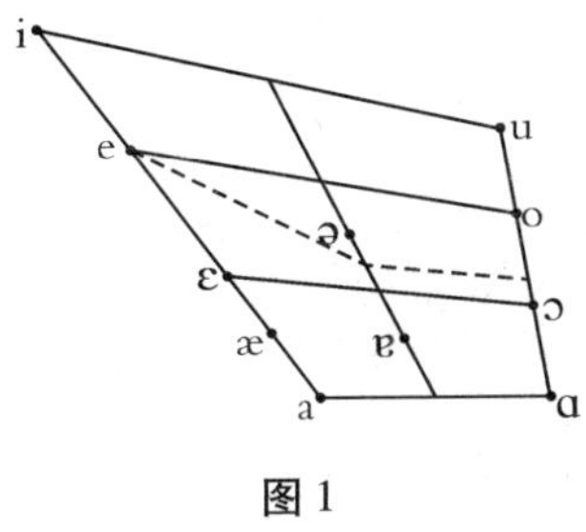

图1

纵使罗常培的理论长期以来备受争议，至今仍未有定论，但学者们（高本汉、董同龢、李荣、王力、陆志韦、马丁、蒲立本、周法高、余乃永，转引自余乃永，1974/1993）对中古音韵腹音值的构拟，仍相当一致地反映为两类（见表1）：高韵腹型摄和低韵腹型摄[①]。

表1

韵腹属性	韵尾					
	＊ －ø	＊-i	＊-u	＊-m/p	＊-n/t	＊-ŋ/k
高韵腹型摄	遇	止	流	深	臻	曾通
低韵腹型摄	果假	蟹	效	咸	山	梗宕江

而中古音为现代大多数方言的共同祖语，因此韵腹的自然类对立在这些现代方言上基本可以体现出来，罗常培（1936/2008）初步指出它们之间的对应关系，后来，张日昇、张群显（1992）以珠江三角洲方言为例，进一步指出中古摄类与现代方言的音长和音色的关系（见表2）。

表2

	现代方言韵腹音色	现代方言韵腹音长
中古高元音韵腹	高	短（同时较高）
中古低元音韵腹	低	长（同时较低）

中古为高元音韵腹的，于现代都为高或短（同时较高）元音；相反，中古为低元音韵

① 由于“内外转”的意义至今未定论，故本文只按各家对中古音拟值归纳为“高韵腹型摄”和“低韵腹型摄”，并非以此去对应传统音韵学上的“内外转”。

腹的，于现代则为低或长（同时较低）元音。

而在现代广州话，有四组配对的韵腹，即 aː ~ ɐ、ɛː ~ e、œː ~ ɵ、ɔː ~ o（Kao，1971；转引自李行德，1985），它们各组之间属性的关系，除了是长短配对外，还有舌位高低的不同（见图2）。

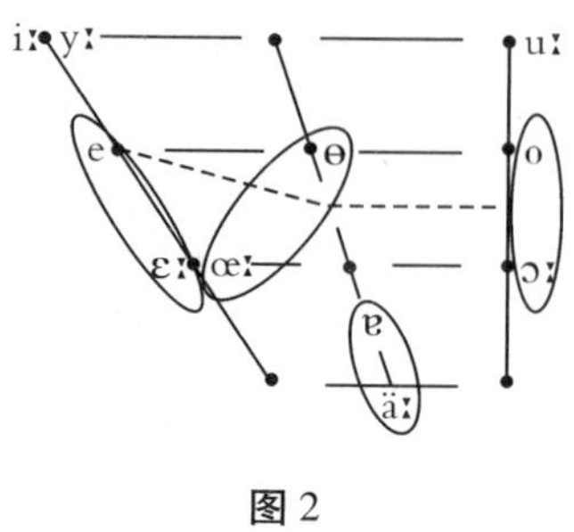

图 2

可见在 ɛː ~ e、œː ~ ɵ、ɔː ~ o 三组的配对中，短元音都在罗常培划定的“内转”位置，长元音都在“外转”位置，但当中比较值得注意是 aː ~ ɐ 一组，因为两个长短配对的元音都是低舌位，可见，元音的高低已经由绝对（以虚线为界）变为相对。另外，现代广州话中有大量以 ɐ 为韵腹的字，而且 aː ~ ɐ 的配对又相当完整（见表3）。

表 3

高韵腹型摄	止	流	深	臻	曾
	ɐi	ɐu	ɐm/p	ɐn/t	ɐŋ/k
低韵腹型摄	蟹	效	咸	山	梗
	ɐi aːi	aːu	ɐm/p aːm/p	aːn/t	文：ɐŋ/k 白：aːŋ/k

可见，凡有 aː 韵腹的，都有 ɐ 韵腹（仅没有 ɐ 独自成韵，因有短韵腹不配零韵尾的语音组合限制），而且以 ɐ 为韵腹的韵母基本上是来自中古的高韵腹型摄，只有部分是来自中古低韵腹型摄，而这些摄只相当有限地出现 ɐ 化。所以，本文的研究重点是中古高韵腹型摄（止、流、深、臻、曾）如何发展成低元音韵腹，以及中古低韵腹型摄（蟹、咸、梗）如何变同中古高韵腹型摄于现代广州话的表现。

3 关于韵腹 ɐ 的历史来源

过去对韵腹 ɐ 的来源的说法，主要可以分为多源论和单一来源论两种，其中主张多源论的李新魁（1994）指 ɐ 来自 e、ə、o、ɵ 韵腹，李新魁等（1995）指其来自 e、a、o、ɵ、u，陈卫强（2011）则指其来自韵腹 a、i、ə、ɐ；而陈渊泉和 Newman（1984a，b；1985）以简化中古音系（Simplified Middle Chinese，SMC）（Chen，1976）为框架，并以

“内外互转（The Realignment of Inner and Outer）”来交代了＊a →ə 和＊ə → a（即 ɐ）的音变，即将其归纳为中古韵腹 ə 的低化的单一来源。

刘镇发（2000）指出今粤语源自宋末移民，所以他们带来的音系也就是不晚于宋末的音系。中古音一向被视为现代大多数方言的共同祖语，但中古三四等的区别、重纽的区别在现代广州话中已经不起作用，而重韵也大都不起作用，因此，现代广州话的直接祖语为后期中古音。本文以不区别重纽、重韵，陈渊泉的简化中古音系为基本框架，并把四等并入三等去讨论现代广州话韵腹 ɐ 化的过程。

由 ə 低化而成

现代广州话韵腹为 ɐ 的，除了咸摄字之外，都来自中古高韵腹型摄（止、流、深、臻、曾），以及高韵腹化的摄（蟹、梗），可见现代韵腹 ɐ 大多来自中古的非低元音。

在陈渊泉的 SMC 中，有三个摄的韵腹都为混元音 ə，即深、臻和曾摄，其韵基分别为＊əm/p、＊ən/t 和＊əɲ/c（əŋ/k）。

（1）深、臻、曾、梗摄的 ɐ 化。

在广州话韵腹中只有开口三等的深摄已悉数为 ɐm/p 韵，这是由韵腹 ə 直接低化而成的，在韵腹低化后，广府片去介音化，介音消失，形成今日看到的 ɐm/p 韵：＊iəm/p → iɐm/p → ⁱɐm/p → ɐm/p。

臻摄在现代广州话中除了开口韵的精、来母发展为 ɵn/t 韵外，均作 ɐn/t 韵，这是为了避 lɐn^{2}音而变同合口的 ɵn/t 韵，并扩散到精母，所以明显不是音理条件上的语音变化，反观开口韵配其他声母都无一例外地变为 ɐ，可见其韵腹也是直接由 ə 低化而成，韵基演变路径：＊ən/t → ɐn/t。

（2）流摄的 ɐ 化。

流摄在《韵镜》中被列为“开”，在《七音略》中被列为“重中重”，《四声等子》将其列为“全重无轻韵”，全为开口韵，无合口韵，《切韵指掌图》虽也指其为独韵，但无标示为开口还是合口，可是其在《切韵指南》中则被列为“独韵合口呼”，这明显和过去的韵图不同，当中是涉及合口化的音变。

在早期中古音中，流摄的两个三等韵幽、尤韵是重韵，幽韵音值为＊iəu（李荣，1956），后来除“彪 piːu^{1}”一字外，所有字韵腹低化为 ɐ，成为＊iɐu。尤韵音值为＊iu（李荣，1956），其细音介音＊i 受圆唇韵腹＊u 影响而合口化为＊y 成为＊yu 韵，后来除“富副妇负”外，韵腹裂化为＊yəu 韵，其后归并入字少的幽韵。

至于一等的侯韵为＊əu，后来在粤语音系中，除了少部分明母字的韵腹弱化而脱落为 u 韵，并在近代再裂化为 ou 韵，如“母”、“戊”外，大部分韵腹低化为 ɐ 成为 ɐu 韵。

流摄在《切韵指南》中标示为“独韵合口呼”，可见一度出现大量以圆唇元音为开头的韵母。一等的侯韵在今北京话中就保留了不少圆唇开头的韵母，如“某 mou^{3}”、“母 mu^{3}”、“走 tsou^{3}”、“狗 kou^{3}”等。至于三等的两韵中字多的尤韵，由于帮组出现轻唇化为非组，这是帮组合口三等的特征，在“轻唇十韵”中，除尤韵外，九韵都在韵图中标示为合口三等，而这个合口化并不存在于幽韵中，其帮组的“彪”就没有轻唇化，而今日流摄三等在不少方言中都不见合口痕迹，可见后来字多的尤韵归并入字少的幽韵，成为今天的格局。

侯一：　＊əu　→　ᵊu　→　u　→　ou（母戊）
　　　　　　↘
　　　　　　ɐu

尤三：　＊iu　→　yu　→　u（ː）（富副妇负）
　　　　　　　　　↘
　　　　　　　　　yəu
　　　　　　　　　　　↘
幽三：　＊iəu　　　　→　　　　iəu　→　iɐu　→　ⁱɐu　→　ɐu
　　　　　　↘
　　　　　　iᵊu　→　i（ː）u（彪）

（3）曾、梗摄的 ɐ 化。

曾、梗摄虽分别属同韵尾发音部位的高低韵腹对立的两个摄，但它们的发展却是殊途同归。两摄对应在粤语等不少现代方言中，都已经合流，是梗摄并入曾摄，文读发展为高或短（同时较高）韵腹，白读则发展为低或长（同时较低）韵腹。其实这个合流在中古已经有迹象。在《韵镜》中，登、蒸韵被列为“内转”的第四十二和第四十三，而庚、清、耕、青韵则被列为“外转”的第三十三至第三十六，而在后来的《四声等子》中则被列为同图，并标示为“内外混等”。可见在不晚于《四声等子》音系的时代，梗摄的低韵腹变同曾摄的高韵腹的情况已经出现，同为 ə 韵腹，后来再低化为 ɐ：

曾开一：　＊əɲ/c（əŋ/k）　→　əŋ/k　→　ɐŋ/k
　　　　　　　　　　　　　↗
梗开二：　＊aɲ/c（aŋ/k）

（4）止、蟹摄的 ɐ 化。

蟹摄在今广州话为 ɐi 韵的，主要在中古的三四等开口及合口的唇、牙、喉音，它们与一、二等主要为 ɔːi 和 aːi 的韵形成了一、二等为长韵腹，三四等为短韵腹的配对，可见蟹摄三四等出现了韵腹高化的音变。蟹摄三四等的韵腹高化早在中古时期已经出现，在《韵镜》的第九和第十图，蟹摄的废韵就和止摄的微韵同列为一图，并标示为“去声寄此”，可见当时高韵腹化的条件就在唇、牙、喉音，而在今广州话中，韵腹高化扩大到三四等开口所有字，以及合口的唇、牙、喉音，换句话说，即不只单单限于唇、牙、喉音。

止摄所经历的 ɐ 化音变和蟹摄有一定关系，止摄在今广州话中为 ɐi 韵的，主要分布在合口韵的唇、牙、喉音，而这些字都经历了洪音化，这是和蟹摄相呼应的，但唯一不同的是，止摄的音变只维持在合口的唇、牙、喉音。

如上文所述，蟹摄在《韵镜》中已有高韵腹化的迹象，《韵镜》作者在编图安排上，把废韵以“去声寄此”方式列为与微韵同图，而且两韵的共通点是只有唇、牙、喉音，可见废韵和微韵在当时的表现是已经在某程度上相近。止摄 ɐ 化的条件在洪音化的合口三四等，这亦只出现在唇、牙、喉音，又和微韵管字的发音部位吻合，所以止、蟹摄率先洪音化应发生在只有唇、牙、喉音的废韵和微韵。而今广州话蟹摄三四等开口所有字及合口的唇、牙、喉音字已经 ɐ 化，止摄则只有合口三四等的唇、牙、喉音 ɐ 化，可见率先发生变化的条件也在合口三四等的唇、牙、喉音。

由于止、蟹摄合口三等帮组在今广州话中出现了轻唇化，而蟹摄的一、二等帮组不曾轻唇化，因此洪音化出现在轻唇化之后，如此可以把音变推断为：蟹摄废韵韵腹率先高化，在非组出现后，止、蟹摄合口三等的唇、牙、喉音才出现洪音化，最后经历洪音化的字的韵腹再 ɐ 化。至于止摄开口韵在今广州话中只表现为 iː 和裂化的 ei，没有像蟹摄那样出现 ɐ 化，是因为蟹摄废韵高韵腹化时，止摄微韵亦出现变化，使两韵没有归并；合口韵方面，在今北京话全面洪音化，但在今广州话则只限唇、牙、喉音，所以其洪音化在宋末前还未完成，只停留在唇、牙、喉音。

蟹摄废韵开口的 * iɐi 最初韵腹高化为止摄微韵原先的 * iəi，蟹摄三四等其他开口韵后来亦变同 * iəi，到广东后韵腹低化为 ɐ，最后去介音化为 ɐi 韵；至于合口韵，废韵的 * yɐi最初高韵腹化变同止摄微韵合口的 * yəi 韵，然后扩散到止摄三等和蟹摄三四等合口韵所有的唇、牙、喉音，然后再洪音化为 uəi，到广东后韵腹低化为 ɐ，最后去介音化成为 ɐi 韵。

开口：

微$_{\text{三}}$： * iəi → i^{ə}i → i（ː） → i（ː）

↘ ei

废$_{\text{三}}$： * iɐi → iəi → iɐi → ^{i}ɐi → ɐi

合口（唇、牙、喉音）：

微$_{\text{三}}$： * yəi → yəi → ʉəi → uəi → uɐi → ^{u}ɐi → ɐi

↗

废$_{\text{三}}$： * yɐi

（5）咸摄的 ɐ 化。

在最早记录古代粤语音系的文献《分韵撮要》中，一共有四套唇音韵尾的韵母组合（刘镇发、张群显，2003），包括“金锦禁急”（第十七）、“兼检剑劫”（第二十）、“缄减鉴甲”（第二十四）和“甘敢绀蛤”（第三十一），但发展到今天，则只有 iːm/p、aːm/p 和 ɐm/p 三种组合。

中古音对应现代广州话韵腹在排除特定条件及语音组合限制后，基本上有较一致的规律，就是中古高韵腹型摄发展为 ɐ；中古低韵腹型摄一等开口大多为 ɔː，合口则为 uː；二等则主要为 aː；三四等开口多数为 iː，合口则为 yː。中古深摄和咸摄都有唇音作韵尾，其中除了咸摄三等有开合口对立外，一、二、四等，以及深摄都只有开口，所以相对于其他摄，它们的变化理应比较单一，但事实并不如此（见表4）。

表 4

<table>
<tr><th>中古韵腹型</th><th>摄</th><th>等</th><th>开合</th><th>假设音</th><th>实际音</th></tr>
<tr><td>高</td><td>深</td><td>三</td><td>开</td><td>ɐm</td><td>ɐm</td></tr>
<tr><td rowspan="4">低</td><td rowspan="4">咸</td><td>一</td><td>开</td><td>ɔːm</td><td>ɐm（牙喉音）
aːm</td></tr>
<tr><td>二</td><td>开</td><td>aːm</td><td>aːm</td></tr>
<tr><td rowspan="2">三四</td><td>开</td><td>iːm</td><td>iːm</td></tr>
<tr><td>合</td><td>yːm</td><td>aːn</td></tr>
</table>

就表中所见，咸开一和合三与众不同。咸合三只有唇音字，唇音声母受介音＊y 影响而轻唇化，所以七个今广州话常用字“法泛凡帆範范犯”都是 f-声母配 aː 韵腹，但这七个字都为-n/t 韵尾，显然是一种唇音声母不与-m/p 韵尾相配的语音组合限制，和中古深摄的“禀品”读 pɐn[2]的情况相同，这个现象早在《分韵撮要》中已经存在，咸合三各字被列入“翻反泛发”（第二十五）韵。这种情况在现代方言中普遍存在，在一些方言资料中（詹伯慧、张日昇，1987；北京大学，1989），除三个客家方言点有 f-声母配-m 韵尾外，其他方言点都没有类似情况，这反映了当时粤语受到中州音影响而有一批唇音韵尾齿化。

至于咸开一的变化则比较特别，它本属低韵腹型摄，但在发展上，配牙、喉音声母的竟变同高韵腹型的深摄的 ɐm/p 韵，而非牙、喉音声母的则变同二等的 aːm/p 韵。圆唇韵腹 ɔː 不配-m/p 明显是语音组限制，但到底假设音 ɔːm/p 有没有存在过？而长短韵腹 aːm/p 和 ɐm/p 的界线又为何在牙、喉音？

中古咸开一有齿音端、精组字，牙音见组字和喉音晓、影组字，既然同摄、同等、同开合，语音发展理应相近，然而在现代广州话中，齿音和牙、喉音发展迥异，其中齿音变同二等，牙、喉音变同深摄。

表 5

		咸开一	咸开二
齿音	端组	+	
	精组	+	
	知组		+
	庄组		+
牙音	见组	+	+
喉音	晓组	+	+
	影组	+	+

咸开一只有端、精组及牙喉音字，而二等则只有知、庄组及牙、喉音字，可见对立在牙、喉音，而齿音则是互补，造成了齿音有大片空档。其实咸摄一、二等在后来是合流，在现代北京话中，两等完全合流，同为 a 韵腹（丁声树、李荣，1981/2010），而粤语则只在齿音，并已经在《分韵撮要》中合为“缄减鉴甲”韵，可见一等齿音韵腹变同二等不晚于清初。

而另一个问题是：假设音 ɔːm/p 有没有存在过？如果有，它如何由低、后、圆唇、长元音 ɔː，变成今天看到的低、央、不圆唇、短元音 ɐ？就第一个问题而言，早期粤语阴入声有固定的配对，短韵腹配高阴入，长韵腹配低阴入，因此，在早期粤语凡被标作低阴入的，都应是长韵腹。比较一些过去和现在记录早期粤语的资料，可以看到咸开一牙喉音阴入字的发展情况（见表 6）。

表 6

	Bridgman 1841	Chalmers 1907	Ball 1908	Eitel 1910	Cowles 1965	Meyer & Wempe 1947	陈瑞祺 1931①	黄锡凌 1947	詹伯慧 2002	现代香港语音
急	kap	kup	kap	kap	kap	kap	［kɐp^{1}］	gɐp	gap^{7}	［kɐp^{1}］
甲	káp	kaap$^{\supset}$	káp$_{o}$	káp$_{o}$	kaåp	kaàp	［kaːp^{3}］	ˉgap	gaap^{8}	［kaːp^{3}］
鸽	kóp	kop$^{\supset}$	kòp$_{o}$	kòp$_{o}$	kåp	kòp	［kɐp^{3}］	ˉgɐp	gap^{8}	［kɐp^{3}］ ［kaːp^{3}］
蛤	kóp	kop$^{\supset}$	-	kòp$_{o}$	kåp	kòp	［kɐp^{3}］	ˉgɐp	gap^{8}	［kɐp^{3}］ ［kaːp^{3}］

从存在四套唇音韵尾的文献（Bridgman，1841；Chalmers，1907；Ball，1908；Eitel，1910；Cowles，1965；Meyer & Wempe，1947）中明显看到“鸽蛤”的标示方法都可和长韵腹的“甲”联系，而不与短韵腹的“急”联系，可知当时应为长韵腹，到了记录 20 世纪三四十年代语音的陈瑞祺《道汉字音》和黄锡凌《粤音韵汇》，两字已经读作短韵腹，但仍保留了以前配低阴入的特色，可见，短长元音配高低阴入的界线已经模糊，而现代香港语音则因读低阴入而衍生出长韵腹的版本。

就第二个问题，如果由 ɔːm/p 变成 ɐm/p，要经历短化及展唇化，由典型的中古低韵腹型摄特点变成典型的中古高韵腹型摄特点，本应付出很大的代价。李新魁（1994：169）指“近几十年来，这个［om］韵母在一些地方如广州市区、番禺、花县、从化等地进一步变为［ɐm］韵母了”，这提出了两个重点，一为出现过与 ɔːm/p 不同的 om/p 韵母，二为 om/p 韵母出现的地点广泛，在珠江三角洲广泛出现（詹伯慧、张日昇，1987），因此有理由相信 om/p 韵是 ɔːm/p 与 ɐm/p 之间的过渡。赵元任（1948）指出中山话韵腹 ɔː 配

① 原书以“道字”记音，本文以国际音标表示。

牙喉音时有裂化为复合韵腹 oɔ 的倾向，这可以作为一个单韵腹裂化为复合韵腹的借镜。近代粤语 ɔː 韵腹在配-m/p 韵尾时裂化成为 ɔum/p 韵，现代广州话亦有残留 ɔum 韵，如 kɔum^{2}、kɔum^{3}及作拟声词的 pɔum^{4}、tɔum^{2}。由于 ɔu 韵腹是复合韵腹，现代广州话音系不容许复合韵腹出现，于是韵腹单元音化为 o，同时它亦变成一个短韵腹。

ɐm/p 韵的出现有迹可循，在 Eitel（1910）、Cowles（1965）和 Meyer & Wempe（1947）中有几个有意思的字例（见表 7）：

表 7

	Eitel 1910	Cowles 1965	Meyer & Wempe 1947
鹌	òm	om，am	om，am
庵	òm	om	om
暗	òm	òm，àm	òm
揞	òm，am	óm，ám；òm，àm	óm，ám

这个情况只出现在配零声母的时候，可见有部分零声母字已经出现 ɔum 韵与 ɐm 韵的竞争。然而，这种情况不是偶然，只以“金锦禁急”和“甘敢绀蛤”配牙喉音的分布来看，会见到和音系内部有一定的关系（见表 8）：

表 8

声母	调类	金锦禁急				甘敢绀蛤			
		平	上	去	入	平	上	去	入
[k-]	阴	+	+	+	+	+	+	+	+
[kʰ-]	阴	+			+				
	阳	+			+				
[h-]	阴				+	+	+	+	+
	阳					+		+	+
[Ø-]	阴					+	+	+	

从表 8 中可见，最主要的对立在 k-声母，h-声母是大部分互补，而 kʰ-和零声母是完全互补，所以以上几个字就填补了“金锦禁急”配零声母的空档，成为率先 ɐ 化的一组，后来，因为-m/p 韵尾不配圆唇韵腹的语音组合限制逐渐成形，ɐ 化就迅速扩大到其他“甘敢绀蛤”字。咸摄开口等一牙喉音的 ɐ 化路径为：

*ɑm/p → ɒ（ː）m/p → ɔːm/p →（牙喉音）ɔum/p → om/p → ɐm/p

↘（其他）aːm/p

（6）小结。

经过归纳后，可以看到现代广州话 ɐ 韵腹的来源有两个，一是由混元音 ə 低化而成，二是由 o 央化及展唇化而成。前者的 ɐ 化形成时间很早，在不晚于清初的《分韵撮要》中已经完成，而后者的 ɐ 化则形成得比较晚，只在这几十年间才出现。

4 音系的改变

中古音系以韵腹的自然类划分，形成低舌位和非低舌位的配对，这在现代大多汉语方言中都可以对应得到，但在现代广州话中，这个“规则”就出现了一些变化，因为本属高韵腹的摄，在现代广州话中大都变成了低元音 ɐ。由于这种情况不只在现代广州话中出现，它更普遍地出现在现代广府片和香山片中，因此，本节的讨论范围将由现代广州话扩大到现代广府片。

宋末时，后期中古音随移民迁徙而流入广东地区（刘镇发，2000），令本来的自然类属性出现了变化，但要发展到不再以低和非低韵腹作配对界线，而改以其他属性去区分，是要付出很大代价的。李新魁（1994）、千岛英一（2002）和王福堂（2008、2010）指出现代广府片和壮侗语有一定关系，因为它们都有/aː/和/a/的韵腹配对（见表9）。

表9

现代广府片		龙州土语（李方桂，1940）		武鸣壮语（韦庆稳、曹国生，1980；转引自千岛英一）		贵州榕江章鲁侗语（王福堂，2008）	
aː		aː		aː		aː	
aːi	ɐi	aːi	ɐi	aːi	ɐi	aːi	
aːu	ɐu	aːu	ɐu	aːu	ɐu	aːu	
			ɐɯ	aːɯ	ɐɯ		
aːm	ɐm	aːm	ɐm	aːm	ɐm	aːm	ɐm
aːp	ɐp	aːp	ɐp	aːp	ɐp	aːp	ɐp
aːn	ɐn	aːn	ɐn	aːn	ɐn	aːn	ɐn
aːt	ɐt	aːt	ɐt	aːt	ɐt	aːt	ɐt
aːŋ	ɐŋ	aːŋ	ɐŋ	aːŋ	ɐŋ	aːŋ	ɐŋ
aːk	ɐk	aːk	ɐk	aːk	ɐk	aːk	ɐk

沈钟伟（2007）指出壮语的语音特征是透过语言转换带进粤语音系中的。所谓语言转换，是指多个语言系统内部发展产生的变化，更进一步指出在语言的历史发展中，外来语对某个语言的影响，而这些影响包括词汇、句法和语音，当中前两者的影响可能较零散，但语音方面则较有系统。所以中古音流入广东地区后，受当地土话影响，与土话融合，改变了其原本面貌，形成了现代广府片和香山片的直接祖语。由于壮侗语有/aː/和/a/的韵

腹配对，以此作为借镜，中古音的低和非低韵腹配对的界线就逐渐消失，为高韵腹型摄的韵腹低化带来了契机，由于韵腹属性的舌位限制大大放宽，ɐ 韵腹形成了一大片空档，导致 ə 进入 ɐ 的填补空白情况。

但这条虚拟界线的“破坏”，并未对音义造成混淆，因为音系有长短元音配对的自然类划分在发挥作用，作为音义的区别特征，音系就由中古时期的腹属绝对高低配对，变为相对高低配对，促成了 aː 和 ɐ 配对的出现。

5 余 论

现代广州话有大量以 ɐ 为韵腹的韵母，对应到中古音系，它们大多本属于中古高韵腹型摄，并由 ə 低化而成，它是宋末移民把中古音带到广东地区，和当地壮侗土话融合而成的“混血儿”，并早在清初《分韵撮要》前已经形成；而咸摄开口等一牙喉音的 ɐ 化则形成得比较晚，在 ɔː 裂化后几十年间迅速形成。

了解了韵腹 ɐ 化之后，对现代广州话韵母的其他音变就能掌握得更好，尤其是在去介音化的过程中，中古介音如何对 ɐ 韵腹造成影响，这可以统合出某一时段中音变路径的某一步骤，从而有助于将来进一步了解从中古音到现代广州话的发展。

参考文献

北京大学中国语言文学系语言学教研室编　1989　《汉语方音字汇》（第 2 版），北京：文字改革出版社。

陈瑞祺　1931　《道汉字音》，香港：道字总社。

陈卫强　2011　《广州地区粤方言语音研究》，广州：暨南大学出版社。

丁声树、李荣　2010　《汉语音韵学讲义》，上海：上海教育出版社。

黄锡凌　1947　《粤音韵汇》，上海：中华书局。

蓝庆元　1999　《桂北壮语后中古层次汉语关系词与平话的渊源关系》，《桂林市教育学报》（综合版）第 4 期，第 44 ~ 48 页。

李方桂　1940　《龙州土语》，上海：商务印书馆。

李　荣　1956　《切韵音系》，北京：科学出版社。

李行德　1985　《广州话元音的音值及长短对立》，《方言》第 1 期，第 28 ~ 38 页。

李新魁　1994　《广东的方言》，广州：广东人民出版社。

李新魁等　1995　《广州方言研究》，广州：广东人民出版社。

刘镇发　2000　《现代粤语源于宋末移民说》，《第七届国际粤方言研讨会论文集》，北京：商务印书馆，第 76 ~ 83 页。

刘镇发、张群显　2003　《清初的粤语音系〈分韵撮要〉的声韵系统》，《第八届国际粤方言研讨会论文集》，北京：中国社会科学出版社，第 206 ~ 233 页。

罗常培　1933　《释内外转》，《中央研究院历史语言研究所集刊》，第 209 ~ 226 页。

罗常培　2008　《方言中的内外转》，载于王均主编　《罗常培文集》（第九卷），济南：山东教育出版社。

沈钟伟　2007　《语言转换与方言底层》，载于丁邦新主编　《历史层次与方言研究》，上海：上海教育出版社，第 106 ~ 134 页。

千岛英一　2002　《粤语杂俎》，东京：好文出版社。

王福堂　2008　《广州方言韵母中长短元音和介音的问题》，《汉藏语学报》第 2 期，第 76 ~ 94 页；又载王福堂（2010）　《汉语方言论集》，北京：商务印书馆。

余乃永　1993　《新校互注宋本广韵》，香港：中文大学出版社。

詹伯慧、张日昇主编　1987　《珠江三角洲方言字音对照》，香港：新世纪出版社。

詹伯慧　1990　《珠江三角洲方言说略》，载于《王力先生纪念论文集》，北京：商务印书馆，第 477 ~ 498 页。

詹伯慧主编　2002　《广州话正音字典》，广州：广东人民出版社。

张日昇、张群显　1992　《从现代方言看内外转》，《中国境内语言暨语言学》（第 1 辑），台北："中央" 研究院，第 305 ~ 322 页。

赵元任　1948　《中山方言》，《中央研究院历史语言研究所集刊》，第 49 ~ 73 页。

Ball, J. D.　1908　*The Cantonese Made Easy Vocabulary* (Third Edition). Hong Kong: Kelly & Walsh LTD.

Bridgman, E. C.　1841　*A Chinese Chrestomathy in the Canton Dialect.* Macao: S. W. Williams.

Chalmers, J.　1907　*An English and Cantonese Dictionary* (Seventh Edition). Hong Kong: Kelly & Walsh LTD.

Chen Y.　1976　From middle Chinese to modern Peking. *Journal of Chinese Linguistics*, 4 (2 – 3): 113 – 277.

Chen Y., and Newman J.　1984a　From middle Chinese to modern Cantonese, Part 1. *Journal of Chinese Linguistics*, 12 (1): 148 – 198.

Chen Y., and Newman J.　1984b　From middle Chinese to modern Cantonese, Part 2. *Journal of Chinese Linguistics*, 12 (2): 334 – 388.

Chen Y., and Newman J.　1985　From middle Chinese to modern Cantonese, Part 3. *Journal of Chinese Linguistics*, 13 (1): 122 – 170.

Cowles, R. T.　1965　*The Cantonese Speaker's Dictionary.* Hong Kong: Hong Kong University Press.

Eitel, E. J.　1910　*A Chinese-English Dictionary in the Cantonese Dialect.* London: Ganesha Publishing LTD.

Meyer B. F., and Wempe T. F.　1947　*The Student's Cantonese-English Dictionary* (Third Edition). New York: Catholic Foreign Mission Society of America.

The Aspectual Function of the Adverbial Modifier *ging*^{6} 劲 in Colloquial Hong Kong Cantonese*

Ken S. K. CHENG

(The Hong Kong Polytechnic University)

Abstract: This paper attempts to explore the extension from degree to aspect of the function of the adverbial modifier *ging*^{6}劲 and the like in colloquial Hong Kong Cantonese. Their usage among five situation types (i. e. state, activity, accomplishment, semelfactive and achievement) are investigated. It is found that *ging*^{6} as an adverb of degree has existed for two decades or more and that it is an established device in present-day colloquial Hong Kong Cantonese. Compared to the traditional adverb of degree *hou*^{2}好, *ging*^{6} has a wider usage and has become the most popular adverb of degree across various situation types. In regard to its aspectual function, *ging*^{6} is mainly used to denote durative in the situation of state when it modifies a verb and both durative and incessant in the situation of state when it modifies an adjective. For other situation types, the aspectual function is mostly borne by *song*^{3}丧 and *maang*^{5}猛, which are in competition with each other at the moment.

Key words: adverbial *ging*^{6} aspect durative incessant

1 Introduction

Ging^{6}劲 often appears as an adjective in Cantonese meaning "supreme" or "powerful". Here are examples taken from Cheung and Ni (1999):

(1) 佢英文好劲。
keoi^5 Jing^{1}man^2 hou^2 ging^6.
s/he English very supreme
S/he speaks excellent English.

(2) 呢一脚真系好劲。
ni^1 jat^1 goek^3 zan^1 hai^6 hou^2 ging^6.
this one leg really is very powerful
This is really a powerful kick.

---

* I am grateful to Miss Chan Wai Ming, my former student, for inspiring me on this topic and to the anonymous reviewer for useful comments. Of course, I alone am responsible for any errors it may contain.

Recently, it has come to scholars' attention (Tse, 2007; Au Yeung, 2008; Leung, 2011) that *ging*^{6} began to be used as an adverbial modifier in colloquial Hong Kong Cantonese denoting degree, i. e. "very" or "to a large extent", a function that is usually performed by the adverb *hou*^{2} 好. Here is a typical example of *ging*^{6} in this respect:

(3) 我劲钟意呢位老师。

ngo^5 ging^6 zung^{1}ji^3 ni^1 wai^2 lou^{5}si^1.

I very like this CL teacher

I like this teacher very much.

In (3), *ging*^{6} modifies the verb *zung*^{1}*ji*^{3}, and functions to denote the degree of liking. In these works, *ging*^{6} is often compared with other modifiers with a similar function, such as *ciu*^{1} 超, *gik*^{1} 激, *baau*^{3} 爆, *song*^{3} 丧, etc., and they are all regarded as trendy expressions (*ciu*^{4}*jyu*^{5} 潮语).

To my observation, in certain cases, the denotation of *ging*^{6} seems to extend from degree to aspect. Compare the following examples:

(4) 我琴晚劲讲电话。

ngo^5 kam^{4}maan^5 ging^6 gong^2 din^{6}waa^2.

I last night "very" talk telephone

I had been talking on the phone for hours last night.

(5) 我琴晚讲电话。

ngo^5 kam^{4}maan^5 gong^2 din^{6}waa^2.

I last night talk telephone

I talked on the phone last night.

In (4), *ging*^{6} does not refer to talking on the phone, say, loudly (the dimension of degree). Rather, it indicates the case of talking on the phone continuously for a substantial period of time (progressive aspect). By contrast, when *ging*^{6} is absent in (5), the aspectual meaning concerned is lost. This reveals clearly that *ging*^{6} is the item bearing the aspectual function in (4). In this regard, *ging*^{6} does not only compete with *hou*^{2} as an adverbial modifier, but also goes beyond it and carries an aspectual function.

Interestingly, in some cases, both the reading of degree and the reading of aspect are possible. For example:

(6) 琴晚劲落雨。

kam^{4}maan^5 ging^6 lok^{6}jyu^5.

last night very rain

It rained heavily last night/It had been raining last night/It had been raining heavily last night.

This paper attempts to provide a more detailed analysis of the aspectual function of *ging*^{6} by investigating its use in different types of aspectual situations. Generalizations will be made on conditions or factors that trigger aspectual interpretation for the adverbial modifier *ging*^{6}.

2 The Rise of *ging*^{6} as an Adverbial Modifier: A Retrospect

As shown above, not until the 2000s did Cantonese researchers notice the extension of *ging*^{6} from an adjective to an adverbial modifier. The time when this linguistic phenomenon first occurred, however, is yet unknown. To trace the development of this usage in Hong Kong Cantonese, I conducted an investigation into written Cantonese materials over the past two centuries.

From the 19th and early 20th centuries Cantonese materials collected in the "Early Colloquial Cantonese Texts: A Database" by HKUST (2012a), only two cases of *ging*^{6} are found, and both of them are used as an adjective, meaning "supreme" or "powerful"[1].

(7) 劲敌(*Vocabulary of the Canton Dialect*, 1828:53)
king tik
Bitter enemy

(8) 纵腕宜曲劲(*Chinese Chrestomathy in the Canton Dialect*, 1841:34)
tsung$^{\supset}$ $^{\subset}$ún, $_{\subseteq}$í k'uk$_{\supset}$ king$^{\supseteq}$.
The long hooked line in characters of this form ought to be bent and strong.

Another time period for investigation is mid-20th century. From "A Linguistic Corpus of Mid-20th Century Hong Kong Cantonese" by HKIEd (2013), one case is spotted and it is again an adjective rather than an adverbial modifier:

(9) 整铺噉劲嘅畀我哋叹? [*Yi Hou San Wang*(《一后三王》), acted by Zheng Junmian (郑君绵)]
zing^{2} pou^{1} gam^{2} ging^{6} ge^{3} bei^{2} ngo^{5}dei^{6} taan^{3}?
make CL such strong GE give to we enjoy
You left us with such a huge problem?

The next search is down to the 1980s. The material I studied is one of the most successful Cantonese novel by that time called *Diary of the Little Man* (A Foon, 1988), which is indeed the scripts of the radio program of the same name (Snow, 2004: 160 – 161). Two cases of *ging*^{6} are found and both are not used as adverbial modifiers:

① Another corpus, Early Cantonese Tagged Database (HKUST, 2012b), was also consulted but no cases of *ging*^{6} were found.

(10)我哋都戴晒拳套,劲!(Week 8,Tue.)
ngo^{5}dei^{6} dou^{1} daai^{3} saai^{3} kyun^{4}tou^{3}, ging^{6}!
we all wear entirely boxing gloves,powerful
We all wore boxing gloves,super!

(11)我本来想同佢去 Regent 食餐劲劲地。(Week 15,Mon.)
ngo^{5}bun^{2}loi^{4}soeng^{2}tung^{4} keoi^{5}heoi^{3}Regent sik^{6}caan^{1}ging^{6}ging^{2}dei^{2}.
I original want together she go Regent Hotel eat CL strong-strong-ish
Originally I wanted to go Regent Hotel with her for a rather expensive meal.

To sum up,until the 1980s,there had been no proof of *ging*^{6} extending its usage from adjective to adverbial modifier. Then it comes to the 1990s. According to Snow(2004:148),one of the most significant developments of written Cantonese from the 1980s to the 1990s was increasing use of Cantonese in Hong Kong newspapers. At the beginning of 1990s,virtually,all of Hong Kong's major newspapers used some Cantonese regularly. In this regard,I have conducted a search of Hong Kong's newspapers through WiseNews,a rather comprehensive database of Chinese newspapers and magazines. The database was first available in 1998,and it is found that the use of *ging*^{6} as an adverbial modifier was already quite popular by that time,at least a decade earlier than its coverage in works by academics. Examples in newspaper are provided below:

(12)美国排骨王豪饮劲食。(*Tin Tin Daily*,1998-11-03)
Mei^{5}gwok^{3} paai^{4}gwat^{1}wong^{4} hou^{4} jam^{2} ging^{6} sik^{6}.
American king of ribs heavily drink "very" eat
Drink and eat a lot in the American King of Ribs.

(13)甘愿冒险劲食。(*Apple Daily*,1998-12-22)
gam^{1}jyun^{6}mou^{6}him^{2} ging^{6} sik^{6}.
willing take a risk "very" eat
Willing to take a risk to eat a lot.

(14)我已经劲食,但食极都唔肥。(*Tin Tin Daily*,1999-04-09)
ngo^{5}ji^{5}ging^{1} ging^{6} sik^{6}, daan^{6} sik^{6} gik^{6} dou^{1} m^{4} fei^{4}.
I already "very" eat, but eat extreme even not fat
I have already eaten a lot,but still cannot get fat.

(15)呢首歌是近日卡拉 OK 的劲热之选。(*Apple Daily*,1999-03-07)
ni^{1} sau^{2}go^{1} si^{6}gan^{6}jat^{6} kaa^{1}laai^{1}ou^{1}kei^{1} dik^{1} ging^{6} jit^{6} zi^{1} syun^{2}.
this CL song is recently karaoke POSS "very" hot POSS selection
This is a very hot song in karaoke recently.

(16)请人放开歌喉一阵劲唱。(*Hong Kong Commercial Daily*,1999-04-06)
ceng^{2} jan^{4} fong^{3}hoi^{1} go^{1}hau^{4} jat^{1} zan^{6} ging^{6} coeng^{3}.
request person release voice soon "very" sing

Invite people to sing freely for a while.

(17)我知道劲开心。(*Sing Tao Daily*,1999-06-09)

ngo⁵ zi¹dou³ ging⁶ hoi¹sam¹.

I know "very" happy

I was very happy when I knew that.

(18)潮流人劲钟意。(*Apple Daily*,1999-06-23)

ciu⁴lau⁴ jan⁴ ging⁶ zung¹ji³.

trendy person "very" like

The trendy people like it very much.

It seems that the use of *ging⁶* as adverbial modifier has already been widely adopted by the newspapers since late 1990s. Assuming that a new linguistic phenomenon has to gain a considerable popularity before being adopted by the media, the findings may suggest that the usage concerned in Hong Kong Cantonese came into existence at least in early 1990s, a period much earlier than noticed. In other words, *ging⁶* as adverbial modifier has probably existed in Hong Kong Cantonese for more than two decades. It is not just a "trendy" expression (which may imply temporariness) as recognized by the literature, but an established device in present-day colloquial Hong Kong Cantonese.

3 Research Design

3.1 The Questionnaire

A questionnaire was designed to elicit responses from native speakers on their interpretation on the aspectual function of the adverbial modifier *ging⁶* and the like. First of all, five situation types were selected as a framework of reference (Vendler, 1957; Smith, 1997):

Table 1

Situation Type	Dynamicity	Durativity	Telicity	Examples Used in the Questionnaire
State	–	+	–	Verb-*zung¹ji³*钟意(to like) Adj-*hoi¹sam¹*开心(happy)
Activity	+	+	–	*coeng³ kei¹*唱K(to sing karaoke)
Accomplishment	+	+	+	*sik⁶ baau²*食饱(be full from eating)
Semelfactive	+	–	–	*haau¹ mun⁴*敲门(knock on a door)
Achievement	+	–	+	*daa² tyun⁵*打断(to break)

From Table 1, it can be seen that situation types can be characterized by three perspectives: whether the event is dynamic or static, whether it is durative or punctual, and whether it is telic or atelic. Examples were selected for each situation type (for "state" type, two examples were included because it can be described in either a verb or an adjective) as the basis of the questionnaire.

Apart from situation types, aspectual system was also an important concern for the design of questionnaire. In this regard, Yue-Hashimoto's (1993) inventory of different kinds of aspects in Chinese dialects was taken into consideration:

Table 2

1. Perfective	9. Habitual
2. Affirmative	10. Incessant
3. Progressive	11. Compensative
4. Durative	12. Change
5. Experiential	13. Tentative
6. Inchoative	14. Continuative
7. Instantive	15. Resumative
8. Partitive	16. Completive

However, it does not seem feasible to have a lengthy questionnaire on each of the above aspectual types, therefore I have chosen two aspectual types—durative and incessant—to be the foci of investigation. To my observation, the two are seemingly related to the use of *ging*6 as adverbial modifier in Hong Kong Cantonese.

Table 3

1a. 下面哪句表达了"我昨天吃得非常饱"的意思? (可选多于一句) □我寻日好食饱。 □我寻日超食饱。 □我寻日劲食饱。 □我寻日激食饱。 □我寻日爆食饱。 □我寻日丧食饱。 □我寻日猛食饱。 □全部都不能表达原句意思。	1a. Which of the following sentences entail the meaning "I ate very full yesterday"? (More than one answer is allowed) □I ate "*hou*2" full yesterday. □I ate "*ciu*1" full yesterday. □I ate "*ging*6" full yesterday. □I ate "*gik*1" full yesterday. □I ate "*baau*3" full yesterday. □I ate "*song*3" full yesterday. □I ate "*maang*5" full yesterday. □None of the above.

(continued)

1b. 下面哪句表达了"我昨天吃饱，并且吃了一段较长时间"的意思？ （可选多于一句） □我寻日好食饱。 □我寻日超食饱。 □我寻日劲食饱。 □我寻日激食饱。 □我寻日爆食饱。 □我寻日丧食饱。 □我寻日猛食饱。 □全部都不能表达原句意思。	1b. Which of the following sentences entail the meaning "I ate full and took a long time to eat yesterday"? (More than one answer is allowed) □I ate "*hou*^{2}" full yesterday. □I ate "*ciu*^{1}" full yesterday. □I ate "*ging*^{6}" full yesterday. □I ate "*gik*^{1}" full yesterday. □I ate "*baau*^{3}" full yesterday. □I ate "*song*^{3}" full yesterday. □I ate "*maang*^{5}" full yesterday. □None of the above.
1c. 下面哪句表达了"我昨天一次又一次地吃饱"的意思？ （可选多于一句） □我寻日好食饱。 □我寻日超食饱。 □我寻日劲食饱。 □我寻日激食饱。 □我寻日爆食饱。 □我寻日丧食饱。 □我寻日猛食饱。 □全部都不能表达原句意思。	1c. Which of the following sentences entail the meaning "I ate full again and again yesterday"? (More than one answer is allowed) □I ate "*hou*^{2}" full yesterday. □I ate "*ciu*^{1}" full yesterday. □I ate "*ging*^{6}" full yesterday. □I ate "*gik*^{1}" full yesterday. □I ate "*baau*^{3}" full yesterday. □I ate "*song*^{3}" full yesterday. □I ate "*maang*^{5}" full yesterday. □None of the above.

Using the examples listed in Table 1, I made up a series of sentences for each situation type (two for the "state" situation), with mere differences in the choice of adverbial modifiers, and provided three ways of interpretations (degree, durative aspect and incessant aspect) in layman's language as far as possible. The selection of adverbial modifiers was a mixture of older ones (*hou*^{2} 好 and *maang*^{5} 猛①) and newer ones (*ciu*^{1} 超, *ging*^{6} 劲, *gik*^{1} 激, *baau*^{3} 爆 and *song*^{3} 丧). The respondents were required to indicate which sentences entail these interpretations (more than one answer is allowed). Table 3 is the example of the adjective *sik*^{6} *baau*^{2} of the "accomplishment" situation type②. In the table, question 1a refers to a "degree" interpretation, question 1b to the "durative aspect" interpretation, and 1c to the "incessant aspect" interpretation.

① Cases of *maang*^{5} as adverbial modifier such as *maang*^{5} *jam*^{2} 猛饮 (drink a lot), *maang*^{5} *ning*^{6} *tau*^{2} 猛拧头 (shake one's head vigorously), etc. can be found in "A Linguistic Corpus of Mid-20th Century Hong Kong Cantonese" (HKIEd, 2013).

② English translation is not provided in the real questionnaire.

3.2 The Sample

The sample of this study consists of 32 subjects ranging from 15 to 26 years of age, of which 7 are males and 25 are females. All of them are native speakers of Hong Kong Cantonese and have resided in Hong Kong continuously for the past decade or more.

As proposed in section 2, the language phenomenon concerned occurred about two decades ago. The present sample is composed of young native speakers below 27. It is believed that the findings can capture their intuition on the latest development of Hong Kong Cantonese in this respect.

4 Findings and Discussion

In the following, the findings will be presented according to the situation types mentioned above. Comparison among various adverbial modifiers will be provided and their aspectual function will be discussed.

4.1 State (Adjective)

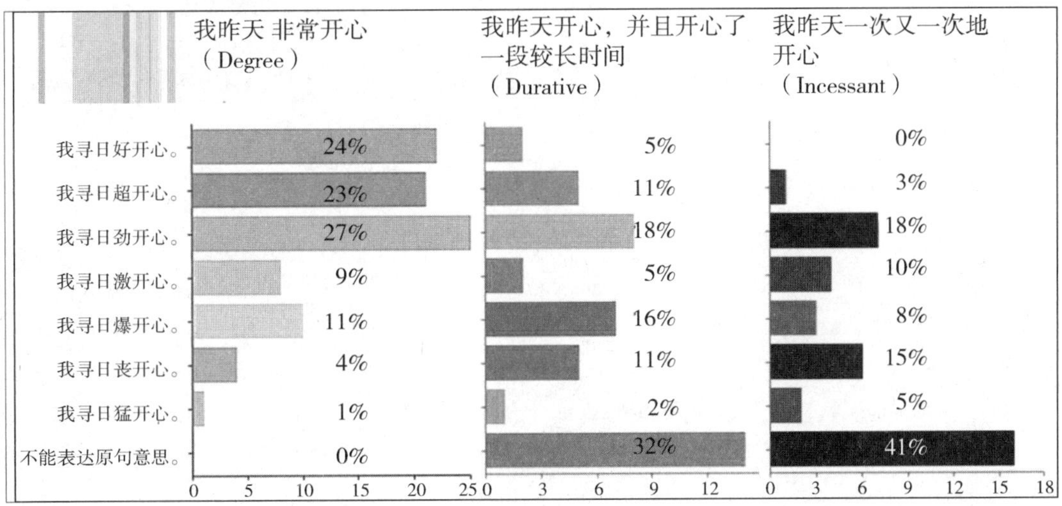

Figure 1

From Figure 1, it can be seen that as far as the "degree" interpretation is concerned, three adverbial modifiers were mostly adopted by the respondents: *hou*² (24%), *ciu*¹ (23%) and *ging*⁶ (27%). It is worth noting that *ging*⁶ outnumbered the older modifier *hou*² as the most accepted modifier for this purpose, supporting the notion that *ging*⁶ as an adverbial modifier has become an established device in Hong Kong Cantonese.

As for the durative and incessant aspects, apart from those who did not opt for any given sentences, most respondents picked the sentence with *ging*^{6} for the interpretations durative and incessant aspects (18% for both), and *baau*^{3} (16%) and *song*^{3} (15%) appeared as the second most popular modifier for the two aspects respectively.

In short, *ging*^{6} is no doubt the most popular all-purpose adverbial modifier that functions to denote degree, durative aspect and incessant aspect for this situation type.

4.2 State(Verb)

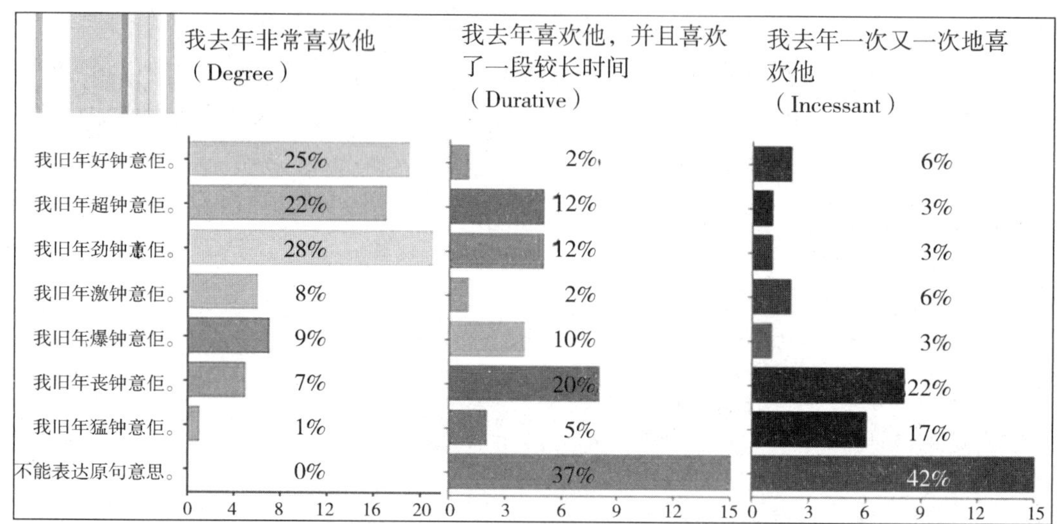

Figure 2

Figure 2 shows that as far as the "degree" interpretation is concerned, this case is very much similar to the last one: the adverbial modifiers *hou*^{2} (25%), *ciu*^{1} (22%) and *ging*^{6} (28%) were widely accepted by the respondents, among them *ging*^{6} has gained the highest rate of acceptance.

Nevertheless, when considering the aspectual interpretations, the picture differs. For the durative aspect, *song*^{3} (20%) was mostly preferred among other adverbial modifiers, while *ging*^{6} and *ciu*^{1} both came next (12%). *Song*^{3} was also the most preferred adverbial modifier for the incessant aspect, but *ging*^{6} has become one of the least preferred at this occasion.

4.3 Activity

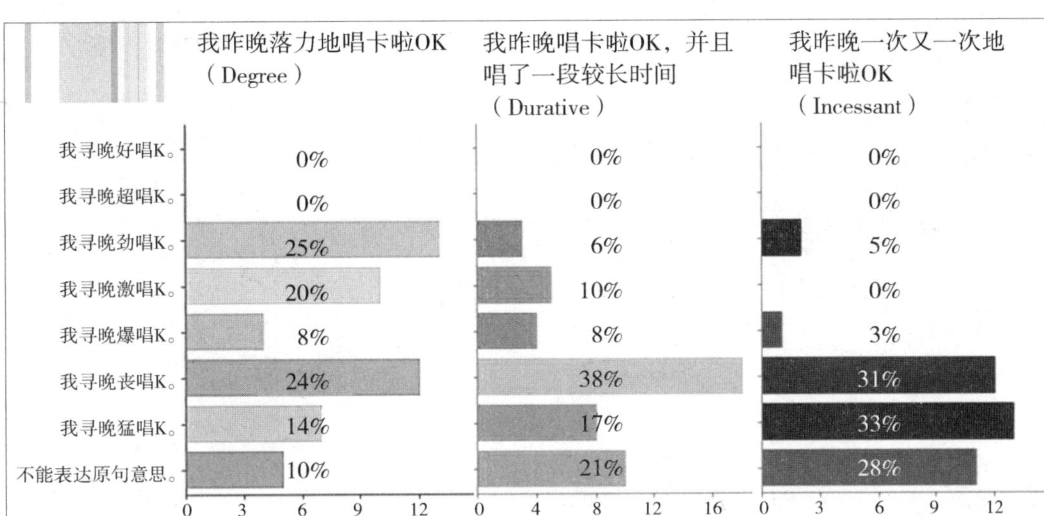

Figure 3

Figure 3 reveals that the traditional adverbial modifier *hou*^{2} plays no role in this situation type. Instead, *ging*^{6} (25%), *song*^{3} (24%) and *gik*^{1} (20%) take up the responsibility for expressing the "degree" interpretation. The finding suggests that the newer modifiers have expanded the conventional scope of the older adverbs of degree to situation types other than "state".

It is another story, however, when their aspectual function is considered. *Ging*^{6} plays a minimal role in expressing both durative and incessant aspects (6% and 5% respectively). *Song*^{3}, on the other hand, plays a dominant role in expressing the durative aspect, and the older modifier, *maang*^{5}, comes next (17%). They come very close when considering their function of expressing the incessant aspect (31% for *song*^{3} and 33% for *maang*^{5}).

4.4 Accomplishment

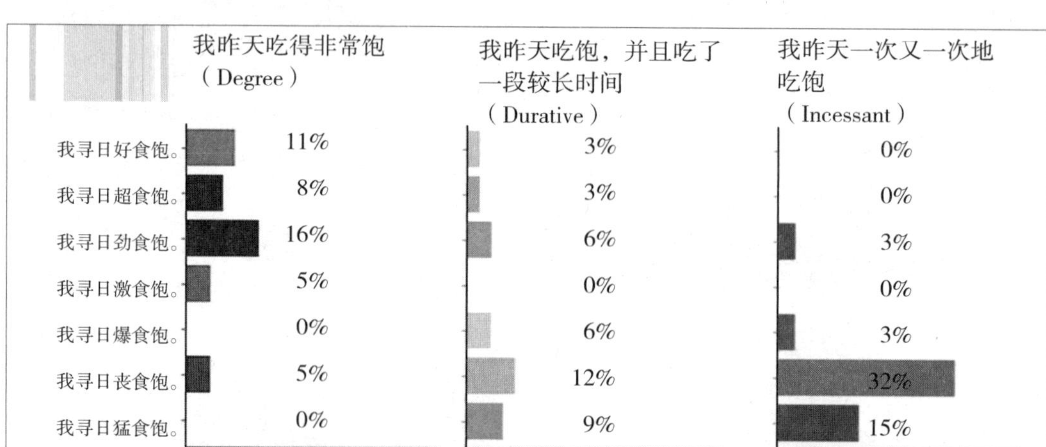

Figure 4

Figure 4 indicates that the older adverbial modifier *hou*^{2} (11%) and the newer modifier *ging*^{6} (16%) are the most accepted options for the "degree" interpretation. Surprisingly, however, there are a considerable number of respondents (55%) replying that none of these options could express the "degree". This may be due to the fact that for V-R constructions, the adverb of degree is usually placed before the resultative complement with *dak*^{1} 得 (Matthews and Yip, 1994: 179 – 180), e. g. "*ngo*^{5} *cam*^{4}*jat*^{6} *sik*^{6} *dak*^{1} *hou*^{2} *baau*^{2}我寻日食得好饱", therefore sentences like "*ngo*^{5} *cam*^{4}*jat*^{6} *hou*^{2} *sik*^{6}*baau*^{2}我寻日好食饱" were regarded less preferred.

The acceptance rates for the aspectual interpretations are rather low as well. The result may again be influenced by the location of the adverbial modifiers. Even so, it is found that *song*^{5} has comparatively higher acceptance rates than the others for both "durative" and "incessant" interpretations (12% for the former and 32% for the latter).

4.5 Semelfactive

	我今早使劲地敲门。(Degree)	我今早敲门一下，并且用了一段较长时间敲那一下 (Durative)	我今早一下又一下地敲门 (Incessant)
我今朝好敲门。	0%	0%	0%
我今朝超敲门。	0%	0%	0%
我今朝劲敲门。	35%	0%	7%
我今朝激敲门。	4%	5%	0%
我今朝爆敲门。	7%	8%	2%
我今朝丧敲门。	17%	37%	27%
我今朝猛敲门。	20%	21%	24%
不能表达原句意思。	17%	29%	39%

Figure 5

From Figure 5, one can tell that the respondents mostly preferred to use *ging*^{6} (35%) to express the "degree" interpretation, while *song*^{3} (17%) and *maang*^{5} (20%) have also got considerable support. The traditional adverb of degree *hou*^{2}, nevertheless, has gained no support from the respondents in this regard.

Semelfactive is punctual by nature (see Table 1), implying that it should be incompatible with the durative aspect. However, the result shows that 37% and 21% of the respondents chose sentences with *song*^{3} and *maang*^{5} respectively for the durative. Given the fact that the respondents gave similar responses for the incessant aspect (27% for *song*^{3} and 24% for *maang*^{5}), a possible explanation is that the respondents applied the same interpretation for both – both are about keeping knocking on the door, rather than spending a long time to make one knock.

4.6 Achievement

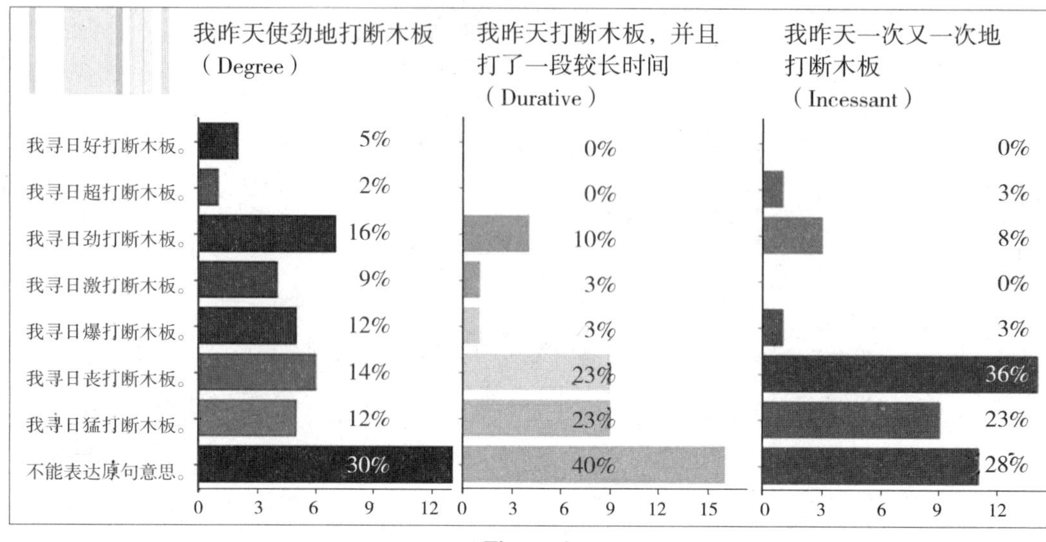

Figure 6

It can be seen from Figure 6 that *ging*⁶ (16%) again has obtained the highest rate of acceptance for the "degree" interpretation, while the following three have got considerable support as well: *baau*³ (12%), *song*³ (14%) and *maang*⁵ (12%).

As far as the aspectual interpretations are concerned, it should be noted that the achievement situation type is punctual and telic (see Table 1), which again implies incompatibility with the durative aspect. Similar to the previous case, the respondents picked *song*³ and *maang*⁵ as the most adopted adverbial modifiers for the two aspects (23% and 36% for *song*³; 23% for *maang*⁴ in both cases). And the explanation given is that the respondents interpreted them as repetition of a series of actions, rather than a single action requiring a long time to complete.

5 Conclusions

In this paper, evidence is given to support the notion that *ging*⁶ as an adverb of degree has existed for two decades or more and that it is an established device in present-day colloquial Hong Kong Cantonese.

The table below summarizes the major results of this study. The most popular adverbial modifiers[①] among different situation types and with different interpretations are listed in descending order.

① Only those selected by more than 10% respondents of the total are included in the table.

Table 4

Situation Type	Interpretation		
	Degree	Durative Aspect	Incessant Aspect
State(Adjective)	1. *ging*^{6}劲 2. *hou*^{2}好 3. *ciu*^{1}超	1. *ging*^{6}劲 2. *baau*^{3}爆 3. *song*^{3}丧/ *ciu*^{1}超	1. *ging*^{6}劲 2. *song*^{3}丧
State(Verb)	1. *ging*^{6}劲 2. *hou*^{2}好 3. *ciu*^{1}超	1. *song*^{3}丧 2. *ging*^{6}劲/ *ciu*^{1}超	1. *song*^{3}丧 2. *maang*^{5}猛
Activity	1. *ging*^{6}劲 2. *song*^{3}丧 3. *gik*^{1}激 4. *maang*^{5}猛	1. *song*^{3}丧 2. *maang*^{5}猛	1. *maang*^{5}猛 2. *song*^{3}丧
Accomplishment	1. *ging*^{6}劲 2. *hou*^{2}好	1. *song*^{3}丧	1. *song*^{3}丧 2. *maang*^{5}猛
Semelfactive	1. *ging*^{6}劲 2. *maang*^{5}猛 3. *song*^{3}丧	1. *song*^{3}丧 2. *maang*^{5}猛	1. *song*^{3}丧 2. *maang*^{5}猛
Achievement	1. *ging*^{6}劲 2. *song*^{3}丧 3. *maang*^{5}猛/ *baau*^{3}爆	1. *song*^{3}丧 2. *maang*^{5}猛	1. *song*^{3}丧 2. *maang*^{5}猛

It can be seen from Table 4 that, in terms of the "degree" interpretation, *ging*^{6} has a wider usage compared to the traditional adverb of degree *hou*^{2} and has become the most popular adverb of degree across various situation types.

In regard to its aspectual function, *ging*^{6} is mainly used to denote durative in the situation of state when it modifies a verb and both durative and incessant in the situation of state when it modifies an adjective. For other situation types, the aspectual function is mostly borne by *song*^{3} and *maang*^{5}. From the figures, it can be seen that the newer modifier *song*^{3} and the older modifier *maang*^{5} overlap in many occasions. It is believed that they are in competition with each other at the moment, and the ultimate winner will be in complementary distribution with *ging*^{6} in terms of their aspectual function among various situation types.

References

A Foon 阿宽　1988　《小男人周记》，香港：友禾制作事务所。

Au Yeung, Wai Hoo 欧阳伟豪　2008　《粤讲粤法》，香港：明窗出版社。

Cheung, Lai Yin, and Ni Liehuai 张励妍、倪列怀　1999　《港式广州话词典》，香港：万里机构。

HKIEd 香港教育学院　2013　《香港二十世纪中期粤语语料库》，http://corpus. ied. edu. hk/hkcc/。

HKUST 香港科技大学　2012a　《早期粤语口语文献资料库》，http://pvs0001. ust. hk/Candbase/。

HKUST 香港科技大学　2012b　《早期粤语标注语料库》，http://pvs0001. ust. hk/WTagging/。

Leung, Wai Mun 梁慧敏　2011　《潮语解密》，香港：万里机构。

Tse, Yiu Kay 谢耀基　2007　《从"潮"谈起——香港的"潮流"用语》，《语文建设通讯》第63期，第1~5页。

Matthews, S., and V. Yip　1994　*Cantonese: A Comprehensive Grammar.* London: Routledge.

Smith, C. S.　1997　*The Parameter of Aspect* (2nd edition). The Netherlands: Kluwer Academic Publishers.

Snow, Don.　2004　*Cantonese as Written Language: The Growth of a Written Chinese Vernacular.* Hong Kong: Hong Kong University Press.

Vendler, Z.　1957　Verbs and times. *The Philosophical Review*, 66:143 – 160.

Yue-Hashimoto, A.　1993　*Comparative Chinese Dialectal Grammar: Handbook for Investigators.* Paris: Ecole des Hautes Etudes en Sciences Sociales, Centre de Recherches Linguistiques sur l'Asie Orientale.

Cantonese *zaa* and *ze*: Focus Function and Discontinuous Constructions*

Siu-Pong CHENG

(The Chinese University of Hong Kong)

Abstract: In light of the system for focus analysis, the decompositional hypothesis for sentence-final particles, the prosodic theories, and the theory of discontinuous constructions, this paper studies the focus function and syntactic status of sentence-final focus particles, and argues that such sentence-final particles as *ze* and *zaa* combine both the focus and mood elements. The focus element restricts the focus. It exerts within its scope the exclusive function on the focus bearing exhausted alternatives and combines with the mood element in the Phonetic Form. Except the topic, these post-verbal elements are irrelevant to the focus position, which is determined by the general principles of stress assignment. According to the decompositional hypothesis for sentence-final particles and the theory of discontinuous constructions, the focus element in a sentence-final particle and its pre-verbal counterpart are "redundant". For their apparent "redundancy", it is reasonable to argue for the locality between the pre-verbal and post-verbal elements. The decompositional hypothesis allows the post-verbal focus element to form a phrase with the pre-verbal one as the former is not fixed to a certain syntactic position.

Key words: sentence-final particle　restrictive focus　discontinuous construction　cartography

1　Meaning and Function of *zaa* and *ze*

In Hong Kong Cantonese (hereafter "Cantonese"), many pre-verbal and post-verbal elements are so similar in their meaning that they form some kind of "mirror" image on the two sides of a verb. Their semantic similarities or apparent "redundancy" leads us to wonder if the two of them have a closer syntactic relationship. It is in this context that the notion of "Cantonese discontinuous constructions" (粤语框式结构) came about. In addition to semantic "redundancy", syntactic locality is another feature of such constructions. Previous discussions on locality include examples like *zaa* 咋 and its corresponding pre-verbal elements, such as *zaai* 斋, *zing* (*hai*) 净 (系), and *dak* 得

* Special thanks go to Sze-Wing Tang for his comments and suggestions, an anonymous reviewer for the detailed comments, and James Huang and Lawrence Cheung for their guest lectures at City U. I am also indebted to the conference participants for their useful comments and discussions in the writing of this paper. The author acknowledges the support from the GRF project "On the Discontinuous Constructions in Cantonese" (CUHK 5493/10H) and the project of the National Social Science Foundation of China, namely the "Studies of Global Chinese Grammar" (11& ZD128). The usual disclaimer applies.

(Tang,2007:266). This paper extends previous work by also including *ze* 啫 and discusses the "focus function" of *zaa* and *ze* as well as their syntactic position. It further studies the semantic and syntactic relationship between pre-verbal and post-verbal focus particles and the way they form a "discontinuous construction".

1.1 Meaning of *zaa* and *ze*

Rao et al. (1998) indicate that *zaa* is a modal word(*yuqici*) used to "remind, confirm or declare", and it corresponds to Mandarin *jinjin* (*zhi*, cai)...*ne* (*a*)[仅仅(只、才)……呢(啊)]. Example sentences include *dak nggo wai zaa* (得五个位咋/there are five seats only)(1998:252). Mai and Tan (1997:441) classify *zaa* as a sentence-final modal word used to narrate, confirm, and so on. It means "restricted as such", referring to a smaller quantity or scope. An example given is *jatgo jyt saambaak man zaa* (一个月三百蚊咋/three hundred yuan for one month only)(1997:443). As for *ze*, Rao et al. also state that it is a modal word used to "defend or refute" in a milder way, e. g., *gam jik dak ze* (噉亦得啫/It's also fine)(1998:255). Mai and Tan classify *ze* the same way as *zaa*, yet giving three definitions: ①it means "nothing more than this" and is used to reject a certain statement, e. g., *hou saijy ze*, *msai daam ze* (好细雨啫,唔使担遮/It's just a little rain. There's no need to use an umbrella). ②It is used to refute what another person has said, e. g., *nei zoudak jandei jau zoudak ze* (你做得人哋又做得啫/You can do it, so can someone else). ③It indicates that some idea is his/her own or only to his/her knowledge, e. g., *sat hai keoi ze* (实系佢啫/It must be him)(1997:443). Description of *zaa* and *ze* is also found in monographs on Cantonese sentence-final particles. Fang (2006) discusses the two elements in the section "Effect on Focus by Sentence-final Particles", and indicates that they "add the modality to the focus" (2006:54). However, the modality that they add differs. *Zaa* is used to explain the reason or "to explain a low quantity or a restricted scope of action so as to avoid misunderstanding" (2006:62). *Ze* conveys the modality of "light-heartedness" (轻描淡写), "and in general it downplays an event." Her examples include *doze matje ze* (多谢乜嘢啫/There's nothing to thank for)(2006:65). Some other scholarly works did not create a separate entry for *zaa*. It is discussed under the item of *ze*, with *zaa* being thought of as phonetically combining *ze* and *aa* 呀. Cheung[2007(1972)] indicates that usages of *ze* are many: ①It means "just" or "only". ②It tells the addressee something unexpected for him/her, with a sense of pride. ③It is a feminine usage, often spoken as *zek*(2007:193-195). Rather than discussing *zaa* separately, Cheung suggests that it is generated when *ze* and *aa* are joined together and "merge into one sound unit" (2007:190). As for *aa*, he indicates that it has multiple meanings and can be used for doubt, imperative, emphasis, promise, calling, listing, and pause(188-190). Leung[2005(1992)] also believes that *zaa* and *ze* are of the same origin, and that *zaa* is formed from the merging of syllables. He indicates that *ze* imposes a lower limit for the predicate regarding its category, extent, quantity, time, scope, and condition. He also states that it combines with *aa*, which sets a mild tone. This mild-toned *zaa* is similar to *gaa* in that they have a tendency of being lexicalized (2005:60). Probably for this reason, some general works on Cantonese grammar do not mention *zaa* at all. Matthews and Yip (1994:354) suggest that *ze* is used to play down an idea, usually a quantity, and means something like "only" and "just". Earlier works like Chao (1969) do not have *zaa* either. As for *ze*, he suggests that it conveys a force similar to that of "only", "that's all", and "that's all there is to it" in English (1969:86).

1.2 Focus Function of *zaa* and *ze*

What is focus? The *Chinese Terms in Linguistics* defines it as such (2011:69): A term in semantics and pragmatics, it is used by the functional school to analyze the information structure of a sentence. Generally, it is classified into natural focus and contrastive focus. The former one is posited in the sentence-final position in many languages. The latter one can be found in any position of the sentence and is marked by stress or any other particular means. For example, in *shi Xiao Wang guan de deng* (是小王关的灯/It's Xiao Wang switching off the light), "Xiao Wang" is the contrastive focus, represented by the marker *shi...de*.

Other than "natural focus vs. contrastive focus", focus can be named differently in other classification schemes. É. Kiss (1998) classifies it into Identificational Focus (or contrastive focus, a term used hereafter) and Information Focus. Contrastive focus expresses exhaustive identification, and information focus expresses the non-presupposed nature of new information, which is not limited to a certain position. "It is a function of constituents marked by pitch accents (1998:251)." Contrastive focus, on the other hand, has a fixed position and may carry [+contrastive] feature besides the expression of exhaustivity. In English, a sentence with *only* contains an exhaustive, contrastive focus. É. Kiss (1998), among others, indicate that focus goes with an exhaustive reading, and particles like *only* conveys contrast as well. To understand this, the meaning of such sentence consists of two parts (König, 1991; Krifa, 1999, etc.). Take the sentence below as an example (from Neeleman and Vermeulen, 2012:12):

(1) John read only *The Selfish Gene.*

In the spirit of Rooth (1985) and the following works on focus, this sentence is analyzed as consisting of two components. The first one is the prejacent, basically conveying the meaning of the sentence without *only*. The second one expresses the situation where the alternatives are restricted. As for the sentence above, it indicates that there is not any alternative other than *The Selfish Gene*. The logical form of the two components is given as follows (Neeleman and Vermeulen, 2012:13):

(2) <λx[John read x], The Selfish Gene, {The Blind Watchmaker, The Ancestor's Tale, The Extended Phenotype, ...}>

(3) $\neg\ \exists y, y \in$ {The Blind Watchmaker, The Ancestor's Tale, The Extended Phenotype, …}, [John read y]

Put it simply, the first component expresses "exhaustivity", and the second one expresses "exclusiveness". Through exhaustion and exclusion, the reading that "John read *The Selfish Gene* but not the other books" arises. Cantonese *zaa* and *ze* are thought of as "focus particles" because they also exert an exclusive function on the exhausted alternatives, effecting a restricted focus:

(4) jatbaak man zaa

一百蚊咋。

100 dollars only.

Exhaust: …20 dollars…50 dollars…100 dollars…120 dollars…

Exclude: …~~20 dollars~~…~~50 dollars~~…100 dollars…12~~0 dollars~~…

(5) jatbaak man ze

一百蚊啫。

100 dollars only.

Exhaust: …20 dollars…50 dollars…100 dollars…120 dollars…

Exclude: …~~20 dollars~~…~~50 dollars~~…100 dollars…12~~0 dollars~~…

However, native speakers of Cantonese might find that (4) and (5) mean something more than that. Although both sentences have the same interpretation that there is not any value other than 100 dollars, it appears that the stress is laid on the exclusion of value *over* 100 dollars; a value under 100 dollars is not what is supposedly eliminated:

(6) msai saambaak man, jatbaak man zaa / ze.

唔使三百蚊，一百蚊咋/啫。

There's no need for 300 dollars, just 100 dollars only.

(7) * msai ngsap man, jatbaak man zaa / ze.

唔使五十蚊，一百蚊咋/啫。

There's no need for 50 dollars, just 100 dollars only.

While *jatbaak man zaa / ze* excludes the alternative of "50 dollars", in actual practice it embeds an additional meaning equivalent to the use of *just*. This has been noticed in the previous literature. Kwok (1984:51) indicates that *zaa* conveys the idea of insufficiency and *ze* the idea of not being excessive. As mentioned above, Leung (2005) argues that *ze* (as well as its derived form *zaa*) imposes a lower limit. In other words, both elements do not only exclude but also impose a restriction on the magnitude. This is understood to be relevant to "scale" and "rank order". In English, *only* corresponds to *zaa* and *ze* in that it also has a rank-order reading and often implies something like "no more than that" —not quite exerting an exclusive function. Regarding this, Coppock and Beaver (2014:378) give the following sentence:

(8) John is only/just a graduate student.

This sentence is not meant to say that the person concerned does not carry other identities (male, citizen, etc.). It is interpreted to the effect that "he is just a graduate student but no more than that". What is excluded is a status "higher" than "graduate student", e. g., post-doctoral fellow or professor, depending on the encyclopedic views regarding which identity is "higher" than a graduate student. Same, a sentence with *zaa* or *ze* can refer to the same meaning:

(9) keoi hai jingausang zaa / ze.
佢系研究生咋/啫。
He is just a graduate student.

Riester (2006), Coppock and Beaver (2014), among others, indicate that rank order and exclusiveness are not opposing concepts. In a broad sense, both convey a scalar reading. For example, Coppock and Beaver (2014) argue that a sentence with a restrictive particle embeds two components, namely, "at least" and "at most". Having the component of "at least", the sentence above means that "at least he is a graduate student". The "at most" situation, on the other hand, is supposed to exist, but it is rejected with the use of the restrictive word. In a typical "exclusive" sentence, like the one below, both the "at least" (At least he is British) and the "at most" situations are construed; the entailed situations (He is both British and American) are seen as belonging to the case of "at most" and rejected:

(10) keoi hai jinggwokjan zaa / ze.
佢系英国人咋/啫。
He is only/just a British.

Other works suggest that it is restriction that gives rise to scalar reading (König, 1991, etc.). Nonetheless, it is fair to say that the focus function of *zaa* and *ze* is embodied in their being exclusive. Scalar and rank-order reading is associated with exclusiveness; the "no-more-than-that" reading also arises as a result of using them.

1.3 Difference between *zaa* and *ze*

As described above, *zaa* and *ze* have the function of restricting focus, and so they are put under one category. Fang (2006) further differentiates them only when she sub-categorizes them: *zaa* is used to explain reason, and *ze* is for light-heartedness. Leung [2005 (1992)] points out that *zaa* combines *ze* and *aa*, and it is milder in tone than *ze*. There are also different views. From König

(1991), Fung (2000) states that restrictive particles tend to induce scalar and evaluative senses. She further argues that the difference between *zaa* and *ze* is due to different assumptions in their evaluation: *zaa* assumes a higher value while *ze* assumes a lower one. Two representative examples are taken from Fung (2000:60) and shown as follows:

(11) msai saambaak man gam do, jatbaak man zaa / *ze.
唔使三百蚊咁多,一百蚊咋/*啫。
(It) does not cost three hundred buck. It's one hundred buck only.

(12) gwai hai gwaizo di, batgwo dou hai jatbaak man ze / *zaa.
贵系贵咗啲,不过都系一百蚊啫/*咋。
(True,) it's a bit expensive. Even so, it's just one hundred buck only.

Fung argues that the lower value assumed by *ze* disallows its use in (11), and the higher value assumed by *zaa* has the same effect in (12). While it may or may not hold true for the variety studied by Fung, my intuition and that of other native speakers consulted suggest that *zaa* and *ze* can be used in either sentence. In (12), it is certain that *ze* sounds better than *zaa*, but the use of *zaa* is not quite infelicitous. It follows that the difference between *zaa and ze* is not due to the different assumptions in their evaluations. In line with Coppock and Beaver (2014), the two elements both set a lower value, which is taken for granted. The higher value (or "at most") is scrutinized with the result of being rejected. "100 dollars" is the "at least" case in both sentences; what are rejected are the "higher" cases (value), e.g., "300 dollars". Note that (12) is a concessive complex sentence, the meanings of the two clauses are opposing or contrasting (Huang and Liao, 2007:131). The higher plausibility of using *ze* than *zaa* may be due to the fact that *ze* is better suited to convey opposition than *zaa*. Recall the usage notes in Rao et al. (1998) and other dictionaries that *zaa* is mostly for "confirmation" and *ze* is mostly for "refutation". Fung (2000:60) also indicates that one of the functions of *ze* is to downplay a result. Therefore, the "light-hearted" modality (in Fang's terms) better fits the concessive semantics of (12). Also note that with the value diminished or augmented, the acceptability of the sentences varies:①

(13) gwai hai gwaizo di, batgwo dou hai sap man ze / $^{OK/?}$zaa.
贵系贵咗啲,不过都系十蚊啫/$^{OK/?}$咋。
(True,) it's a bit expensive. Even so, it's just ten buck only.

(14) gwai hai gwaizo di, batgwo dou hai jatjik jingbong ze / $^{??}$zaa.
贵系贵咗啲,不过都系一亿英镑啫/$^{??}$咋。
(True,) it's a bit expensive. Even so, it's just 100 million pounds only.

① As expected, my judgment of (13) and (14) might differ from Fung's vis-à-vis (11) and (12).

Obviously, the acceptability of sentences in relation to the use of *zaa* and *ze* is not necessarily related to their core semantics. It is relevant to the context and even one's encyclopedic understanding of the world. To illustrate, if (14) came from the mouth of a billionaire, it would be as natural to use either *zaa* or *ze*. ① Summing up, the difference between *zaa* and *ze* is a difference in mood, but not the focus function. König (1991) is right in saying that focus particles induce evaluation. That is to say, the difference between *zaa* and *ze* is a difference in evaluation, and the very concept of "evaluation" is an element pertaining to "mood".

1.4 Focalization of *zaa* and *ze*

First consider a term similar to *zaa / ze*, i. e., *eryi* in Mandarin. Erlewine (2010) finds that in terms of Association with Focus (AWF), the focus of *eryi* can be on the object or the verb, but not the subject. Association with Focus is a term originated from Jackendoff (1972) and indicates the inter-relation between focus operator and focus. Erlewine offers the following examples (2010: 20): ②

(15) wo (zhi) ai [ni] (eryi).
　　我(只)爱[你](而已)。
　　I only love [you]...I love no one else.

(16) wo (zhi) hui [nian] Hanzi (eryi).
　　我(只)会[念]汉字(而已)。
　　I only can [read] Chinese characters...I cannot write them.

(17) * [wo] (zhi) ai ni (eryi).
　　[我](只)爱你(而已)。
　　[I] love you...no one else loves you.

The use of *zhi* (and its Cantonese pre-verbal equivalents) aside, Cantonese *zaa* and *ze* also demonstrate the same phenomenon. AWF cannot be done between *zaa / ze* on the one hand and the subject on the other. Take *zaa* as the example: ③

(18) ngo oi [nei] zaa.
　　我爱[你]咋。

---

① The "confirmation" nature of *zaa* allows it to have a greater effect than *ze* in affirming the "at least" case. In (14), for example, the use of *zaa* shows that the value is not only accepted, but also affirmed in a positive, optimistic manner. Therefore, our world knowledge leads us to conclude that only a super billionaire is capable of making such a statement without feigning confidence.

② The "implicature" here and also in the rest of this paper does not include all implied meanings. It merely shows which of the alternatives are eliminated.

③ To control the length of this paper, from here on only *zaa* is illustrated in the example sentences.

I only love [you]... I love no one else.

(19) ngo wui [duk] Honzi zaa

我会[读]汉字咋。

I only can [read] Chinese characters...I cannot write them.

(20) * [ngo] oi nei zaa

[我]爱你咋。

[I] love you...no one else loves you.

In an earlier observation, Tang (1998:45,46) notices that in sentences with *zaa*, the subject is not a focalized constituent. There are also opposing views, such as the view that the subject can also be focalized in *zaa*-sentences (Law, 2002). The following parts study the AWF between *zaa / ze* and different constituents. Tang's observation includes elements such as verbs, post-verbal elements like direct and indirect objects, and pre-verbal elements like manner adverbs, temporal adverbs, instrumental PPs, and subjects. I will selectively revisit it and also take "topics" into consideration.

1.4.1 Direct Object and Indirect Object

Tang (1998) discovers that both direct and indirect objects can be focalized with the use of *zaa*. He also shows that neither one is necessarily the focus (1998:45,46):①

(21) ngo bei pin man bei Siu Ming zaa. (DO/IO)

我畀篇文畀萧明咋。

I gave (only) the paper (only) to Siu Ming.

(22) ngo manzo Siu Ming jat tiu mantai zaa. (DO > ?? IO)

我问咗萧明一条问题咋。

I asked Siu Ming only one question.

(23) ngo manzo loeng go jan ni tiu mantai zaa. (IO > DO)

我问咗两个人呢条问题咋。

I asked only two people this question.

To this, Tang suggests that an indefinite nominal seems to attract the focus of *zaa*. This agrees to the observation results. More precisely, cardinal nominals seem to be more "focus-attractive" than non-cardinal indefinite nominals [e. g., "bare" classifier-noun sequence; see Cheng and Sybesma (1999) for details]:

(24) ngo manzo go jan loeng tiu mantai zaa. (DO > ?? IO)

我问咗个人两条问题咋。

---

① The greater-than symbol " > " used in Tang's examples indicates that the focalization of the item preceding " > " is preferred over that of the following item. My examples of (24) to (26) follow suit.

I asked a person only two questions.

(25) ngo manzo loeng go jan tiu mantai zaa. (IO > ?? DO)

我问咗两个人条问题咋。

I asked only two people a question.

If the direct object and indirect object are both cardinal, it naturally follows that both attract the focus; and apparently, the direct object is more easily focalized.

(26) ngo manzo loeng go jan loeng tiu mantai zaa. (DO > IO)

我问咗两个人两条问题咋。

I asked two people two questions only.

1.4.2 Indefinite Bare Object

A brief note is made on the focalization of the indefinite bare object, or the object in the "pseudo noun incorporation" (after Massam, 2001; quoted in Huang, to appear):

(27) ngo jauzo seoi zaa.

我游咗水咋。

I have swum only.

Following Lu (1957), *jauseoi* (swim) can also be understood as a separable word, or *liheci*. This "object" is not a regular one. Here is a sentence with a regular object:

(28) ngo zyuzo jidaaileifan zaa

我煮咗意大利粉咋。

I have cooked spaghetti only.

The focus falls on the object *jidaaileifan* (spaghetti). On the other hand, it is more likely for a verb to get focalized if the object is the general object of a verb:

(29) ngo zyuzo je zaa

我煮咗嘢咋。

I have cooked only... I didn't do anything else.

1.4.3 Subject

Tang (1998) notes that manner adverbs, such as *manmangam* (慢慢咁/slowly), locative adverbs, such as *hai tousyugun* (系图书馆/in library), temporal adverbs, such as *kamjat* (琴日/yesterday), and instrumental PPs, such as *jung ni zi bat* (用呢支笔), may also be focalized. This being less objectionable, the focalization of these elements will not be further pursued in this paper. As for the subject, Tang's many examples show that it cannot be the focalized constituent in a *zaa*-sentence. Opposing views, however, indicate that the subject can be focalized under certain circumstances. Law (2002:388) offers the following sentence to illustrate this view:

(30) Lousi: bingo waak faa bung coeng?
老师:边个画花㨃墙?
Teacher: Who did the graffiti?
Billy: m gwaan ngo si aa. Aaming waak faa bung coeng zaa.
Billy:唔关我事呀。阿明画花㨃墙咋。
Billy: It's not me! It's only Aaming who did it.

Law argues that when stress is placed on *Aaming*, the reading as seen above is acceptable. In other words, subject can be focalized in a *zaa*-sentence. I share the same intuition with Law regarding this example scenario. As she mentioned, a stress should be placed on subject; otherwise, a stress-less subject cannot be focalized—different from the previous examples, such as the focalization of verbs and objects, in which case an audible and intentional stress is unnecessary. Revisit (20). It is found that a subject with a stress placed on it can indeed be focalized:①

(31) [ngo] oi nei zaa
[我]爱你咋。
[I] love you...no one else loves you.

In contrastive sentences, the subject is not focalized either unless it is stressed:

(32) * di sailou gongsiu zaa, di daaijan mou gongsiu.
啲细路讲笑咋,啲大人无讲笑。
It is only those kids who joked...the adults didn't joke.

(33) [di sailou] gongsiu zaa, di daaijan mou gongsiu.
[啲细路]讲笑咋,啲大人无讲笑。
It is only those kids who joked...the adults didn't joke.

This is how one can understand the observation results by Tang (1998) and Law (2002): Tang's assertion that the subject is not focalized in *zaa*-sentences refers to the general situation where there is no noticeable stress and/or the utterance is given in an "out-of-the-blue" manner. Law's claim that the focus of a *zaa*-sentence can fall on the subject holds true only when the subject carries the stress, or in some cases where the response is so short that a subject can

① From here on, a stressed element will be given in boldface.

become the focus without one's conscious placement of stress on it. Take the following scenario as an example:

(34) A: bingo heoi Dungzikmat Gungjyun?
A: 边个去动植物公园?
A: Who goes to the Zoological and Botanical Gardens?
B: ngo heoi zaa.
B: 我去咋。
B: Only I go.

1.4.4 Topic

Law (2002:389) exemplifies the impossibility of focalizing topics in *zaa*-sentences:

(35) si le, ngo tai gwo zaa.
诗呢,我睇过咋。
a. * I have only read poetry (not novels).
b. I have only read poetry (but not written any).

From her example, it is shown that although the topic (poetry) is the logical object, this nominal cannot be focalized after being topicalized. For the so-called "gapless" topic sentence, the topic cannot be the focus either, as in Law's example (2002:390):

(36) dungmat le, ngo zungji touzai zaa.
动物呢,我钟意兔仔咋。
As for animals, I only like rabbits.

The topic, *animal*, is not within the scope of focalization. Based on Law (2002), I use the "stress test" to confirm that the topic cannot be focalized even when stressed:

(37) * [daance], ngo zouzo zaa.
[单车],我租咗咋。
I have only rented bicycles...nothing else.

Notice that the subject can be focalized when it carries the stress:

(38) daance, [ngo] zouzo zaa.
单车,[我]租咗咋。
Only I have rented bicycles...nobody else.

1.5 Analysis

Tang (1998:47) summarized his observation on *zaa* as follows:

(39) Properties of *zaa* in Cantonese

a. Verbs and post-verbal elements could be focalized in the transitive.

b. Verbs and pre-verbal adverbs (below the subject) could be focalized in the intransitive.

c. Subject and any pre-subject elements (adverbs and topics) cannot be focalized.

d. Focalization of *zaa* is sensitive to indefinite nominals.

First, let's consider the generalized rules of (39)c and (39)d. Generally speaking, the focalization of *zaa*-sentences is as what Tang (1998) describes in as much as it does not fall on the subject and the pre-subject elements. In most cases, only when a stress is placed on the subject can it become the focus. In accordance with the classification by Feng (1997:64), stress can be classified into four sub-categories: ①emphatic stress; ②contrastive stress; ③response stress; ④normal stress. The first three subtypes can be understood as "not normal" and grouped together as "special focus stress". Special focus stress and normal stress are the two top-level subdivisions. Unlike an element in the predicate, subject must carry special focus stress in order to be focalized.① That is not to say that a predicate element cannot carry the special stress. What distinguishes subject and such predicate elements as objects is that a special stress is needed for the focalization of subjects. Pre-subject topic can by no means be focalized even when an audible stress is placed on it. Therefore, it should be handled separately. As for (39)d, it tells a significant part of the whole story. As far as Mandarin is concerned, some elements require a weak stress and some a strong one. Feng (1997:84) gives a rank of nominals arranged from weak-stressed to strong-stressed:

(40) pronouns < definites < "a few" N < "two or three" N < cardinal nouns

From a cross-linguistic perspective, the rank above should still hold true. The so-called "weak" elements, e.g., pronouns, tend to convey old information, whereas the "strong" ones tend to convey new information. Therefore, for a numeral or cardinal expression, once it appears, there is a high tendency for it to become the focus. (39)d states that indefinites are close to the "strong"

① A reviewer suggests that the subject as in (32) can be focalized without stress, and offers a supporting example: *di sailou sikzo je zaa, di fumou zau mou sik laa* (啲细路食咗野咋,啲父母就无食喇/Only the kids ate … the parents didn't eat). (Context: There is very limited food available. The parents all give up their own portion for their children) A possible explanation for this intuitional difference is that a silent *zijau* (只有/only) or *dak* [得/(it) IS] is found in the variety of those who accept a focused "subject" (now turned into part of the predicate) without a special focus stress.

end, and as a result, they become sensitive to focalization. In addition, the stress placement rules also play a role in determining which element is focalized. Assuming all Chinese varieties share the same basic rules of stress placement, we can resort to Chao's (1968:35) generalized rule that the "strongest stress falls on the last" ①. In this regard, (39)a and (39)b can be easily explained. Generally in the transitives, objects are posited in the final position, preceded by verbs. The stress falls on the object. In the intransitive, stress naturally falls on the sentence-final verb. On the other hand, there are instances showing that stress does not fall on the last. Feng's (1997:66) example below is used to prove that the "stress on the last" is brought about by the verb head (1997:68).

(41) wo kanwanle shu le.
我看完了书了。
I have finished reading the book.

The sentence-final *le* is the last but not the strongest. Instead, *shu* generally carries the stress. According to Feng (1997), the verb assigns stress to an element of the same phrase (verb phrase), which explains why a normal stress falls on the object. In (39)a, it indicates that the verb can be focalized. This is possibly because the following object is insensitive to stress, such as pronouns (1997:71). This object has a bleached meaning, such as the one in (29). As for (39)b, it indicates that a modifier (or some pre-verbal element) can carry stress. And it is the modifying element which shows a prosodic structure different from the one used for the normal stress placement (Feng, 1997: 73). Given that functional words basically do not carry stress (as "prosodic invisible element"; see Feng, 2000:45), Tang's (1998) generalization can now be re-stated with the input from the prosodic theory:

(42) Properties of *zaa* in Cantonese
a. Post-subject elements are assigned stress according to the stress placement principles. Above the basic structure, such element can itself carry stress.
b. Subject is focalized only when a special focus stress is placed on it.
c. Topic can by no means be focalized.
d. The focus in *zaa*-sentences is more sensitive to a "stronger" nominal.

---

① One major drawback of this assumption is that Cantonese is well conceived as a stress-less language or at the least a language which lacks a noticeable stress. Following the traditions, I define "stress" as relative prominence, and the formulation of my assumption resorts to Duanmu's (2007:144) "Information-Stress Principle" which states that "(a) word or phrase that carries more information than its neighbour (s) should be stressed". This paper draws on recent and ongoing research on the acoustic cues of Cantonese "information stress"—a topic that is beyond the capacity of this paper. Prima facie evidence, however, shows that Mandarin and Cantonese share the kind of contrastive stress that has the same syntactic relevance, as in (Mandarin) *ta gao* * (*wo ai*) 他高(我矮) vs. (Cantonese) *keoi gou* * (*ngo ai*) 佢高(我矮) "He's tall (and I'm short)". Prosodically speaking, Mandarin and Cantonese are different, but not totally unconnected.

e. Functional words are hardly focalized.

As can be seen, the subject can be focalized only when it carries special focus stress because normal stress is not an alternative, given the "verb-based" stress placement principles. In all generalized rules, only (42) c has to do with the special feature of sentence-final focus particles; others can be simplified as the reflection of the general principles of focus/stress occurrence. It is (42) c that relates to the syntax of *zaa* / *ze*.

2 Syntactic Status of *zaa* and *ze* and their Discontinuous Constructions

In line with traditional assumptions (Tancredi, 1990; Aoun and A. Li, 1993; Büring and Hartmann, 2001; H. Li, 2011, etc.), a focus particle c-commands the focused constituent XP. At this point, it is only confirmed that the topic is not within the c-command domain given that it can by no means be focalized. Based on the Split-CP Hypothesis by Rizzi (1997), Law (2002) suggests that the position of *zaa* is below the topic, and the scope of *zaa* does not cover it. For (36), Law offers this account:

(43) [$_{TopP}$ dungmat "animal" [$_{SFP}$ zaa [$_{VP}$ ngo zungji touzai "I love rabbit"]]]

It appears that Law's (2002) proposal is a simple answer that also conforms to the linguistic data. Yet there are still some problems associated with her proposal.

2.1 C or T?

Law divides sentence-final particles into two groups, SFP_1 and SFP_2. The syntactic position of SFP_1 is higher than that of SFP_2. Here is part of her list (2002:380):

(44) SFP_1: aa, bo, wo, ze...
SFP_2: zaa, tim, laa

An immediate problem of this classification is that *ze*, like *zaa*, is also used for the restrictive focus. Treating *zaa* and *ze* differently at two layers fails to explain their focal homogeneity. Later works like Li (2006:118) adopt the Split-CP Hypothesis to a greater extent and separate various sentence-final particles into different layers:

(45) $Epist_1$ > Evid > $Epist_2$ > Disc > Eval > Mood > Deik > Foc > Fin
1,4 5 *k* *aa*, *o* *ne* *me* *le* *ze* *ge3*

The labels above include Epist(emic), Evid(ential), Disc(ourse), Eval(uative), Mood, Deik (related to time; Li refers to Sybesma, 1997), Foc(us), and Fin(ite). Li does not consider sentence-final particle as a simplex unit. Instead, she treats them in a way that they are decomposed into different components. For example, *zaa* is re-analyzed and decomposed into "z(e) + aa": *z* is the focus element, and *aa* is within the discourse layer. By the same token, *ze* is also decomposed into "ze + 1", in which tone 1 is the epistemic element. The claim that both *zaa* and *ze* contain a component in the Foc layer explains their focal homogeneity. On the other hand, Tang (1998) suggests that *zaa* is the head T of TP. He bases this claim on three pieces of evidence: ①the focused constituents are all within TP; ②*zaa* is incompatible with other T elements, e.g., *lai*; ③English T is also used for emphasis. As mentioned, Tang's first evidence reflects the general situation. However, the possible focalization of subject needs further elaboration. Besides, it is without doubt that *zaa* is incompatible with *lai* under certain conditions, like Tang's example below (1998:47):

(46) ngo tausin saizo gaa ce (*zaa) lai (*zaa).
我头先洗咗架车(*咋)嚟(*咋)。
I just (*only) washed the car.

In this sentence, my intuition (unlike Tang's) shows that although placing *zaa* after *lai* is still ungrammatical, it sounds less infelicitous than placing it before *lai*. If the object is replaced with a cardinal expression that "attracts the focus", the acceptability of the sentence will greatly increase, even to the extent that it is deemed grammatical:

(47) $^{OK/?}$ngo tausin saizo saam gaa ce lai zaa.
我头先洗咗三架车嚟咋。
I just only washed three cars.

Again, it can be explained with the general principles of stress placement. It is fair to say that Tang's (1998:48) claim that the scope of *zaa* is vP reflects the general condition. This scope is uncontroversial, although a scope larger than this is also possible. There is another advantage of putting *zaa* and *lai* into the same category. First, it has been found that *lai* can be found in the embedded clause (Tang, 1998:49):

(48) nei zi m zidou [zingwaa lokgwo jyu lai] aa?
你知唔知道[正话落过雨嚟]呀?
Do you know it just rained?

Same, *zaa* can also be found inside the embedded clause:

(49) nei zi m zidou [gin saam zik jatbaak man zaa]?

你知唔知道[件衫值一百蚊咋]?
Do you know the shirt costs 100 dollars only?

The focus is found inside the embedded clause, so it is natural to say that restrictive focus element *zaa* is also inside it. Of course, a proposal based on *zaa* being C also explains the case of focalization above: *zaa* c-commands the embedded element from a position in the root clause. This is not completely impossible, but in many languages, a restrictive focus particle located in the root clause is incompatible with a question. Take Mandarin as an example (Yang, 2008:9):

(50) * zhiyou Zhangsan chile shenme?
只有张三吃了什么?
What did Zhangsan only eat?

Cantonese *zaa* is not acceptable either in a similar question:

(51) * Zoengsaam sikzo matje zaa?
张三食咗乜嘢咋?
What did Zoengsaam only eat?

Yang (2008) and Li (2011) call this phenomenon the "focus intervention effect". The grammaticality of (52) shows that there is no intervention—*zaa* is not in the root clause but in the embedded one:

(52) jau bingo zidou [gin saam zik jatbaak man zaa]?
有边个知道[件衫值一百蚊咋]?
Who knows that the shirt costs 100 dollars only?

Tang (1998) classifies sentence-final particles into two categories, namely, inner particles and outer particles: inner particles include *laa*, *lei*, *zaa*, etc.; outer particles include *maa*, *me*, *aa*, *ne*, *bo*, etc. (1998:42). Law (2002) shows that the scope of *zaa* includes subject. It is now shown that this is possible when the subject carries audible stress. Further discoveries also show that *zaa* can co-occur with *lai*. That is to say, "inner particles" lack homogeneity. However, if inner and outer particles are differentiated by their ability to enter the embedded clause, then their categorical difference can still hold true. Inner particles can be found in an embedded clause, whereas the outer ones cannot. It is still theoretically possible to call *zaa* a C element: inner particles include both "low C" (following Paul, 2011) and T; outer particles are "high C". It is trivial to ask if low C can be thought of as T.

2.2 Hurdles and Solutions

Treating *zaa* as an inner particle explains why it can enter the embedded clause, as in (49).

However, the presence of *zaa* in embedded clauses is not without constraints. Not all embedded clauses allow *zaa*. For example, *lai* is acceptable in a relative clause:

(53) [lokjyun jyu lai] ge hunghei zeoi cingsan.
[落完雨嚟]嘅空气最清新。
The air after rain is the freshest.

Inner particle *lai* is inside the relative clause. This is not possible for *zaa*:

(54) * [sik juk zaa] ge dungmat jau sizi.
[食肉咋]嘅动物有狮子。
The animals that only eat meat include lions.

If the relative clause becomes a complement clause, *zaa* allows two scopes:

(55) ngo zidou sizi sik juk zaa.
我知道狮子食肉咋。
I (only) know lions eat (only) meat.

There are two readings in the absence of special stress. The first one refers to the situation where "lions eating meat" is the only thing known to the speaker. The second one means that "meat" is the only thing lions eat. In the first reading, the focus-restricting function of *zaa* takes effect on a root-clause component, i. e., the complement of *zidou* (know). In the second reading, the focus is on "meat". For pre-verbal focus particles like *zinghai* (only), its effect does not cross the clause boundary:

(56) * ngo zinghai zidou sizi sik juk.
我净系知道狮子食肉。
Intended: I know lion eat only meat.

The reading of "eating meat only" is disallowed even if *juk* (meat) carries stress. All these observations lead to the following paradox:

(57) Focus particle can be non-root, but should be found in the root (final) position.

Cross-linguistic data show that it is common for restrictive focus particles to occur in non-root clauses. Cantonese should be no exception. The reason why Cantonese post-verbal focus particles create the exception might be explained by the above-mentioned fact that they are not "purely" focus particles. Leung (2005) states that *zaa* combines *ze* and *aa*. Li (2006) divides *zaa* and *ze* into "z + aa" and "ze + 1". In the same vein, Tang (2006b: 229) decomposes *zaa* into focus particle *za* and mood particle *a* and argues that *zaa* combines the two of them. This explains why *zaa* should appear in the sentence-final position. Assuming that Tang (2006b) is on the right track, *za* must combine with *a*, and it is *a* that is posited in the root position. As a result, *zaa* is always in the sentence-final position. The ungrammaticality of (54), as compared to the grammatical (49), shows that the combination process should be done when *za* and *a* neighbor each other. In the spirit of the Minimalist Program, I argue that the "neighboring" requirement is a requirement after the overt syntax. Only after Spell-Out when the linear order becomes relevant. In accordance with Chomsky (1995a, 1995b), the Phonetic Form (PF) is where linearization takes places. Given that "neighboring" is the prerequisite for the combination of focus element *za* and modal *a*, it is argued that this is performed in PF. What is involved is PF movement as follows:

(58)

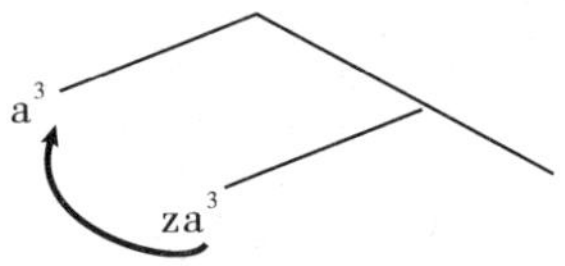

a3

za3

The decompositional analysis of Tang (2006b) explains the claims made in Fung (2000). The restrictive focus particles differ in sounds because the same focus element combines with different mood elements. Given the clear modality as shown in *ze*, it is suggested that *ze* is also decomposable as it combines the focus and mood elements, contra Leung (2005).

2.3 Discontinuous Constructions

It has been noted that in Cantonese, several pre-verbal and post-verbal elements are similar in their meaning. Together they are termed "discontinuous constructions", and their examples and properties have been well studied (see Tang, 2002a, 2002b, 2003, 2006a, 2006b, 2006c, 2007, 2008a, 2008b, 2009a, 2009b, 2009c, 2012). In addition to thc apparent semantic "redundancy", discontinuous construction also "forms an integral relation between pre-verbal and post-verbal elements" (Tang and Cheng, 2014: 621). As mentioned in the beginning of this paper, both pre-verbal *zaai* and post-verbal *zaa* and *ze* have the function of bringing out a restrictive focus. Both eliminate the exhausted alternatives until there is one remaining. They have the same semantic function, and their semantic "redundancy" is evident. Given their "redundancy", the omission of either one does not affect the core sentence meaning:

(59) ngo zaai tai syu zaa.
　　我斋睇书咋。
　　I only read (books).

(60) ngo zaai tai syu.
　　我斋睇书。

I only read (books).

(61) ngo tai syu zaa.

我睇书咋。

I only read (books).

However, according to the decompositional analysis here, such post-verbal focus particles as *zaa* and *ze* also contain a mood element. Therefore, the sentence without *zaa* should lack some sort of mood, e. g., a mild tone (see above). Pre-verbal *zaai* and post-verbal *zaa* are not semantically equivalent. This fits the sense of their being apparently redundant. Moreover, pre-verbal elements display different syntactic behavior. In general, the scope of post-verbal focus particles includes the predicate. The subject may be focalized when it carries a special focus stress. On the other hand, *zaai* only scopes over the following verb. Even when a cardinal expression serves as an object, the focalization of this object is marginal.

(62) OK/? ngo zaai tai saam bun syu.

我斋睇三本书。

I only read three books.

So, which pre-verbal focus particles are "freer" in their syntactic positioning? This freer element should be *zing* (or *zinghai*). It precedes various kinds of constituents:

(63) keoi zinghai hai tousyugun duk syu. (PP)

佢净系系图书馆读书。

He studies in the library only.

(64) keoi zinghai ling ngo m gouhing. (causative construction)

佢净系令我唔高兴。

He angers me only.

(65) keoi zinghai m tai syu. (negative construction)

佢净系唔睇书。

He does not read (books) only.

(66) zinghai Zoengsaam tai syu. (subject)

净系张三睇书。

Only Zoengsaam reads (books).

It is without doubt that the term *zinghai* contains a restrictive focus element. At issue is whether *zing* or the whole *zinghai* is the element concerned. On the one hand, *zing* almost always co-occurs with *hai*, and it rarely precedes another morpheme. But on the other hand, if *hai* corresponds to Mandarin *shi* (be), it can be understood as a focus word on its own merits (Tang, 1983; He, 2011, etc.). Tang (2007) argues that *zing* is an independent element. Based on the test of "omission", it is argued here that *zinghai* is instead one single lexicon.

(67) Zoengsaam zinghai mhai lousi.
张三净系唔系老师。
Zoengsaam is not a teacher only.

(68) * Zoengsaam [ ] hai mhai lousi.
张三[ ]系唔系老师。
Zoengsaam is not a teacher.

If *hai* in (67) is an independent focus word equivalent to *shi*, omitting *zing* does not affect its grammaticality as it simply serves as a modifier. The ungrammaticality of (68) shows that there is an integral relation between the two morphemes. Therefore, it is considered a single lexicon. Given this, the scope of *zinghai*, as compared to the post-verbal particles, is clearer in that the focus falls on the following constituent:

(69) Zoengsaam hai canteng zinghai sik saam wun faan. (* Subj/ * PP/Obj)
张三系餐厅净系食三碗饭。
In the restaurant, Zoengsaam ate three bowls of rice only.

(70) Zoengsaam zinghai hai canteng sik saam wun faan. (* Subj/PP/ ? Obj)
张三净系系餐厅食三碗饭。
Zoengsaam ate three bowls of rice in the restaurant only.

(71) Zinghai Zoengsaam hai canteng sik saam wun faan. (Subj/ * PP/ * Obj)
净系张三系餐厅食三碗饭。
Only Zoengsaam ate three bowls of rice in the restaurant.

As shown, *zinghai* is most likely to undergo AWF with the neighboring constituent. This might be related to the "Closeness Principle" applied on focus particles (for details, see Büring and Hartmann, 2001: 257). Further addition of *zaa* does not change the focus position. No matter whether it is the "C-headed proposals" by Law (2002) and Li (2006) or "T-headed proposal" by Tang (1998), post-verbal *zaa* c-commands the focused constituent at a high-up position. In (69), *zinghai* is posited at a lower position. Regardless of which proposal is adopted, the locality of *zinghai* and *zaa* fails to be established, which undermines the supposed "integral relation" between them. Now with the decompositional hypothesis, it is shown that the focus element of the post-verbal particle, i. e., *za*, does not differ in its semantic function from the pre-verbal one. If the pre-verbal element occurs in various syntactic positions, it is also reasonable to assume that the post-verbal one exhibits the same syntactic behaviour. Given that focus particle is in the periphery because the mood element is there, it now follows that the focus element might not be fixed to a certain position. In the case of *zinghai...za*, they exhibit locality in the overt syntax, and only after Spell-

Out does the focus element *za* combines with the mood element *a*. The "floating" account for post-verbal focus element is an alternative to the C- or T-headed proposals. With due considerations of the locality between *zinghai* and *za*, and given the assumption of the headedness of *za*, I propose the following configuration in (72)b, which resonates with a similar formulation by Tang (2007). The left diagram, (72)a, captures the essence of the other proposals:

(72) a.

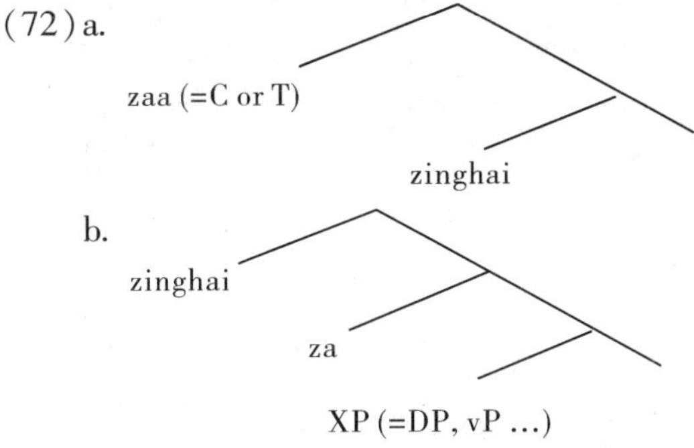

In conjunction with (58), the surface word order of *zinghai* ... *zaa* (not *za*) can be derived when *za* moves out to and combines with *a* at the root position in PF. (71) also suggests that *zinghai*, as well as *za*, goes with a subject DP and forms part of the nominal. If (72)b is on the right track, it leads to the conclusion that *za* can "float" as much as its pre-verbal counterpart *zinghai*.

3 Conclusion

This paper is based on the theories in relation to focus and focus particles, with an emphasis on Cantonese sentence-final focus particles as well as their discontinuous constructions. It is found that *zaa* and *ze* have the same focus function, i. e., the function of eliminating the exhausted alternatives until only one remains. Their exclusive function is the function of restricting the focus. The difference between *zaa* and *ze* is a difference in mood, but not in the focus function. Syntactic tests show that the subject can be focalized only when it carries special focus stress. The pre-subject topic can never be the focus, and the post-subject elements can be focalized under some general principles such as "the strongest stress falls on the last". In line with the prosodic theory (Feng, 1997), the "focalization principles" of sentence-final particles can be simplified as the embodiment of stress placement principles. The only specific feature about the sentence-final focus particles lies on the fact that the topic can never be focalized. It is argued that their largest scope is below the topic. With this in mind, this paper indicates that these particles can c-command the embedded elements. Considering the cases of questions and pre-verbal elements, I suggest that in such an occasion the focus element itself is inside the embedded clause. In accordance with Leung (2005), Tang (2006b), and Li (2006), a sentence-final particle can be analysed in a decompositional way so that *zaa*, as well as *ze*, combines both the focus and mood elements. At the time when they are spoken, they are in the periphery. This is because of the peripheral mood element that combines with the focus element in PF. Under this analysis, the paradox between its effect within an embedded clause and its final, "root" position can now be satisfactorily explained. Previous studies on the discontinuous constructions show that post-verbal *zaa* corresponds to pre-verbal *zaai* (Tang, 2007). In this paper, it is proposed that *zinghai* also forms a discontinuous construction with the post-verbal counterpart given their apparent redundancy. The locality issue can be explained by resorting to the "floating" nature of the post-verbal focus element. In other words, the post-verbal focus element (not the whole particle) is not fixed to a certain position. A non-decompositional account can only assume that there is a fixed position for the restrictive focus element.

References

Aoun, Joseph, and Audrey Yen-Hui Li 1993 Wh-elements in situ: syntax or LF? *Linguistic Inquiry*, 24: 199 – 238.

Büring, Daniel, and Katharina Hartmann 2001 The syntax and semantics of focus-sensitive particles in German. *Natural Language & Linguistic Theory*, 19: 229 – 281.

Chao, Yuen Ren 1968 *A Grammar of Spoken Chinese.* Berkeley and Los Angeles: University of California Press.

Chao, Yuen Ren 1969 *Cantonese Primer.* New York: Greenwood Press.

Cheng, Lisa Lai-shen, and Rint Sybesma 1999 Bare and not-so-bare nouns and the structure of NP. *Linguistic Inquiry*, 30: 509 – 542.

Cheung, Samuel Hung-nin 张洪年 1972/2007 《香港粤语语法的研究》,香港:香港中文大学出版社。

Chomsky, Noam 1995a Bare phrase structure. In Gert Webelhuth ed., *Government and Binding Theory and the Minimalist Program.* Cambridge, MA: Blackwell.

Chomsky, Noam 1995b *The Minimalist Program.* Cambridge, MA: MIT Press.

Coppock, Elizabeth, and David Beaver 2014 Principles of the exclusive muddle. *Journal of Semantics*, 31(3): 371 – 432.

Duanmu, San 2007 *The Phonology of Standard Chinese.* Oxford: Oxford University Press.

É. Kiss, Katalin 1998 Identificational focus versus information focus. *Language*, 74: 245 – 273.

Erlewine, Michael Yoshitaka 2010 Sentence-final only and the interpretation of focus in Mandarin Chinese. In L. E. Clemens, and C. -M. L. Liu eds., *Proceedings of the 22nd North American Conference on Chinese Linguistics (NACCL – 22) & the 18th International Conference on Chinese Linguistics (IACL – 18) Volume 2.* Cambridge, MA: Harvard University. pp. 18 – 35.

Fang, Xiaoyan 方小燕　2003　《广州方言句末语气助词》,广州:暨南大学出版社。

Feng, Shengli 冯胜利　1997　《汉语的韵律 · 词法与句法》,北京:北京大学出版社。

Feng, Shengli 冯胜利　2000　《汉语韵律句法学》,上海:上海教育出版社。

Fung, Suk-Yee Roxana　2000　*Final Particles in Standard Cantonese: Semantic Extension and Pragmatic Inference.* Doctoral dissertation, Columbus: Ohio State University.

He, Yuanjian 何元建　2011　《现代汉语生成语法》,北京:北京大学出版社。

Huang, Borong, and Liao Xudong 黄伯荣、廖序东　2007　《现代汉语》(下册),北京:高等教育出版社。

Huang, C. -T. James　2015　To appear. Syntactic analyticity and parametric theory. In Audrey Li. ed., *Chinese Syntax in a Cross-Linguistic Perspective.* Oxford and New York: Oxford University Press.

Jackendoff, Ray S.　1972　*Semantic Interpretation in Generative Grammar.* Cambridge, Mass: MIT Press.

König, Ekkehard　1991　*The Meaning of Focus Particles: A Comparative Perspective.* London: Routledge.

Krifka, Manfred　1999　Additive particles under stress. *Proceedings of Semantics and Linguistic Theory 8.* Cornell: CLC Publications. pp. 111 – 128.

Kwok, Helen　1984　*Sentence Particles in Cantonese.* Hong Kong: Centre of Asian Studies, University of Hong Kong.

Law, Ann　2002　Cantonese sentence-final particles and the CP domain. *UCL Working Papers in Linguistics*, 14: 375 – 98.

Law, Sam Po　1990　*The Syntax and Phonology of Cantonese Sentence-final Particles.* Doctoral dissertation, Boston: Boston University.

Leung, Chung-sum 梁仲森　1992　《香港粤语语助词的研究》,香港:香港理工大学硕士学位论文。

Leung, Chung-sum 梁仲森　2005　《当代香港粤语语助词的研究》,香港:香港城市大学语言信息科学研究中心。

Li, Boya　2006　*Chinese Final Particles and the Syntax of the Periphery.* Utrecht: LOT.

Li, Haoze　*Focus Intervention Effects in Mandarin.* M. Phil. thesis, Hong Kong: The Chinese University of Hong Kong.

Lu, Zhiwei 陆志韦　1957　《汉语的构词法》,北京:科学出版社。

Mai, Yun, and Tan Buyu eds. 麦耘、谭步云编　1997　《实用广州话分类词典》,广州:广东人民出版社。

Massam, Diane　2001　Pseudo noun incorporation in Niuean. *Natural Language & Linguistic Theory*, 19: 153 – 197.

Matthews, Stephen, and Virginia Yip　1994　*Cantonese: A Comprehensive Grammar.* London and New York: Routledge.

Neeleman, Ad, and Reiko Vermeulen 2012 The syntactic expression of information structure. In Ad Neeleman, and Reiko Vermeulen eds., *The Syntax of Topic, Focus, and Contrast*. Berlin: Mouton De Gruyter. pp. 1 – 38.

Paul, Waltraud 2011 Why particles are not particular: sentence-final particles in Chinese as heads of a split CP. Ms.

Rao, Bingcai, Ouyang Jueya, and Zhou Wuji 饶秉才、欧阳觉亚、周无忌 1998 《广州话方言词典》(修订版),香港:商务印书馆。

Riester, Arndt 2006 Only scalar. In Janneke Huitink, and Sophia Katrenko eds., *Proceedings of the Eleventh ESSLLI Student Session*. pp. 64 – 75.

Rizzi, Luigi 1997 The fine structure of the left periphery. In Liliane Haegeman ed., *Elements of Grammar*. Dordrecht: Kluwer Academic Publishers. pp. 281 – 337.

Rooth, Mats 1985 *Association with Focus*. Ph. D. dissertation, Amherst: University of Massachusetts.

Sybesma, Rint 1997 *The deictic function of TP and sentence-le in Mandarin Chinese*. Paper presented at the 9th North American Conference on Chinese Linguistics (NACCL – 9), University of Victoria.

Tancredi, Christopher 1990 Syntactic association with focus. In Denise Meyer, Satoshi Tomioka, and Leyla Zidani-Eroglu eds., *Proceedings from the First Meeting of the Formal Linguistic Society of Mid-America*. Madison: University of Wisconsin. pp. 289 – 303.

Tang, Sze-Wing 1998 *Parametrization of Features in Syntax*. Ph. D. dissertation, Irvine: University of California.

Tang, Sze-Wing 邓思颖 2002 《粤语句末助词的不对称分布》,《中国语文研究》第 2 期,第 75 ~ 84 页。

Tang, Sze-Wing 2003 Properties of *ngaang* and the syntax of verbal particles in Cantonese. *Journal of Chinese Linguistics*, 31(2): 245 – 269。

Tang, Sze-Wing 邓思颖 2006a 《粤语"得滞、乜滞、咁滞"是否属于同一个家族?》,《中国语文研究》第 1 期,第 1 ~ 11 页。

Tang, Sze-Wing 邓思颖 2006b 《粤语疑问句"先"的句法特点》,《中国语文》第 3 期,第 225 ~ 232 页。

Tang, Sze-Wing 邓思颖 2006c 《粤语框式虚词结构的句法分析》,《汉语学报》第 2 期,第 16 ~ 23 页。

Tang, Sze-Wing 邓思颖 2007 《粤语框式虚词的局部性和多重性》,载于张洪年、张双庆、陈雄根主编 《第十届国际粤方言研讨会论文集》,北京:中国社会科学出版社,第 262 ~ 276 页。

Tang, Sze-Wing 邓思颖 2008a 《为甚么问"乜"?》,《中国语文研究》第 1 期,第 9 ~ 19 页。

Tang, Sze-Wing 邓思颖 2008b 《粤语框式虚词"咪……啰"的句法特点》,《中国语言学集刊》第 3 卷第 1 期,第 145 ~ 159 页。

Tang,Sze-Wing 邓思颖　2009a　《粤语句末"住"和框式虚词结构》,《中国语文》第 3 期,第 234 ~ 240 页。

Tang,Sze-Wing 邓思颖　2009b　《粤语句末助词"罢啦"及其框式结构》,载于钱志安、郭必之、李宝伦、邹嘉彦编　《粤语跨学科研究:第十三届国际粤方言研讨会论文集》,香港:香港城市大学语言信息科学研究中心,第 415 ~ 427 页。

Tang,Sze-Wing　2009c　The syntax of two approximatives in Cantonese: discontinuous constructions formed with *zai*[6]. *Journal of Chinese Linguistics*,37(2): 227 –256.

Tang,Sze-Wing,and Cheng Siu-Pong　2014　Aspects of Cantonese Grammar. In C. -T. James Huang, Y. -H. Audrey Li, and Andrew Simpson eds., *Handbook of Chinese Linguistics*. Hoboken,NJ: Wiley-Blackwell. pp. 601 –628.

Tang,Ting-Chi　1983　Focusing constructions in Chinese: cleft sentences and pseudo-cleft sentences. In Ting-Chi Tang,Robert L. Cheng,and Ying-Che Li eds., *Studies in Chinese Syntax and Semantics*,*Universal Scope*: *Presupposition and Quantification in Chinese*. Taipei: Student Book Co. pp. 127 –226.

Yang,C. -Y. Barry　2008　Intervention effects and covert component of grammar. Ph. D. dissertation,Taipei: National Tsing Hua University.

Yuyanxue Mingci Shending Weiyuanhui 语言学名词审定委员会　2011　《语言学名词》,北京:商务印书馆。

Acquisition of Cantonese Relative Clauses by Typically Developing and Deaf Children*

Scholastica LAM

Abstract: Acquisition studies on Cantonese relative clauses are limited and no consensus is reached on whether subject-object asymmetry is present. This study explores the acquisition of Cantonese relative clauses by Cantonese-speaking children from age 3;10 to 5;10 in order to contribute further to our understanding to how children comprehend and produce Cantonese relative clauses. Another goal of this study is to examine how deaf children perform similar to or different from their hearing peers. Two methods, an elicited production task and a picture pointing task were designed. The results show that subject advantage is observed with typically developing children but not with deaf children in elicited production task. By contrast, object advantage is observed in picture pointing task for both groups of children. The result can be explained by the fact that the elicited production task tends to elicit passive object relatives (evidenced by responses of adult participants). If children are still learning passive structures, they may not be able to produce adult-like responses for object-gapped relatives. As a result, object-gapped relatives are not performed as good as subject-gapped relatives in elicited production task, even though both groups of children are able to comprehend them.

Key words: prenominal relative clauses　Cantonese　subject-object asymmetry　first language acquisition

1 Introduction

This study examines how typically developing and deaf children comprehend and produce Cantonese relative clauses. Relative clause is a complex structure that has been widely studied in language acquisition. Acquisition studies began as early as 1970s. Now a substantial body of research studying how typically developing children acquire relative clauses in different languages

* This paper is supported by the CUHK Direct Grant for Research 2011 – 2012 (Project no. :2010376). I would like to thank the kindergartens for the venue of data collection, the children and their family and the adult participants for supporting this research project and the Jockey Club Sign Bilingualism and Co-enrolment in Deaf Education Programme for allowing me to do research with the deaf students in the programme. Thanks also go to the helpers of this project. They are: Jia Li, Wingie Tang, Susanna Leung, Leslie Tsoi, Ka Wing Ng. I would like to thank Angel Chan, Chris Yiu and Gladys Tang for their comments on the design of the experiments and the insightful comments from the audience at Annual Research Forum, Linguistic Society of Hong Kong 2012, the 21th International Association of Chinese Linguistics (IACL 21) and the 18th International Conference on Yue Dialects.

is accumulated [Sheldon (1974), Tavakolian (1981), Hamburger and Crain (1982), Diessel and Tomasello (2000) for English; Friedmann and Novogrodsky (2004) for Hebrew, Brandt et al. (2009) for German; Lee (1992), Hsu et al. (2009) for Mandarin Chinese; Guasti and Cardinaletti (2003), Contemori and Belletti (2013) for Italian; Varlokosta (1997), Stavrakaki (2001, 2002) for Greek, to name just a few]. Cross-linguistically, it has been observed that the age of emergence of relative clauses varies. While internally-headed relative clauses appear at around age 2 [e. g. Isobe (2003, 2005), Ozeki and Shirai (2007) for Japanese], postnominal externally-headed relative clauses emerge much later at around age 4 (cf. Guasti et al., 2012). The complexity of relative clauses also affects the developmental sequence of different kinds of relative clauses. Diessel and Tomasello (2005) note that English-speaking children initially use relatives in copular construction [e. g. This is the sugar *that goes in there* (Nina 3;0)] and later in main clause construction (e. g. The horse *that pushed the goat* stands on the lion). Relative clauses containing a resumptive pronoun also appear earlier than those containing a gap (Labelle, 1990, 1996).

Acquisition studies on relative clauses largely focus on whether certain types of relative clauses are more difficult than the other. Dated back to 1974, Sheldon identifies four types of relative clauses which differ in whether they are center-embedded and whether the head noun and the gap have parallel function (p. 275):

(1) a. SS: **The dog$_i$** [that ____$_i$ jumps over the pig] bumps into the lion.
b. SO: **The lion$_i$** [that the horse bumps into ____$_i$] jumps over the giraffe.
c. OS: The pig bumps into **the horse$_i$** [that ____$_i$ jumps over the giraffe].
d. OO: The dog stands on **the horse$_i$** [that the giraffe jumps over ____$_i$].

SS, SO, OS and OO in (1) refer to four types of relative clauses. The first and the second alphabets of each type of relative clauses represent the grammatical roles (Subject or Object) of the head noun [i. e. the bolded noun phrase in (1)] and of the gap [i. e. "____" in (1)] respectively. Different findings in different studies reveal that methodological designs are highly important in exploring children's knowledge of relative clauses. A number of factors facilitating children's comprehension have been reported, including felicity condition (Hamburger and Crain, 1982), use of intransitive verbs and inanimate object in the relative clauses [Arosio et al. (2011) for Italian; Goodluck and Tavakolian (1982) for English; Lee (1992) for Chinese]. Recent study conducted by Adani (2010) also points out that pragmatic conditions, factors related to the lexicon and visual inspection of the scene are factors facilitating children's performance in production task.

Over the decades, acquisition studies of relative clauses focus on subject-object asymmetry. It is observed that subject relatives are easier to comprehend and produce in languages having postnominal relative clauses [Adani (2010), Adani et al. (2010), Arosio et al. (2006, 2009), Belletti and Contemori (2010) for Italian; Arnon (2010), Friedmann et al. (2009) for Hebrew; Booth et al. (2000) for English, to name just a few]. Three hypotheses, Canonical Word Order

Hypothesis, Filler-Gap Linear Distance Hypothesis and Structural Distance Hypothesis, have been proposed to capture the subject-object asymmetry. Canonical Word Order Hypothesis (Bever, 1970) states that children recognize input utterances by using the canonical sentence in the target language. Children may find structures following the canonical order easier than those do not. In English, the order of subject-gapped relatives is the same as the canonical word order and hence subject-gapped relatives are easier than object-gapped relatives [see example (2)].

(2) English (Hsu et al., 2009:327)

S V O

a. The girl likes the cat.

S V O

b. The girl, [that ____ likes the cat] (subject-gapped relative)

O S V

c. The cat [that the girl likes ____] (object-gapped relative)

Filler-Gap Linear Distance Hypothesis makes the same prediction, but based on a different reason. This hypothesis states that the greater the linear distance between the filler (the head noun in the case of relative clause) and gap, the higher the processing load and the difficulty. In English, the linear distance between the head noun and the gap is short for subject-gapped relatives, but long for object-gapped relatives [see example (3)]. The processing load for object-gapped relatives is high. Object-gapped relatives are therefore difficult.

(3) English (Hsu et al., 2009:329)

filler ------------ gap

a. The girl [who ____ likes the boy] (subject-gapped relative)

filler -------------------------------- gap

b. The boy [who the girl likes ____] (object-gapped relative)

Structural Distance Hypothesis proposes that the order of difficulty follows Keenan and Comrie's (1977) Noun Phrase Accessibility Hierarchy (NPAH), that is, the lower the ranking of the grammatical role of the gap, the higher the degree of difficulty. Hence subject relatives are easier than object relatives; object relatives are easier than oblique relatives and so on. Two new approaches emerge recently, one is frequency/usage-based approach (cf. Brandt et al., 2009) and the other is grammatical/intervention approach [Friedmann et al. (2009), Grillo (2009)]. The first approach explains children's performance with input frequency and children's own spontaneous speech. The second approach, inspired by Rizzi's (1990) Relativized Minimality, states that the intervening subject NP between the head noun and the gap in object relatives serves as a competitor with the object NP and causes difficulty. Hence object-gapped relatives are more difficult. All these approaches are attempts to explain the subject-object asymmetry, if any.

While previous studies on relative clauses are largely on postnominal relative clauses in SVO languages, little is known on the acquisition of prenominal relative clauses. Cantonese relative clauses are prenominal. An acquisition study of Cantonese relative clauses will therefore fill in this gap. To the best of my knowledge, only few studies, Lau (2006), Tsou et al. (2009) and Chan et al. (2011), provided some preliminary findings in this area. This paper attempts to add to the literature on how typically developing children acquire Cantonese relative clauses by investigating subject-gapped and object-gapped via a comprehension task and a production task. The results may help determine whether subject-object asymmetry occurs in the acquisition of Cantonese relative clauses. The second goal of this paper is to explore whether deaf children demonstrate knowledge of Cantonese relative clauses. Deaf children generally have problem with complex structure like relative clauses. Friedmann and Szterman (2006) suggest that the problem is resulted from deaf children's lack of knowledge of syntactic movement. When the head noun is subject or object, the relative clauses generally contain a gap in Cantonese, suggesting the presence of wh-movement (see discussion below). We will see if deaf children could produce relative clauses containing gaps which imply the presence of the knowledge of syntactic movement.

In the following sections, the adult grammar of Cantonese relative clauses will be introduced. Then a brief review on previous studies on the acquisition of Cantonese relative clauses by typically developing monolingual Cantonese children and deaf children will be presented.

1.1 Cantonese Relative Clauses: Adult Grammar

Cantonese relative clauses are typologically rare because Cantonese, being an SVO language, has prenominal relative clauses while almost all SVO languages have postnominal relative clauses (Yip and Matthews, 2007a, b). They may occur either in a copular construction or in a main clause construction (Lau, 2006: 33 – 34): ①

(4) a. Relative clauses in copular construction

li^1 zek^3 hai^6 zuk^1 zyu^6 zo^2 tou^3zai^2 go^2 zek^3 si^1zi^2

this CL is catch ASP ASP rabbit that CL lion

This is the lion that has caught the rabbit.

b. Relative clauses in main clause construction

[sik^6 zo^2 tiu^4 jyu^5] go^2 zek^3 $maau^1maau^1$ $haang^4$ zo^2 $heoi^3$

eat ASP CL fish that CL cat walk ASP to

① Cantonese data are represented with jyutping, a romanization developed by Linguistic Society of Hong Kong. Aspect markers are coded as ASP, classifiers as CL, passive as PASS, particles as PRT, sentence final particles as SFP.

laap^{6}saap^{3}tung^2 go^{2}dou^6
rubbish-bin there
The cat that ate the fish walked to the rubbish bin.

While the relative clauses in main clause construction involve embedding, those in copular construction serve as the complement of the copular verb *hai*^{6} (be).

Cantonese relative clauses have two subtypes, the *ge*^{3} relatives and classifier relatives. While the *ge*^{3} relatives are used in high register, the classifier relatives are more colloquial (Matthews and Yip, 2001):

(5) a. Classifier relatives
keoi^5 sik^6 go^2 lap^1 tong^2
s/he eat that CL candy
the candy s/he eats
b. *Ge*^{3} relatives
keoi^5 sik^6 ge^3 tong^2
s/he eat that candy
the candy(ies) s/he eats

Similar to many natural languages, the gaps in the relative clauses may be of different grammatical roles. When the gaps are canonical subjects and objects, no resumptive pronouns are required (Matthews and Yip, 1994:110):

(6) a. Subject-gapped relatives
[$\_\_\__i$ sik^1 ngo^5] ge^3 jan^4_i
know me that people
people that know me
b. Object-gapped relatives
[ngo^5 sik^1 $\_\_\__i$] ge^3 jan^4_i
I know that people
people that I know

When we look at the surface word order, subject relatives and object relatives contrast with each other. The surface word order of subject relatives is VOS while that of object relatives is SVO. Note that object relatives may be expressed by passive object relatives:

(7) a. Object-gapped relative
[maa^{5}lau^1 zeoi^1 $\_\_\__i$] go^2 zek^3 gau^{2}zai^2_i
monkey chase that CL dog
the dog that the monkey is chasing

b. Passive object relative

[___$_{i}$ bei^{2} maa^{5}lau^{1} zeoi^{1}] go^{2} zek^{3} gau^{2}zai$^{2}_{i}$

PASS monkey chase that CL dog

the dog that was chased by the monkey

Though passive object relatives are structurally more complex, adults' preference to them may be resulted from the need of disambiguating garden path sentences [see Lee (2006) for a discussion on garden path effects in Chinese].

In addition to subject-gapped and object-gapped relatives, Cantonese relative clauses may contain indirect object [i. e. example (8)], object of coverb [i. e. example (9)] or the possessor of the head noun [i. e. example (10)] as the gaps and these relative clauses all require resumptive pronouns (adapted from Matthews and Yip, 1994:112):

(8) Indirect object relatives

[ngo^{5}dei^{6} sung^{3} faa^{1} bei^{2} keoi$^{5}_{i}$] go^{2} go^{3} beng^{6}jan$^{4}_{i}$

we send flowers give him that CL patients

the patient whom we sent flowers to

(9) Oblique

[ngo^{5} tung^{4} keoi^{5}dei$^{6}_{i}$ king^{1}gai^{2}] go^{2} go^{3} hok^{6}saang$^{1}_{i}$

I with them chat that CL student

the students I chat with have left

(10) Genitive

[ngo^{5} zong^{6} dou^{2} keoi$^{5}_{i}$ gaa^{3} ce^{1}] go^{2} go^{3} neoi^{5}jan$^{2}_{i}$

I bump PRT her CL car that CL woman

the woman whose car I bumped into

The examples above show that resumptive pronouns are needed in indirect object relatives, oblique relatives as well as genitive relatives. All these relative clauses are more complex than the subject relatives and object relatives. The construction of indirect object relatives requires the grammatical knowledge of dative construction; forming of oblique and genitive relatives also requires grammatical knowledge of coverb and possessive phrases.

Relative clauses have been studied under the context of wh-questions in generative grammar. While English relative clauses are derived via wh-questions, are Cantonese relative clauses derived via wh-movement as well? He (2007), to my best knowledge, is the first paper that discusses the syntax of Cantonese relative clauses. He divides Cantonese relative clauses into three types: (i) relative clauses that require a syntactic head, (ii) relative clauses that have optional syntactic heads and (iii) relative clauses that are obligatorily headless. While *ge*^{3} relatives are of the first type, classifier relatives mentioned above are of the second and third type. The author proposes that (i) is a complex NP and no movement is involved (see Figure 1). The classifier relatives involve syntactic movement from complex NP to Spec, DP for (ii) (see Figure 2a and 2b) and to Spec, ClP for (iii) (see Figure 3). Note that classifier relatives always contain *ge*[3] in the underlying structure, the presence/absence of the *ge*[3] at the surface form depends on whether the CP containing *ge*[3] undergo PF deletion (He, 2007: 20 – 24):

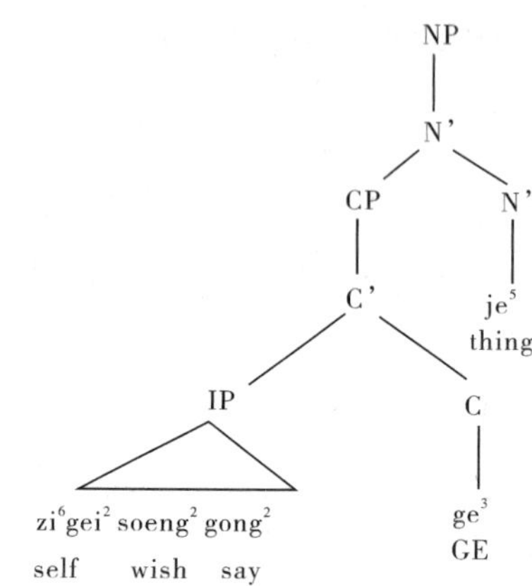

Figure 1 Derivation of (i) "Things (That Oneself Wishes to Say)"

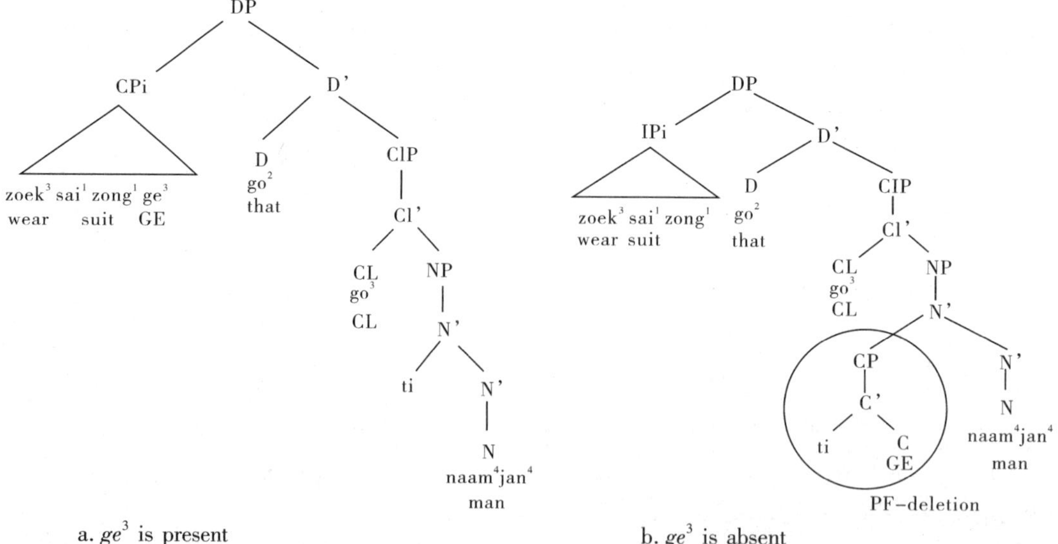

Figure 2 Derivation of (ii) "the Man (That Wears a Suit)"

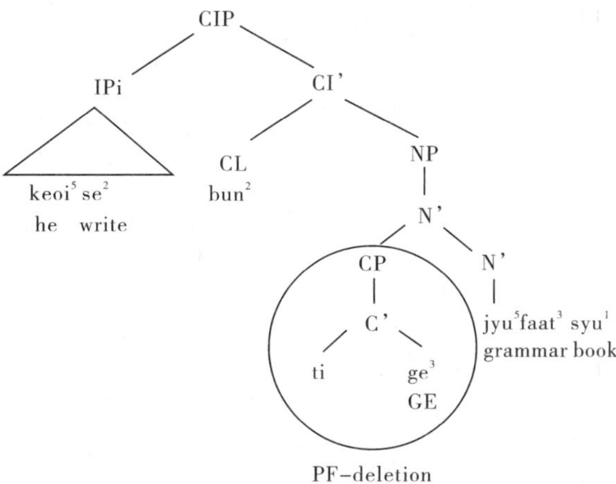

Figure 3 Derivation of (iii) "the Grammar Book (Which He Wrote)"

In other words, ge^3 relatives do not involve syntactic movement while classifier relatives involve syntactic movement.

1.2 Monolingual Acquisition of Cantonese Relative Clauses

As noted above, subject-object asymmetry is the major focus of acquisition studies on relative clauses in the literature. Four approaches, Canonical Word Order Hypothesis, Filler-Gap Linear Distance Hypothesis, grammatical/intervention approach and Structural Distance Hypothesis, have also been proposed to capture the acquisition patterns. Consider the predictions made by these approaches one by one. Canonical Word Order Hypothesis predicts that object relatives are easier than subject relatives given the fact that the order of object relatives resembles the canonical SVO order in Cantonese (Slobin and Bever, 1982):

(11) Subject-gapped relatives

V O S

[____$_i$ sek^3 gung^{1}gai^1 go^2 zek^3 lou^{5}syu^2_i] hai^2 bin^{1}dou^6 aa^3

kiss chicken that CL mouse is where SFP

Where is the mouse that is kissing the chicken?

(12) Object-gapped relatives

S V O

[joeng^{4}zai^2 teoi^1____$_i$ go^2 zek^3 tou^{3}zai^2_i] hai^2 bin^{1}dou^6 aa^3

sheep push that CL rabbit is where SFP

Where is the rabbit that the sheep is pushing?

Filler-Gap Linear Distance Hypothesis also makes the same prediction because the linear distance between the filler and gap is shorter with object-gapped relatives (Gibson, 1998, 2000):

(13) Subject-gapped relatives

gap ---------------------- filler

[____$_i$ sek^3 gung^{1}gai^1 **go^2 zek^3 lou^{5}syu$_i^2$**] hai^2 bin^{1}dou^6 aa^3

kiss chicken that CL mouse is where SFP

Where is the mouse that is kissing the chicken?

(14) Object-gapped relatives

gap ---------- filler

[joeng^{4}zai^2 teoi^1 ____$_i$ **go^2 zek^3 tou^{3}zai$_i^2$**] hai^2 bin^{1}dou^6 aa^3

sheep push that CL rabbit is where SFP

Where is the rabbit that the sheep is pushing?

The grammatical/intervention approach also predicts that object-gapped relatives are easier because there is a NP intervening the gap and the head noun for subject-gapped relatives but no competitor NP is present for object-gapped relatives:

(15) Subject-gapped relatives

gap intervening NP head noun

[____$_i$ daa^2 gau^{2}zai^2 go^2 zek^3 maau^{1}zai$_i^2$] zi^2 zyu^6 ngau^{4}zai^2

hit dog that CL cat point ASP cow

The cat that is hitting the dog (is pointing at the cow).

(16) Object-gapped relatives

gap head noun

[zyu^{1}zai^2 pou^5 ____$_i$ go^2 zek^3 maau^{1}zai$_i^2$] zi^2 zyu^6 ngau^{4}zai^2

pig hold that CL cat point ASP cow

The cat that the pig is holding (is pointing at the cow).

Structural Distance Hypothesis, by contrast, predicts subject advantage because subject is of the highest position in the NPAH.

A question follows is which of these accounts capture the acquisition of Cantonese relative clauses. How Cantonese-speaking children acquire relative clauses is an understudied area. Only few studies, Lau (2006), Tsou et al. (2009) and Chan et al. (2011), provided some preliminary findings on this area. Lau (2006) is the first study exploring the acquisition of Cantonese relative clauses by young children. She studied a total of 31 native Cantonese monolingual children from the age of 4;0 to 6;1. A total of 48 test sentences were designed on the basis of Diessel and Tomasello's (2005) classification of relative clauses. The test sentences include both relative clauses occurring in copular and main clause constructions. The gaps are of six types: subject, agent, patient, indirect object, oblique and genitive. These test sentences were randomly divided into two groups, forming the stimuli for the act-out task (comprehension) and an elicited imitation task (production). The results show that children performed best with subject relatives with intransitive verb, followed by agent relatives (i. e. subject relatives with transitive verb), patient relatives, genitive relatives, oblique relatives and lastly indirect object relatives in the production task. The accuracy rate in comprehension task is generally higher for all types of relative clauses. The children also performed best with subject relatives, but genitive relative clauses instead of the agent relatives have higher accuracy, showing evidence against the predictions made by Keenan and Comrie's (1977) NPAH. However, Lau's study does not provide conclusive results due to a number of factors. First, it has been reported in the literature that transitivity, animacy and power relations would affect children's test performance. The comparison of relative clauses containing intransitive verbs (i. e. subject relatives) with those containing transitive verbs (i. e. agent relatives, patient relatives, indirect relatives, oblique relatives, genitive relatives) is not fair because relative clauses containing intransitive verbs are easier for children. The animacy cues and power relations were also not systematically controlled. The use of act-out task may also miss out other interpretations children have. All the experimental flaws weaken her claim that there is a subject advantage in the acquisition of Cantonese relative clauses.

Tsou et al. (2009), on the other hand, aim at exploring how Cantonese-speaking children understand function words and complex constructions. The study of relative clauses is part of their bigger research project that documents Cantonese development of Hong Kong school children via an assessment tool, the Hong Kong Cantonese Oral Language Assessment Scale (HKCOLAS). While SS, OO and OS were tested in a picture pointing task, the genitive relatives and indirect object relatives were tested in a sentence production task. The results show that Cantonese-speaking children could only reach the accuracy rate of 70% or higher when they reach age 6. The performance on SS and OO is better than OS in the picture pointing task, given the fact that even children aged at 11;0 may not be able to comprehend OS well. In the sentence production task, children showed knowledge on genitive relative clauses as early as age 7;0, but they could not reach 70% accuracy for indirect object relative clauses even at 11;0. Though Tsou et al. (2009) report data from children with wider age range, the uneven types and test items designed for comprehension and production tasks and the small number of test items (only seven test items for five types of relative clauses) only allow us to have some preliminary ideas on the development of Cantonese relative clauses.

In their review on the acquisition of Cantonese relative clauses, Chan et al. (2011) mentioned two studies, one on production and the other on comprehension. Both studies explore the order of difficulty by adapting Diessel and Tomasello's (2005) classification of relative clauses. While the elicited imitation task shows no subject or object advantage in production, the picture pointing task shows that Cantonese-speaking children performed significantly better in comprehending object relatives than subject relatives. Though Lau (2006) and the studies noted in Chan et al. (2011)

both used elicited imitation task, the results are different. One possibility is that Chan et al. (2011) neturalized the animacy cues. Additional evidence to the object advantage comes from Yip and Matthews' (2007a) study of Cantonese-English bilinguals. They report that Cantonese relative clauses emerge at age 2;01.1, 2;04.28 and 2;09.5 for their three bilingual children and all these relative clauses are object relatives. Yip and Matthews suggest that the isomorphism between object relatives and word order in main clause may explain the early emergence of object relatives. In sum, the results in previous studies conform to the predictions made by Canonical Word Order Hypothesis, Filler-Gap Linear Distance Hypothesis and grammatical/intervention approach.

1.3 Acquisition of Cantonese Relative Clauses by Deaf Children

Studies on acquisition of relative clauses of spoken language by the deaf are scarce. De Villiers (1988) conducted an elicited production task with deaf children aged 11 through 18 and found that relative clauses are acquired late. The developmental pattern conforms to that of normally hearing children. The errors like the use of resumptive pronouns and relativization of the wrong noun phrase, however, suggest that deaf children have incomplete grammar. Friedmann and Szterman's (2006) study on Hebrew orally-trained deaf children, who have moderate to profound hearing loss, contributes further to our understanding on deaf children's development of relative clauses. The results come from a series of experiments (i. e. sentence-matching task, preference task and picture description task) on comprehension and production of relative clauses by deaf children aged from 7;7 to 11;3. The major findings show that orally-trained deaf children have language deficit in object relative clauses derived via syntactic movement and they perform better with relative clauses containing a resumptive pronoun than those containing a gap. Subsequent studies of this research team report similar results with other deaf children acquiring Hebrew (Friedmann et al., 2008; Friedmann et al., 2010; Friedmann and Costa, 2011) and Palestinian Arabic (Friedmann et al., 2010; Friedmann and Costa, 2011).

Hong Kong deaf children are often exposed to Cantonese and not to signed languages due to the fact that the Hong Kong government adopts the oral-only language policy for deaf education. Only two studies, Yiu (2004) and Tam (2011) on how deaf children acquire Cantonese relative clauses have been conducted.

Yiu (2004) investigated both comprehension and production of relative clauses by deaf children who had profound hearing loss and no exposure to Hong Kong Sign Language. 20 profoundly deaf children and 36 hearing children aged 4;0 – 6;11 participated in two experiments, an act-out task and an elicited production task. While only SS relatives were tested in an elicited production task, stimuli in the act-out task contained SS, SO and SIO (i. e. gap = indirect object) relatives. The results of the act-out task show that SS and SIO are easier for profoundly deaf children and these relatives are acquired at age 4. SO is the most difficult and it is not fully acquired even by age 6. Treating relative clauses as conjoined clauses and use of wrong actor were two errors observed in the act-out task. In the production task, many deaf children did not produce any relative clause (62.5% of total responses). This happened most with four-year-old children. A handful of sentences produced (21.3% of total responses) contain conjoined clauses instead of relative clauses.

Tam (2011) used the data collected from Hong Kong Cantonese Oral Language Assessment Scale (HKCOLAS), the same tool used in Tsou et al. (2009). 4 test stimuli (2 items on SS, 1 on OO and 1 on OS) were studied in a picture selection task (i. e. comprehension task) and 3 items (2 items on SS and 1 item on OS) in an elicited production task. A total of 69 mild to profound deaf children aged 8;0 – 12;11, with the hearing age ranged from 1;10 – 9;5, were studied. Tam reports that deaf children generally perform better with SS than SO in the production task. The comprehension data, however, show that deaf children do better with OO than SS and the performance with SS is better than OS, refuting the claim that object relatives would be easier in comprehension.

The two pieces of work on deaf children's acquisition of relative clauses described above report some preliminary findings on the acquisition of Cantonese relative clauses by deaf children. However, these studies are limited in various aspects. Yiu's (2004) study, though focused, examines only SS in the production task and hence order of difficulty cannot be shown from the production data. It is unclear whether order of difficulty can be solely determined by comprehension data collected from act-out task, especially when the results show that even normally hearing children aged between 6;0 and 6;11 do not reach 100% accuracy. Tam (2011) explores acquisition of relative clauses by deaf children with a wider range of hearing loss and with different linguistic background. The types of relative clauses tested in comprehension task do not match those in production task. The number of items are also too few to make generalizations.

This study attempts to contribute further to our understanding on acquisition of relative clauses by investigating how typically developing monolingual Cantonese children and deaf children comprehend and produce subject-gapped and object-gapped relative clauses. In particular, two experiments, elicited production task (production) and picture pointing task (comprehension), were designed. The two sets of data will allow us to have a more comprehensive picture on the knowledge of Cantonese relative clauses of the two groups of children.

2 Experiment 1: Elicited Production Task

2.1 Participants

Three groups of participants, (i) adult, (ii) typically developing Cantonese-speaking children and (iii) deaf children, participated in this experiment. Group (i) contained eighteen Cantonese-speaking adults (Mean = 20;8; Range = 19 – 24) who were undergraduate students from different disciplines of the same university. Fifty Cantonese-speaking children (Mean = 4; 8; Range: 3;10–5;10)(21 Males and 29 females) participated in the experiment as Group (ii). They were divided into two levels in the kindergarten: K2(age range:3;10 to 4;10) and K3(4;11 to 5;10). All of them were monolingual and had no disabilities. The third group consisted of twenty-four severely and profoundly deaf students [Mean = 10;2; Range:6;7 to 13;11(chronological age); Mean = 8;6; Range:4;9 to 11;11(hearing age)]① with normal intelligence. The average hearing thresholds of these children was higher than 70dB (Range: 72 – 120dB). Seven students wore hearing aids at both ears and seventeen students wore cochlear implant on either left or right ear. Five of these students had deaf parents and other students had hearing parents. All of these children were exposed to Hong Kong Sign Language (HKSL) as one of the first languages if their parents were deaf or as a second language if their parents were hearing when they were enrolled in a school that adopted a sign bilingual approach in which Hong Kong Sign Language (HKSL) and Cantonese were the mediums of instruction. The participants' biodata is given in Appendix.

Since the speech abilities of deaf students showed a high degree of diversity regardless of age of onset and years of exposure, a cluster analysis was done to group the students by using the scores of Cantonese grammar in HKCOLAS, the standardized assessment tool on Cantonese. Two groups were formed: Group A consisted of 15 deaf students and the score ranged from 20 to 42; Group B had 9 deaf students and the score ranged from 51 – 69. 3 youngest deaf children of deaf parents were grouped in Group A and 2 older deaf children of deaf parents were grouped in Group B.

2.2 Method and Test Procedures

This study uses a picture description task developed by Zukowski (2001), a task used to elicit language data from children with William Syndrome. The same task has successfully elicited production of normal hearing children acquiring Indonesian (Tjung, 2006) and Mandarin (Hsu et al., 2009). A similar task developed by Friedmann and Szterman (2006) could also elicit language production of orally-trained deaf children. In current design, test sentences are generated from 6 animal charactersi[e. tou^{3} zai^{2} (rabbit), maa^{5} lau^{1} (monkey), maau^{1} zai^{2} (cat), gau^{2} zai^{2} (dog), hung^{4} zai^{2} (bear), zyu^{1} zai^{2} (pig) and 5 verbs daa^{2} (hit), naau^{6} (scold), pou^{5} (hold), tek^{3} (kick), bei^{2} (give)]. 5 items each for SS, SO, OO and OS are created. Animacy and transitivity effects are neutralized. The complexity of the target sentence is also minimized by using only one character[i. e. ngau^{4} (cow)] in the matrix clause. Examples of expected answers are given in Table 1 below:

① Hearing age refers to the years of exposure of speech after the fitting of hearing devices.

Table 1　Examples of Expected Answers in Elicited Production Task

Expected Answers	Grammatical Roles in Matrix Clause	Grammatical Roles in Relative Clause
____$_i$ daa2 gau2zai2 go2 zek3 maau1zai2$_i$ (zi2 zyu6 ngau4zai2) hit dog that CL cat point ASP cow The cat that is hitting the dog (is pointing at the cow).	Subj	Subj
zyu1zai2 pou5 ____$_i$ go2 zek3 maau1zai2$_i$ (zi2 zyu6 ngau4zai2) pig hold that CL cat point ASP cow The cat that the pig is holding (is pointing at the cow).	Subj	Obj
(ngau4zai2 zi2 zyu6) maa5lau1 daa2 ____$_i$ go2 zek3 zyu1zai2$_i$ cow point ASP monkey hit that CL pig (The cow is pointing at) the pig that the monkey is hitting.	Obj	Obj
(ngau4zai2 zi2 zyu6) ____$_i$ pou5 tou3zai2 go2 zek3 maau1zai2$_i$ cow point ASP hold rabbit that CL cat (The cow is pointing at) the cat that is holding the rabbit.	Obj	Subj

The test procedure goes like this. Experimenter 1 first introduced the pairs of identical characters and the action involved in the base picture in order to set up the context of using relative clauses. Experimenter 1 then showed the child the question picture which showed a minimal difference with the base picture. The minimal difference was always a cow being pointed at or a cow is pointing at another animal. Experimenter 1 then asked the child to tell Experimenter 2 (who could not see the pictures on the computer) which X (an animal character) the cow was pointing at in object questions and which X was pointing at the cow in subject questions (see Table 2 for a sample item).

Table 2　Sample Item of the Elicited Production Task

Steps	Pictures	Test Procedures
Lead-in description		1. Introduction of characters: Lead-in description: *jat1 zek3 tou3zai2 naau6 hung4zai2, ling6 jat1 zek3 tou3zai2 daa2 hung4zai2* A rabbit is scolding a bear. Another rabbit is hitting another bear.

(continued)

Steps	Pictures	Test Procedures
Elicited production		2. Experimenter 1 asked the child to tell Experimenter 2 which rabbit was pointing at the cow. Expected answer: *naau⁶ hung⁴zai² go² zek³ tou³zai² (zi² zyu⁶ ngau⁴zai²)* The rabbit that is scolding the bear (is pointing at the cow).

2.3 Results: Typically Developing Children

2.3.1 Adult-like RC Responses

The group of typically-developing Cantonese-speaking children produced 980 responses in the elicited production task. 700 out of 980 responses (71.43%) contain relative clauses while all responses in adult group are relative clauses. Among the relative clauses produced, 306 out of 700 responses (43.71%) are adult-like[see examples (17) to (20)]:

(17) naau^6 hung^{4}hung^2 go^2 zek^3 tou^{3}zai^2 zi^2 zyu^6 ngau^{4}zai^2
scold bear that CL rabbit point ASP cow
The rabbit that is scolding the bear is pointing at the cow.
(NTKK3_hCHY 5;3)

(18) naau^6 hung^{4}zai^2 go^2 zek^3
scold bear that CL
(the rabbit) that is scolding the bear
(NTKK2_hCCY 4;8)

(19) naau^6 go^2 go^3
scold that CL
(the rabbit) that is scolding (the bear)
(NTKK3_hZCP 5;0)

(20) bei^2 zyu^{1}zai^{2}pou^5 zyu^6 go^2 zek^3 hung^{4}zai^2
PASS pig hold ASP that CL bear
the bear that is held by the pig
(LYMK3_hWTM 4;11)

Children from both K2 (age range: 3;10 to 4;10) and K3 (age range: 4;11 to 5;10) were able to produce target relative clauses, though individual differences are observed. Note that while adults uniformly produced passive object relatives, only two children (one from K2, age 4;1 and one from K3, age 4;11) produced passive object relatives [example (20)].

133 out of 700 responses (19.00%) are unexpected but grammatical relative clauses, exemplified in the following examples where children used adjectival predicate [example (21)], directional phrase [example (22)], oblique relative clause [example (23)] and genitive relative clause [example (24)]:

(21) a. Child form
hoi1sam1 go2 go3 tou3zai2
happy that CL rabbit
the rabbit that is happy
(LYMK3_hCCY 5;6)
b. Adult form
zyu1zai2 pou2 go2 zek3 tou3zai2
pig hold that CL rabbit
the rabbit that the pig is holding

(22) a. Child form
zo2bin1 go2 zek3 tou3zai2
left-side that CL rabbit
the rabbit on the left
(LYMK3_hWHK 5;0)
b. Adult form
naau6 hung4zai2 go2 zek3 tou3zai2
scold bear that CL rabbit
the rabbit that is scolding the bear

(23) a. Child form
tung4 hung4 naau6gaau1 go2 go3 tou3zai2
with bear argue-with that CL rabbit
the rabbit that is arguing with the bear
(NTKK2_hYTC 4;7)
b. Adult form
naau6 hung4zai2 go2 zek3 tou3zai2
scold bear that CL rabbit
the rabbit that is scolding the bear

(24) a. Child form
maa5lau1 daa2 keoi5 faai3 min6 go2 zek3 zyu1zai2
monkey hit him CL face that CL pig
the pig's face that the monkey is hitting

(LYMK3_hLHT 5;0)

b. Adult form

maa^{5}lau^1 daa^2 go^2 zek^3 zyu^{1}zai^2

monkey hit that CL pig

the pig that the monkey is hitting

Subject-object asymmetry is one of the major focuses in acquisition studies of relative clauses. As noted in Section 1, no consensus has been reached on whether subject advantage is observed in children's performance on elicited imitation task. The data obtained in the present study, however, show that subject-gapped relatives (84.03%) are performed significantly better than object-gapped relatives (40.52%) [$t(49) = 6.959, p = 0.000$]. This is true regardless of whether the subject-gapped relative clauses occur in subject condition [$t(49) = 6.779, p = 0.000$] or object condition [$t(49) = 6.012, p = 0.000$].

2.3.2 Non-adult-like RC Responses

Now let us consider the errors produced by the Cantonese-speaking children and explore how these errors reflect the properties of child Cantonese. Errors produced in children's relative clauses fall into five groups: (i) wrong order of the relative clauses, (ii) resumptive NP, (iii) wrong head noun, (iv) wrong thematic role of the head noun and (v) missing constituents: ①

(25) Wrong order

a. Child form

ngau^{4}zai^2 zi^2 zyu^6 baak^{6}tou^3 naau^6 maau^{1}zai^2 go^2 zek^3

cow point ASP rabbit scold cat that CL

The cow is pointing at the cat that the rabbit is scolding.

(LYMK3_hWWL 5;2)

b. Adult form

tou^{3}zai^2 naau^6 go^2 zek^3 maau^{1}zai^2

rabbit scold that CL cat

the cat that the rabbit is scolding

(26) Resumptive NP

a. Child form

zek^3 gau^{2}zai^2 daa^2 maau^{1}maau^1 go^2 zek^3 maau^1 zi^2 zyu^6 ngau^{4}zai^2

① Responses showing wrong head errors are largely responses showing a change of the type of relative clauses too. The subject-gapped relatives become object-gapped relatives and object-gapped relatives become subject-gapped relatives when wrong head errors occur. Only three tokens of responses contain *ngau^{4}zai^2* (cow) as the wrong head. These tokens responses do not involve a change of the type of relative clauses. Other responses are like example (27) which demonstrates wrong head error and the use of subject-gapped relative rather than the intended object-gapped relative.

CL dog hit cat that CL cat point ASP cow

The cat that the dog is hitting is pointing at the cow.

(LYMK3_hKWS 5;10)

b. Adult form

gau2zai2 daa2 go2 zek3 maau1zai2

dog hit that CL cat

the cat that the dog is hitting

(27) Wrong head noun

a. Child form

zi2 zyu6 daa2 zyu1zai2 go2 go3 maa5lau1zai2

point ASP hit pig that CL monkey

(The cow) is pointing at the monkey that is hitting the pig.

(NTKK2_hCCY 4;8)

b. Adult form

maa5lau1 daa2 go2 zek3 zyu1zai2

monkey hit that CL pig

the pig that the monkey is hitting

(28) Wrong thematic role

a. Child form

naau6 baak6 tou3 go2 zek3 maau1zai2

scold rabbit that CL cat

the cat that is scolding the rabbit

(LYMK3_hSHC 5;4)

b. Adult form

tou3zai2 naau6 go2 zek3 maau1zai2

rabbit scold that CL cat

the cat that the rabbit is scolding

(29) Missing constituent

a. Child form

hai2dou3 naau6 go2 go3 tou3 zai2 zi2 zyu6 ngau4

now scold that CL rabbit point ASP cow

The rabbit that is scolding (someone) is pointing at the cow

(LYMK3_hKWS 5;10)

b. Adult form

naau6 hung4zai2 go2 zek3 tou3zai2

scold bear that CL rabbit

the rabbit that is scolding the bear

These errors may vary in the number of tokens produced. Table 3 lists the distribution of different kinds of errors:

Table 3 Distribution of Different Types of Errors by Typically Developing Children

Types of Non-adult-like RC Responses	Token (Percentage)
(i) Wrong order	128/259 (49.42%)
(ii) Resumptive NP	37/259 (14.29%)
(iii) Wrong head noun	70/259 (27.03%)
(iv) Wrong thematic role of the head noun	9/259 (3.47%)
(v) Missing constituents	15/259 (5.79%)

Error (i) is the most common error observed for both K2 and K3 children. The order of the children's answer is always S-V-O-that-CL. The demonstrative *go*^{2} (that), the classifier *zek*^{3} and the NP *maau*^{1} *zai*^{2} (cat) are analyzed as the head noun, but the NP may be omitted in adult grammar. Assuming that children have no problem with the syntactic order within DP, the order S-V-O-that-CL described by error (i) may be analyzed as S-V-resumptive NP-that-CL-null head noun. While this analysis may capture the error associated with object-gapped relatives (50.50%), it is not entirely clear how the same analysis explains the errors occurring with subject-relatives (45.61%) where the V-O-S-that-CL order is expected. Given the fact that children use S-V-O-that-CL order for both subject-gapped and object-gapped relatives, it is speculated that the entire NP containing S, V and O has moved up from the complex NP to Spec, DP. Such error suggests the presence of syntactic movement, though it is not adult-like.

2.3.3 Non-RC Responses

As noted earlier, Cantonese-speaking children also produced sentences not containing relative clauses. A small number of children refused to answer the question in Cantonese. They instead point to the picture. Excluding the responses in pointing, three types of responses that do not contain relative clauses are observed: (i) determiner phrases containing demonstratives or ordinal noun (109/264, 41.29%), (ii) simple declaratives (62/264, 23.48%) and (iii) conjoined clauses (93/264, 35.23%):

(30) Determiner phrase: demonstrative

a. Child form

zi^{2} zyu^{6} li^{1} jat^{1} zek^{3}

point ASP this one CL

Point at this one.

(NTKK2_hLHK 3;10)

b. Adult form

tek^{3} maau^{1}zai^{2} go^{2} zek^{3} maa^{5}lau^{1}
kick cat that CL monkey
the monkey that is kicking the cat

(31) Determiner phrase: ordinal

a. Child form
dai^{6}ji^{6} zek^{3} hung^{4}zai^{2}
the second CL bear
the second bear
(LYMK3_hTWH 4;10)

b. Adult form
zyu^{1}zai^{2} pou^{5} go^{2} zek^{3} hung^{4}zai^{2}
pig hold that CL bear
the bear that the pig is holding

(32) Simple declarative

a. Child form
ngau^{4}zai^{2} zi^{2} zyu^{6} gau^{2}zai^{2} pou^{5} hei^{2} zo^{2} maa^{5}lau^{1}
cow point ASP dog hold up ASP monkey
The cow is pointing at the event "dog lifted up the monkey".
(NTKK3_hYSL 5;1)

b. Adult form
gau^{2}zai^{2} pou^{5} go^{2} zek^{3} maa^{5}lau^{1}
dog hold that CL monkey
the monkey that the dog is holding

(33) Conjoined clauses

a. Child form
go^{2} zek^{3} hung^{4}zai^{2} naau^{6} zyu^{1}zai^{2}, go^{2} zek^{3} zyu^{1}zai^{2} ne^{1}
that CL bear scold pig that CL pig PRT
zau^{6} zi^{2} zyu^{6} ngau^{4}zai^{2}
then point ASP cow
That bear is scolding the pig. Then that pig is pointing at the cow.
(LYMK3_hYHK 5;0)

b. Adult form
hung^{4}zai^{2} naau^{6} go^{2} zek^{3} zyu^{1}zai^{2}
bear scold that CL pig
the pig that the bear scolds

The examples above show that the Cantonese-speaking children avoided using adult-like relative clauses under the restrictive context. It is observed that children tended to ignore whether Experimenter 2 could identify which animal was pointing at the cow when they provided answers like determiner phrase containing a demonstrative. They may also label the two referents with ordinal like "first" and "second" such that they did not need to produce relative clauses. Though the use of ordinal phrase is possible under the given context, no adult subjects produced this kind of answers with the same set of materials. Cantonese-speaking children also produced simple declarative sentence describing the event associated with the target relative clauses, as shown in example (32). Since the two referents in the stimuli differ only on the verb, such answer could still help the hearer to identify the referent and hence is marginally acceptable. The last type of response not containing relative clauses is conjoined clauses. Instead of giving a sentence embedded with relative clauses, the children described the events with two conjoined clauses. Similar errors have also been reported in Hsu et al. (2009) where the same method is used to elicit Mandarin relative clauses of young children.

2.4 Results: Deaf Children

2.4.1 Adult-like RC Responses

The deaf children produced 480 responses in the elicited production task. 22 out of 480 (4.58%) responses are unintelligible due to low speech intelligibility of the deaf children. Excluding the unintelligible tokens, 283 out of 458 (61.79%) responses do not contain relative clauses and 175 (38.21%) contain relative clauses. 18 deaf children produced adult-like responses. Eight of them are from Group A (with lower Cantonese proficiency) and nine of them are from Group B (with higher Cantonese proficiency) (see Table 4 for the number of adult-like RC responses). While all students from Group B produced adult-like relative clauses, only some students from Group A did.

Table 4　Adult-like RC Responses Produced by Groups A and B

Groups	HKCOLAS: CG Score Range	Adult-like RC Responses
Group A	20 – 42	25/278 (8.99%)
Group B	51 – 69	96/180 (53.33%)

Adult-like RC responses produced by deaf children may occur in a main clause construction [example(34)]. They may contain null head noun [example (35)] or in the form of passive object relatives [example (36)]:

(34) ngau^{4} zi^{2} zyu^{6} pou^{5}, zyu^{1} pou^{5} zyu^{6} ge^{3} hung^{4}zai^{2}
cow point ASP hold pig hold ASP GE bear
The cow is pointing at the bear that the pig is holding.
(Group A: C4-5-GTC, DD, hearing age: 8;3)

(35) tek^{3} maa^{5}lau^{1} go^{2} go^{3} (zyu^{1}zai^{2})
kick monkey that CL (pig)
(the pig) that is kicking the monkey
(Group A: C4-6-LYC, DH, hearing age: 5;10)

(36) bei^{2} zyu^{1} pou^{5} go^{2} zek^{3} tou^{3}zai^{2} zi^{2} zyu^{6} ngau^{4}zai^{2}
PASS pig hold that CL rabbit point ASP cow
The rabbit that is held by the pig is pointing at the cow.
(Group B: C1-1-CTY, DH, hearing age: 10;4)

Six deaf children also produced unexpected but grammatical relative clauses by using a directional phrase [example (37)], non-target object in relative clauses [example (38)] or relative clauses containing instrument [example (39)]:

(37) Relative clauses with directional phrase (2 tokens)
a. Child form
zo^{2} (bin^{1}) zek^{3} maau^{1} zi^{2} zyu^{6} ngau^{4}
left CL cat point ASP cow
The cat on the left is pointing at the cow.
(Group A: C6-6-THY, DD, hearing age: 5;10)
b. Adult form
daa^{2} gau^{2}zai^{2} go^{2} zek^{3} maau^{1}zai^{2}
hit dog that CL cat
the cat that is hitting the dog

(38) Non-target object in relative clauses (3 tokens)
a. Child form
li^{1} zek^{3} hai^{6} daa^{2} ge^{3}, daa^{2} tou^{3}, daa^{2} zek^{3} gau^{2} ge^{3} tau^{4} ge^{3} maau^{1}
this CL be hit GE hit rabbit hit CL dog GE head GE cat
This is hitting, hitting the rabbit, the cat that is hitting the dog's head.
(Group A: C3-2-CKW, DH, hearing age: 8;6)
b. Adult form
daa^{2} gau^{2}zai^{2} go^{2} zek^{3} maau^{1}zai^{2}
hit dog that CL cat
the cat that is hitting the dog

(39) Subject-gapped relative clause containing instrument (1 token)
a. Child form
daa^{2} gau^{2}, jung^{6} zek^{3} sau^{2} daa^{2} gau^{2}zai^{2} go^{2} zek^{3} maau^{1} zi^{2} zyu^{6} ngau^{4}
hit dog, use CL hand hit dog that CL cat point ASP cow
Hit the dog, the cat that used the hand to hit the dog is pointing at the cow.

(Group B: C2-5-WCY, DH, hearing age: 9;0)

b. Adult form

daa2 gau2zai2 go2 zek3 maau1zai2

hit dog that CL cat

the cat that is hitting the dog

The data suggest that deaf children studied here demonstrate knowledge of Cantonese relative clauses. A question follows is whether their performance demonstrate subject-object asymmetry. See the adult-like RC responses produced by the deaf students in Table 5 below:

Table 5 Adult-like RC Responses Produced by Groups A and B

Groups	HKCOLAS: CG Score Range	Subject-gapped	Object-gapped
Group A	20 – 42	15/141 (10.64%)	13/137 (9.49%)
Group B	51 – 69	49/90 (54.44%)	50/90 (55.56%)

Deaf students from Group B clearly performed much better than those from Group A, suggesting that Cantonese proficiency is tied to deaf students' performance. No significant difference, however, is observed between deaf children's performance on subject-gapped versus object-gapped relatives [$t(15) = 0.131, p = 0.898$].

2.4.2 Non-adult-like RC Responses

Similar to the typically developing children, deaf children also made non-adult-like RC responses. These non-adult-like RC responses have also been observed with typically developing children acquiring Cantonese as the first language. A total of 175 responses contain relative clauses, 49 of them (28.00%) are non-adult-like. 30 responses are produced by Group A and the remaining responses from Group B. The following examples demonstrate the non-adult-like RC responses produced by deaf children:

(40) Wrong demonstrative

a. Child form

siu2gau2 daa2 maau1 go2bin1 zi2 ngau4

dog hit cat there point cow

The side where the dog is hitting the cat is pointing at the cow.

(Group A: C1-3-LKY, DH, hearing age: 11;10)

b. Adult form

gau2zai2 daa2 go2 zek3 maau1zai2

dog hit that CL cat

the cat that the dog is hitting

(41) Wrong order

a. Child form

gau^{2} pou^{5} maa^{5}lau^{1} go^{2} go^{3}

dog hold monkey that CL

the monkey that the dog is holding

(Group A: C4-6-LYC, DH, hearing age: 5;10)

b. Adult form

gau^{2}zai^{2} pou^{5} go^{2} zek^{3} maa^{5}lau^{1}

dog hold that CL monkey

the monkey that the dog is holding

(42) Resumptive NP error

a. Child form

go^{2} zek^{3} maau^{1} bei^{2} zyu^{1} pou^{5} go^{2} zek^{3} maau^{1} zau^{6} zi^{2} zyu^{6} ngau^{4} lo^{1}

that CL cat PASS pig hold that CL cat then point ASP cow SFP

the cat that is held by the pig is pointing at the cow

(Group B: C1-1-CTY, DH, hearing age: 10;4)

b. Adult form

zyu^{1}zai^{2} pou^{5} go^{2} zek^{3} maau^{1}zai^{2}

pig hold that CL cat

the cat that the pig is holding

(43) Wrong head error①

a. Child form

ngau^{4} zi^{2} zyu^{6} maau^{1} pou^{5} zyu^{6} ge^{3} tou^{3}zai^{2}

cow point ASP cat hold ASP GE rabbit

The cow is pointing at the rabbit that the cat is holding.

(Group A: C3-2-CKW, DH, hearing age: 9;3)

b. Adult form

pou^{5} tou^{3}zai^{2} go^{2} zek^{3} maau^{1}zai^{2}

hold rabbit that CL cat

the cat that is holding the rabbit

(44) Wrong subject

a. Child form

hung^{4}maau^{1} daa^{2} ge^{3} zyu^{1} lo^{1}

panda hit GE pig SFP

① As noted above, responses containing wrong head are largely responses involving change of the type of relative clauses, either from subject-gapped to object-gapped relatives or vice versa. All wrong head errors observed in the deaf children group involve the change of the type of relative clauses.

the pig that the panda is hitting

(Group A: C3-2-CKW, DH, hearing age: 9;3)

b. Adult form

maa^{5}lau^1 daa^2 go^2 zek^3 zyu^{1}zai^2

monkey hit that CL pig

the pig that the monkey is hitting

(45) Wrong thematic role①

a. Child form

daa^2 maa^{5}lau^1 go^2 zek^3 zyu^{1}zai^2

hit monkey that CL pig

the pig that is hitting the monkey

(Group B: C3-6-TSM, DH, hearing age: 9;6)

b. Adult form

maa^{5}lau^1 daa^2 go^2 zek^3 zyu^{1}zai^2

monkey hit that CL pig

the pig that the monkey is hitting

Examples (40) through (45) illustrate the six types of non-adult-like RC responses produced by deaf children. The distribution of these types of responses is summarized as Table 6 below. Wrong order, resumptive NP error and wrong head error are the most common non-adult-like RC responses. In particular, resumptive NP error and wrong head error are the most common errors. But wrong order is mainly produced by deaf children from Group A.

Table 6 Distribution of Different Types of Non-adult-like RC Responses

Non-adult-like RC Responses	Group A	Group B	Group A + B
(i) Wrong demonstrative	1/29 (3.45%)	0/20 (0.00%)	1/49 (2.04%)
(ii) Wrong order	16/29 (55.17%)	1/20 (5.00%)	17/49 (34.69%)
(iii) Resumptive NP error	6/29 (20.69%)	9/20 (45.00%)	15/49 (30.61%)
(iv) Wrong head error	5/29 (17.24%)	7/20 (35.00%)	12/49 (24.49%)
(v) Wrong subject	1/29 (3.45%)	2/20 (10.00%)	3/49 (6.12%)
(vi) Wrong thematic role	0/29 (0.00%)	1/20 (5.00%)	1/49 (2.04%)

2.4.3 Non-RC Responses

As noted earlier, the majority of responses produced by deaf children do not contain relative clauses. What did they produce in place of relative clauses? They either used a simple declarative

① This example also involves a change of the type of the relative clause from intended object-gapped relative to subject-gapped relative. However, the number of token is too small to make any claim associated with subject-object asymmetry.

(with or without an overt subject) or described the events with conjoined clauses, as shown in the following examples:

(46) Simple declaratives

a. Child form

siu^{2}gau^2 naau^6 siu^{2}zyu^1

dog scold pig

The dog is scolding the pig.

(Group A: C4-1-CNW, DD, hearing age: 8;1)

b. Adult form

naau^6 zyu^{1}zai^2 go^2 zek^3 gau^{2}zai^2

scold pig that CL dog

the dog that is scolding the pig

(47) Conjoined clauses

a. Child form

maa^{5}lau^1 tek^3 siu^{2}hung^4, maa^{5}lau^1 zi^2 zyu^6 ngau^4

monkey kick bear, monkey point ASP cow

The monkey is kicking the bear, the monkey is pointing at the cow.

(Group A: C1-5-TKH, DH, hearing age: 12;8)

b. Adult form

tek^3 hung^{4}zai^2 go^2 zek^3 maa^{5}lau^1

kick bear that CL monkey

the monkey that is kicking the bear

Both types of non-RC responses are observed with both groups. However, the use of simple declaratives constitutes the majority of non-RC responses (see Table 7).

Table 7 Non-RC Responses Produced by Groups A and B

Groups	Number of Students	HKCOLAS: CG Score	Simple Declaratives	Conjoined Causes
Group A	15	20 – 42	196/221 (88.69%)	25/221 (11.31%)
Group B	9	51 – 69	61/62 (98.39%)	1/62 (1.61%)

3 Experiment 2: Picture Pointing Task

One shortcoming of production task is that children may avoid producing the target relative clauses. In order to explore further whether the typically developing and deaf children have the knowledge of relative clauses, children were tested on their comprehension of relative clauses.

3.1 Participants

The participants in Experiment 2 are the same group of participants in Experiment 1. All participants participated Experiment 1 first and then Experiment 2.

3.2 Method and Test Procedures

A picture pointing task is designed to explore whether children have knowledge of relative clauses. This task consists of 24 test sentences, 9 are subject-gapped relative clauses, 9 are object-gapped relative clauses and 6 are fillers. All relative clauses occur in copular construction. The test procedure is as follows. The experimenter first introduced pairs of identical characters involved in order to provide the restrictive context for Cantonese relative clauses. Then the experimenter read out a test sentence (e. g. *Li*^{1} *zek*^{3} *hai*^{6} *maau*^{1}*maau*^{1} *daa*^{2} *go*^{2} *zek*^{3} *zyu*^{1}*zai*^{2}. This is the pig that the cat is hitting.). Meanwhile, the child looked at two pictures, one matched the picture (e. g. the cat is hitting the pig), the other described relativization of the wrong noun phrase (e. g. the pig is hitting the cat) (see Figure 4). The child needed to choose the picture that matched the test sentence.

a.Target Answer　　b.Wrong Head Error

Figure 4　Sample Question in Picture Pointing Task

3.3 Results

The results show that typically developing children generally perform better with object-gapped relatives (K2: 85.51%; K3: 89.56%) than subject-gapped relatives (K2: 61.35%; K3:

67.11%).[①] Paired-sample t test shows that there is a significant difference between the accuracy of the subject-gapped and object-gapped relative clauses [$t(49) = -8.191$, $p = 0.000$]. Deaf children from Group B generally perform better than Group A. The average accuracy rate of subject-gapped relatives and object-gapped relatives are close for Group B (90.12% versus 98.77%). The performance is also close to the adult group (subject-gapped relatives: 95.00%, object-gapped relatives: 97.78%). But performance with object-gapped relatives (90.37%) is much better than subject-gapped relatives (43.70%) for Group A. The overall performance object-gapped relatives is also significantly better than subject-gapped relatives [$t(23) = -5.139$, $p = 0.000$].

4 Discussion and Conclusions

This study explores how typically developing and deaf children comprehend and produce Cantonese relative clauses. In particular, whether children perform better with subject-gapped relatives or with object-gapped relatives are examined. Consider typically developing children first. While the accuracy rate on object-gapped relatives is significantly higher than the subject-gapped relatives in the picture pointing task, an opposite result is observed in the elicited production task. While the results of comprehension task may be explained by the Canonical Word Order Hypothesis, Filler-Gap Linear Distance Hypothesis and the grammatical/intervention approach, the results of production task are captured by the Structural Distance Hypothesis. A question arises here is why typically developing children perform better with subject-gapped relatives in production but object-gapped relatives in comprehension.

The comprehension task consists of test sentences which are structurally simpler. All relative clauses occur in copular construction. By contrast, the full answers of the which-question in the elicited production task are all main clause construction which is structurally more complex. Though children can only reply with a DP selected by the verb "point at", the presence of two action verbs may complicate the task, resulting in higher degree of difficulty. Another possible explanation to fewer adult-like responses of object-gapped relatives may be associated with passive. As noted, all adult participants produced passive object relatives in both subject and object condition, though they also accept the use of standard object relatives. The performance of the adult participants suggests that it may be more natural to produce passive object relatives in the context designed in the task. Deen (2011) notes that Cantonese-speaking children rarely produced passives in

① An anonymous reviewer notes that the object advantage is expected in the picture pointing task because children only need to point at the matching picture. The task can be improved by asking the children to point at the head noun rather than the matching picture. Then it will become clearer on whether the children are able to identify the head noun after listening to a sentence containing relative clause. This change will also help confirming if children made wrong head error, a common error observed in comprehension task in the literature.

longitudinal data. But three-year-old and four-year-old children performed well in a picture selection task testing actional and non-actional passives. The correct responses are higher than 70% for actional passives and just under 70% for non-actional passives for both groups of children. Though this experiment shows that Cantonese-speaking children have knowledge of passive, it is not clear whether children of the same age could produce passives. The corpus data, however, suggest that Cantonese-speaking children rarely produce passives. Assuming Cantonese-speaking children in the present study is still acquiring Cantonese passives, their low responses rate on object-gapped relatives may be explained by the fact that they have difficulty in producing passive object relatives. This speculation, however, requires further tests on children's knowledge on passives.

This study also examines deaf children's knowledge of relative clauses. Deaf children generally develop at a slower rate than typically developing children. Similar to typically developing children, deaf children studied in this paper also perform better with object-gapped relative clauses in comprehension while no such advantage is observed in elicited production task. The types of adult-like RC responses, non-adult-like RC responses and non-RC responses produced by deaf children are also observed in the data of the typically developing children. In other words, the data on deaf children only show quantitative but not qualitative difference from the typically developing children.

Note that the test sentences presented in this paper are largely classifier relatives which are derived via syntactic movement of relative clause up to DP/ClP and PF deletion of *ge*[3]. The adult-like RC responses suggest that syntactic movement is present for both groups of children. The errors on wrong order, however, call for the question on whether syntactic movement is always present in the child grammar. The wrong order S-V-O-that-CL is the major error for both groups of children. As noted earlier, such error may be analyzed as S-V-resumptive NP-that-CL-null head noun. While such analysis is possible with object-gapped relatives, it cannot explain the subject-gapped relatives which have the V-O-S-that-CL order. An alternative analysis is the NP housing S, V and O moves up as a phrase to Spec, DP, resulting in S-V-O-that-CL order for both subject-gapped and object-gapped relatives. If this analysis is correct, the child grammar derives relative clauses with syntactic movement, though such movement is not adult-like. Contrary to Friedmann and Szterman's (2006) claim, our study shows that deaf children, like their hearing peers, have the knowledge of syntactic movement. But the type of movement is the same as what is observed with normal-hearing children, but different from that of the adult grammar.

Appendix

Biodata of Deaf Children

Deaf Students	Chron. Age	Hearing Age	M/F	Lv.	I[a]	II[b]	III[c]	IV[d]	V[e]	VI[f]	Ⅶ[g]	Ⅷ[h]
C1-1-CTY	11 ; 1	10 ; 4	F	P6	88	No	CI	0 ; 9	0 ; 9	4 ; 11	6 ; 2	69
C1-2-HST	13 ; 5	11 ; 5	F	P6	118	No	CI	n/a	2 ; 0	7 ; 2	6 ; 2	32
C1-3-LKY	13 ; 1	11 ; 10	M	P6	105	CI	No	1 ; 6	3 ; 2	6 ; 11	6 ; 2	29
C1-4-SMC	12 ; 3	11 ; 8	M	P6	93	HA	HA	0;6	0;6	6 ; 0	6 ; 2	69
C1-5-TKH	13 ; 11	11 ; 11	M	P6	108	No	CI	2 ; 0	2 ; 0	7 ; 8	6 ; 2	30
C2-1-CYF	10 ; 2	8 ; 8	M	P5	108	CI	HA	2 ; 6	1 ; 9	5 ; 0	5 ; 2	27
C2-2-SMY	10 ; 9	8 ; 2	F	P5	72	HA	HA	2;7	2;7	5 ; 6	5 ; 2	63
C2-3-TWK	12 ; 3	9 ; 1	M	P5	107	HA	HA	3 ; 6	3 ; 2	7 ; 1	5 ; 2	68
C2-5-WCY	12 ; 0	9 ; 0	M	P5	87	HA	HA	3 ; 0	3 ; 0	6 ; 9	5 ; 2	51
C2-6-WSY	11 ; 10	11 ; 7	F	P5	120	HA	HA	0 ; 3	0 ; 3	6 ; 8	5 ; 2	38
C3-1-CKY	9 ; 8	7 ; 6	F	P4	93	HA	HA	2 ; 0	2 ; 0	5 ; 6	4 ; 2	69
C3-2-CKW	10 ; 1	8 ; 6	F	P4	97	CI	HA	1 ; 6	1 ; 6	5 ; 10	4 ; 2	37
C3-5-OTN	10 ; 0	8 ; 1	F	P3	118	CI	No	1 ; 11	n/a	5 ; 10	4 ; 2	26
C3-6-TSM	9 ; 5	8 ; 9	F	P4	108	CI	HA	0 ; 7	0 ; 7	5 ; 2	4 ; 2	65
C4-1-CNW	8 ; 7	7 ; 4	F	P3	88	No	CI	1 ; 6	1 ; 3	5 ; 5	3 ; 2	27
C4-2-CWK	9 ; 4	7 ; 4	F	P3	120	No	CI	n/a	2 ; 0	6 ; 2	3 ; 2	42
C4-3-CWL	9 ; 4	7 ; 4	F	P3	120	CI	No	2 ; 0	n/a	6 ; 2	3 ; 2	51
C4-4-CHY	9 ; 0	6 ; 3	F	P2	80	CI	HA	2 ; 10	2 ; 9	5 ; 10	3 ; 2	23
C4-5-GTC*	8 ; 9	8 ; 3	F	P3	95	HA	CI	0 ; 6	0 ; 6	5 ; 6	3 ; 2	41
C4-6-LYC	6 ; 7	5 ; 10	F	P1	106	CI	HA	1 ; 3	0 ; 9	5 ; 5	1 ; 2	37
C5-3-PTY	8 ; 4	4 ; 9	M	P3	87	HA	HA	3 ; 7	3 ; 8	6 ; 2	2 ; 2	60
C5-4-SLY	8 ; 0	6 ; 7	F	P2	117	CI	HA	1 ; 5	n/a	5 ; 10	2 ; 2	20
C6-2-HYT	9 ; 11	7 ; 5	F	P2	110	CI	HA	2 ; 6	2 ; 6	8 ; 9	1 ; 2	33
C6-6-THY	7 ; 1	5 ; 10	M	P1	113	HA	CI	0 ; 6	n/a	5 ; 10	1 ; 2	30

a: Hearing status (better ear); b: Hearing device (left ear), HA = hearings aids, CI = cochlear implants; c: Hearing device (right ear); d: Age of fitting (left ear); e: Age of fitting (right ear); f: Age of initial exposure of HKSL; g: Years of HKSL exposure; h: HKCOLAS: CG (raw score).

References

Adani, Flavia 2010 Re-thinking the acquisition of relative clauses in Italian: Towards a grammatically-based account. *Journal of Child Language*, 22: 1 – 25.

Adani, Flavia, Heather van der Lely, Matteo Forgiarini, and Maria Teresa Guasti 2010

Grammatical feature dissimilarities make relative clauses easier: A comprehension study with Italian children. *Lingua*, 120(9): 2148 – 2166.

Arnon, Inbal 2010 Re-thinking child difficulty: The effect of NP type on children's processing of relative clauses in Hebrew. *Journal of Child Language*, 37: 27 – 57.

Arosio, Fabrizio, Flavia Adani, and Maria Teresa Guasti 2006 Children's processing of subject and object relatives in Italian. In Adriana Belletti, Elisa Bennati, Cristiano Chesi, Elisa Di Domenico, and Ida Ferrari eds., *Language Acquisition and Development: Proceedings of GALA 2005*. Cambridge: Cambridge Scholars Press. pp. 15 – 27.

Arosio, Fabrizio, Flavia Adani, and Maria Teresa Guasti 2009 Grammatical features in the comprehension of Italian relative clauses by children. In José M. Brucart, Anna Gavarrò, and Jaume Solà eds., *Merging Features: Computation, Interpretation and Acquisition*. Oxford: Oxford University Press. pp. 138 – 155.

Arosio, Fabrizio, Maria Teresa Guasti, and Natale Stucchi 2011 Disambiguating information and memory resources in children's processing of Italian relative clauses. *Journal of Psycholinguistic Research*, 40: 137 – 154.

Belletti, Adriana, and Carla Contemori 2010 Intervention and attraction: On the production of subject and object relatives by Italian (young) children and adults. In João Costa, Ana Castro, Maria Lobo, and Fernanda Pratas eds., *Language Acquisition and Development: Proceedings of GALA* 2009. Cambridge: Cambridge Scholars Press. pp. 39 – 52.

Bever, Thomas G. 1970 The cognitive basis for linguistic structures. In John R. Hayes ed., *Cognition and Development of Language*. New York: Wiley. pp. 279 – 362.

Booth, James R., Brian Mac Whinney, and Yasuaki Harasaki 2000 Developmental differences in visual and auditory processing of complex sentences. *Child Development*, 71: 981 – 1003.

Brandt, Silke, Evan Kidd, Elena Lieven, and Michael Tomasello 2009 The discourse bases of relativization: An investigation of young German and English-speaking children's comprehension of relative clauses. *Cognitive Linguistics*, 20(3): 539 – 570.

Chan, Angel, Stephen Matthews, and Virginia Yip 2011 The acquisition of relative clauses in Cantonese and Mandarin. In Evan Kidd ed., *The Acquisition of Relative Clauses: Processing, Typology and Function*. Amsterdam: John Benjamins. pp. 197 – 225.

Contemori, Carla, and Adriana Belletti 2013 Relatives and passive object relatives in Italian speaking children and adults: Intervention in production and comprehension. *Applied Psycholinguistics First View*. pp. 1 – 33.

De Villiers, Peter A. 1988 Assessing English syntax in hearing-impaired children: Eliciting production in pragmatically motivated situations. In Richard R. Kretschmer and Laura W. Kretschmer eds., *Communication Assessment of Hearing-impaired Children: From Conversation to Classroom. Monograph Supplement*. Mt. Pleasant: Academy of Rehabilitative Audiology.

pp. 41 – 71.

Deen, Kamil 2011 The acquisition of the passive. In Jill de Villiers and Tom Roeper eds., *Handbook of Generative Approaches to Language Acquisition*. Dordrecht: Springer. pp. 155 – 187.

Diessel, Holger, and Michael Tomasello 2000 The development of relative clauses in spontaneous child speech. *Cognitive Linguistics*, 11: 131 – 151.

Diessel, Holger, and Michael Tomasello 2005 A new look at the acquisition of relative clauses. *Language*, 81(4): 882 – 906.

Friedmann, Naama, and João Costa 2011 Last resort and no resort: Resumptive pronouns in Hebrew and Palestinian Arabic hearing impairment. In Alain Rouveret ed., *Resumptive Pronouns at the Interfaces*. Amsterdam: John Benjamins. pp. 223 – 239.

Friedmann, Naama, and Rama Novogrodsky 2004 The acquisition of relative clause comprehension in Hebrew: A study of SLI and normal development. *Journal of Child Language*, 31: 661 – 681.

Friedmann, Naama, and Ronit Szterman 2006 Syntactic movement in orally trained children with hearing impairment. *Journal of Deaf Studies and Deaf Education*, 11(1): 56 – 75.

Friedmann, Naama, Adriana Belletti, and Luigi Rizzi 2009 Relativized relatives: Types of intervention in the acquisition of A-bar dependencies. *Lingua*, 119: 67 – 88.

Friedmann, Naama, Rama Novogrodsky, Ronit Szterman, and Omer Preminger 2008 Resumptive pronouns as a last resort when movement is impaired: Relative clauses in hearing impairment. In Sharon Armon-Lotem, Gabi Danon, and Susan Rothstein eds., *Current Issues in Generative Hebrew Linguistics*. Amsterdam: John Benjamins. pp. 267 – 290.

Friedmann, Naama, Ronit Szterman, and Manar Haddad-Hanna 2010 The comprehension of relative clauses and Wh questions in Hebrew and Palestinian Arabic hearing impairment. In João Costa, Ana Castro, Maria Lobo, and Fernanda Pratas eds., *Language Acquisition and Development: Proceedings of GALA 2009*. Cambridge: Cambridge Scholars Publishing. pp. 157 – 169.

Gibson, Edward 1998 Linguistic complexity: Locality of syntactic dependencies. *Cognition*, 68: 1 – 76.

Gibson, Edward 2000 The dependency locality theory: A distance-based theory of linguistic complexity. In Yasushi Miyashita, Alec Marantz, and Wayne O'Neil eds., *Image, Language, Brain. Cambridge*, MA: MIT Press. pp. 95 – 126.

Goodluck, Helen, and Susan Tavakolian 1982 Competence and processing in children's grammar of relative clauses. *Cognition*, 11: 1 – 27.

Grillo, Nino 2009 Generalized minimality: Feature impoverishment and comprehension deficits in agrammatism. *Lingua*, 119: 1426 – 1443.

Guasti, Maria Teresa, and Anna Cardinaletti 2003 Relative clause formation in Romance child's production. *Probus*, 15: 47 – 89.

Guasti, Maria Teresa, Stavroula Stavrakaki, and Fabrizio Arosio 2012 Cross-linguistic differences and similarities in the acquisition of relative clauses: Evidence from Greek and Italian. *Lingua*, 122: 700 - 713.

Hamburger, Henry, and Stephen Crain 1982 Relative acquisition. In Stan A. Kuczaj ed., *Language Development Vol. 1: Syntax and Semantics.* Hillsdale, NJ: Lawrence Erlbaum Associates, Inc., pp. 245 - 274.

He, Yuan-Jian 2007 Headless relatives in Cantonese: A derivational account. In Joanna Ut-Seong Sio and Sze-Wing Tang eds., *Studies in Cantonese Linguistics 2.* Hong Kong: Linguistic Society of Hong Kong, pp. 17 - 32.

Hsu, Chun-chieh Natalie, Gabriella Hermon, and Andrea Zukowski 2009 Young children's production of head-final relative clauses: Elicited production data from Chinese children. *Journal of East Asian Linguistics*, 18: 323 - 360.

Isobe, Miwa 2003 Head-internal relative clauses in child Japanese. In Barbara Beachley, Amanda Brown, and Frances Conlin eds., *Proceedings of the 27th Annual Boston University Conference on Language Development (BUCLD).* Somerville, MA: Cascadilla Press. pp. 358 - 369.

Isobe, Miwa 2005 *Language Variation and Child Language Acquisition: Laying Ground for Evaluating Parametric Proposals.* Doctoral dissertation, Tokyo: Keio University.

Keenan, Edward L., and Bernard Comrie 1977 Noun phrase accessibility and universal grammar. *Linguistic Inquiry*, 8: 63 - 99.

Labelle, Marie 1990 Predication, wh-movement, and the development of relative clauses. *Language Acquisition*, 1(1): 95 - 119.

Labelle, Marie 1996 The acquisition of relative clauses: Movement or no movement? *Language Acquisition*, 5(2): 65 - 82.

Lau, Elaine 2006 *The Acquisition of Relative Clauses by Cantonese Children: An Experimental Approach.* M. Phil. thesis, Hong Kong: The University of Hong Kong.

Lee, Thomas Hun-tak 1992 The inadequacy of processing heuristics: Evidence from relative clause acquisition in Mandarin Chinese. In Thomas Hun-tak Lee ed., *Research on Chinese Linguistics in Hong Kong.* Hong Kong: Linguistic Society of Hong Kong. pp. 47 - 85.

Lee, Thomas Hun-tak 2006 A note on garden-path sentences in Chinese. In Dah-an Ho, Samuel Cheung, Wuyun Pan, and Fuxiang Wu eds., *Linguistic Studies in Chinese and Neighboring Languages: Festschrift in Honor of Professor Pang-hsin Ting on His Seventieth Birthday.* Taipei: Institute of Linguistics, Academia Sinica. pp. 491 - 518.

Matthews, Stephen, and Virginia Yip 1994 *Cantonese: A Comprehensive Grammar.* London: Routledge.

Matthews, Stephen, and Virginia Yip 2001 The structure and stratification of relative clauses in contemporary Cantonese. In Hilary Chappell ed. *Sinitic Grammar: Synchronic and Diachronic Perspectives.* Oxford: Oxford University Press. pp. 266 - 281.

Ozeki, Hiromi, and Yasuhiro Shirai 2007 Does the noun phrase accessibility hierarchy predict the difficulty order in the acquisition of Japanese relative clauses? *Studies in Second Language Acquisition*, 29: 169 – 196.

Rizzi, Luigi 1990 *Relativized Minimality.* Cambridge, MA: MIT Press.

Sheldon, Amy 1974 The role of parallel function in the acquisition of relative clauses in English. *Journal of Verbal Learning and Verbal Behavior*, 13: 272 – 281.

Slobin, Dan I., and Thomas G. Bever 1982 Children use canonical sentence schemas: A crosslinguistic study of word order and inflections. *Cognition*, 12: 229 – 265.

Stavrakaki, Stavroula 2001 Comprehension of reversible relative clauses in specifically language impaired and normally developing Greek children. *Brain and Language*, 77: 419 – 431.

Stavrakaki, Stavroula 2002 Eliciting relative clauses from specifically language impaired and normally developing children. *Proceedings of the 14th International Symposium of Theoretical and Applied Linguistics.* Thessaloniki: School of English, Aristotle University of Thessaloniki. pp. 395 – 411

Tam, Kit Ying 2011 *Acquisition of Cantonese Relative Clauses by Deaf and Hard of Hearing (D/HH) Children in Hong Kong.* M. A. thesis, Hong Kong: The Chinese University of Hong Kong.

Tavakolian, Susan L. 1981 The conjoined-clause analysis of relative clauses. In Susan L. Tavakolian ed., *Language Acquisition and Linguistic Theory.* Cambridge, MA: MIT Press. pp. 167 – 187.

Tjung, Yassir 2006 *The Formation of Relative Clauses in Jakarta Indonesian: A Subject-object Asymmetry. Doctoral dissertation*, Newark: University of Delaware.

Tsou, Benjamin K., Thomas Hun-tak Lee, Hintat Cheung, and Peter Tung 2009 Some highlights from the HKCOLAS project: Explorations in language development in a linguistically complex society. Paper presented at the workshops on *Milestones in the First Language Acquisition of Chinese.* Hong Kong: The Chinese University of Hong Kong.

Varlokosta, Spyridoula 1997 The acquisition of relative values in modern Greek: A movement account. In Antonella Sorace, Caroline B. Heycock, and Richard Shillcock eds., *Proceedings of GALA* 1997. Edinburgh: Human Communication Research Center, University of Edinburgh. pp. 184 – 187.

Yip, Virginia, and Stephen Matthews 2007a Relative clauses in Cantonese-English bilingual children: Typological challenges and processing motivations. *Studies in Second Language Acquisition*, 29: 277 – 300.

Yip, Virginia, and Stephen Matthews 2007b *The Bilingual Child: Early Development and Language Contact.* Cambridge: Cambridge University Press.

Yiu, Kun-man 2004 *Acquisition of Restrictive Relative Clauses by Orally-trained Profoundly Hearing-impaired Children.* M. A. thesis, Hong Kong: The Chinese University of Hong Kong.

Zukowski, Andrea 2001 *Uncovering Grammatical Competence in Children with Williams Syndrome.* Doctoral dissertation, Boston: Boston University.

Classification of Yue and Pinghua: A Lexicostatistical Approach

Pui Yiu SZETO

(The Chinese University of Hong Kong)

Abstract: This paper addresses the classification debate over Yue and Pinghua by adopting lexicostatistical analysis, a method of language classification seldom employed in Chinese Dialectology. By comparing the core vocabulary of 15 dialects of Yue and Pinghua, the preliminary results of this study support the classification schemes which treat Yue and Southern Pinghua as a single group, and Northern Pinghua as another group (e. g. Qin, 2000; Wu, 2001). However, the results also reveal an unexpectedly high degree of diversity among the Goulou subgroup of Yue dialects, which, given the subgroup's special status in the classification problem of Yue and Pinghua (Li, 2001, 2005; Qin, 2000; Wu, 2001), potentially has a huge impact on the classification problem. Instead of providing a definite answer to the classification debate, this study argues that further studies on Goulou Yue are required to settle the dispute.

Key words: Yue Pinghua Goulou classification lexicostatistics

1 Introduction

Since being recognized as a major dialect group by the Language Atlas of China in 1987, Pinghua has attracted an unprecedented level of attention in Chinese Dialectology. The relationship between Yue and Pinghua remains controversial nowadays, and most Chinese Dialectology textbooks (e. g. Li and Xiang, 2009) only consider Pinghua a subgroup of Yue. While phonological comparison, primarily based on the categories listed in the Chinese rime dictionary *Qieyun*, plays the most important role in the classification of different spoken Chinese varieties in traditional Chinese Dialectology (Simmons, 1999), this study attempts to employ lexicostatistics to shed new light on this controversial classification problem in Chinese Dialectology.

2 Literature Review

2.1 Classification Schemes of Chinese Dialect Groups

Spoken Chinese has long been known to vary geographically, especially in speech sounds; and systematic classification work on Chinese languages began in late 19th century (for further details, see Li and Xiang, 2009; Xiang and Cao, 2013). 4 representative classification schemes, 2 from Chinese scholars and 2 from western scholars, are briefly introduced here.

2.1.1 10-group Scheme

The 10-group scheme proposed by the Language Atlas of China classifies Chinese languages into Mandarin, Jin, Xiang, Gan, Wu, Hui, Min, Hakka, Yue, and Pinghua. In the second edition of the atlas (Institute of Linguistics, Chinese Academy of Social Sciences, The Institute of Ethnology and Anthropology, Chinese Academy of Social Sciences and Language Information Sciences Research Centre, City University of Hong Kong, 2012), the tenth group is renamed as Pinghua and Tuhua(平话和土话). Although this classification scheme is highly influential, its decision to consider Jin, Hui, and Pinghua and Tuhua to be on the same par with other major Chinese dialect groups has caused controversies (Xiang and Cao, 2013).

2.1.2 7-group Scheme

The 7-group scheme is adopted by most reference books about Modern Chinese or Chinese Dialectology (such as Hu, 2011; Zhai, 2003). Compared with the 10-group scheme, this scheme considers Jin a branch of Mandarin, Hui a branch of Wu, and Pinghua a branch of Yue.

2.1.3 3-major group, 11-subgroup Scheme

In his classification scheme, Norman (1988) classifies Chinese into 3 major groups and 11 subgroups, namely Northern (Northern Mandarin, Northwest Mandarin, Southern Mandarin, Southwest Mandarin), Central (Xiang, Gan), and Southern (Wu, Hui, Min, Hakka, Yue). The 3-major group classification is believed to be able to capture the significant differences among the major groups of Chinese varieties, and has been highly influential in the study of Chinese Dialectology (Li, 2010; Xiang, 2010).

2.1.4 13-group Scheme

This scheme, proposed by the Ethnologue 17th edition (Paul et al., 2014), considers Chinese a macrolanguage and further classifies it into 13 languages (Mandarin, Jin, Xiang, Gan, Wu, Hui, Min Bei, Min Dong, Min Nan, Min Zhong, Pu-Xian, Hakka, Yue) primarily based on mutual intelligibility. A distinguishing feature of this scheme is that it classifies Min into 5 languages (Min Bei, Min Dong, Min Nan, Min Zhong, Pu-Xian), which is consistent with the general consensus that Min is a group with a high degree of internal diversity (Norman, 1988). Notice that Pinghua is not identified as a distinct group in this scheme.

2.2 Relationship between Yue and Pinghua

As shown in the Language Atlas of China, the geographical distributions of Yue and Pinghua overlap in many areas of Guangxi. According to Mai (2010), Yue and Pinghua may share a common origin—both were developed from Ancient Lingnan Chinese, which formed as a result of population migrations of Han Chinese people to the Lingnan region during the Qin dynasty and Han dynasty. Influence from Middle Chinese in the Southern Song dynasty may have played a significant role in the diversification of Yue and Pinghua. While Yue is a well-recognized Chinese variety widely spoken in Guangdong, Guangxi, Hong Kong, Macau, and many overseas Chinese communities, the status of Pinghua is still a matter for debate.

Previous studies, primarily based on phonological comparison, fail to reach a general consensus on the affiliation issue of Pinghua. Zhang (1982), Wei (1996), and Liang and Zhang (1999) identify a number of phonological characteristics which can distinguish the Pinghua dialects from the Yue dialects in question, and therefore maintain that Pinghua should be classified as a distinct dialect group. Meanwhile, scholars like Qin (2000) and Wu (2001) notice the remarkable internal diversity of Pinghua, and argue that Southern Pinghua is inseparable from Yue, especially the Goulou subgroup (勾漏片). Li (2000, 2005) also recognize the close connection between Goulou Yue and Pinghua. But instead of classifying Pinghua as a subgroup of Yue, Li (2000, 2005) suggest that the Goulou subgroup should be considered a variety of Pinghua instead of Yue. By contrast, based on 7 phonological characteristics of Northern Pinghua, Liang (1997) concludes that Pinghua is highly consistent with Yue, and both the Northern and Southern varieties of Pinghua should be classified as Yue dialects. See Qin (2012) for a detailed review of the debate.

2.3 Criteria for Language Classification

Phonology, lexicon, and grammar are all linguistic criteria commonly used in language classification (Campbelland Poser, 2008). In western dialectology, all these linguistic criteria are considered in the study of dialects (Chambers and Trudgill, 1998). Meanwhile, in Chinese Dialectology, phonological comparison is usually the focus (Li and Xiang, 2009; Xiang and Cao, 2013). More specifically, the categories listed in the Chinese rime dictionary *Qieyun* are widely used to analyze correspondence between Chinese dialects (Simmons, 1999). It is not surprising given the fact that phonological differences are arguably the most salient feature among Chinese languages and dialects; and China has a long history of phonological study, which helps lay a solid foundation for phonology-based classification.

While previous work on language classification has provided invaluable information about the relationship between different languages, in order to improve the accuracy, precision, and reliability of language classification, it is important to make the classification scheme as scientific as possible. As traditional language classification methods typically involve qualitative analysis based on the linguist's experience (Dengand Wang, 2009), the testability and replicability criteria, which are crucial to all types of scientific study, can hardly be met. This paper proposes that a scientific language classification scheme must fulfill the following 6 criteria: (i) take reliable and representative linguistic data into account; (ii) reflect the genetic relationship between the languages/dialects in question; (iii) be consistent; (iv) be measurable; (v) be testable; (vi) be repeatable. Among these criteria, (iv) to (vi) are difficult to fulfill by using traditional comparative methods because subjective judgments are often hardly avoidable when using traditional comparative methods. Therefore, to increase the objectivity of language classification, quantitative methods are a good complement (but not a replacement) to traditional methods.

2.4 Quantitative Methods for Language Classification

2.4.1 Introduction

Computational tools can help to analyze a large quantity of language data in ways which would be impossible for humans without computer assistance (Campbell, 2013), and find interesting phenomena for further investigation. In the case of language classification, quantification of the degree of relatedness between languages makes subgrouping more reliable and consistent. Moreover, measurable results are more favored by other related disciplines (e. g. evolutionary anthropologists and genetics), which can facilitate interdisciplinary collaboration (for example, Cavalli-Sforza and Wang, 1986; Deng and Wang, 2009).

As there are significant parallels between the evolution of language and that of organisms (Atkinsonand Gray, 2005; Wang, 1994), some methods adopted by biology to address historical questions can potentially be applied to the study of language change and classification. Common quantitative methods relevant to language classification include distance-based methods, character-based methods, and network methods (Campbell, 2013; McMahon and McMahon, 2005). In this study, we focus on the Neighbor Joining (NJ) method (Saitou and Nei, 1987), the most widely used distance-based method in which an algorithm is applied to a distance matrix to produce an unrooted phylogenetic tree (i. e. a phylogenetic tree which only specifies the degree of relatedness among the taxa, without indicating the direction of evolution) (Hall, 2011). An example of an unrooted tree comprising various strains of bacteria estimated by the NJ method is shown in Figure 1a (based on data provided by Hall, 2011). The branch length between the different bacteria is proportional to their degree of relatedness. It is noteworthy that the radiation format is preferred in this study despite the fact that the rectangular format (Figure 1b) may look more familiar to most people. The reason for choosing the radiation format is that, although actually presenting the same information, the rectangular format tends to lead us to interpret the leftmost node as the root, which is in fact non-existent in an unrooted tree. An unrooted is a tree which shows the degree of relatedness without implying the existence of a common ancestor and the direction of evolution. Therefore, a tree diagram in the radiation format is less likely to mislead people to interpret an unrooted tree as a rooted one.

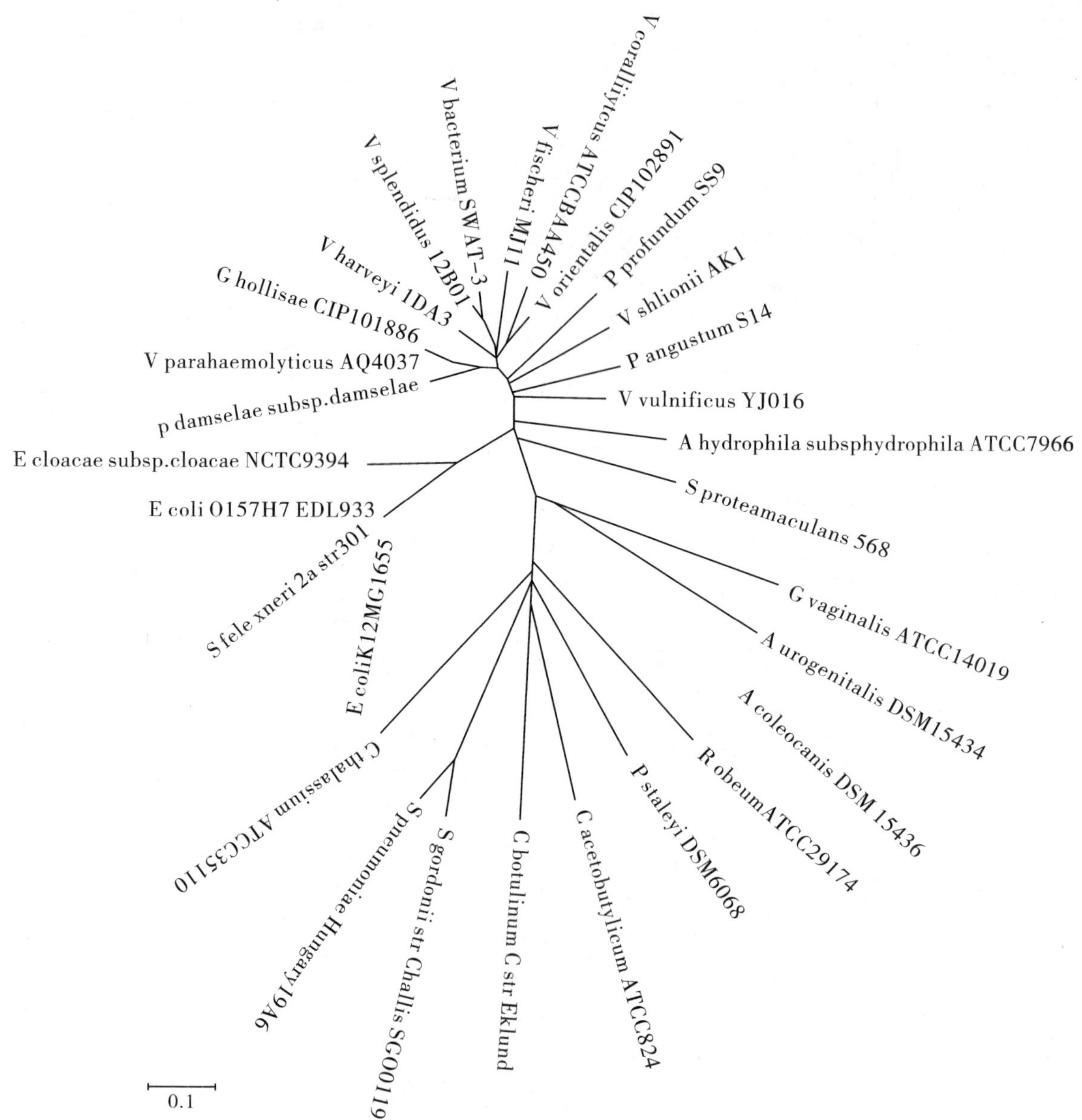

Figure 1a. An Unrooted Tree Displayed in the Radiation Format

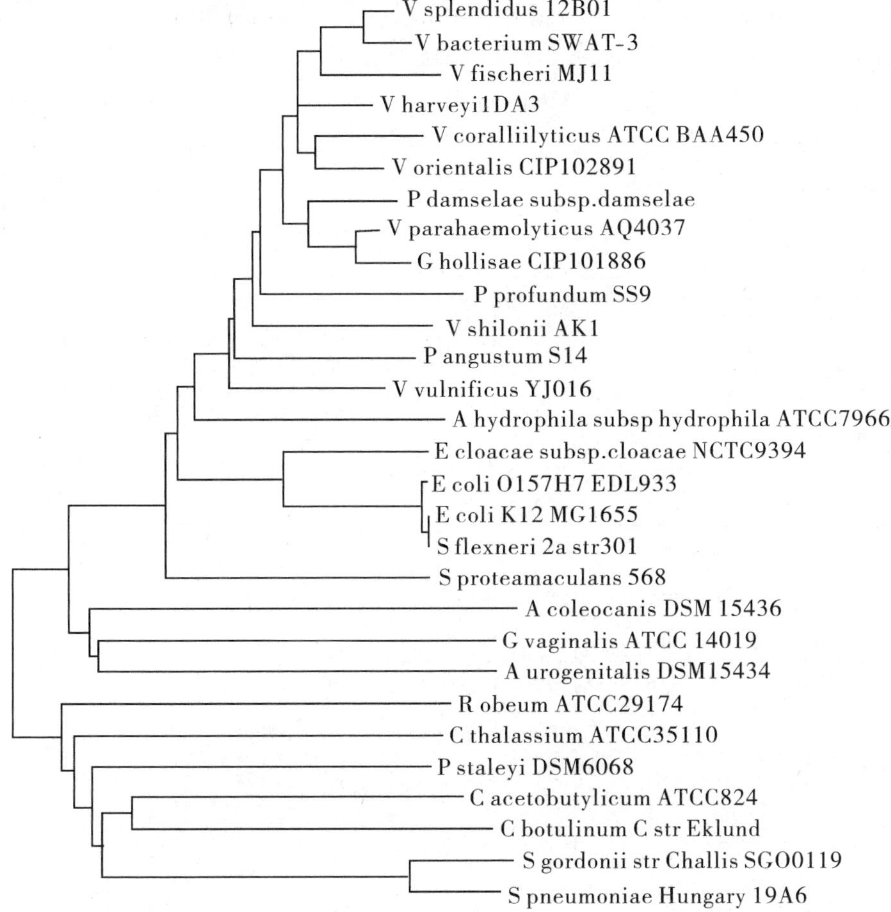

Figure 1b. An Unrooted Tree Displayed in the Rectangular Format

2. 4. 2 Lexicostatistics

Lexical comparison is a prerequisite to the distance-based method mentioned above as the distance matrix is generated from lexicostatistical analysis. Lexicostatistics is the earliest developed and best known quantitative method in comparative linguistics, which was originally developed to estimate the time at which 2 languages split from their last common ancestor, i. e. glottochronology (Wang, 1994). As glottochronology involves a number of highly controversial assumptions, nowadays lexicostatistics is often used to quantify relatedness instead of estimating time of divergence (Wang, 1994). In this study, no attempt is made to infer time depth from lexical distance. The basic assumption of lexicostatistics is the presence of a core vocabulary, which is relatively universal and culture-free. Such vocabulary items are frequently used, acquired early, and resistant to linguistic change (especially borrowing) (Campbell, 2013). Further, as Burling (2012) and Mufwene (2014) illustrate, lexicon is the most central component of language and must have been the first component which made linguistic evolution possible to begin. Although these two studies are not directly concerned with lexicostatistics and language classification, they can help to justify the use of core lexicon, arguably the most evolutionarily ancient and central component of language, to study the phylogenetic relationship between different languages. The Swadesh 100-word list (Swadesh, 1955) is the best known and most widely used word list for lexical comparison (see Table 1).

Table 1 Swadesh 100-word List

1	all	21	ear	41	horn	61	nose	81	stone
2	ashes	22	earth	42	I	62	not	82	sun
3	bark	23	eat	43	kill	63	one	83	swim
4	belly	24	egg	44	knee	64	person	84	tail
5	big	25	eye	45	know	65	rain	85	that
6	bird	26	fat	46	leaf	66	red	86	this
7	bite	27	feather	47	lie	67	road	87	thou
8	black	28	fire	48	liver	68	root	88	tongue
9	blood	29	fish	49	long	69	round	89	tooth
10	bone	30	fly	50	louse	70	sand	90	tree
11	breast	31	foot	51	man	71	say	91	two
12	burn	32	full	52	many	72	see	92	walk
13	claw	33	give	53	meat	73	seed	93	warm
14	cloud	34	good	54	moon	74	sit	94	water
15	cold	35	green	55	mountain	75	skin	95	we
16	come	36	hair	56	mouth	76	sleep	96	what
17	die	37	hand	57	name	77	small	97	white
18	dog	38	head	58	neck	78	smoke	98	who
19	drink	39	hear	59	new	79	stand	99	woman
20	dry	40	heart	60	night	80	star	100	yellow

When doing lexicostatistical analysis, we first fill in each slot by a word which corresponds to the meaning on the list. Afterwards, we compare the items that occupy the same slot cross-linguistically, and determine whether those items are cognates (the decision relies on prior historical linguistic research work). The number of cognates reflects the degree of relatedness between the languages in question.

Lexicostatistics has its limitations. First, it is extremely difficult to devise a word list (or sometimes called meaning list) which is truly universal and culture-neutral. Therefore, variations of the list which suit specific language or culture groups exist. Furthermore, as Trask (1996) argues, lexicostatistics is only for quantifying the degree of relatedness between languages which are already known to have a genetic link, but not for deciding whether languages with no known genetic link are related or not. In our case, as the Chinese dialects concerned are known to share a common ancestry, the application of lexicostatistics is justified.

3 Objectives

Given the lack of general consensus on the status of Pinghua in relation to Yue, this study aims to employ lexicostatistical analysis, a method not commonly used in Chinese Dialectology, to shed light on the classification controversies from a new angle.

4 Methodology

4.1 Introduction

As outlined by Deng and Wang (2009), lexicostatistical analysis involves 5 basic steps, namely (i) compile a word list, (ii) identification the cognates between each language pair, (iii) calculate the percentage of cognates between each language pair, (iv) sort out a distance matrix, and (v) estimate a tree diagram which fits the distance matrix best; in which steps (iii)—(v) are processed by computer programmes. This study follows these basic steps, and the details of the procedures are described below.

4.2 Data Source

Analysis of a fairly large amount of lexical data is required in this study. At this stage, *Linguistic Atlas of China* (Cao, 2008) acts as the primary data source. Linguistic Atlas of China is the most large-scale, comprehensive, and systematic work on Chinese dialect data collection so far, which covers different types of linguistic data (phonology, lexicon, grammar) of 930 Chinese dialects collected from fieldwork. Data from the lexicon volume and grammar volume (which contains some function words) are relevant to this study.

4.3 Word List

The Swadesh 100-word list (Swadesh, 1955) has been widely used in lexicostatistical analyses, including those involving Chinese dialect groups, such as Xu (1991), Wang and Wang (2004). However, it is noteworthy that the Swadesh list was compiled primarily based on experience and intuition, instead of empirical evidence for its cross-linguistic validity. In view of the weakness of the Swadesh list, the Leipzig-Jakarta list of basic vocabulary (Tadmor, 2009), a product of the Loanword Typology Project (Haspelmath and Tadmor, 2009), is compiled to serve as a better alternative. Unlike the Swadesh list, the Leipzig-Jakarta list is an empirically-based basic word list which takes all the factors of basic vocabulary into account, namely stability, universality, simplicity, and resistance to borrowing. Establishing a worldwide sample of languages, the project makes use of the powers of computational linguistics and academic collaboration to compile a 100-word basic vocabulary list which can serve as an invaluable tool for determining whether and how languages are related to each other. Because of its obvious strengths, the lexicostatistical analysis carried out in this study will be based on the Leipzig-Jakarta list.

Among the 100 words on the list, 40 of them show reasonable variation among different Chinese varieties and are covered by the Linguistic Atlas of China①. These 40 words, as shown in Table 2, are used for the lexicostatistical analysis of this study.

Table 2 The 40-word List Used in This Study

1	1SG pronoun	11	bird	21	to eat	31	to run
2	2SG pronoun	12	child	22	to drink	32	to hide
3	3SG pronoun	13	eye	23	house	33	to fall
4	this	14	nose	24	to see	34	to give
5	who?	15	mouth	25	to say	35	to know
6	what?	16	tongue	26	to cry	36	small
7	not	17	neck	27	to bite	37	thick
8	in	18	foot	28	to hit	38	wide
9	dog	19	breast	29	to carry	39	black
10	egg	20	to tie	30	to stand	40	one

4.4 Identification of Cognates

This study chiefly relies on the sinograms (Chinese characters) and/or the pronunciation corresponding to the specific meaning given by the Linguistic Atlas of China to judge whether the words involved are cognates (words which share a common origin). The use of sinograms to identify cognates may seemingly be questionable as the historical comparative methods are usually employed in studies concerning other languages. However, it is noteworthy that the determination of original sinograms (*benzi* 本字) actually relies on the historical comparative methods. Given that

① A few lexical items on the Leipzig-Jakarta list, namely "wing", "hair", and "yesterday", are known to have variable forms in different Chinese varieties, but the relevant data is not found in the Linguistic Atlas of China. Because of the lack of complete data of these 3 words, they are omitted from the word list used in this study. This is admittedly a limitation of this study which can be overcome by the collection of relevant data from other sources in the future.

Cao (2008) has put careful effort into the determination of original sinograms, their judgment is arguably a reliable and invaluable source of information.

4.5 Computation of Lexical Distance and Tree Diagrams

MEGA6 (Tamura et al., 2013) is an integrated phylogenetics package which can compute genetic data and estimate phylogenetic trees by a variety of distance-based and character-based methods. As the software package is originally designed to analyze genetic data, we have to devise a way to make it able to analyze linguistic data as well. There are 20 proteinogenic amino acids which are directly encoded by the universal genetic code, namely alanine (A), cysteine (C), aspartic acid (D), glutamic acid (E), phenylalanine (F), glycine (G), histidine (H), isolecine (I), lysine (K), leucine (L), methionine (M), asparagine (N), proline (P), glutamine (Q), arginine (R), serine (S), threonine (T), valine (V), tryptophan (W), and tyrosine (Y); in the case of lexical comparison, when filling in each meaning slot, a particular amino acid is used to represent a group of words which are cognates. For example, among the 7 dialects selected to represent each well-recognized Chinese dialect group (Beijing for Mandarin, Changsha for Xiang, Nanchang for Gan, Shanghai for Wu, Xiamen for Min, Meizhou for Hakka, Guangzhou for Yue), there are 4 different kinds of words which express the meaning "this". The amino acid short forms A, C, D, and E are used to represent the 4 different groups of cognates, as shown in Table 2. After filling in all the meaning slots of a particular word list, a distance matrix displaying the lexical distance between each language pair is generated (Figure 2), where 0.525 indicates a 52.5% lexical difference, 0.650 indicates a 65.0% lexical difference, and so on. The average lexical difference among the Chinese dialects is 59.2%, with a range from 32.5% (Changsha vs. Nanchang) to 77.5% (Beijing vs. Xiamen). Eventually, a tree diagram which fits the distance matrix best is estimated using the NJ method (Figure 3). The distance between each dialect pair in the diagram indicates their lexical difference. For example, the distance between Beijing and Shanghai is slightly more than 10 times the length of the 0.05-scale bar, which is consistent with their lexical difference as indicated in the distance matrix, i.e. 0.55. Notice that the distance displayed in the tree diagram is not necessarily identical to the one in the distance matrix, because while the tree diagram serves as the best graphical representation of the distance among the dialects in question, the exact value is often inevitably subject to minor discrepancies. It is therefore important to refer to both the distance matrix and the tree diagram when it comes to data interpretation.

Table 3 The Words Corresponding to "This" in the 7 Chinese Dialects

Beijing	Changsha	Nanchang	Shanghai	Xiamen	Meizhou	Guangzhou
这	个	个	底	这	个	你/尔
A	C	C	D	A	C	E

	1	2	3	4	5	6
1. Beijing						
2. Changsha	0.525					
3. Nanchang	0.650	0.325				
4. Shanghai	0.550	0.375	0.475			
5. Xiamen	0.775	0.750	0.625	0.675		
6. Meizhou	0.750	0.575	0.500	0.675	0.550	
7. Guangzhou	0.700	0.525	0.625	0.600	0.675	0.525

Figure 2　Distance Matrix of the 7 Chinese Dialects

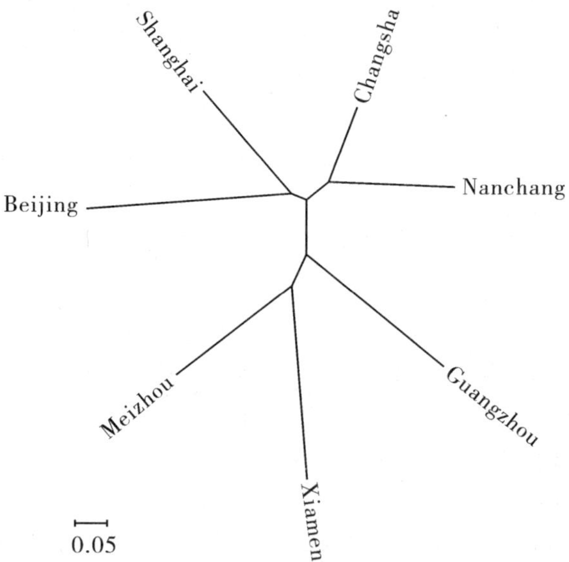

Figure 3　Tree Diagram of the 7 Chinese Dialects

To ensure that the 40-word list is suitable for Chinese dialect classification, we repeat the above procedures with 3 additional dialects (Chengdu, Fuzhou, Taishan) which are well-agreed to belong to Mandarin, Min, and Yue, respectively. It is expected that Chengdu and Beijing will form a Mandarin cluster, Fuzhou and Xiamen a Min cluster, and Taishan and Guangzhou a Yue cluster. The results, as shown in Figures 4 and 5, are in good agreement with the expectations.

	1	2	3	4	5	6	7	8	9
1. Beijing									
2. Changsha	0.525								
3. Nanchang	0.650	0.325							
4. Shanghai	0.550	0.375	0.475						
5. Xiamen	0.775	0.750	0.625	0.675					
6. Meizhou	0.750	0.575	0.500	0.675	0.550				
7. Guangzhou	0.700	0.525	0.625	0.600	0.675	0.525			
8. Chengdu	0.400	0.375	0.500	0.375	0.775	0.750	0.600		
9. Fuzhou	0.825	0.800	0.700	0.725	0.250	0.600	0.750	0.825	
10. Taishan	0.667	0.436	0.538	0.538	0.667	0.487	0.179	0.564	0.744

Figure 4　Distance Matrix of the 10 Chinese Dialects

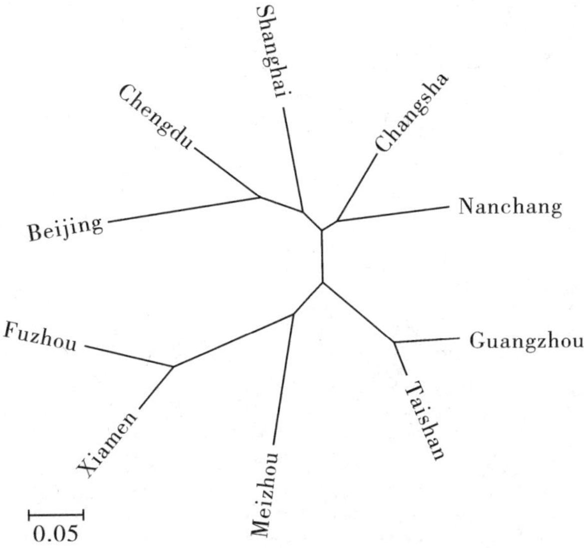

Figure 5 **Tree Diagram of the** 10 **Chinese Dialects**

5 Case Study

5.1 Introduction

After outlining the procedures involved in this study, we now move on to address the classification issues of Yue and Pinghua.

5.2 Dialect Selection

According to the Language Atlas of China, Yue is classified into 7 subgroups, namely Guangfu 广府片, Siyi 四邑片, Gaoyang 高阳片, Wuhua 吴化片, Goulou 勾漏片, Yongxun 邕浔片, and Qinlian 钦廉片. Pinghua is classified into the Northern subgroup and Southern subgroup, known as Guibei 桂北片 and Guinan 桂南片 respectively. Considering the high relevance of Goulou Yue and Pinghua to the purpose of this study, the 15 dialects selected for this study are as follows:

Yue: Guangzhou 广州(Guangfu), Taishan 台山(Siyi), Gaozhou 高州(Gaoyang), Wuchuan 吴川(Wuhua), Yulin 玉林, Cangwu 苍梧, Yangshan 阳山(Goulou), Nanning 南宁(Yongxun), Qinzhou 钦州(Qinlian)

Pinghua: Guilin 桂林, Pingle 平乐, Hezhou 贺州(Guibei), Baise 百色, Nanning 南宁, Laibin 来宾(Guinan)

5. 3 Results

After filling in the corresponding words of the Yue and Pinghua dialects onto the 40-word list①(see Appendix), the data is processed by MEGA6 and the distance matrix and tree diagram generated are as follows:

	1	2	3	4	5	6	7	8	9	10	11	12	13	14
1. Guangzhou														
2. Taishan	0.179													
3. Gaozhou	0.300	0.231												
4. Wuchuan	0.275	0.154	0.100											
5. Yulin	0.425	0.333	0.250	0.175										
6. Cangwu	0.325	0.282	0.300	0.250	0.375									
7. Yangshan	0.333	0.316	0.385	0.333	0.385	0.487								
8. Nanning(Yue)	0.250	0.256	0.275	0.275	0.425	0.275	0.410							
9. Qinzhou	0.385	0.289	0.231	0.231	0.333	0.333	0.395	0.282						
10. Guilin	0.525	0.462	0.500	0.450	0.400	0.475	0.513	0.550	0.513					
11. Pingle	0.450	0.385	0.400	0.350	0.275	0.350	0.513	0.450	0.410	0.325				
12. Hezhou	0.436	0.421	0.385	0.359	0.359	0.308	0.421	0.513	0.447	0.487	0.359			
13. Baise	0.436	0.342	0.359	0.333	0.385	0.385	0.368	0.410	0.342	0.538	0.487	0.474		
14. Nanning(Pinghua)	0.350	0.282	0.325	0.275	0.325	0.375	0.385	0.350	0.308	0.450	0.350	0.436	0.231	
15. Laibin	0.385	0.263	0.282	0.205	0.282	0.282	0.421	0.359	0.289	0.385	0.333	0.368	0.316	0.256

Figure 6 Distance Matrix of the Yue and Pinghua Dialects

In Figure 7a, each Goulou Yue dialect is marked with a black circle, Northern Pinghua dialect a black square, and Southern Pinghua dialect a black triangle; while the unmarked ones are the other Yue dialects.

5. 4 Data Analysis and Discussion

5. 4. 1 Introduction

As shown in the tree diagram, the Southern Pinghua dialects and Yue dialects (excluding the Goulou subgroup) somehow form 2 clusters of their own, suggesting they are 2 groups with relatively low internal diversity. Such a finding is consistent with the data from the distance matrix—while the average lexical difference among the Yue and Pinghua dialects is 35.6%; the within-group difference among the Southern Pinghua dialects is 26.8%, and that among the Yue dialects is 21.4%, both are considerably smaller than the overall difference. On the other hand, the Northern Pinghua dialects and Goulou Yue dialects show higher degrees of internal diversity—39.0% for the former and 41.6% for the latter. For clarity, a tree diagram with a reduced number

① As suggested by a reviewer, the Swadesh 100-word list may also be used here to see whether it works well on Pinghua classification. While it would be interesting to test whether the empirically-based Leipzig-Jakarta list really works better than the Swadesh list in language classification, we are of the view that such tests should be done on a broad range of languages with well-established relationship. As the classification problem of Yue and Pinghua remains a disputed issue, it might not be an ideal case for making such a comparison. To avoid confusion, we only adopt the Leipzig-Jakarta list in this study, assuming that its stronger empirical foundation will make it superior for the present purpose.

of dialects is provided below.

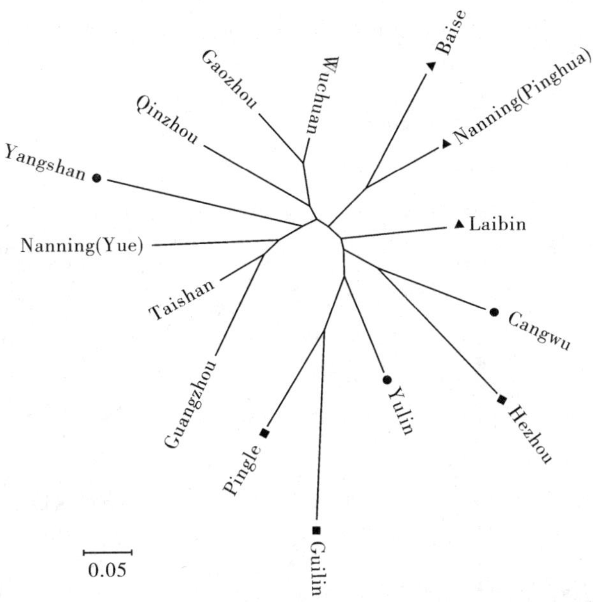

Figure 7a. Tree Diagram of the Yue and Pinghua Dialects

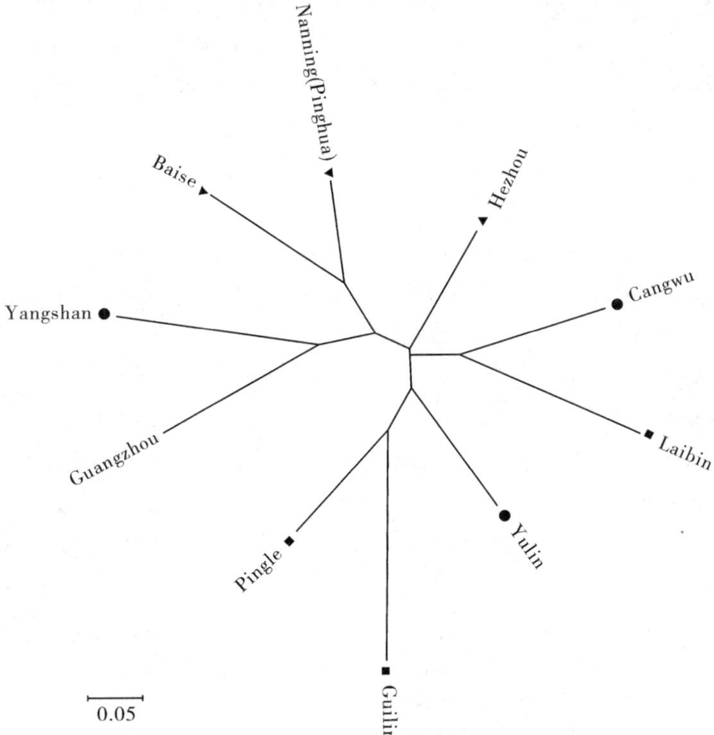

Figure 7b. Tree Diagram of the Yue and Pinghua Dialects (with Some Less Relevant Dialects Omitted)

5. 4. 2 Implications For the Classification Debate

As mentioned in Section 2. 2, there have been debates over the status of Pinghua in relation to Yue. This section discusses the rationality of various classification schemes based on the lexicostatistical results of this case study.

(a) Yue and Pinghua as a single group

To evaluate whether it is appropriate to regard Yue and Pinghua as a single group, it would be helpful to refer to the data about the lexical distance between various well-recognized dialect groups presented in Section 4. 5. As many previous studies notice the similarity between Yue and Southern Pinghua, The major dispute over classifying Yue and Pinghua as a singlegroup may lie on the difference between Yue and Northern Pinghua. If we take Guangzhou as the representative dialect of Yue and Guilin as the one of Northern Pinghua, the difference between Yue and Pinghua is 52. 5%, which is the same as that between Yue and other major dialect groups, such as Xiang and Hakka. Therefore, given such a large difference, it does not seem appropriate to classify Yue and Pinghua as a single group.

(b) Yue as a group, Pinghua as a group

While it makes sense to regard Yue and Pinghua as different groups, the considerable internal diversity of Pinghua may render this classification scheme problematic. If we take Nanning as the representative dialect of Southern Pinghua, its difference with Guilin, the representative dialect of Northern Pinghua, is 45. 0%. Such a difference is comparable to that between Gan and Wu, and even greater than that between Xiang and Gan, and that between Xiang and Wu. Therefore, such a classification scheme should still be subject to further modification.

(c) Yue and Southern Pinghua as a group, Northern Pinghua as a group

Taking the representative dialects into account, Southern Pinghua is closer to Yue (35. 0%) than Northern Pinghua (45. 0%). Grouping Yue and Southern Pinghua seems to be a feasible scheme.

(d) Classification schemes which involve special treatment of Goulou Yue

Studies such as Li (2001, 2005), Qin (2000), and Wu (2001) highlight the special status of Goulou Yue when discussing the classification problem of Yue and Pinghua. Given its widespread distribution in western Guangdong and eastern Guangxi, it may seem natural to consider Goulou Yue a "bridge" between Yue and Pinghua. However, as the results of this study suggest, Goulou Yue has an abnormally high degree of internal diversity, especially given that it is usually considered a subgroup of dialects only. Given the considerable diversity among Goulou Yue dialects found in this study, we take all the 3 dialects into account. As shown in the distance matrix (Figure 6), while Cangwu and Yangshan are relatively close to Yue, Yulin is relatively close to both Northern Pinghua and Southern Pinghua. Given that Yulin is often considered the representative dialect of Goulou Yue, the results are somehow consistent with the studies which suggest a close link between Goulou Yue and Pinghua. However, the internal diversity of Goulou Yue is hardly addressed in previous studies, which may have led to the premature conclusion that Goulou Yue is closely associated with Pinghua. In fact, although Cangwu and Yangshan are both relatively close to Yue, these 2 dialects are not particular close to each other. As shown in the radiation-format tree diagram (Figure 9), these Goulou Yue dialects do not form a close cluster. Therefore, it does not seem appropriate to treat Goulou Yue as a close-knit group when dealing with the classification problem of Yue and Pinghua.

	1	2	3	4	5	6
1. Yulin						
2. Cangwu	0.375					
3. Yangshan	0.385	0.487				
4. Guangzhou	0.425	0.325	0.333			
5. Guilin	0.400	0.475	0.513	0.525		
6. Nanning(Pinghua)	0.325	0.375	0.385	0.350	0.450	

Figure 8 Distance Matrix of the Goulou Yue Dialects and Other Representative Yue and Pinghua Dialects

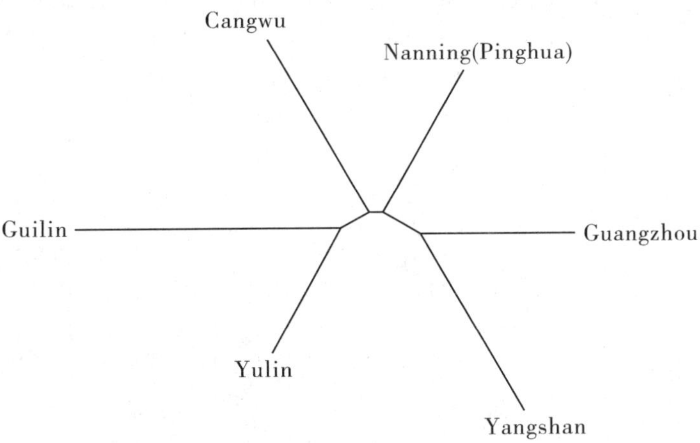

Figure 9 Tree Diagram of the Goulou Yue Dialects and Other Representative Yue and Pinghua Dialects

6 Conclusion

Putting the problem of Goulou Yue aside, the results of this study are in favor of the position that Yue and Southern Pinghua should be grouped together while Northern Pinghua should be classified as a separate group. Nonetheless, adopting the lexicostatistical approach, this study manages to identify an important (and unexpected) problem not addressed in previous studies, namely the high internal diversity of Goulou Yue. Therefore, we argue that it would be premature to jump to conclusions about the classification problem of Yue and Pinghua, without sorting out the intriguing complexity of Goulou Yue first. Further studies on a larger range of Goulou Yue dialects are required to reevaluate the status of Goulou Yue as a dialect subgroup. It seems likely that the current classification scheme of Yue requires some modification to accurately reflect the diversity among Yue dialects. Only after doing so can we give a more definite answer to the classification problem concerning Yue and Pinghua.

Appendix

Corresponding Words of the Yue and Pinghua Dialects on the Word List①,②

	GuZ	TS	GaZ	WC	YL	CW	YS	NNY	QZ	GL	PL	HZ	BS	NNP	LB
1SG	我	我	我	我	我	我	我	我	我	我	我	我	我	我	我
2SG	你	你	你	你	你	你	你	你	你	你	你	你	你	你	你
3SG	渠	渠	渠	渠	渠	渠	渠	渠	渠	他	渠	渠	渠	渠	渠
this	尔	个	个	个	个	个	尔	a/e/ei	个	个	个	个	那	尔	个
who?	边个	阿谁	物谁	阿	什人	边个	哪	边个	哪	哪	么	何	哪	哪	哪
what?	物	物	物	物	什	物	物	物	么	什	啥	啥	哪	哪	啥
not	唔	唔	冇	冇	冇	冇	唔	冇	冇	ȵia	冇	冇	mi	冇	唔
in	系	到	在	在	在	在	度	系	跟	在	在	*③	在	在	在
dog	狗	狗	狗	狗	狗	狗	狗	狗	狗	狗	狗	狗	狗	狗	狗
egg	春	蛋	蛋	蛋	蛋	蛋	春	蛋	蛋	蛋	蛋	春	蛋	蛋	蛋
bird	雀	雀	雀	雀	鸟	雀	雀	雀	雀	鸟	鸟	雀	雀	鸟	鸟
child	细蚊	细蚊	农	农	农	细子	*	细老	小儿	小巴戏	*	细子	细蚊	细蚊	农
eye	眼	眼	眼	眼	眼	眼	眼	眼	眼	眼	眼	眼	眼	眼	眼
nose	鼻	鼻	鼻	鼻	鼻	鼻	鼻	鼻	鼻	鼻	鼻	鼻	鼻	鼻	鼻
mouth	嘴	嘴	嘴	嘴	嘴	嘴	口	口	口	嘴	嘴	嘴	嘴	嘴	嘴
tongue	利	利	利	利	利	利	舌	利	利	舌	舌	舌	利	利	舌
neck	颈	颈	颈	颈	颈	颈	颈	颈	颈	颈	颈	颈	颈	颈	颈
foot	脚	脚	脚	脚	脚	脚	脚	脚	脚	脚	脚	脚	脚	脚	脚
breast	辈	辈	辈	辈	辈	奶	辈	咪	nɛu	奶	奶	辈	pɛ	妈	*

(continued)

① Abbreviations used: GuZ-Guangzhou, TS-Taishan, GaZ-Gaozhou, WC-Wuchuan, YL-Yulin, CW-Cangwu, YS-Yangshan, NNY-Nanning (Yue), QZ-Qinzhou, GL-Guilin, PL-Pingle, HZ-Hezhou, BS-Baise, NNP-Nanning (Pinghua), LB-Laibin.

② For the sake of clarity, only the key morphemes are shown. For example, different dialects may use words like 雀,雀儿,雀仔 to stand for "bird"; but as 雀 is clearly the key morpheme for cognacy determination, only the word 雀 is shown on the table. Please refer to Cao (2008) for the exact word of each dialect corresponding to each meaning on the word list.

③ An asterisk refers to a word which is not specified in Cao (2008), i. e. labelled as 其他 (others) in the atlas.

	GuZ	TS	GaZ	WC	YL	CW	YS	NNY	QZ	GL	PL	HZ	BS	NNP	LB
to tie	绑	绑	缚	绹	绹	扎	绑	绑	缚	绹	捆	绹	缚	绑	绹
to eat	iak	吃	食	吃	吃	吃	吃	食	吃	吃	吃	吃	吃	吃	吃
to drink	饮	饮	饮	饮	饮	饮	呷	饮	饮	吃	ɕyE	饮	饮	饮	饮
house	屋	屋	屋	屋	屋	屋	屋	屋	屋	屋	屋	屋	屋	屋	屋
to see	睇	睇	睇	睇	睇	睇	望	睇	睇	望	看	看	lEi	看	睇
to say	讲	讲	讲	讲	讲	讲	讲	讲	讲	讲	讲	讲	讲	讲	讲
to cry	喊	哭	哭	哭	哭	啼	哭	哭	哭	哭	哭	啼	哭	哭	哭
to bite	咬	咬	咬	咬	咬	咬	咬	咬	咬	咬	咬	咬	咬	咬	咬
to hit	打	打	打	打	撅	打	撅	打	打	撅	撅	撅	打	打	打
to carry	抬	抬	扛	扛	扛	抬	扛	抬	扛	抬	抬	扛	扛	扛	扛
to stand	徛	徛	徛	徛	徛	徛	徛	徛	徛	立	徛	徛	徛	徛	徛
to run	走	走	走	走	走	跳	走	适	走	走	走	跳	溜	走	逸
to hide	收	偋	收	收	收	收	藏	收	收	藏	收	藏	*	放	抽
to fall	跌	跌	跌	跌	lɐŋ	跌	lɐŋ	跌	跌	跌	跌	跌	lɐŋ	跌	跌
to give	畀	畀	畀	畀	分	畀	畀	畀	畀	得	分	分	xei	xei	畀
to know	晓	*	知	知	知	识	知	识	识	晓	晓	晓	识	识	识
small	细	细	细	细	泥	细	细	细	*	小	泥	细	细	细	细
thick	厚	厚	厚	厚	厚	厚	厚	厚	厚	厚	厚	厚	厚	厚	厚
wide	阔	阔	宽	阔	阔	阔	阔	阔	大	阔	阔	宽	阔	阔	阔
black	黑	黑	黑	黑	黑	黑	乌	黑	黑	黑	黑	黑	乌	黑	黑
one	一	一	一	一	一	一	一	一	一	一	一	一	一	一	一

References

Atkinson, Q. D., and R. D. Gray 2005 Curious parallels and curious connections? Phylogenetic thinking in biology and historical linguistics. *Systematic Biology*, 54: 513 – 26.

Burling, R. 2012 Words came first: Adaptations for word-learning. In M. Tallerman and K. R. Gibson eds., *The Oxford Handbook of Language Evolution.* Oxford: Oxford University Press. pp. 406 – 416.

Campbell, L. 2013 *Historical Linguistics: An Introduction* (*3rd edition*). Edinburgh: Edinburgh University Press.

Campbell, L., and W. J. Poser 2008 *Language Classification: History and Method.* Cambridge: Cambridge University Press.

Cavalli-Sforza, L. L., and W. S.-Y. Wang 1986 Spatial distance and lexical replacement. *Language*, 62: 38 – 55.

Chambers, J. K., and P. Trudgill 1998 *Dialectology* (2nd edition). Cambridge:

Cambridge University Press.

Hall, B. G. 2011 *Phylogenetic Trees Made Easy: A How-to Manual* (4th edition). Sunderland, MA: Sinauer Associates.

Haspelmath, M., and U. Tadmor 2009 The Loanword Typology project and the World Loanword Database. In M. Haspelmath and U. Tadmor eds., *Loanwords in the World's Languages: A Comparative Handbook*. Berlin: De Gruyter Mouton. pp. 1－34.

McMahon, A., and R. McMahon 2005 *Language Classification by Numbers*. Oxford: Oxford University Press.

Mufwene, S. S. 2014 What Dwight L. Bolinger probably would have contributed to evolutionary linguistics. Paper presented at the 10th International Conference on the Evolution of Language (EVOLANG X), University of Vienna. pp. 14－17.

Norman, Jerry 1988 *Chinese*. Cambridge: Cambridge University Press.

Paul, L. M., G. F. Simons, and C. D. Fennig 2014 *Ethnologue: Languages of the World* (17th edition). Dallas, Texas: SIL International. Online version. http://www.ethnologue.com.

Saitou, N., and M. Nei 1987 The neighbor-joining method: A new method for reconstructing phylogenetic trees. *Molecular Biology and Evolution*, 4: 406－25.

Simmons, R. V. 1999 On Chinese dialect classification: A case study examining the relationship of the Harngjou and Jennjiang dialects. In R. V. Simmons ed., *Issues in Chinese Dialect Description and Classification*. New Brunswick: Journal of Chinese Linguistics. pp. 204－34.

Swadesh, M. 1955 Towards greater accuracy in lexicostatistic dating. *International Journal of American Linguistics*, 21: 121－37.

Tadmor, U. 2009 Loanwords in the world's languages: Findings and results. In M. Haspelmath and U. Tadmor eds., *Loanwords in the World's Languages: A Comparative Handbook*. Berlin: Mouton De Gruyter. pp. 55－75.

Tamura, K., G. Stecher, D. Peterson, A. Filipski, and S. Kumar 2013 MEGA6: Molecular Evolutionary Genetics Analysis Version 6.0. *Molecular Biology and Evolution*, 30: 2725－29.

Trask, R. L. 1996 *Historical Linguistics*. London: Arnold.

Wang, F., and W. S.-Y. Wang 2004 Basic words and language evolution. *Language and Linguistics*, 5(3): 643－62.

Wang, W. S.-Y. 1994 Glottochronology, lexicostatistics, and other numerical methods. In R. E. Asher ed., *The Encyclopedia of Language and Linguistics* (Vol. 3). Oxford; New York: Pergamon Press. pp. 1445－50.

Cao, Zhiyun ed. 曹志耘编 2008 《汉语方言地图集》，北京：商务印书馆。

Deng, Xiaohua, and W. S.－Y. Wang 邓晓华、王士元 2009 《中国的语言及方言的分类》，北京：中华书局。

Hu, Yushu 胡裕树编　2011　《现代汉语》（重订本），上海：上海教育出版社。

Institute of Linguistics, Chinese Academy of Social Sciences, Institute of Ethnology and Anthropology, Chinese Academy of Social Sciences, and Language Information Sciences Research Centre, City University of Hong Kong 中国社会科学院语言研究所、中国社会科学院民族学与人类学研究所、香港城市大学语言信息科学研究中心编　2012　《中国语言地图集》（第2版），北京：商务印书馆。

Li, Lianjin 李连进　2000　《平话音韵研究》，南宁：广西人民出版社。

Li, Lianjin 李连进　2005　《勾漏方言的归属》，《民族语文》第1期，第34~41页。

Li, Rulong 李如龙　2010　《罗杰瑞先生对汉语方言分区的贡献》，载于余霭芹、柯蔚南编　《罗杰瑞先生七秩晋三寿庆论文集》，香港：吴多泰中国语文研究中心，第87~277页。

Li, Xiaofan, and Xiang Mengbing 李小凡、项梦冰　2009　《汉语方言学基础教程》，北京：北京大学出版社。

Liang, Jinrong 梁金荣　1997　《桂北平话语音研究》，暨南大学博士学位论文。

Liang, Min, and Zhang Junru 梁敏、张均如　1999　《广西平话概论》，《方言》第1期，第24~32页。

Mai, Yun 麦耘　2010　《粤语的形成、发展与粤语和平话的关系》，载于潘悟云、沈钟伟编　《研究之乐——庆祝王士元先生七十五寿辰学术论文集》，上海：上海教育出版社，第227~243页。

Mei, Zulin 梅祖麟　2000　《梅祖麟语言学论文集》，北京：商务印书馆。

Qin, Yuanxiong 覃远雄　2000　《桂南平话研究》，暨南大学博士学位论文。

Qin, Yuanxiong 覃远雄　2012　《平话和土话》，载于中国社会科学院语言研究所、中国社会科学院民族学与人类学研究所、香港城市大学语言信息科学研究中心编　《中国语言地图集》（第2版），北京：商务印书馆，第152~159页。

Wei, Shuguan 韦树关　1996　《试论平话在汉语方言中的地位》，《语言研究》第2期，第95~101页。

Wu, Wei 伍巍　2001　《论桂南平话的粤语系属》，《方言》第2期，第133~141页。

Xu, Tongjiang 徐通锵　1991　《历史语言学》，北京：商务印书馆。

Zhang, Junru 张均如　1982　《广西中南部地区壮语中的老借词源于古"平话"考》，《语言研究》第1期，第197~219页。

Xiang, Mengbing 项梦冰　2010　《评罗杰瑞教授的汉语方言分区方案》，载于余霭芹、柯蔚南编《罗杰瑞先生七秩晋三寿庆论文集》，香港：吴多泰中国语文研究中心，第289~303页。

Xiang, Mengbing, and Cao Hui 项梦冰、曹晖　2013　《汉语方言地理学——入门与实践》，北京：中国书籍出版社。

Zhai, Shiyu 翟时雨　2003　《汉语方言学》，重庆：西南师范大学出版社。

后 记

由香港科技大学中国语言学研究中心主办的第十八届国际粤方言研讨会，于2013年12月7日至8日在香港科技大学举行。来自中国内地、香港、澳门、台湾以及美国、日本的六十多位学者参加了会议。大会共设四场专题演讲、十三场分会报告，此外还有香港语言学会主持的“粤拼”及其他粤语拼音系统专场、优秀学生论文竞赛专场，共计报告论文48篇。会议规模虽然不大，但涵盖了粤语研究的方方面面，举凡语音、音系、词法、句法、语义、词汇，以及对外粤语教学、粤语水平考试、粤语习得、方言划分、方言文字等，与会论文均有相当广泛而深入的探讨。从研究方法上看，这些论文多以语料丰富见长，既重历时文献，又重共时口语，且多从类型学的角度出发，以比较的眼光，借鉴最新研究方法去处理材料，分析问题，是以成果丰富，体现了粤语研究的最新发展。

会议结束不久，我们即着手论文汇编事宜。组稿通知发出后，与会学者热烈响应，纷纷惠寄稿件。为确保学术水准，除专题报告之外，所有论文均送外审。论文作者根据修改意见认真改进，有的甚至在修改两三遍之后才最后定稿。严谨求实的科学态度、不辞辛劳的勤奋精神，实在令人感佩。文集共收学术论文17篇，其中中文11篇，英文6篇。论文共分三组，第一组是专题演讲，第二组是参加优秀学生论文竞赛的论文，会议论文的主体则归为第三组。组内论文依作者音序排列。

文集出版颇多头绪，幸得师友鼎力相助，才能在较短时间内顺利完成。包睿舜（Robert S. Bauer）、陈咏珊、邓思颖、郭必之、梁仲森、欧阳伟豪、单韵鸣、汪锋、萧敬伟、张钦良（顺序依汉语拼音）等先生和女士不辞辛劳，拨冗审读，提出精到的修改意见。我中心吴和德博士从会议筹备举行到论文编辑出版，劳心劳力，始终其事。暨南大学出版社的李战副编审专业敬业，确保出版流程环环相扣，了无延宕；黄少君老师细心耐心，编排校读，补苴订正，多所建议，为本文集增色不少。值此文集付梓之际，谨向以上诸位表示诚挚的谢意，同时亦期待因诸位协助而问世的本集研究成果，能为粤语研究的发展发挥积极的作用。

孙景涛

2015年3月25日